MW01247669

Table of Contents

AN INTRODUCTION AND STATUS REPORT

The appearance of this year's *Top American Research Universities* marks another transition in the life of The Center for Measuring University Performance (MUP). As our readers know, last year we lost our long-time colleague, Betty Capaldi Phillips, a founding director of our Center whose leadership and academic distinction served to guide us from the first publication in 2000. With the advice of our Advisory Board and the generous continuing support of the University of Massachusetts Amherst and the substantial re-engagement in co-sponsorship by the University of Florida, we have been able to maintain the work of the MUP Center and anticipate its continuation. The MUP Center benefited greatly for many years from the remarkably strong support from Arizona State University where Betty Capaldi Phillips served as provost. We have always relied on the home institutions of our staff at the University at Buffalo, the University of Florida, and for a time the Louisiana State University System.

These institutions have allowed us to sustain the consistency and stability of the data structure that has over many years provided the reliable indicators of research university performance that underlie the *Top American Research Universities* annual report. Along with an essay on various topics of research university interest that appears at the beginning of each annual report, the data we use all exists in downloadable format on our website. The transition from ASU's webspace to the UMass Amherst webspace took place without major problems thanks to the expert assistance of the technical staffs of both institutions.

The published hard copy report reaches about 1400 recipients each year, and the website [http://mup.umass.edu] continues to draw an average of over 300 hits per day, a significant number for such a specialized resource. Research institutions and other organizations interested in research university performance continue to use the data in reports, evaluations, and presentations, fulfilling our goal of providing a useful and reliable resource to the academic community. Our staff is often asked to participate in conferences and other activities that contribute to the always lively discussion about the purpose and performance of America's research universities.

We continue to rely on the advice of our Advisory Board, reflecting a wide range of academic expertise from across the country and from multiple institutional perspectives. We could not have maintained the vitality and significance of this work without them.

The Center for Measuring University Performance Staff
November 2018

America's Research Universities: Is the Enterprise Model Sustainable?

John V. Lombardi and Diane D. Craig

INTRODUCTION

Since at least the second world war, the top American research universities, both public and private, have enjoyed remarkable success, not only in capturing significant shares of the federal dollars available to support research but also in expanding their influence and significance within the context of American higher education. This success is reflected today in multiple ways from the growing undergraduate population seeking admission to these institutions to the prestige conferred by multiple ranking publications of varying methodological quality.[1]

Indeed, almost all colleges and universities that aspire to any distinction at all support some variety of research enterprise, even if some are relatively modest in scale. A reflection of the almost universal significance of research achievement appears in the web pages and alumni publications of prestigious and highly selective liberal arts colleges whose claim to distinction rests primarily on the quality of their undergraduate educational programs but whose web pages nonetheless wax eloquent over the research accomplishments of their faculty.[2]

Yet over the past decades, as the financial circumstances of all colleges and universities have changed, with declining public tax-based support, increased tuition and fee structures, complex tuition discounting programs, sophisticated need-based financial aid mechanisms at the state and federal levels, and competition for fee-paying international students, some may worry that the research enterprises of these institutions may be at risk. This perception of possible risk reflects several circumstances particular to the university research enterprise.[3]

The Center for Measuring University Performance Staff

THE RESEARCH UNIVERSITY MODEL

University research, especially scientific research, with few exceptions, is an institutional loss leader. The revenue generated by research grants and contracts does not pay for the costs of producing the research. Indirect costs exceed any external reimbursement, and a wide variety of other research support provided by the university, whether for released time from teaching, unfunded facility, equipment and personnel costs, support structures for graduate students, or institutionally supported research work, receives no external funding. In a resource-constrained environment, some observers worry that the financial model that has

supported the current scale of America's dynamic and productive research university environment cannot continue.[4]

However, even if the data may indicate that research generates an increasing net cost to institutions, it may not follow that all current research universities will reduce their commitment to research in pursuit of a more economically rational model of institutional finance. The most successful research universities, moreover, compete not to get rich but rather to generate the funds needed to accumulate the highest level of quality elements within their institutional boundaries as possible. The external marketplace for their goods and services serves primarily as a venue for acquiring the resources to continue expanding their internal quality.

Indeed, this characteristic of the research university model deserves more attention than it usually receives. These institutions function as quality engines, that is they operate to capture the largest amount of nationally competitive quality elements within their institutional boundaries. These quality elements include students, faculty, staff, facilities, and programs, but above all they seek to acquire research faculty and associated personnel. Research capable faculty and staff bring with them or attract a wide range of other quality assets, whether graduate students, competitive grants, research publications, post-docs, or high-level scientific staff. Because these high performing faculty are in short supply relative to the demand from many research-competitive institutions for their services, they can command a significant university investment. This investment is less about salaries or individual faculty compensation and more about facilities, support personnel, institutional research infrastructure, graduate student support, and availability of related high-quality faculty and programs. The prestige and significance of any research university is the result of the cumulative impact of these high performing people supported by the infrastructure and research-related personnel of the institution.[5]

For this reason, the primary indicator of research university success has generally been the annual amount of federally sponsored science and engineering research expenditures. This number is useful for this purpose not because it reflects a monetary accounting unit but because it reflects the annual research activity funded through the national peer review process of the various federal funding agencies. Annual federal expenditure data is a particularly useful indicator, as opposed to federal research awards, because it reflects annual direct activity on research billed to a federal research grant. It is also useful as a general proxy for the scale of institutional investment required to sustain that level of federal research activity. This funding model for American research activity has some consequences for the way research institutions operate.

The model is based, in simplified terms, on a competition that pits individual faculty research proposals against each other in a peer reviewed context. These proposals are not institutional proposals but individual faculty proposals (although of course they all carry a substantial component of institutional support that underlies the quality and strength of the proposal). The awards when they come are primarily faculty awards, although they may have a wide range of linked institutional commitments. In practice of course, many individual proposals have multiple faculty participants, may well involve individuals from a number of institutions in a collaborative framework, and can include linkages to corporations or other outside entities. Nonetheless, the core competencies that drive the success of the research university are the high performing faculty and associated staff whose records of achievement and whose reputations validate the likelihood of a successful research result from the funding proposed.[6]

This model places a significant burden on the research university that must recruit and retain nationally significant faculty in order to build the capacity to compete successfully in the peer review process for the national grants that define research university success. The institution's investment is, in many cases, a high-risk investment. Although it may be advantageous to recruit faculty who already have funded federal research grants, the marketplace does not offer a sufficient number of these individuals to meet the demand, and as a result institutions must also recruit younger promising faculty whose work offers the expectation of a successful research career. Sometimes the promise is fulfilled, and sometimes it is not, so the institutional investment in promising high performing faculty carries a significant risk.

Research universities cover this risk in a number of ways. The most obvious is through the tenure process that attempts over a relatively short window of time to identify which newly hired faculty members will have the greatest likelihood of continued long-term future research success. Those that pass this review are deemed to be more likely to have a significant long-term competitive research career than those who do not pass. While this process lowers somewhat the risk associated with hiring and supporting a particular faculty member, the time for decision is relatively short, perhaps five years, so some significant risk remains. This risk is covered in a variety of ways by institutions, depending on their circumstances.

In institutions with substantial undergraduate populations teaching and other functions associated with extensive undergraduate and masters or certificate programs provide a useful occupational niche for faculty whose research potential may not have reached or no longer can be sustained at the anticipated level of productivity. By shifting faculty effort from research to teaching and other institutional support activities, high quality faculty whose competitive research strengths are not quite up to the national level, remain productive and their cost compensated by the work they do on behalf of the undergraduate, masters, or certificate programs.

This model is particularly relevant for the large public research universities whose research accomplishments have elevated many of them into the top levels of national and international competition. The size of the undergraduate student body and the growth of profitable masters and certificate programs serve public universities especially as a buffer against the risk associated with providing tenure to candidates early in their research careers. Large undergraduate and pre-doctoral student populations in public universities also provide other advantages. While tuition and fee revenue for undergraduates generally do not pay for the full cost of their education, in most states, public funding tends to be driven by calculations closely related to student credit hours or their derivatives. In addition, since institutions rarely discount masters and certificate tuition and fees, these programs more than pay their own way. Some infrastructure and other operating costs of the institution, subsidized by the undergraduate and non-PhD graduate student economy, also subsidize research infrastructure, whether related to buildings, core support of energy costs, basic accounting and other business services, security, legal, technology, and the like. The larger the university budget from all sources, the better able the institution will be to support the special costs of sustaining highly competitive research faculty. Further illustrating this process, private research universities have also grown their undergraduate and master's level programs in recent years.[7]

For all research universities, public or private, funding from annual gifts and endowment earnings also serve to cover unfunded costs, whether for educational or research expenses. Long a staple of the private institutional financial model, all public institutions now seek private funding with highly professional staffs and systems. They generate large amounts from annual giving and accumulate endowments that range into the billions of dollars. This support, too, is a required element of the research university financial structure, for without this revenue, the scale of institutional activity could not be sustained.

In short, the current research model seeks out all types of revenue to create a financial base capable of sustaining the substantial unfunded costs of highly competitive research faculty, staff, and facilities. This university quality engine, fueled by this financial base, seeks to acquire the highest level and volume of quality within its boundaries. It uses this engine to attract students, faculty, alumni, donors, granting agencies, foundations, and others to participate in and with the accumulated quality. These people engage primarily to participate in various ways with the quality assembled inside the boundaries of the institution. They individually receive various intellectual, social, or personal benefits unique to each participant's needs and interests, and they use these primarily intangible benefits to enhance their marketability or significance outside the university.[8]

CHARACTERISTICS OF RESEARCH UNIVERSITIES

While it is useful to take a broad, high level look at the research university marketplace, such a perspective can lull us into imagining a more homogeneous world of universities participating in the research marketplace than exists in reality. The profiles of successful American research universities are significantly varied. Over the years we have explored a wide range of topics related to university competition and improvement through the work of The Center for Measuring University Performance (MUP), and we have tested a number of different perspectives for understanding this competition.

Given the American mania for ranking, we have looked in various ways at what we call the *Search for Number One*. This Quixotic effort to bring some rationality to the ranking conversation has been helped by many others in the field. We have all sought to impress on our colleagues and outside observers that any methodology that offers a rank ordering of institutions from Number One on down, using a variety of measures combined into a single index number is sure to be methodologically unsound and theoretically flawed.

There is no best university. What we have are clusters of similar universities that share many of the same characteristics, that compete with each other, sometimes improving over time and sometimes not, but all of whom operate within groups that are substantially and often indistinguishably similar. In America we struggle to determine what we mean by a "good" university, and since we cannot make up our minds, we collect data of varying quality and imagine that by using clever statistical methods we can turn incompatible data into a single golden number that will tell us that the number 5 university is twice as good as the number 10 university. This is magical thinking but immensely popular and profitable for those who pursue such alchemy.[9]

CHANGE AND STABILITY IN THE AMERICAN RESEARCH UNIVERSITY MARKETPLACE

Recognizing the many changes and much innovation taking place throughout American higher education, the sector of highly competitive research university remains nonetheless remarkably stable. In our latest annual report (2017), we have identified some 158 universities (public and private) with over $40 million in federal science and engineering expenditures in 2015. This group represents about 19% of the academic institutions spending federal research funds and captures about 92% of the federal research expenditures reported by all these institutions. This relationship with minor variations has remained stable for over at least

a decade and a half.[10]

This stability is all the more remarkable given the many innovations and changes that have characterized the instructional and financial context of all of American higher education. Research universities constitute a special category among the many components of the American post-secondary marketplace. Their significance and visibility sometimes appear much greater than their participation levels in many parts of the higher education community. For example, out of the 2,317 four-year higher education institutions (excluding for profit enterprises), the top group of 158 research universities in our data used for this discussion constitutes only 7% of the institutions and enrolls something on the order of 3.6 million students, representing only about 28% of the 12.8 million students enrolled at all levels of public and private non-profit 4-year and above institutions. However, because they represent a highly visible and prestigious cluster of universities, many capturing exceptional visibility through their intercollegiate sports programs, and because their doctoral programs produce a constant stream of instructors and faculty throughout the higher education industry and with a significant presence in may sectors of the national economy, what takes place on these campuses often dominates the public conversation about higher education.[11]

There are many ways to highlight the stability of these research universities, and to recognize their long-standing significance within the post-secondary marketplace. The model of research university success that focuses on the capture of federal and other research dollars, the acquisition of highly qualified and productive faculty, and the development of other related assets, encouraged us to review the performance of the top research institutions over time to illustrate their success in maintaining their preeminence.[12]

THE PLACE OF THE TOP RESEARCH UNIVERSITIES IN THE RESEARCH MARKETPLACE

For this illustration we have taken our top group of academic research institutions in 2015 (defined by MUP as those with over $40M in annual federal research expenditures) and looked back in time to see if their dominant position remained stable over the last decade or so when much of the current conversation about institutional transformations and the restructuring of the academic marketplace has taken place. Some 158 fall into our top category of over $40M in 2015. We compare the performance of these 158 institutions, tracked back at intervals through 2003 on our measures, to the 962 institutions that spent any federal research funds within a five-year period between 2011 and 2015.

In our data we start with federal research expenditures as reported by NSF and adjusted by the MUP staff to ensure a consistent single-campus comparison. In recent years, NSF guidelines have more closely matched our definition of single campus institutions for reporting purposes, thereby reducing the number of adjustments we needed to make. Table 1 below illustrates that the top academic institutions, representing 19% of the research university pool, captured a stable share of federal research from 2003 through 2015 at 90% to 92%.[13]

Total research expenditures include both federal and non-federal funds (state and local and other sourced expenditures reported by institutions, some of which are peer reviewed and some of which are not). These resources reflect a larger pool of funds, many from local and state sources, and their distribution offers a profile similar to the more competitive federal research expenditures as illustrated by the following Table 2. Over time, the percent share of the top institutions has declined from 25% in 2003 to 18% in 2015, likely the result in part of intense competition from less research-intensive institutions with good access to local and state funds and in part the consequence of an increase in the number of institutions from which data are collected.

Because a strong institutional financial base is necessary for the support of highly competitive research universities, we have used endowment assets as a proxy for institutional wealth. This is of course only an indicator since a number for the true wealth of institutions is exceptionally difficult to acquire in any consistent or comparable fashion. Nonetheless, this indicator offers an illustration of the ability of these institutions to capture a strong position within the domain of private fund raising for endowment at a steady 75% of all endowment assets recorded for institutions that participate in the research marketplace despite making up less than one-fourth of the research university population as is illustrated in Table 3 below. Not surprisingly, the data on annual giving shows a similar pattern.[14]

Faculty quality is another indicator of research university competitive success. While it is difficult to identify fully reliable measures of the achievements of university faculty in a comparative context, we have two indicators that serve to highlight the concentration of nationally recognized faculty in research institutions. One is the number of National Academy members in each institution. As the following table illustrates, National Academy members are heavily concentrated in the top research group as we might expect. A steady proportion of 97% of the National Academy members are in the over $40M group, although only 68% of the institutions in this group have faculty with these distinc-

Table 1. Federal Research

Institutions Reporting Any Federal Research in 2011-2015	2015 (in 000s)	Percent Share	2011 (in 000s)	Percent Share	2007 (in 000s)	Percent Share	2003 (in 000s)	Percent Share
Total Federal Research Expenditures	$36,815,202		$39,614,834		$30,374,171		$24,700,369	
Over $40M Group*	$33,730,208	92%	$35,496,476	90%	$27,194,103	90%	$22,182,180	90%
Number of Institutions with Federal Research	853		879		667		627	
Over $40M Group	158	19%	158	18%	157	24%	156	25%

*Institutions with more than $40 million in 2015 federal research expenditures.

Table 2. Total Research

Institutions Reporting Any Federal Research in 2011-2015	2015 (in 000s)	Percent Share	2011 (in 000s)	Percent Share	2007 (in 000s)	Percent Share	2003 (in 000s)	Percent Share
Total Research Expenditures	$65,024,118		$61,832,669		$49,374,619		$39,971,165	
Over $40M Group	$58,639,298	90%	$54,560,851	88%	$43,887,088	89%	$35,556,791	89%
Number of Institutions with Any Research	874		890		670		631	
Over $40M Group	158	18%	158	18%	157	23%	156	25%

Table 3. Total Endowment and Annual Giving

Institutions Reporting Any Federal Research in 2011-2015	2015 (in 000s)	Percent Share	2011 (in 000s)	Percent Share	2007 (in 000s)	Percent Share	2003 (in 000s)	Percent Share
Total Endowment Assets	$498,497,085		$384,567,427		$388,083,120		$211,499,504	
Over $40M Group	$374,223,994	75%	$287,447,059	75%	$290,816,235	75%	$153,511,476	73%
Number of Institutions Reporting Endowment	707		695		678		664	
Over $40M Group	154	22%	154	22%	153	23%	152	23%
Total Annual Giving	$32,068,451		$24,803,431		$23,556,287		$18,642,760	
Over $40M Group	$25,138,592	78%	$18,853,365	76%	$17,197,735	73%	$13,327,450	71%
Number of Institutions Reporting Giving	614		629		621		630	
Over $40M Group	153	25%	153	24%	144	23%	148	23%

tions as is illustrated in Table 4. This is a reflection of the concentration of National Academy members in a small number of institutions. About half of these individuals are in the 14 institutions that have over 100 National Academy members.

A second faculty indicator includes faculty who have received a variety of scholarly awards (outlined in detail on the MUP website and in the annual publication). These awards are for distinction in a wide range of fields, not just those in the sciences and engineering. Again, the over $40M institutions capture around 79% of the faculty awards even though they represent only 35% of all institutions having faculty with these awards as seen in Table 5. Of particular note here, 271 institutions not in the over $40M group nonetheless have high quality faculty who win these awards.

These indicators of quality concentration within the top research institutions focus primarily on elements associated with what we could call the published research enterprise. That is, the activities of the university's people that end up as published books and articles contributing to the advancement of knowledge. Much of that is identified by the proxy of federal research and other elements associated with the faculty who are the primary drivers of this work. At the

same time, however, these institutions sustain undergraduate enterprises, often of large size, and compete with other research institutions as well as liberal arts colleges for outstanding students. Again, data on the quality of incoming students is elusive, but the selectivity of colleges is often linked to the scores on the SAT or its equivalent. While of course the SAT has many defects as an indicator of likely undergraduate student success it does serve as a surrogate indicator of institutional undergraduate selectivity.

In our observation of research universities it appears likely that many high performing research faculty and staff not only seek institutions that can support their research ambitions but likely prefer to participate in the life of institutions with high quality students. The following table provides a glimpse into the differential attractiveness of research universities for high SAT students. Note, however, that in this case the research university advantage is relatively less impressive, as many colleges with minimal research profiles nonetheless capture a significant number of high SAT applicants. The over $40M group has an SAT advantage of only 145 points over institutions outside this group, a premium of around 13%. See Table 6 below. Not all universities that fall into our group of research institutions require or provide SAT data, so these numbers should only be taken as general indicators.

Table 4. National Academy Members

Institutions Reporting Any Federal Research in 2011-2015	2015	Percent Share	2011	Percent Share	2007	Percent Share	2003	Percent Share
Total Academy Members	4,747		4,350		3,937		3,584	
Over $40M Group	4,590	97%	4,204	97%	3,818	97%	3,479	97%
Number of Institutions with Members	214		210		197		186	
Over $40M Group	146	68%	147	70%	142	72%	133	72%

Table 5. Faculty Awards

Institutions Reporting Any Federal Research in 2011-2015	2015	Percent Share	2011	Percent Share	2007	Percent Share	2003	Percent Share
Total Faculty Awards	2,391		2,450		2,489		2,370	
Over $40M Group	1,896	79%	1,914	78%	1,976	79%	1,848	78%
Number of Institutions with Awards	415		433		422		442	
Over $40M Group	144	35%	148	34%	148	35%	149	34%

Table 6. Median SAT Score

Institutions Reporting Any Federal Research in Past Five Years	2015	Net Difference	2011	Net Difference	2007	Net Difference	2003	Net Difference
Average Median SAT	1102		1103		1095		1107	
Over $40M Group	1247	145	1231	128	1210	115	1207	100
Number of Institutions Reporting SAT	693		765		782		692	
Over $40M Group	125		126		129		127	
Percent Premium for Over $40M Group		13%		12%		11%		9%

Scale is an important element underlying research university success, in large part because sufficient scale helps spread the costs of research support and infrastructure over a larger number of projects, faculty, and research programs. Many research institutions have significant undergraduate student bodies whose numbers drive resources and support the teaching and other work associated with instruction that often provide an employment buffer for faculty whose research productivity may have declined but whose intellectual vitality remains strong. In many cases, as well, research faculty with highly successful programs and full funding nonetheless teach students at the undergraduate and graduate level, and offset some costs associated with their faculty salaries.

As the following table illustrates, the top research universities have over a third of the undergraduate and graduate students enrolled in all the institutions with any federal research expenditures. These top institutions have a somewhat lower percentage of undergraduates than the entire group, but a higher percentage of graduate students. However, the top research universities have about three times the median size of undergraduate population and about four times the median size of graduate population than the group as a whole. See Table 7.

Reflecting this emphasis on graduate education, the next table shows the expected distribution of degrees, with the top institutions in the over $40M group producing the smallest percentage of associate degrees, over a third of the bachelor's degrees, almost half the master's degrees, just over half the professional degrees, and over three quarters of the doctorate degrees. Since the over $40M group is just under one-fifth of the institutions included in this illustration, it is clear that they make a major impact on the degree production of all institutions with any participation in the federal research competition. See Table 8.

IMPACT OF THE CONTEMPORARY CONTEXT FOR HIGHER EDUCATION

These illustrations highlight the distinctiveness of the top American research universities within the context of the US higher education marketplace. They help us understand that general concerns about the trends and transformations affecting post-secondary schooling do not necessarily affect all institutions in the same way. Some vulnerabilities highlighted in the popular press do not apply to these institutions. Unlike many business enterprises, universities and especially research universities are generally long-term

Table 7. Student Enrollment

Institutions Reporting Any Federal Research in 2011-2015	2015 Total Students	2015 Total Undergraduates	2015 Total Graduate	Percent Undergraduate	Percent Graduate
Total Students	9,352,140	7,219,690	2,132,450	77%	23%
Over $40M Group	3,578,592	2,534,000	1,044,592	71%	29%
Percent Share for Over $40M Group	38%	35%	49%		
Median Fall Enrollment	5,826	4,743	1,412	81%	24%
Over $40M Group	23,104	17,498	5,926	76%	26%

Table 8. Degrees

Institutions Reporting Any Federal Research in 2011-2015	2015 Associate's	2015 Bachelor's	2015 Master's	2015 Doctorate	2015 Professional
Total Degrees	38,056	1,535,078	546,001	61,468	89,367
Over $40M Group	4,778	598,434	253,081	46,103	47,066
Percent Share for Over $40M Group	13%	39%	46%	75%	53%
Median Degrees	39	993	347	48	145
Over $40M Group	30	3,799	1,332	244	307

operations, and except for the smallest, usually private, colleges they are not at risk of economic collapse. Only a few non-profit institutions, especially small private colleges, heavily dependent on tuition revenue and without significant endowment, face the risk of imminent failure. The table included here provides a sense of the scale of institutional failures in recent years. Although these occurrences occasion much comment, the numbers, within the context of over 2,400 four-year institutions is not large as is clear in Table 9 below. [15]

Nonetheless, the major research institutions, while at no risk of failure and operating stable competitive enterprises, struggle constantly with the challenge of maintaining the scale of their operations through continuous adjustments on the margin. They engage in constant innovation, pursue opportunities of every kind made available by expanding technological capabilities, seek economies in operation through outsourcing, pursue revenue opportunities wherever they can be found, and constantly adjust their undergraduate programs to continue to capture the best possible students while expanding the diversity of their student bodies.[16]

Taken as productive organizations, research universities manage a wide range of product lines of dramatically varying profitability. Some generate net costs to the institution such as research and, for most institutions, intercollegiate sports. Some generate profits for the college such as undergraduate enrollment for public institutions with state funding and significant alumni support, stock market returns for private universities and private fund raising for all institutions. Of the characteristics that define these institutions, their resiliency over the years in the face of financial challenges is perhaps one of the most interesting.

A rational model of university operation that focused on return on investment or some other measurable utility function derived from commercial business enterprises would surely underestimate the value of the intangible products of the institutions that help explain their long-term behavior. It is possible that the stress of the current financial condition of American higher education will change the commitment to research that currently characterizes many institutions, but how these changes could produce a major re-framing of the American higher education marketplace is not yet clear.

LIKELY RESTRUCTURING OF THE HIGHER EDUCATION MARKETPLACE

In addressing these issues, it is important to emphasize again that American higher education is composed of quite distinct sectors. While they may have fuzzy boundaries, they are nonetheless substantially different in their organization, personnel composition, financial structures, opportunities, and expectations. Each of these sectors will respond to the current and likely future financial and demographic constraints by readjusting their operational models to meet changing public and private expectations in significantly different ways. Some will reconfigure their activities to acquire the efficiencies of sophisticated technologies and generate revenue by capturing currently under-served populations with low cost high volume enterprises. The traditional model of tenured professors defining the substance of the academic enterprise is already seriously modified at many institutions below the most prestigious and the ability of many universities to sustain a significant research presence will decline. Demographic trends will also have an impact although NCES projects continued stability and growth in the college age population through 2025.

Perhaps the most significant impact on the higher education marketplace will be the continued challenge in the public sector as states struggle to find sufficient revenue to meet their many required obligations, leaving in many cases little discretionary tax-based income for colleges. In any event, over time, the current higher education marketplace will continue to evolve into distinct operational sectors following different priorities (whatever their public relations rhetoric), with considerable turmoil at the boundaries. A wide range of quantitative indicators illustrate how much of that transformation is already well underway, even though the process is obscured by a media focus on elite institutions competing for small advantages among themselves and on exemplary or crisis driven individual institutional cases.

Table 9. Closures Among 4-Year Non-Profit Postsecondary Institutions

Year Closed	Public	Private
2010-11	0	6
2011-12	0	2
2012-13	1	2
2013-14	1	3
2014-15	0	3
2015-16	0	5
Six-Year Total	**2**	**21**

The top American research universities will continue their dominance of the upper end of the higher education spectrum. The current model as described here is surely sustainable. Those already among the top 150 to 200 institutions will likely continue to prosper although a few at the lower edges of this group may find it difficult to continue to keep pace with the top producers. Their faculty will remain highly tenured and predominately full-time although we may see various types of rolling term contracts for faculty in some fields. Moreover, it is possible that the context for major fund raising, a critical element in the financial structure of all major research universities, will encounter political difficulties as legislators seek the elimination of various tax deductions that have benefited research universities as a means to generate revenue that would support the campaigns to reduce tax rates on businesses and individuals.[17]

Another group of primarily public, comprehensive universities with some significant research presence will also prosper by diversifying into a wide range of occupational, masters, and technology enabled programs. They will have substantial undergraduate programs, extensive masters and certificate programs, and many professional programs. They will sponsor research in some areas but not at the intensity of the top universities. Their faculty will become more heavily contingent with the development of a variety of term contract faculty arrangements, in most cases developed through extensive negotiations with unions.

A group of smaller public and private institutions will struggle to maintain sufficient enrollment to prosper. They will expand into masters and certificate programs, seek economies with extensive outsourcing of a wide range of university services, and continue the trend to increasingly contingent faculty. They will experiment with various tuition/fee arrangements and discount and financial aid processes. Some private institutions in this group may fail and close or be absorbed by competitors, but the public institutions on the margin will more likely be consolidated into larger system entities rather than disappear.

A special category of small prestigious and heavily endowed private colleges will continue to prosper with an emphasis on highly qualified tenured faculty, elaborate programs and facilities, and high demand from students. These elite institutions will also continue to compete with the top research universities (public and private) for the most qualified undergraduate students. Many will also develop master's programs in many areas.

These categories will be very confusing at the boundaries, and many institutions will compete partially in one category and partially in another. However, in every case, the American higher education marketplace is likely to continue the trend that emphasizes the spread between elite institutions and non-elite institutions, between primarily academic and primarily occupationally centered institutions. Throughout, the controversies over elitism, diversity, inclusion, employability, and cost will remain a constant subtext in all discussions about the US higher education industry.[18]

Recent work has highlighted the economic basis for these changes, illustrating through sophisticated modeling the relationships between enrollment, tuition, other funding sources, and institutional expense categories. Such a model clearly shows that while the research university elite is likely to be able to continue to dominate the top echelon of name brand higher education, other institutions will find it increasingly difficult to compete within the tradition model defined by the research university sector. Major change will surely characterize those institutions below the top prestige institutions, with much creativity, innovation, new styles of instruction, higher investments in technology enable instruction, and an increased emphasis on occupational specialties within the traditional college and master's degree curricula.[19]

None of the innovations taking place below the top university level are likely to challenge the dominance of the major institutional performers. Any innovation that offers an opportunity for increased revenue or enhanced brand value, that reaches a new and profitable audience, will in almost all cases be immediately adopted and branded by a high prestige institution, often allowing the top institutions to siphon off some of the highest value transactions associated with these new ventures. This has occurred already with the evolution of some forms of distance education, and has been characteristic of high value, high priced niche certificate programs.

Finally, it is important to reemphasize that American higher education is a very stable industry with institutions with long histories and deep constituencies. While much is written about crisis and the challenges of rapid change, the American higher education industry has weathered a wide range of cultural, economic, political, and demographic changes over its long history with remarkable staying power. Even as the critiques about the value and cost of an American higher education multiply, the demand for a college education continues to rise. The simple lifetime earnings premium that a college education provides individuals guarantees that even as the higher education industry adapts tomorrow as it did yesterday to many changes in its environment, it will remain a core component of the American economic system.[20]

1 The Center for Measuring University Performance (MUP) has had a continuing interest in the process of university rankings. See the following series of papers from the MUP Center on this topic: Diane D. Craig and John V. Lombardi. "The Best American Research Universities, Rankings: Four Perspectives, *The Top American Research Universities* (TARU) (2013), Craig and Lombardi; "Measuring Research Performance: National and International Perspectives," TARU (2012); Lombardi, "In Pursuit of Number ONE," *TARU* (2010); Lombardi and Elizabeth D. Capaldi," Rankings, Competition, and the Evolving American University," *TARU* (2007); Lombardi, Craig, Capaldi, and Denise S. Gater, "The Myth of Number One: Indicators of Research University Performance, *TARU* (2000). Institutional selectivity is variously measured, sometimes by rejection/acceptance rates (with the possibility of institutional manipulation) and more commonly by median SAT (or equivalent) scores of admitted students. For data on SAT for research universities see: "SAT Scores (2003-2013)," MUP website [http://mup.umass.edu]. See also Gater, "The Competition for Top Undergraduates by America's Colleges and Universities," *TheCenter Reports* (May 2001) [http://mup.umass.edu/publications].

2 The following quotes from some of these websites are illustrative (emphasis added). From the Williams College website [https://employment.williams.edu/faculty/ (10/20/2017)] we have this general statement: "The members of Williams College's accomplished and diverse faculty are strongly committed to original **research** and artistic creation and to teaching undergraduates from a rich variety of backgrounds and experiences." The Amherst College website highlights this competitive context with the following general statement and some characteristic faculty profiles [https://employment.williams.edu/faculty/ (10/20/2017) "Amherst College faculty are foremost authorities in their fields, yet are exceptionally approachable." Amherst College Faculty Profiles: on a Professor of Economics: "Her **research** focuses on public health and social impacts of environmental pollution, malpractice and physician behavior, factors influencing judicial decision-making, and other topics in applied microeconomics. " On an Assistant Professor: "my **research** focuses on the intersection of market culture, institutions and state formation during this transitional period, in particular the relationship between court and commerce in the Low Countries where the aforementioned issues came together in dramatic and critical fashion." On another Professor:"My **research** focuses on Latin American cinema, and my contributions to the field include a book on Cuba's foremost film director … and the first comprehensive history of Latin American narrative cinema …" Another Professor: "Most of my research involves algebraic geometry, which is the field of mathematics that studies geometric objects by means of algebra. Some aspects of my work are very abstract, while others are more computational and applied. "Similar credentials are offered online [https://www.oxy.edu/faculty (10/20/2017)] for the faculty of a west coast competitor, Occidental College Professor: "Environmental Economist whose **research** falls into three areas: recycling, evaluation of environmental programs, and energy and climate policy." Associate Professor: "Her **research** interests include synapse formation, axon transport, and regulation of neuronal microtubules. She uses a combination of genetic, molecular biology, and cell biology techniques to study nervous system development using the nematode C. elegans as a model organism." Professor: "...**Research** areas are computational aerodynamics, scientific computation, numerical analysis, mathematical modeling of physical phenomena, and applying mathematics to 'real world' situations. He has published several articles in various peer-reviewed journals," [https://www.oxy.edu/faculty (10/20/2017)]

3 On state support see *State Higher Education Finance (SHEF) FY 2017*, State Higher Education Executive Officers, 2018; and Ingrid Schroeder, et al. *Federal and State Funding of Higher Education: A Changing Landscape*, (Pew Charitable Trusts, 2015). Of particular interest is the current controversy over funding the University of California System, see: Kevin Cook, "A Long-term View of Higher Education Funding," Public Policy Institute of California (August 16, 2018) and John Aubrey Douglass and Zachary Bleemer, "Approaching a Tipping Point? A History and Prospectus of Funding for the University of California," University of California, Berkeley, August 20, 2018. On tuition and fees over time see: "Tuition and Fees, 1999-2000 to 2012-2013," *Chronicle of Higher Education*, (October 24, 2012). For the current structure of tuition discounting see: *NACUBO 2017 Tuition Discounting Study*, National Association of College and University Business Officers, (Washington, DC, 2018); Lucie Lapovsky, "Phantom Dollars: Findings from 1996 NACUBO Tuition Discounting Survey," *NACUBO Business Officer*, March 1997; Sandy Baum, Lucie Lapovsky, and Jennifer Ma, *Tuition Discounting: Institutional Aid Patterns at Public and Private Colleges and Universities, 2000-01 to 2008-09* (The College Board, 2010). An example of the controversies over university debt load see Charlie Eaton, et al. "Swapping our Future: How Students and Taxpayers are Funding Risky UC Borrowing and Wall Street Profits" in "Critical Approaches to Financialization (*Berkeley Journal of Sociology*, 57, 2013), pp. 178-199; and Josh Freedman, "The Hidden College Problem: When Universities, Not Just Students, Take On Debt," Forbes (March 19, 2014). See also Robert C. Lowry, "Subsidizing Institutions vs. Outputs vs. Individuals: States' Choices for Financing Public Postsecondary Education," *Journal of Public Administration Research and Theory*, (2016). A labor union perspective on public funding for higher education is in *A Decade of Neglect. Public Education Funding in the Aftermath of the Great Recession*, AFT (2018).

4 Heidi Ledford, "Keeping The Lights On. Every Year, the US Government Gives Research Institutions Billions of Dollars Towards Infrastructure And Administrative Support. A Nature Investigation Reveals Who Is Benefiting Most," Nature (19 November 2014) [http://www.nature.com/news/indirect-costs-keeping-the-lights-on-1.16376] *Basic Scientific and Engineering Research at U.S. Universities, AAU Data and Policy Brief* (February 2015, No 1) [https://www.aau.edu/sites/default/files/AAU%20Files/AAU%20Documents/BasicResearchPaper-FINAL.pdf]

5 Lombardi, Craig, Capaldi, Gater, Sarah L. Mendonça,"Quality Engines: The Competitive Context for Research Universities," *The Top American Research Universities, 2001 Annual Report*.

6 Federal expenditures is but one of nine measures used and The MUP Center has produced these data since its first publication as described in Lombardi, Craig, Capaldi, and Gater, "The Myth of Number One: Indicators of Research University Performance," *TARU* (2000) cited above. Over the years we have revisited these indicators, and viewed the data from different perspectives. See for example Lombardi, Capaldi, Denise S. Mirka, Craig W. Abbey, "Deconstructing University Rankings: Medicine and Engineering, and Single Campus Research Competitiveness," (*TARU*, 2005 Corrected). See also the review of the results of including non-Science and Engineering federal funding in a measure of research university competitiveness in Craig and Lombardi, "Tracking Academic Research Funding: The Competitive Context for the Last Ten Years," *TARU* (2014). In the Source Notes and Data Notes included in each edition of the *Top American Research Universities* [http://mup.umass.edu] we provide a discussion of the validity of the data used in these publications and web-based data tables as well as a review of any data adjustments made. For some considerations on the various data elements for measuring research university performance see: Gater, "Using National Data in University Rankings and Comparisons," (TheCenter Reports, June 2003); Gater, "A Review of Measures Used in U.S. News & World Report's America's Best Colleges" (TheCenter, Summer 2002); Gater and Lombardi, "The Use of IPEDS/AAUP Faculty Data in Institutional Peer Comparisons," (TheCenter Reports, 2001).

7 Of the 158 academic institutions in our top group of over $40M in federal research expenditures in our most recent report (2017, reflecting 2015 expenditures), 70 percent or 110 are public [http://mup.umass.edu/University-Data].

8 It is exceptionally difficult to get good comparable data on university finance. Public and private institutions report their results differently, accounting standards vary, state funding structures for public institutions also differ by state with some items carried as state general obligations in some places and on the institution's books in others. While it is clear that money matters and research universities require a substantial financial base to compete effectively, some creative estimates are necessary to approximate an analysis. We attempted such an analysis in Lombardi, Craig, Capaldi-Phillips, and Gater, "University Organization, Governance, and Competitiveness," *The Top American Research Universities, 2002 Annual Report*. In this experiment, which also included a discussion of the impact of institutional organizational structure, we could illustrate the close relationship between university wealth and competitive research performance.

9   In addition to the items in note 1 above, the following offer some perspective on the challenges associated with various ranking schemes. See for example: Christopher Claassen, "Measuring University Quality," *Scientometrics* (2015, 104); Shari L. Gnolek, Vincenzo T. Falciano, and Ralph W. Kuncl, "Modeling Change and Variation in U.S. News & World Report College Rankings: What Would It Really Take to be in the Top 20?" *Research in Higher Education* (May 2014); Ellen Hazelkorn, "Reflections on a Decade of Global Rankings: What We've Learned and Outstanding Issues," *European Journal of Education* (9:1, 2014); Andrejs Rauhvargers, "Global University Rankings and their Impact: Report II European University Association," 2013; *IREG Ranking Audit Manual*, IREG Observatory on Academic Ranking and Excellence. International Ranking Expert Group, Warsaw, Poland (November 2011); Michael Sauder and Wendy Nelson Espeland, "The Discipline of Rankings: Tight Coupling and Organizational Change," *American Sociological Review* (74, 2009).

10 The apparent stability of the top research university group does not, however, mean that they are exempt from competition among themselves. In a study published in the MUP 2011 annual report we explored a number of the elements characterizing the competition within this top group and charted the changes in the indicator of federal research expenditures over time. In that study it is clear that the barriers to dramatic changes in the composition of this group are quite significant. Craig and Lombardi, "Moving Up: The Marketplace for Federal Research in America," *The Top American Research Universities, 2011 Annual Report*.

11 The total number of students is taken from NCES *Digest of Education Statistics*, 2016 Tables and Figures, Table 317.40, for Fall 2015. The number of students in the top research universities is taken from the IPEDS 2015 Fall Enrollment Survey. Note that NCES uses the Carnegie Classifications for research universities (see the note to the table cited above from NCES) which is similar to our own Top American Research Universities, but not identical. In the 2003 MUP annual report, we produced a thorough analysis of "The Sports Imperative in America's Research Universities" (Lombardi et al., MUP, 2003) The general analysis and conclusions of this report remain even more relevant today as the significance of the intercollegiate sports enterprise continues to expand and research universities appear determined to capture a predominant place in this domain.

12 For another related perspective on the stability of America's top research universities see Lombardi and Craig, "American Research University in an Era of Change: 2006-2015," *The Top American Research Universities, 2016 Annual Report*.

13 Federal research expenditure data is influenced by the fields for which congress appropriates money to federal agencies. Over the recent decades, the investment in medically related research has been the dominant field above all others. Of the almost $70 billion in Federal R&D obligations estimated for 2017 about $33 billion is in life sciences areas. Institutions with research intensive medical centers or standalone academic medical centers have an advantage in the competition for this large segment of federal research funds. See: Table 19. Federal obligations for research, by detailed field of science and engineering: FYs 2015–17 at [https://ncsesdata.nsf.gov/fedfunds/2015/html/FFS2015_DST_019.html]. However, not all academic institutions with medical schools benefit since many medical schools are not research intensive. For a discussion of the impact of medical schools on university research funding see "University Rankings: Medicine and Engineering, and Single Campus Research Competitiveness," (2005 Corrected) cited in note 6 above.

14 For a discussion of the challenges involved in calculating institutional wealth see note 9 above. NCES data on the financial structure of colleges and universities has many difficulties, most indicated in the notes to the tables published there. Of particular concern are the expenditure data, much used in the popular press and key to the often cited work of the Delta Cost Project of the American Institutes for Research (Washington, DC, 2017). The accounting systems of the individual universities on which the NCES and Delta Cost Project expenditure data are based, do not have sufficient detail or consistency between public and private institutions to support clear analysis of institutional expenses by such categories as instruction and research. See: Ozan Jaquette, and Edna Parra, "The Problem with the Delta Cost Project Database," *Research in Higher Education*, (March 30, 2015).

15 The specter of college failure is of such interest in large part because so few actually die. In recent years the number of small college failures has attracted considerable attention from the higher education press as is evident in the following selection of articles: Kellie Woodhouse, "Mills College Struggles with Financial Difficulty, Faculty Unrest as President Calls it Quits," *Inside Higher Ed* (May 12, 2015); Dawn Lyken-Segosebe and Justin Cole Shepherd. "Learning from Closed Institutions: Indicators of Risk for Small Private Colleges and Universities," *Higher Education Leadership and Policy Studies*, Vanderbilt University, (July 2013); Stephen R. Porter, "Why do colleges fail? An Analysis of College and University Closings and Mergers, 1975-2005," Department of Educational Leadership and Policy Studies, Iowa State University, 2009; Lawrence Biemiller, "Is Sweet Briar's Closure a Warning Sign for Other Small Colleges?" *The Chronicle of Higher Education* (March 3, 2015); Biemiller, "Survival at Stake In the Aftermath of the Recession, Small Colleges Adapt to a New Market," *The Chronicle of Higher Education* (March 2, 2015); Eric Kelderman,."The Plight of the Public Regional College," *The Chronicle of Higher Education* (November 19, 2014); Ry Rivard." Public HBCUs, Facing Tests on Many Fronts, Fight for Survival," *Inside Higher Ed* (June 24, 2014); Scott Jaschik, "Deal Will Save Sweet Briar College," *Inside Higher Ed* (June 20, 2015); Kellie Woodhouse, "Enrollment Declines Drove Closure of Marian Court College," *Inside Higher Ed* (June 18, 2015); Beth McMurtrie,"Why Is It So Hard to Kill a College?" *The Chronicle of Higher Education* (June 29, 2015); Amemona Hartocollis, "At Small Colleges, Harsh Lessons About Cash Flow," *The New York Times* (April 29, 2016); James Rushing Daniel, "Crisis at the HBCU," *Composition Studies* (44.2, 2016). The table is drawn from Table 317.50 of the NCES *Digest of Education Statistics*, 2016 highlights the issue of college closing, a primarily private, small college phenomenon.

16 One of the key indicators of the challenge of maintaining the financial base of the highly competitive research universities is the expansion of ambitious fund raising campaigns. Although private universities have been in the many million to billion dollar campaign business for many years, the top public research universities, recognizing the weakness of their state funding base, have also developed outstanding fund raising organizations over the past decades. Today, multi-billion dollar comprehensive fund raising campaigns are the norm for public research universities. See Rick Seltzer, "Colleges And Universities Set High Targets in Latest Fund-Raising Campaigns," *Inside Higher Ed* (October 17, 2017).

17 Many institutions seek to participate at the highest levels of research performance and to improve their status within the research university environment. See for some commentary on this subject, Gary A. Olson, "What Institutions Gain From Higher Carnegie Status," *The Chronicle of Higher Education* (July 29, 2018); Eric Kelderman, "Is Climbing the Carnegie Research Rankings Worth the Price Tag?" *The Chronicle of Higher Education* (July 29, 2018).

18 The research universities also find themselves in a constant conversation on improving the quality and effectiveness of their graduate programs, with initiatives proposed that will no doubt raise the costs of graduate education, at least in the STEM fields, substantially. See Alan Leshner and Layne Scherer, Eds., *Graduate STEM Education for the 21st Century*, A Consensus Study Report of the National Academies of Science, Engineering, and Medicine (2018).

19 On modeling and predicting university futures see William B. Rouse, *Universities as Complex Enterprises: How Academia Works, Why It Works These Ways, and Where the University Enterprise Is Headed*. John Wiley & Sons (2016) and the forthcoming article mentioned above William B. Rouse, John V. Lombardi, and Diane D. Craig, "Modeling Research Universities: Predicting Probable Futures of Public vs. Private and Large vs. Small Research Universities" in the *Proceedings of the National Academy of Sciences* (ca. 2018).

20 The conversation about the constant institutional adjustment to challenges is reflected in two items from the higher education press: Eric Kelderman, "A Regional Public University Scales Back Its Research Ambitions," *The Chronicle of Higher Education* (October 20, 2011) and Lee Gardner "Public Regional Colleges Never Die. Can They Be Saved?" *The Chronicle of Higher Education* (April 30, 2017).

Part I – The Top American Research Universities

The Center for Measuring University Performance determines the Top American Research Universities by their rank on nine different measures: Total Research, Federal Research, Endowment Assets, Annual Giving, National Academy Members, Faculty Awards, Doctorates Granted, Postdoctoral Appointees, and SAT scores. (The Source Notes section of this study provides detailed information on each of the nine indicators.) The tables group research institutions according to how many times they rank in the top 25 on each of these nine measures. The top category includes those universities that rank in the top 25 on all nine indicators. The bottom category includes universities with only one of the nine measures ranked in the top 25. Within these groups, institutions are then sorted by how many times they rank between 26 and 50 on the nine performance variables, with ties listed alphabetically. A similar methodology produces a second set of institutions—those ranked 26 through 50 on the same nine measures.

For the purpose of this study, *The Center for Measuring University Performance* includes only those institutions that had at least $40 million in federal research expenditures in fiscal year 2015. This is the same dollar cutoff used since the 2008 report. There were 158 institutions who met our criteria, 110 public and 48 private.

The first two tables list each institution with the most current data available for each measure and its corresponding national rank (i.e., rank among all institutions regardless of whether they are privately or publicly controlled). The third through sixth tables provide the same nine data measures but with the groupings determined by the control rank (i.e., rank among all private or all public institutions). Institutions ranking in the top 25 on at least one measure are included in the tables with the (1-25) identifier, while those ranking 26 through 50 are found in the tables labeled with the (26-50) header. Many research universities rank highly both nationally and among their public or private peers, and therefore appear in more than one table.

- **The Top American Research Universities (1-25)** identifies the 51 institutions (26 private, 25 public) that rank in the top 25 nationally on at least one of the nine measures.

- **The Top American Research Universities (26-50)** identifies the 23 institutions (5 private, 18 public) that rank 26 through 50 nationally on at least one of the nine measures.

- **The Top Private Research Universities (1-25)** identifies the 31 private institutions that rank in the top 25 among all private universities on at least one of the nine measures.

- **The Top Private Research Universities (26-50)** identifies the 7 private institutions that rank 26 through 50 among their private counterparts on at least one of the nine measures.

- **The Top Public Research Universities (1-25)** identifies the 43 public institutions that rank in the top 25 among all public universities on at least one of the nine measures.

- **The Top Public Research Universities (26-50)** identifies the 28 public institutions that rank 26 through 50 among their public counterparts on at least one of the nine measures.

- **The Top Medical and Specialized Research Universities** tables identify the institutions that have at least one measure that ranks in the top 50 nationally or among their private and public counterparts.

Data found in these tables may not always match the figures published by the original source. *The Center for Measuring University Performance* makes adjustments, when necessary, to ensure that the data reflect the activity at a single campus rather than that of a multiple-campus institution or state university system. When data are missing from the original source, *The Center for Measuring University Performance* may substitute another figure, if available. A full discussion of this subject, and the various adjustments or substitutions made to the original data, is in the Data Notes section of this report.

The Center for Measuring University Performance presents these tables, along with prior years' top universities, in Microsoft Excel spreadsheets on its website [http://mup.umass.edu].

Top American Research Universities (1-25)		Number of Measures in Top 25 Nationally	Number of Measures in Top 26-50 Nationally	Research				Private	
Institutions in Order of Top 25 Score, then Top 26-50 Score, then Alphabetically		Number of Measures in Top 25 Nationally	Number of Measures in Top 26-50 Nationally	2015 Total Research x $1000	2015 National Rank	2015 Federal Research x $1000	2015 National Rank	2016 Endowment Assets x $1000	2016 National Rank
Private	Columbia University	9	0	826,010	18	577,833	7	9,041,027	11
Private	Harvard University	9	0	955,246	9	530,382	13	34,541,893	1
Private	Massachusetts Institute of Technology	9	0	858,917	12	486,650	15	13,181,515	5
Private	Stanford University	9	0	969,643	8	645,633	4	22,398,130	3
Private	University of Pennsylvania	9	0	828,649	17	597,791	6	10,715,364	7
Public	University of Michigan - Ann Arbor	8	1	1,300,340	2	728,712	3	9,743,461	9
Private	Yale University	8	1	792,953	19	471,381	17	25,408,600	2
Public	University of California - Los Angeles	8	0	992,009	7	482,771	16	3,849,133	22
Private	Duke University	7	2	1,029,193	6	558,566	9	6,839,780	14
Private	Johns Hopkins University	7	2	2,299,057	1	1,988,993	1	3,381,281	28
Public	University of California - Berkeley	7	2	748,139	21	342,042	26	3,845,281	23
Public	University of Washington - Seattle	7	1	1,101,078	4	851,573	2	2,968,013	30
Public	University of Wisconsin - Madison	7	1	938,366	11	506,910	14	2,739,728	33
Private	Northwestern University	6	3	627,320	29	385,868	24	9,648,497	10
Private	University of Southern California	6	3	650,457	27	408,105	21	4,608,714	19
Public	Ohio State University - Columbus	6	2	745,238	22	406,941	22	3,578,562	25
Public	University of Minnesota - Twin Cities	6	2	844,016	14	468,482	18	3,280,681	29
Public	University of North Carolina - Chapel Hill	6	2	939,252	10	577,574	8	2,889,679	32
Private	University of Chicago	5	3	402,777	53	290,776	39	7,001,204	13
Public	University of California - San Diego	5	2	1,093,784	5	601,184	5	1,176,581	70
Private	Cornell University	4	5	637,404	28	277,163	41	4,524,419	20
Public	University of Texas - Austin	4	4	551,654	35	331,388	29	10,935,781	6
Private	Washington University in St. Louis	4	4	680,150	26	424,723	20	6,461,717	15
Public	Pennsylvania State Univ. - Univ. Park	4	3	683,003	25	447,956	19	1,912,254	45
Private	Princeton University	4	3	272,379	80	157,867	75	22,152,580	4
Public	Texas A&M University - College Station	4	3	836,250	15	291,714	38	9,944,936	8
Private	Emory University	3	5	574,472	34	346,534	25	6,401,650	16
Private	New York University	3	5	505,071	41	326,691	32	3,487,702	27
Public	University of Florida	3	4	699,750	24	281,317	40	1,461,347	62
Public	University of Illinois - Urbana-Champaign	3	4	614,011	31	330,479	30	1,489,991	59
Public	University of Pittsburgh - Pittsburgh	3	4	852,333	13	554,658	10	3,524,904	26
Private	Vanderbilt University	3	4	619,866	30	390,701	23	3,822,187	24
Private	University of Notre Dame	3	1	171,148	108	82,615	112	8,374,083	12
Public	Georgia Institute of Technology	2	5	757,116	20	548,063	11	1,843,764	46
Private	California Institute of Technology	2	4	350,833	61	269,156	44	2,106,724	39
Public	Purdue University - West Lafayette	2	4	498,887	43	209,005	56	2,254,541	36
Public	University of California - Davis	2	4	706,087	23	322,919	34	965,805	90
Private	Dartmouth College	2	1	203,660	98	145,807	79	4,474,404	21
Private	Rice University	2	0	141,935	120	73,817	122	5,324,289	18
Public	University of Colorado - Boulder	1	5	403,654	52	341,828	27	583,190	154
Public	University of Maryland - College Park	1	5	503,368	42	332,079	28	466,075	183
Private	Boston University	1	3	372,267	58	256,562	49	1,654,531	52
Private	Brown University	1	3	286,332	78	127,886	83	2,963,366	31
Private	Carnegie Mellon University	1	3	241,829	86	187,259	64	1,708,618	49
Public	North Carolina State University	1	3	462,347	45	196,058	60	998,600	87
Public	Rutgers University - New Brunswick	1	3	607,257	32	320,311	35	865,867	101
Public	University of Virginia	1	2	339,813	64	186,676	66	5,852,309	17
Public	Arizona State University	1	1	403,708	51	186,890	65	612,590	148
Private	Northeastern University	1	0	115,664	137	78,379	119	693,025	128
Private	Tufts University	1	0	162,510	113	120,181	88	1,562,968	57
Public	University of California - Santa Barbara	1	0	213,537	95	114,596	94	273,679	253

Support		Faculty				Advanced Training				Undergraduate	
2016 Annual Giving x $1000	2016 National Rank	2016 National Academy Members	2016 National Rank	2016 Faculty Awards	2016 National Rank	2016 Doctorates Granted	2016 National Rank	2015 Post Docs	2015 National Rank	2015 Median SAT	2015 National Rank
584,809	6	136	5	25	15	587	21	1,249	7	1475	11
1,187,530	1	382	1	66	1	713	12	5,674	1	1500	6
419,752	16	267	3	33	8	646	17	1,493	4	1505	5
951,149	2	340	2	48	2	763	7	2,264	2	1485	8
542,851	7	118	9	34	7	540	25	901	14	1465	13
433,776	14	113	12	48	2	848	3	1,299	5	1390	38
519,146	9	117	10	28	9	411	44	1,157	10	1515	4
498,800	11	100	15	22	19	775	6	1,016	12	1325	71
506,441	10	67	19	25	15	537	26	584	31	1455	19
657,293	4	101	14	21	21	528	30	1,679	3	1445	21
348,865	20	230	4	36	5	576	23	1,184	9	1380	45
541,444	8	110	13	35	6	632	18	1,205	8	1245	117
318,828	23	77	16	27	12	870	2	765	17	1300	83
401,679	17	42	29	25	15	467	40	746	19	1440	25
666,641	3	48	25	21	21	714	11	475	43	1385	41
386,112	18	33	35	21	21	807	4	619	27	1300	83
332,851	22	41	30	27	12	804	5	752	18	1280	94
308,694	24	38	31	28	9	542	24	803	16	1360	51
443,305	13	70	17	21	21	396	46	586	30	1520	2
206,873	35	119	8	25	15	529	29	1,250	6	1335	68
427,089	15	63	20	20	25	497	35	502	39	1430	30
345,992	21	70	17	18	30	896	1	370	49	1290	90
269,877	26	48	25	16	35	266	80	615	28	1460	15
147,570	56	28	43	22	19	659	16	366	50	1195	183
267,876	27	126	7	20	25	373	50	526	38	1490	7
276,475	25	32	36	8	69	705	13	615	28	1190	190
192,700	38	31	38	18	30	251	84	642	24	1380	45
461,150	12	56	22	18	30	489	37	680	20	1360	51
243,666	30	26	49	15	41	723	10	679	21	1260	109
159,693	47	56	22	38	4	726	9	542	36	1280	94
127,155	66	32	36	17	33	461	41	664	22	1265	104
143,605	58	34	34	13	46	322	62	629	26	1485	8
371,762	19	4	111	16	35	216	93	124	112	1460	15
129,304	64	31	38	19	28	531	28	237	77	1405	34
182,869	41	114	11	8	69	190	105	552	35	1550	1
151,217	53	28	43	27	12	727	8	389	48	1205	160
129,224	65	46	27	14	45	513	34	833	15	1205	160
227,038	32	16	62	9	63	87	185	204	87	1445	21
102,977	76	24	51	8	69	211	97	263	68	1475	11
160,445	46	29	41	16	35	410	45	911	13	1220	138
146,044	57	27	46	13	46	592	20	496	41	1315	78
156,941	50	19	61	10	58	579	22	421	46	1305	81
207,725	34	21	56	16	35	235	88	252	74	1465	13
155,302	51	43	28	16	35	323	60	193	90	1450	20
129,948	63	21	56	20	25	518	33	497	40	1245	117
118,493	69	36	32	12	51	620	19	306	56	1225	136
245,392	29	23	52	7	81	315	67	420	47	1355	58
140,417	60	22	53	19	28	674	14	257	71	1170	210
56,292	134	3	120	9	63	186	107	114	116	1440	25
60,405	124	12	70	8	69	135	136	182	92	1445	21
101,177	78	58	21	8	69	346	54	306	56	1225	136

Top American Research Universities (26-50)		Number of Measures in Top 26-50 Nationally	Research				Private	
Institutions in Order of Top 26-50 Score, then Alphabetically		Number of Measures in Top 26-50 Nationally	2015 Total Research x $1000	2015 National Rank	2015 Federal Research x $1000	2015 National Rank	2016 Endowment Assets x $1000	2016 National Rank
Public	University of Arizona	7	592,874	33	265,878	46	754,651	117
Public	Michigan State University	6	519,994	37	256,228	50	2,585,841	34
Public	University of Utah	5	509,409	39	270,311	43	1,076,649	80
Public	Indiana University - Bloomington	4	451,508	46	206,263	57	991,134	89
Private	Case Western Reserve University	3	400,167	55	307,960	36	1,662,739	51
Public	University of California - Irvine	3	313,798	70	170,622	72	498,171	169
Public	University of Cincinnati - Cincinnati	3	408,412	50	250,457	51	1,165,522	72
Public	University of Iowa	3	423,528	48	223,730	53	1,259,309	67
Public	University of Alabama - Birmingham	2	509,586	38	325,008	33	431,459	193
Private	University of Rochester	2	344,921	62	261,023	47	1,927,573	43
Public	University of South Florida - Tampa	2	420,002	49	196,215	59	395,324	201
Public	Virginia Polytechnic Institute and State University	2	495,502	44	191,080	63	842,991	103
Public	Florida State University	1	237,427	87	133,569	82	584,529	153
Private	Georgetown University	1	157,308	116	87,268	105	1,483,502	60
Private	Rensselaer Polytechnic Institute	1	102,122	140	59,417	136	634,916	143
Public	University of Colorado - Denver/Anschutz Medical	1	400,515	54	266,147	45	479,474	176
Public	University of Connecticut - Storrs	1	170,730	109	91,837	103	275,335	252
Public	University of Georgia	1	330,273	65	127,825	84	1,016,732	84
Public	University of Kentucky	1	325,558	67	145,097	80	1,117,852	78
Private	University of Miami	1	328,082	66	192,691	62	844,643	102
Public	University of Missouri - Columbia	1	243,430	84	102,852	99	869,566	99
Public	University of Oklahoma - Norman	1	92,075	146	57,455	138	1,003,434	85
Public	University of Tennessee - Knoxville	1	233,650	89	116,928	92	597,475	152

Support		Faculty				Advanced Training				Undergraduate	
2016 Annual Giving x $1000	2016 National Rank	2016 National Academy Members	2016 National Rank	2016 Faculty Awards	2016 National Rank	2016 Doctorates Granted	2016 National Rank	2015 Post Docs	2015 National Rank	2015 Median SAT	2015 National Rank
186,870	40	29	41	13	46	524	32	471	44		
176,131	43	14	63	12	51	533	27	471	44	1170	210
201,854	36	21	56	15	41	331	58	487	42	1130	288
195,908	37	13	67	16	35	485	38	365	51	1175	206
158,323	48	22	53	12	51	230	90	271	66	1400	35
73,657	106	30	40	15	41	393	47	297	60	1160	238
162,076	45	8	87	13	46	284	77	303	58	1170	210
192,262	39	20	59	9	63	468	39	346	54	1170	210
88,043	95	7	94	3	142	149	127	252	74	1150	246
107,297	72	22	53	5	101	301	74	233	80		
45,583	152	8	87	13	46	314	68	282	65	1170	210
100,057	80	14	63	6	92	492	36	225	81	1210	152
75,413	103	8	87	9	63	386	48	202	88	1220	138
153,384	52	9	78	2	178	124	146	109	118	1410	32
37,798	167	7	94	4	121	142	132	83	134	1385	41
106,963	73	14	63	7	81	123	149	288	63	1050	548
65,620	117	1	162	15	41	320	65	109	118	1235	129
133,881	62	7	94	9	63	526	31	250	76	1240	120
163,919	44	2	136	7	81	313	70	221	82	1150	246
236,334	31	13	67	5	101	216	93	258	70	1340	64
113,079	71	9	78	7	81	416	43	165	97	1205	160
252,996	28	1	162	4	121	210	98	133	107	1205	160
91,456	90	6	99	17	33	356	52	136	106	1220	138

Top Private Research Universities (1-25)		Number of Measures in Top 25 Control	Number of Measures in Top 26-50 Control	Research				Private	
Institutions in Order of Top 25 Score, then Top 26-50 Score, then Alphabetically				2015 Total Research x $1000	2015 Control Rank	2015 Federal Research x $1000	2015 Control Rank	2016 Endowment Assets x $1000	2016 Control Rank
Private	Columbia University	9	0	826,010	7	577,833	4	9,041,027	8
Private	Duke University	9	0	1,029,193	2	558,566	5	6,839,780	11
Private	Harvard University	9	0	955,246	4	530,382	6	34,541,893	1
Private	Johns Hopkins University	9	0	2,299,057	1	1,988,993	1	3,381,281	20
Private	Massachusetts Institute of Technology	9	0	858,917	5	486,650	7	13,181,515	5
Private	Northwestern University	9	0	627,320	12	385,868	12	9,648,497	7
Private	Stanford University	9	0	969,643	3	645,633	2	22,398,130	3
Private	University of Chicago	9	0	402,777	18	290,776	17	7,001,204	10
Private	University of Pennsylvania	9	0	828,649	6	597,791	3	10,715,364	6
Private	Washington University in St. Louis	9	0	680,150	9	424,723	9	6,461,717	12
Private	Yale University	9	0	792,953	8	471,381	8	25,408,600	2
Private	Cornell University	8	1	637,404	11	277,163	18	4,524,419	16
Private	Emory University	8	1	574,472	14	346,534	13	6,401,650	13
Private	New York University	8	1	505,071	17	326,691	15	3,487,702	19
Private	University of Southern California	8	1	650,457	10	408,105	10	4,608,714	15
Private	Vanderbilt University	8	1	619,866	13	390,701	11	3,822,187	18
Private	California Institute of Technology	7	2	350,833	22	269,156	20	2,106,724	24
Private	Princeton University	7	2	272,379	29	157,867	29	22,152,580	4
Private	Carnegie Mellon University	6	3	241,829	30	187,259	25	1,708,618	32
Private	Boston University	6	2	372,267	21	256,562	23	1,654,531	34
Private	Brown University	5	4	286,332	28	127,886	33	2,963,366	21
Private	Case Western Reserve University	5	4	400,167	19	307,960	16	1,662,739	33
Private	University of Notre Dame	4	5	171,148	36	82,615	38	8,374,083	9
Private	Dartmouth College	4	4	203,660	33	145,807	31	4,474,404	17
Private	Rice University	3	6	141,935	39	73,817	42	5,324,289	14
Private	University of Rochester	3	5	344,921	23	261,023	21	1,927,573	28
Private	University of Miami	3	4	328,082	24	192,691	24	844,643	62
Private	Northeastern University	2	5	115,664	43	78,379	40	693,025	81
Private	Tufts University	1	8	162,510	37	120,181	34	1,562,968	39
Private	George Washington University	1	7	226,132	31	135,667	32	1,570,278	38
Private	Georgetown University	1	7	157,308	38	87,268	36	1,483,502	40

Support		Faculty				Advanced Training				Undergraduate	
2016 Annual Giving x $1000	2016 Control Rank	2016 National Academy Members	2016 Control Rank	2016 Faculty Awards	2016 Control Rank	2016 Doctorates Granted	2016 Control Rank	2015 Post Docs	2015 Control Rank	2015 Median SAT	2015 Control Rank
584,809	5	136	4	25	6	587	6	1,249	5	1475	11
506,441	8	67	11	25	6	537	9	584	15	1455	19
1,187,530	1	382	1	66	1	713	3	5,674	1	1500	6
657,293	4	101	9	21	9	528	10	1,679	3	1445	21
419,752	12	267	3	33	4	646	5	1,493	4	1505	5
401,679	13	42	18	25	6	467	13	746	8	1440	25
951,149	2	340	2	48	2	763	1	2,264	2	1485	8
443,305	10	70	10	21	9	396	15	586	14	1520	2
542,851	6	118	6	34	3	540	8	901	7	1465	13
269,877	15	48	15	16	16	266	21	615	13	1460	15
519,146	7	117	7	28	5	411	14	1,157	6	1515	4
427,089	11	63	12	20	12	497	11	502	21	1430	30
192,700	20	31	20	18	14	251	23	642	11	1380	43
461,150	9	56	13	18	14	489	12	680	9	1360	48
666,641	3	48	15	21	9	714	2	475	22	1385	39
143,605	26	34	19	13	20	322	19	629	12	1485	8
182,869	21	114	8	8	27	190	32	552	18	1550	1
267,876	16	126	5	20	12	373	17	526	20	1490	7
155,302	24	43	17	16	16	323	18	193	33	1450	20
156,941	23	19	30	10	22	579	7	421	23	1305	69
207,725	19	21	28	16	16	235	24	252	30	1465	13
158,323	22	22	26	12	21	230	25	271	27	1400	34
371,762	14	4	44	16	16	216	26	124	38	1460	15
227,038	18	16	31	9	25	87	62	204	32	1445	21
102,977	31	24	25	8	27	211	29	263	28	1475	11
107,297	29	22	26	5	36	301	20	233	31		
236,334	17	13	32	5	36	216	26	258	29	1340	57
56,292	51	3	48	9	25	186	33	114	41	1440	25
60,405	45	12	34	8	27	135	43	182	34	1445	21
101,391	32	11	35	8	27	264	22	111	42	1290	76
153,384	25	9	37	2	64	124	49	109	43	1410	32

Top Private Research Universities (26-50)		Number of Measures in Top 26-50 Control	Research				Private	
Institutions in Order of Top 26-50 Score, then Alphabetically			2015 Total Research x $1000	2015 Control Rank	2015 Federal Research x $1000	2015 Control Rank	2016 Endowment Assets x $1000	2016 Control Rank
Private	Tulane University	8	140,118	40	84,143	37	1,171,314	46
Private	Brandeis University	7	68,690	48	46,764	48	866,778	61
Private	Drexel University	7	122,366	41	67,226	43	650,252	90
Private	Rensselaer Polytechnic Institute	7	102,122	44	59,417	44	634,916	92
Private	Wake Forest University	7	171,538	35	148,084	30	1,141,211	50
Private	Yeshiva University	6	306,174	27	180,791	26	632,856	93
Private	University of Dayton	2	93,319	45	74,548	41	473,122	109

Support		Faculty				Advanced Training				Undergraduate	
2016 Annual Giving x $1000	2016 Control Rank	2016 National Academy Members	2016 Control Rank	2016 Faculty Awards	2016 Control Rank	2016 Doctorates Granted	2016 Control Rank	2015 Post Docs	2015 Control Rank	2015 Median SAT	2015 Control Rank
98,919	33	2	56	6	34	135	43	133	37	1360	48
57,593	48	11	35	7	31	83	64	95	45	1360	48
60,905	44	8	38	5	36	214	28	93	46	1203	123
37,798	72	7	39	4	44	142	41	83	48	1385	39
88,787	36	6	41	3	50	58	80	87	47		
39,298	71	13	32	4	44	152	37	283	26	1250	88
21,668	117	0	88	0	188	39	110	9	81	1205	111

Top Public Research Universities (1-25)		Number of Measures in Top 25 Control	Number of Measures in Top 26-50 Control	Research				Private	
Institutions in Order of Top 25 Score, then Top 26-50 Score, then Alphabetically		Number of Measures in Top 25 Control	Number of Measures in Top 26-50 Control	2015 Total Research x $1000	2015 Control Rank	2015 Federal Research x $1000	2015 Control Rank	2016 Endowment Assets x $1000	2016 Control Rank
Public	Ohio State University - Columbus	9	0	745,238	14	406,941	12	3,578,562	7
Public	University of California - Berkeley	9	0	748,139	13	342,042	13	3,845,281	6
Public	University of California - Los Angeles	9	0	992,009	5	482,771	9	3,849,133	5
Public	University of California - San Diego	9	0	1,093,784	4	601,184	3	1,176,581	25
Public	University of Michigan - Ann Arbor	9	0	1,300,340	1	728,712	2	9,743,461	3
Public	University of Minnesota - Twin Cities	9	0	844,016	9	468,482	10	3,280,681	9
Public	University of North Carolina - Chapel Hill	9	0	939,252	6	577,574	4	2,889,679	11
Public	University of Wisconsin - Madison	9	0	938,366	7	506,910	8	2,739,728	12
Public	University of Florida	8	1	699,750	16	281,317	23	1,461,347	21
Public	University of Illinois - Urbana-Champaign	8	1	614,011	18	330,479	17	1,489,991	20
Public	University of Texas - Austin	8	1	551,654	21	331,388	16	10,935,781	1
Public	University of Washington - Seattle	8	1	1,101,078	3	851,573	1	2,968,013	10
Public	Georgia Institute of Technology	7	2	757,116	12	548,063	6	1,843,764	17
Public	University of Pittsburgh - Pittsburgh	7	2	852,333	8	554,658	5	3,524,904	8
Public	Texas A&M University - College Station	7	1	836,250	10	291,714	22	9,944,936	2
Public	Pennsylvania State Univ. - Univ. Park	6	2	683,003	17	447,956	11	1,912,254	16
Public	University of Maryland - College Park	6	2	503,368	25	332,079	15	466,075	72
Public	Purdue University - West Lafayette	5	4	498,887	26	209,005	33	2,254,541	14
Public	University of California - Davis	5	4	706,087	15	322,919	19	965,805	34
Public	Michigan State University	5	3	519,994	22	256,228	27	2,585,841	13
Public	University of Arizona	5	3	592,874	20	265,878	26	754,651	46
Public	University of Colorado - Boulder	5	3	403,654	35	341,828	14	583,190	57
Public	University of Utah	5	3	509,409	24	270,311	24	1,076,649	29
Public	Rutgers University - New Brunswick	4	5	607,257	19	320,311	20	865,867	40
Public	University of Virginia	4	4	339,813	41	186,676	41	5,852,309	4
Public	North Carolina State University	3	6	462,347	28	196,058	37	998,600	32
Public	Indiana University - Bloomington	2	6	451,508	29	206,263	34	991,134	33
Public	University of Iowa	2	6	423,528	31	223,730	30	1,259,309	23
Public	Arizona State University	2	5	403,708	34	186,890	40	612,590	53
Public	University of California - Irvine	2	4	313,798	45	170,622	45	498,171	64
Public	University of Alabama - Birmingham	2	1	509,586	23	325,008	18	431,459	79
Public	Virginia Polytechnic Inst. and St. Univ.	1	7	495,502	27	191,080	39	842,991	41
Public	University of Cincinnati - Cincinnati	1	6	408,412	33	250,457	28	1,165,522	26
Public	University of Georgia	1	6	330,273	42	127,825	51	1,016,732	30
Public	University of California - Santa Barbara	1	5	213,537	63	114,596	60	273,679	101
Public	Stony Brook University	1	4	219,485	61	115,031	59	262,191	104
Public	U. of Colorado - Denver/Anschutz Med.	1	4	400,515	36	266,147	25	479,474	69
Public	University of Kentucky	1	3	325,558	43	145,097	49	1,117,852	28
Public	University of Connecticut - Storrs	1	2	170,730	73	91,837	68	275,335	100
Public	University of Oklahoma - Norman	1	2	92,075	101	57,455	93	1,003,434	31
Public	University of Tennessee - Knoxville	1	2	233,650	59	116,928	58	597,475	55
Public	University of Delaware	1	1	167,904	76	109,258	62	1,261,790	22
Public	Virginia Commonwealth University	1	0	196,412	67	123,665	53	1,559,874	19

Support		Faculty				Advanced Training				Undergraduate	
2016 Annual Giving x $1000	2016 Control Rank	2016 National Academy Members	2016 Control Rank	2016 Faculty Awards	2016 Control Rank	2016 Doctorates Granted	2016 Control Rank	2015 Post Docs	2015 Control Rank	2015 Median SAT	2015 Control Rank
386,112	5	33	16	21	13	807	4	619	15	1300	13
348,865	6	230	1	36	3	576	16	1,184	4	1380	3
498,800	3	100	6	22	11	775	6	1,016	6	1325	10
206,873	16	119	3	25	10	529	20	1,250	2	1335	9
433,776	4	113	4	48	1	848	3	1,299	1	1390	2
332,851	8	41	12	27	7	804	5	752	11	1280	16
308,694	10	38	13	28	5	542	17	803	9	1360	4
318,828	9	77	7	27	7	870	2	765	10	1300	13
243,666	14	26	26	15	22	723	9	679	12	1260	25
159,693	26	56	10	38	2	726	8	542	18	1280	16
345,992	7	70	8	18	17	896	1	370	26	1290	15
541,444	2	110	5	35	4	632	13	1,205	3	1245	29
129,304	38	31	19	19	15	531	19	237	47	1405	1
127,155	40	32	17	17	18	461	28	664	13	1265	21
276,475	11	32	17	8	43	705	10	615	16	1190	63
147,570	31	28	23	22	11	659	12	366	27	1195	59
146,044	32	27	25	13	27	592	15	496	20	1315	11
151,217	28	28	23	27	7	727	7	389	25	1205	50
129,224	39	46	11	14	26	513	24	833	8	1205	50
176,131	22	14	32	12	31	533	18	471	22	1170	68
186,870	20	29	21	13	27	524	22	471	22		
160,445	25	29	21	16	20	410	31	911	7	1220	38
201,854	17	21	29	15	22	331	41	487	21	1130	100
118,493	41	36	14	12	31	620	14	306	32	1225	36
245,392	13	23	27	7	51	315	48	420	24	1355	7
129,948	37	21	29	20	14	518	23	497	19	1245	29
195,908	18	13	36	16	20	485	26	365	28	1175	65
192,262	19	20	31	9	39	468	27	346	30	1170	68
140,417	34	22	28	19	15	674	11	257	42	1170	68
73,657	67	30	20	15	22	393	32	297	36	1160	78
88,043	59	7	56	3	93	149	89	252	45	1150	83
100,057	48	14	32	6	59	492	25	225	50	1210	46
162,076	24	8	50	13	27	284	57	303	34	1170	68
133,881	36	7	56	9	39	526	21	250	46	1240	31
101,177	46	58	9	8	43	346	37	306	32	1225	36
76,704	63	14	32	8	43	350	36	263	41	1265	21
106,963	44	14	32	7	51	123	100	288	38	1050	201
163,919	23	2	81	7	51	313	51	221	51	1150	83
65,620	76	1	98	15	22	320	46	109	76	1235	33
252,996	12	1	98	4	78	210	69	133	71	1205	50
91,456	56	6	59	17	18	356	35	136	70	1220	38
56,843	83	8	50	4	78	283	58	132	72	1195	59
69,180	71	6	59	2	115	306	53	194	57	1095	138

Top Public Research Universities (26-50)		Number of Measures in Top 26-50 Control	Research				Private	
	Institutions in Order of Top 26-50 Score, then Alphabetically		2015 Total Research x $1000	2015 Control Rank	2015 Federal Research x $1000	2015 Control Rank	2016 Endowment Assets x $1000	2016 Control Rank
Public	University of South Florida - Tampa	6	420,002	32	196,215	36	395,324	82
Public	Washington State University - Pullman	6	306,989	48	121,627	54	907,828	36
Public	Florida State University	5	237,427	57	133,569	50	584,529	56
Public	Iowa State University	5	295,635	49	113,443	61	760,461	44
Public	University at Buffalo	5	367,133	38	174,146	44	600,961	54
Public	University of Houston - University Park	5	125,973	91	54,516	95	665,001	49
Public	University of Missouri - Columbia	5	243,430	55	102,852	64	869,566	39
Public	Colorado State University - Fort Collins	4	308,785	47	213,685	31	286,348	99
Public	University of Hawaii - Manoa	4	313,046	46	199,818	35	271,180	102
Public	University of Illinois - Chicago	4	344,619	40	192,930	38	287,188	98
Public	University of Oregon	4	65,226	120	56,448	94	758,692	45
Public	University of Kansas - Lawrence	3	172,406	72	85,862	71	1,150,623	27
Public	University of Massachusetts - Amherst	3	197,183	66	97,206	66	287,213	97
Public	University of Nebraska - Lincoln	3	260,152	52	94,763	67	869,874	38
Public	Auburn University	2	132,970	85	47,939	102	646,624	51
Public	Louisiana State University - Baton Rouge	2	274,001	51	82,276	75	416,717	80
Public	Oregon State University	2	242,874	56	150,625	48	492,546	66
Public	University of California - Riverside	2	136,493	83	62,642	90	191,420	127
Public	University of California - Santa Cruz	2	147,518	80	91,249	69	162,211	143
Public	University of New Mexico - Albuquerque	2	224,321	60	151,619	47	393,240	83
Public	University of South Carolina - Columbia	2	181,742	68	84,723	72	655,469	50
Public	Clemson University	1	120,858	93	45,292	105	621,294	52
Public	George Mason University	1	89,845	103	54,113	96	71,566	220
Public	New Jersey Institute of Technology	1	96,386	98	50,554	99	98,006	177
Public	University of Alabama - Huntsville	1	84,745	106	66,564	86	71,053	222
Public	University of Central Florida	1	169,770	75	81,788	76	146,416	148
Public	University of Louisville	1	160,199	78	66,100	87	715,689	47
Public	University of Maryland - Baltimore County	1	67,944	116	47,591	103	78,101	203

Support		Faculty				Advanced Training				Undergraduate	
2016 Annual Giving x $1000	2016 Control Rank	2016 National Academy Members	2016 Control Rank	2016 Faculty Awards	2016 Control Rank	2016 Doctorates Granted	2016 Control Rank	2015 Post Docs	2015 Control Rank	2015 Median SAT	2015 Control Rank
45,583	89	8	50	13	27	314	49	282	39	1170	68
103,845	45	9	42	10	37	322	44	175	60	1030	239
75,413	65	8	50	9	39	386	33	202	56	1220	38
90,148	58	9	42	7	51	327	42	299	35	1150	83
36,219	97	8	50	6	59	340	40	256	43	1160	78
98,449	50	10	38	7	51	358	34	264	40	1150	83
113,079	43	9	42	7	51	416	30	165	63	1205	50
42,798	92	8	50	4	78	249	62	254	44	1150	83
42,209	93	10	38	5	66	204	71	234	49	1080	165
53,815	85	6	59	11	35	346	37	214	52	1090	143
136,295	35	9	42	8	43	159	83	105	79	1115	114
149,771	29	5	62	4	78	314	49	149	65	1150	83
32,805	106	9	42	8	43	298	56	144	69	1220	38
100,542	47	3	73	8	43	307	52	205	55	1150	83
118,477	42	1	98	5	66	272	59	40	121	1220	38
147,998	30	2	81	3	93	344	39	148	66	1170	68
97,101	51	5	62	10	37	214	68	212	53	1105	131
24,369	120	9	42	12	31	239	64	190	58	1095	138
69,052	72	9	42	8	43	174	79	125	74	1175	65
66,077	75	5	62	9	39	200	72	124	75	1030	239
94,103	53	0	137	5	66	317	47	129	73	1200	57
90,623	57	2	81	5	66	233	65	77	91	1250	28
67,940	73	2	81	3	93	322	44	44	115	1145	96
		1	98	3	93	57	151	42	117	1210	46
2,297	342	1	98	0	272	34	184	13	173	1220	38
22,427	128	1	98	8	43	299	55	51	106	1175	65
85,186	60	2	81	1	158	147	90	107	78	1170	68
13,788	167	1	98	3	93	82	129	67	96	1210	46

Top Medical and Specialized Research Universities				Research				Private	
Institutions in Order of Top 25 Score, then Top 26-50 Score, then Alphabetically		Number of Measures in Top 25 National	Number of Measures in Top 26-50 National	2015 Total Research x $1000	2015 National Rank	2015 Federal Research x $1000	2015 National Rank	2016 Endowment Assets x $1000	2016 National Rank
Public	University of California - San Francisco	6	1	1,126,620	3	535,457	12	2,112,014	38
Public	Univ. of Texas MD Anderson Cancer Ctr.	2	1	833,406	16	161,171	74	1,212,099	69
Private	Icahn School of Medicine at Mount Sinai	1	2	508,353	40	329,641	31	659,261	138
Private	Rockefeller University	1	1	323,932	69	81,949	114	1,927,404	44
Public	Univ. of Texas SW Medical Ctr. - Dallas	0	5	438,824	47	183,787	67	1,684,130	50
Private	Baylor College of Medicine	0	4	520,220	36	256,895	48	1,063,678	81
Private	Scripps Research Institute	0	3	384,161	56	274,097	42		
Public	Oregon Health & Science University	0	1	325,268	68	243,876	52	570,485	156
Public	Uniformed Services University of the HS	0	1	361,173	60	299,007	37		
Private	Weill Cornell Medical College	0	1	309,015	72	168,103	73	1,233,303	68

Top Private Medical and Specialized Research Universities				Research				Private	
Institutions in Order of Top 25 Score, then Top 26-50 Score, then Alphabetically		Number of Measures in Top 25 Control	Number of Measures in Top 26-50 Control	2015 Total Research x $1000	2015 Control Rank	2015 Federal Research x $1000	2015 Control Rank	2016 Endowment Assets x $1000	2016 Control Rank
Private	Scripps Research Institute	5	0	384,161	20	274,097	19		
Private	Baylor College of Medicine	4	2	520,220	15	256,895	22	1,063,678	52
Private	Rockefeller University	3	4	323,932	25	81,949	39	1,927,404	29
Private	Weill Cornell Medical College	3	4	309,015	26	168,103	28	1,233,303	45
Private	Icahn School of Medicine at Mount Sinai	3	3	508,353	16	329,641	14	659,261	89
Private	Thomas Jefferson University	0	5	119,631	42	58,536	45	500,943	105
Private	Cold Spring Harbor Laboratory	0	4	84,653	46	49,063	47		
Private	Medical College of Wisconsin	0	4	199,283	34	109,542	35	748,862	72
Private	Woods Hole Oceanographic Institution	0	4	216,592	32	172,995	27		
Private	Rush University	0	3	79,048	47	52,193	46	538,823	102

Top Public Medical and Specialized Research Universities				Research				Private	
Institutions in Order of Top 25 Score, then Top 26-50 Score, then Alphabetically		Number of Measures in Top 25 Control	Number of Measures in Top 26-50 Control	2015 Total Research x $1000	2015 Control Rank	2015 Federal Research x $1000	2015 Control Rank	2016 Endowment Assets x $1000	2016 Control Rank
Public	University of California - San Francisco	7	0	1,126,620	2	535,457	7	2,112,014	15
Public	University of Texas SW Med. Ctr. - Dallas	4	3	438,824	30	183,787	42	1,684,130	18
Public	Univ. of Texas MD Anderson Cancer Ctr.	4	2	833,406	11	161,171	46	1,212,099	24
Public	Uniformed Services University of the HS	1	1	361,173	39	299,007	21		
Public	Oregon Health & Science University	0	5	325,268	44	243,876	29	570,485	58
Public	University of Maryland - Baltimore	0	4	379,465	37	211,773	32	254,733	106
Public	Univ. of Mass. Med. Sch. - Worcester	0	3	250,338	53	183,588	43	183,435	130
Public	University of Texas HSC - Houston	0	1	234,299	58	125,890	52	336,086	89

Support		Faculty				Advanced Training			
2016 Annual Giving x $1000	2016 National Rank	2016 National Academy Members	2016 National Rank	2016 Faculty Awards	2016 National Rank	2016 Doctorates Granted	2016 National Rank	2015 Post Docs	2015 National Rank
595,940	5	133	6	28	9	123	149	1,041	11
208,482	33	11	71	2	178	0	626	637	25
120,327	68	20	59	5	101	23	350	643	23
67,659	115	51	24	7	81	31	315	292	61
181,153	42	36	32	12	51	98	173	562	34
77,605	100	25	50	4	121	94	179	537	37
		27	46	10	58	0	626	573	33
156,961	49	10	74	4	121	44	272	292	61
		4	111	2	178	0	626	33	182
85,207	96	28	43	10	58	58	229	354	52

Support		Faculty				Advanced Training			
2016 Annual Giving x $1000	2016 Control Rank	2016 National Academy Members	2016 Control Rank	2016 Faculty Awards	2016 Control Rank	2016 Doctorates Granted	2016 Control Rank	2015 Post Docs	2015 Control Rank
		27	22	10	22	0	343	573	17
77,605	38	25	24	4	44	94	59	537	19
67,659	41	51	14	7	31	31	129	292	25
85,207	37	28	21	10	22	58	80	354	24
120,327	28	20	29	5	36	23	153	643	10
56,821	50	4	44	0	188	13	196	117	40
		5	42	1	158	0	343	143	36
19,028	132	3	48	0	188	24	148	66	49
		3	48	0	188	0	343	99	44
3,070	424	3	48	0	188	20	163	28	60

Support		Faculty				Advanced Training			
2016 Annual Giving x $1000	2016 Control Rank	2016 National Academy Members	2016 Control Rank	2016 Faculty Awards	2016 Control Rank	2016 Doctorates Granted	2016 Control Rank	2015 Post Docs	2015 Control Rank
595,940	1	133	2	28	5	123	100	1,041	5
181,153	21	36	14	12	31	98	117	562	17
208,482	15	11	37	2	115	0	284	637	14
		4	68	2	115	0	284	33	126
156,961	27	10	38	4	78	44	174	292	37
57,911	82	9	42	2	115	67	141	325	31
7,550	216	7	56	11	35	64	145	348	29
55,453	84	4	68	1	158	113	110	237	47

Part II – The Center for Measuring University Performance – *Research Universities*

The Center for Measuring University Performance's research universities consist of academic institutions that had more than $40 million in federal research expenditures in fiscal year 2015. In the following tables, institutions are listed alphabetically with the most current data available on each measure and their rank on each measure for each year. *The Center for Measuring University Performance* provides both the national rank (rank among all universities) and the control rank (rank within private or public universities). We include five years of data for each measure, which correspond to the same data years used in each of the five prior *The Top American Research Universities* reports. In addition to the nine performance variables presented in Part I tables, these tables also include other institutional characteristics related to student enrollment, medical schools, land grant status, ownership, research focus, and National Merit and Achievement Scholars. The Source Notes section of this report provides detailed information on each data element. Tables in this section include the following:

- **Total Research Expenditures** (2011-2015)

- **Federal Research Expenditures** (2011-2015)

- **Research by Major Discipline** (2015)

- **Endowment Assets** (2012-2016)

- **Annual Giving** (2012-2016)

- **National Academy Membership** (2012-2016)

- **Faculty Awards** (2012-2016)

- **Doctorates Awarded** (2012-2016)

- **Postdoctoral Appointees** (2011-2015)

- **SAT Scores** (2011-2015)

- **National Merit and Achievement Scholars** (2012-2016)

- **Change: Research** presents trend data on total, federal, and non-federal research (2006 and 2015) in constant dollars.

- **Change: Private Support and Doctorates** provides trend data on endowment assets (2007 and 2016) and annual giving (2007 and 2016) in constant dollars, and doctorates awarded (2007 and 2016).

- **Change: Students** includes trend data on median SAT scores (2006 and 2015), National Merit and Achievement Scholars (2007 and 2016), and student headcount enrollment (2006 and 2015).

- **Institutional Characteristics** includes state location, highest degree offered, medical school and land grant status, federal research focus (summary of federal research by discipline), and total student enrollment.

- **Student Characteristics** provides headcount enrollment data broken out by level (i.e., undergraduate and graduate), part-time enrollment by level, and degrees awarded.

- *The Center for Measuring University Performance* measures presents the number of times a university ranks in the top 25 (or 26-50) on the nine quality measures in this year's report as compared to the past five years (i.e., 2012-2016 reports).

Data found in these tables may not always match the figures published by the original source. *The Center for Measuring University Performance* makes adjustments, when necessary, to ensure that the data reflect the activity at a single campus rather than that of a multiple-campus institution or state university system. When data are missing from the original source, *The Center for Measuring University Performance* may substitute another figure, if available. A full discussion of this subject, and the various adjustments or substitutions made to the original data, is in the Data Notes section of this report.

The prior years' data or ranks may differ slightly from our last report due to revised figures or estimates from the data source or institution.

The Center for Measuring University Performance's website [http://mup.umass.edu] provides these same tables in Microsoft Excel spreadsheets for ease of analysis. In addition to the over-$40-million group, the online tables contain data on all institutions reporting any federal research in the past five years.

Total Research

	Institutions with Over $40 Million in Federal Research, Alphabetically	2015 Total Research x $1000	2015 National Rank	2015 Control Rank	2014 Total Research x $1000	2014 National Rank	2014 Control Rank
Public	Arizona State University	403,708	51	34	380,581	55	36
Public	Auburn University	132,970	125	85	140,110	122	83
Public	Augusta University	67,736	165	117	64,116	171	123
Private	Baylor College of Medicine	520,220	36	15	496,314	38	15
Private	Boston University	372,267	58	21	353,850	60	22
Private	Brandeis University	68,690	163	48	67,048	166	48
Private	Brown University	286,332	78	28	291,917	76	28
Private	California Institute of Technology	350,833	61	22	358,137	59	21
Private	Carnegie Mellon University	241,829	86	30	250,497	82	30
Private	Case Western Reserve University	400,167	55	19	417,436	49	18
Public	Clemson University	120,858	134	93	116,871	136	94
Public	Cleveland State University	56,683	176	128	61,291	173	125
Private	Cold Spring Harbor Laboratory	84,653	152	46	76,733	161	47
Public	Colorado State Univ. - Fort Collins	308,785	73	47	300,572	73	47
Private	Columbia University	826,010	18	7	844,766	13	5
Private	Cornell University	637,404	28	11	580,936	32	13
Private	Dartmouth College	203,660	98	33	204,360	97	33
Private	Drexel University	122,366	133	41	124,464	132	41
Private	Duke University	1,029,193	6	2	1,031,404	6	2
Private	Emory University	574,472	34	14	551,556	34	14
Public	Florida International University	124,631	132	92	107,487	140	97
Public	Florida State University	237,427	87	57	231,390	88	58
Public	George Mason University	89,845	148	103	85,493	151	107
Private	George Washington University	226,132	90	31	213,334	93	32
Private	Georgetown University	157,308	116	38	162,983	112	36
Public	Georgia Institute of Technology	757,116	20	12	720,248	21	13
Private	Harvard University	955,246	9	4	875,964	11	4
Private	Icahn School of Med. at Mount Sinai	508,353	40	16	463,429	43	17
Public	Indiana University - Bloomington	451,508	46	29	172,380	107	72
Public	Iowa State University	295,635	76	49	297,293	74	48
Private	Johns Hopkins University	2,299,057	1	1	2,227,536	1	1
Public	Kansas State University	180,082	103	69	178,304	102	68
Public	Louisiana State Univ. - Baton Rouge	274,001	79	51	282,462	79	50
Private	Massachusetts Ins. of Technology	858,917	12	5	815,008	16	6
Private	Medical College of Wisconsin	199,283	99	34	199,713	99	34
Public	Medical University of South Carolina	243,534	83	54	242,594	83	53
Public	Michigan State University	519,994	37	22	492,501	39	24
Public	Mississippi State University	216,817	93	62	200,251	98	65
Public	Montana State University - Bozeman	98,467	141	97	104,646	144	100
Public	Naval Postgraduate School	74,293	161	114	91,400	149	105
Public	New Jersey Institute of Technology	96,386	142	98	94,371	147	103
Public	New Mexico State Univ. - Las Cruces	127,000	129	89	129,124	128	88
Private	New York University	505,071	41	17	490,614	40	16
Public	North Carolina State University	462,347	45	28	440,392	44	27
Private	Northeastern University	115,664	137	43	111,779	137	43
Private	Northwestern University	627,320	29	12	621,504	30	12
Public	Ohio State University - Columbus	745,238	22	14	752,836	20	12
Public	Oregon Health & Science University	325,268	68	44	313,112	71	46
Public	Oregon State University	242,874	85	56	229,456	89	59

2013 Total Research x $1000	2013 National Rank	2013 Control Rank	2012 Total Research x $1000	2012 National Rank	2012 Control Rank	2011 Total Research x $1000	2011 National Rank	2011 Control Rank
367,277	59	38	344,611	62	39	323,567	65	42
143,545	120	81	130,222	125	86	161,785	110	74
64,033	174	126	70,526	168	121	73,486	165	118
508,799	35	14	474,700	36	14	466,061	38	15
359,312	61	22	330,247	66	24	348,593	60	23
69,398	167	48	69,489	169	48	71,638	167	48
222,945	90	30	234,906	86	30	223,455	85	30
333,548	64	24	374,075	57	22	374,636	53	21
270,898	77	28	254,992	79	29	240,956	81	29
422,041	47	18	430,246	43	16	428,206	43	17
116,138	133	92	110,493	137	96	135,681	121	83
67,137	172	124	60,481	180	132	55,044	189	140
78,236	160	47	84,072	152	45	95,984	146	43
303,461	71	47	335,336	65	42	321,130	67	43
845,847	13	5	847,809	11	4	841,173	12	5
556,288	32	12	507,012	34	13	514,843	35	14
198,995	96	32	195,251	98	34	210,274	94	32
118,754	132	41	112,390	135	41	109,729	137	40
987,393	7	2	1,004,759	7	2	1,018,241	5	2
493,734	36	15	474,537	37	15	522,900	32	13
92,463	147	105	83,639	154	109	97,804	144	102
224,425	88	59	208,005	94	63	216,869	90	60
82,849	154	110	79,913	159	113	80,284	161	115
192,152	99	34	187,652	99	35	189,427	101	35
170,503	109	36	171,829	106	36	164,301	107	36
726,377	21	13	683,894	24	16	650,588	25	17
910,569	10	3	753,973	16	7	623,116	26	9
428,654	45	17	400,680	51	19	363,091	59	22
173,464	107	72	151,240	117	79	160,038	112	76
259,320	79	50	252,675	80	51	261,016	77	50
2,149,770	1	1	2,092,999	1	1	2,135,547	1	1
177,525	104	69	169,863	107	71	163,494	108	72
276,748	74	48	279,019	75	48	281,221	72	47
833,884	15	6	770,367	15	6	693,714	19	7
201,237	95	31	209,040	93	31	215,358	91	31
245,451	81	52	236,586	83	54	213,346	93	62
479,145	40	25	471,620	38	23	423,766	45	27
197,359	98	65	222,320	89	59	217,793	88	58
103,144	140	98	113,235	134	94	114,244	134	95
89,616	150	107	124,531	129	90	95,153	147	104
97,088	142	100	91,407	149	105	89,250	151	108
136,254	122	83	135,214	123	84	137,301	120	82
435,095	43	16	425,043	45	17	402,327	50	19
413,524	49	31	400,046	52	33	374,446	54	33
111,134	138	42	102,911	140	42	81,230	158	46
612,009	29	10	602,451	28	10	595,202	28	10
743,321	19	11	720,082	18	11	794,023	14	9
307,134	70	46	305,360	70	46	334,324	63	40
231,342	86	57	239,571	81	52	227,752	84	55

Total Research

	Institutions with Over $40 Million in Federal Research, Alphabetically	2015 Total Research x $1000	2015 National Rank	2015 Control Rank	2014 Total Research x $1000	2014 National Rank	2014 Control Rank
Public	Penn. State Univ. - Hershey Med. Ctr.	91,381	147	102	82,793	154	109
Public	Penn. State University - Univ. Park	683,003	25	17	702,912	23	15
Private	Princeton University	272,379	80	29	287,730	78	29
Public	Purdue University - West Lafayette	498,887	43	26	502,457	37	23
Private	Rensselaer Polytechnic Institute	102,122	140	44	104,844	143	44
Private	Rice University	141,935	120	39	136,419	124	40
Private	Rockefeller University	323,932	69	25	316,368	69	25
Private	Rush University	79,048	156	47	80,551	158	46
Public	Rutgers University - New Brunswick	607,257	32	19	627,076	29	18
Public	San Diego State University	76,131	159	112	77,474	160	114
Private	Scripps Research Institute	384,161	56	20	386,231	54	19
Private	Stanford University	969,643	8	3	912,244	10	3
Public	Stony Brook University	219,485	92	61	210,301	95	63
Public	Temple University	210,371	96	64	206,556	96	64
Public	Texas A&M Univ. - College Station	836,250	15	10	826,152	15	10
Private	Thomas Jefferson University	119,631	136	42	118,378	135	42
Private	Tufts University	162,510	113	37	156,411	115	38
Private	Tulane University	140,118	121	40	148,784	117	39
Public	Uniformed Services Univ. of the HS	361,173	60	39	262,489	80	51
Public	University at Albany	110,284	139	96	129,434	127	87
Public	University at Buffalo	367,133	59	38	370,083	57	37
Public	University of Alabama - Birmingham	509,586	38	23	421,475	48	31
Public	University of Alabama - Huntsville	84,745	151	106	85,994	150	106
Public	University of Alaska - Fairbanks	139,605	122	82	152,352	116	78
Public	University of Arizona	592,874	33	20	575,864	33	20
Public	Univ. of Arkansas for Med. Sciences	132,451	126	86	131,438	125	85
Public	University of California - Berkeley	748,139	21	13	708,485	22	14
Public	University of California - Davis	706,087	23	15	699,689	24	16
Public	University of California - Irvine	313,798	70	45	322,315	65	41
Public	University of California - Los Angeles	992,009	7	5	920,183	9	7
Public	University of California - Riverside	136,493	123	83	128,506	129	89
Public	University of California - San Diego	1,093,784	5	4	1,060,207	5	4
Public	Univ. of California - San Francisco	1,126,620	3	2	1,084,031	4	3
Public	Univ. of California - Santa Barbara	213,537	95	63	225,614	90	60
Public	University of California - Santa Cruz	147,518	118	80	147,536	119	80
Public	University of Central Florida	169,770	111	75	143,063	120	81
Private	University of Chicago	402,777	53	18	378,322	56	20
Public	University of Cincinnati - Cincinnati	408,412	50	33	399,571	52	34
Public	University of Colorado - Boulder	403,654	52	35	362,882	58	38
Public	U. of Colorado - Denv./Anschutz Med.	400,515	54	36	401,230	51	33
Public	Univ. of Connecticut - Health Center	80,891	154	108	105,047	142	99
Public	University of Connecticut - Storrs	170,730	109	73	142,332	121	82
Private	University of Dayton	93,319	144	45	83,409	153	45
Public	University of Delaware	167,904	112	76	169,641	109	74
Public	University of Florida	699,750	24	16	652,341	26	17
Public	University of Georgia	330,273	65	42	313,445	70	45
Public	University of Hawaii - Manoa	313,046	71	46	319,818	67	43
Public	University of Houston - Univ. Park	125,973	131	91	122,163	133	92
Public	University of Idaho	95,459	143	99	92,512	148	104

2013 Total Research x $1000	2013 National Rank	2013 Control Rank	2012 Total Research x $1000	2012 National Rank	2012 Control Rank	2011 Total Research x $1000	2011 National Rank	2011 Control Rank
82,501	155	111	84,338	151	107	99,863	141	99
742,510	20	12	699,556	20	13	677,082	21	14
264,998	78	29	264,980	77	28	255,483	78	28
528,564	34	21	528,140	33	21	520,001	34	21
92,365	148	43	92,348	147	44	84,346	156	45
128,621	129	40	115,235	133	40	109,197	138	41
298,474	72	25	292,896	71	25	272,491	73	26
81,770	157	46	80,300	158	46	79,212	162	47
474,192	41	26	420,737	47	30	415,502	47	29
69,338	168	120	75,670	164	117	91,789	149	106
399,899	53	19	398,673	53	20	400,768	51	20
900,547	11	4	854,580	10	3	868,393	10	3
224,030	89	60	218,209	91	61	206,207	96	63
207,190	94	64	126,288	128	89	117,131	132	93
796,101	16	10	752,775	17	10	757,510	16	11
89,273	151	44	100,506	144	43	104,923	139	42
154,694	116	38	159,140	112	37	154,760	115	37
151,314	117	39	154,196	114	38	154,530	116	38
164,232	111	75	151,392	116	78	175,365	104	69
135,879	123	84	135,673	122	83	146,987	119	81
371,387	57	36	340,930	63	40	337,783	62	39
434,882	44	28	449,108	39	24	497,680	36	22
96,932	143	101	83,076	157	112	72,988	166	119
118,907	131	91	121,640	130	91	132,608	124	86
616,487	28	19	615,434	27	18	597,988	27	18
133,677	126	87	129,056	127	88	122,066	129	91
690,299	25	17	696,904	21	14	670,926	22	15
715,870	24	16	704,999	19	12	698,193	18	12
329,500	66	42	335,874	64	41	328,870	64	41
934,135	9	7	969,682	8	6	942,450	8	6
126,916	130	90	129,609	126	87	125,902	128	90
1,066,979	4	3	1,065,306	4	3	1,003,584	6	4
1,042,841	5	4	1,032,673	5	4	995,226	7	5
225,976	87	58	222,916	88	58	217,877	87	57
145,092	118	79	149,824	118	80	149,702	117	79
108,560	139	97	102,562	141	99	97,309	145	103
389,900	54	20	411,864	49	18	446,512	39	16
414,738	48	30	408,294	50	32	419,456	46	28
369,663	58	37	373,512	58	36	372,034	56	35
400,815	52	34	422,844	46	29	407,517	49	31
102,829	141	99	102,530	142	100	98,638	142	100
133,297	127	88	147,938	119	81	148,614	118	80
82,349	156	45	79,877	160	47	89,037	152	44
170,470	110	74	161,327	111	75	160,503	111	75
642,502	27	18	649,988	26	17	686,048	20	13
308,486	69	45	311,498	68	44	239,594	82	53
326,402	67	43	312,311	67	43	318,316	68	44
112,469	136	95	105,844	138	97	98,231	143	101
93,941	145	103	95,327	146	103	94,345	148	105

Total Research

	Institutions with Over $40 Million in Federal Research, Alphabetically	2015 Total Research x $1000	2015 National Rank	2015 Control Rank	2014 Total Research x $1000	2014 National Rank	2014 Control Rank
Public	University of Illinois - Chicago	344,619	63	40	339,644	63	39
Public	Univ. of Illinois - Urbana-Champaign	614,011	31	18	598,531	31	19
Public	University of Iowa	423,528	48	31	436,852	45	28
Public	University of Kansas - Lawrence	172,406	106	72	169,884	108	73
Public	University of Kansas Medical Center	85,360	150	105	81,302	155	110
Public	University of Kentucky	325,558	67	43	322,313	66	42
Public	University of Louisville	160,199	115	78	163,199	111	76
Public	University of Maryland - Baltimore	379,465	57	37	390,682	53	35
Public	Univ. of Maryland - Baltimore County	67,944	164	116	64,329	169	121
Public	University of Maryland - College Park	503,368	42	25	472,235	42	26
Public	Univ. of Massachusetts - Amherst	197,183	100	66	183,210	100	66
Public	U. of Mass. Med. Sch. - Worcester	250,338	82	53	241,869	84	54
Private	University of Miami	328,082	66	24	342,852	62	24
Public	University of Michigan - Ann Arbor	1,300,340	2	1	1,279,603	2	1
Public	University of Minnesota - Twin Cities	844,016	14	9	850,880	12	8
Public	University of Missouri - Columbia	243,430	84	55	233,613	87	57
Public	University of Nebraska - Lincoln	260,152	81	52	254,879	81	52
Public	Univ. of Nebraska Medical Center	145,009	119	81	139,126	123	84
Public	University of Nevada - Reno	83,385	153	107	81,028	156	111
Public	Univ. of New Hampshire - Durham	130,700	127	87	130,951	126	86
Public	Univ. of New Mexico - Albuquerque	224,321	91	60	221,817	91	61
Public	Univ. of North Carolina - Chapel Hill	939,252	10	6	955,601	8	6
Private	University of Notre Dame	171,148	108	36	160,461	113	37
Public	University of Oklahoma - HSC	135,493	124	84	106,782	141	98
Public	University of Oklahoma - Norman	92,075	146	101	120,322	134	93
Public	University of Oregon	65,226	168	120	77,655	159	113
Private	University of Pennsylvania	828,649	17	6	792,314	18	7
Public	University of Pittsburgh - Pittsburgh	852,333	13	8	835,838	14	9
Public	University of Rhode Island	86,139	149	104	84,393	152	108
Private	University of Rochester	344,921	62	23	347,161	61	23
Public	Univ. of South Carolina - Columbia	181,742	102	68	181,363	101	67
Public	University of South Florida - Tampa	420,002	49	32	436,578	46	29
Private	University of Southern California	650,457	27	10	650,506	27	10
Public	University of Tennessee - Knoxville	233,650	89	59	237,642	85	55
Public	University of Texas - Austin	551,654	35	21	526,173	35	21
Public	University of Texas - El Paso	77,515	158	111	70,475	163	116
Public	University of Texas HSC - Houston	234,299	88	58	233,737	86	56
Public	Univ. of Texas HSC - San Antonio	170,277	110	74	172,716	106	71
Public	U. of Texas MD Anderson Cancer Ctr.	833,406	16	11	794,980	17	11
Public	U. of Texas Med. Branch - Galveston	173,506	105	71	178,014	103	69
Public	Univ. of Texas SW Med. Ctr. - Dallas	438,824	47	30	434,627	47	30
Public	University of Utah	509,409	39	24	476,017	41	25
Public	University of Vermont	114,090	138	95	109,343	139	96
Public	University of Virginia	339,813	64	41	337,732	64	40
Public	University of Washington - Seattle	1,101,078	4	3	1,091,135	3	2
Public	University of Wisconsin - Madison	938,366	11	7	984,830	7	5
Public	University of Wyoming	54,928	179	131	48,736	191	142
Public	Utah State University	173,848	104	70	167,256	110	75
Private	Vanderbilt University	619,866	30	13	659,418	25	9

2013 Total Research x $1000	2013 National Rank	2013 Control Rank	2012 Total Research x $1000	2012 National Rank	2012 Control Rank	2011 Total Research x $1000	2011 National Rank	2011 Control Rank
358,797	62	40	381,918	56	35	373,750	55	34
721,587	22	14	558,022	30	19	522,769	33	20
423,097	46	29	432,980	42	27	433,088	41	25
179,848	102	67	172,615	105	70	156,028	114	78
87,202	152	108	83,695	153	108	118,139	131	92
332,366	65	41	354,132	61	38	364,175	57	36
160,338	112	76	165,319	109	73	166,918	106	71
412,387	50	32	414,754	48	31	391,685	52	32
62,887	178	130	65,628	172	124	83,155	157	112
487,345	37	22	498,417	35	22	485,078	37	23
172,217	108	73	178,207	104	69	176,545	103	68
245,923	80	51	256,090	78	50	262,714	75	48
338,568	63	23	361,772	60	23	321,830	66	24
1,304,074	2	1	1,247,680	2	1	1,212,990	2	1
834,181	14	9	806,832	14	9	824,489	13	8
232,760	85	56	234,975	85	56	130,269	126	88
245,170	82	53	238,471	82	53	220,141	86	56
137,485	121	82	141,619	121	82	133,036	122	84
85,085	153	109	83,137	155	110	86,372	155	111
134,535	124	85	152,276	115	77	128,348	127	89
220,840	91	61	216,218	92	62	217,206	89	59
942,467	8	6	864,748	9	7	762,620	15	10
156,234	115	37	143,328	120	39	121,466	130	39
91,838	149	106	101,648	143	101	76,777	163	116
129,078	128	89	115,529	132	93	87,260	153	109
78,654	159	113	87,656	150	106	87,161	154	110
790,265	17	7	813,210	13	5	851,522	11	4
846,556	12	8	839,793	12	8	880,425	9	7
94,381	144	102	97,845	145	102	101,202	140	98
382,399	55	21	388,401	55	21	428,144	44	18
178,800	103	68	186,559	100	65	196,820	99	65
410,092	51	33	394,694	54	34	343,366	61	38
610,382	30	11	593,003	29	11	579,717	29	11
243,151	83	54	234,188	87	57	214,600	92	61
572,959	31	20	549,312	31	20	558,377	30	19
73,005	163	116	72,033	166	119	67,576	173	125
233,256	84	55	236,250	84	55	261,172	76	49
175,983	105	70	184,298	101	66	198,655	98	64
718,096	23	15	685,814	23	15	663,279	23	16
180,198	101	66	180,888	102	67	193,555	100	66
440,620	42	27	435,085	41	26	431,883	42	26
486,245	39	24	425,558	44	28	410,392	48	30
115,054	134	93	115,569	131	92	132,107	125	87
366,103	60	39	363,569	59	37	287,259	70	46
1,111,508	3	2	1,065,414	3	2	1,112,526	3	2
997,523	6	5	1,030,605	6	5	1,022,723	4	3
63,149	176	128	63,812	175	127	55,320	187	138
156,774	114	78	155,305	113	76	172,563	105	70
548,086	33	13	533,878	32	12	534,806	31	12

Total Research

	Institutions with Over $40 Million in Federal Research, Alphabetically	2015 Total Research x $1000	2015 National Rank	2015 Control Rank	2014 Total Research x $1000	2014 National Rank	2014 Control Rank
Public	Virginia Commonwealth University	196,412	101	67	177,540	104	70
Public	Virginia Polytechnic Inst. and St. U.	495,502	44	27	502,486	36	22
Private	Wake Forest University	171,538	107	35	176,380	105	35
Public	Washington State Univ. - Pullman	306,989	74	48	287,942	77	49
Private	Washington University in St. Louis	680,150	26	9	646,756	28	11
Public	Wayne State University	207,830	97	65	213,253	94	62
Private	Weill Cornell Medical College	309,015	72	26	293,791	75	27
Public	West Virginia University	160,560	114	77	156,946	114	77
Private	Woods Hole Oceanographic Inst.	216,592	94	32	220,016	92	31
Private	Yale University	792,953	19	8	764,002	19	8
Private	Yeshiva University	306,174	75	27	306,826	72	26

2013 Total Research x $1000	2013 National Rank	2013 Control Rank	2012 Total Research x $1000	2012 National Rank	2012 Control Rank	2011 Total Research x $1000	2011 National Rank	2011 Control Rank
175,880	106	71	179,310	103	68	185,566	102	67
487,121	38	23	448,054	40	25	445,302	40	24
182,721	100	35	203,730	97	33	208,460	95	33
273,037	75	49	288,693	74	47	363,678	58	37
665,484	26	9	689,035	22	8	707,404	17	6
217,984	92	62	221,666	90	60	252,620	79	51
284,936	73	26	292,782	72	26	264,966	74	27
159,865	113	77	161,961	110	74	159,206	113	77
198,232	97	33	204,352	96	32	198,775	97	34
787,609	18	8	654,824	25	9	654,259	24	8
271,166	76	27	289,027	73	27	283,673	71	25

Federal Research

	Institutions with Over $40 Million in Federal Research, Alphabetically	2015 Federal Research x $1000	2015 National Rank	2015 Control Rank	2014 Federal Research x $1000	2014 National Rank	2014 Control Rank
Public	Arizona State University	186,890	65	40	186,126	65	39
Public	Auburn University	47,939	149	102	49,739	149	103
Public	Augusta University	50,585	144	98	47,771	151	105
Private	Baylor College of Medicine	256,895	48	22	264,641	47	22
Private	Boston University	256,562	49	23	254,285	48	23
Private	Brandeis University	46,764	152	48	45,800	153	47
Private	Brown University	127,886	83	33	125,005	84	33
Private	California Institute of Technology	269,156	44	20	276,447	43	19
Private	Carnegie Mellon University	187,259	64	25	198,247	61	25
Private	Case Western Reserve University	307,960	36	16	328,548	29	14
Public	Clemson University	45,292	153	105	44,673	155	108
Public	Cleveland State University	41,721	157	109	44,139	156	109
Private	Cold Spring Harbor Laboratory	49,063	148	47	41,845	158	48
Public	Colorado State Univ. - Fort Collins	213,685	54	31	206,958	56	33
Private	Columbia University	577,833	7	4	591,523	8	4
Private	Cornell University	277,163	41	18	299,320	36	17
Private	Dartmouth College	145,807	79	31	145,080	76	30
Private	Drexel University	67,226	126	43	75,557	122	41
Private	Duke University	558,566	9	5	556,847	10	5
Private	Emory University	346,534	25	13	329,254	27	13
Public	Florida International University	67,293	125	83	68,946	126	84
Public	Florida State University	133,569	82	50	140,995	79	49
Public	George Mason University	54,113	141	96	53,775	143	98
Private	George Washington University	135,667	81	32	139,148	82	32
Private	Georgetown University	87,268	105	36	99,567	103	36
Public	Georgia Institute of Technology	548,063	11	6	510,422	14	8
Private	Harvard University	530,382	13	6	554,944	11	6
Private	Icahn School of Med. at Mount Sinai	329,641	31	14	300,667	35	16
Public	Indiana University - Bloomington	206,263	57	34	80,109	117	79
Public	Iowa State University	113,443	95	61	115,285	91	58
Private	Johns Hopkins University	1,988,993	1	1	1,936,953	1	1
Public	Kansas State University	66,632	127	84	64,565	129	87
Public	Louisiana State Univ. - Baton Rouge	82,276	113	75	93,584	105	68
Private	Massachusetts Institute of Tech.	486,650	15	7	480,991	16	7
Private	Medical College of Wisconsin	109,542	96	35	111,241	98	35
Public	Medical University of South Carolina	117,255	91	57	118,649	90	57
Public	Michigan State University	256,228	50	27	247,970	49	26
Public	Mississippi State University	79,181	116	77	70,615	125	83
Public	Montana State University - Bozeman	62,827	132	89	66,770	128	86
Public	Naval Postgraduate School	71,987	123	81	89,284	109	72
Public	New Jersey Institute of Technology	50,554	145	99	51,853	146	100
Public	New Mexico State Univ. - Las Cruces	78,253	120	80	80,247	116	78
Private	New York University	326,691	32	15	314,712	31	15
Public	North Carolina State University	196,058	60	37	177,722	70	44
Private	Northeastern University	78,379	119	40	77,401	120	40
Private	Northwestern University	385,868	24	12	385,888	24	12
Public	Ohio State University - Columbus	406,941	22	12	416,177	21	12
Public	Oregon Health & Science University	243,876	52	29	246,050	50	27
Public	Oregon State University	150,625	77	48	143,815	77	47

2013 Federal Research x $1000	2013 National Rank	2013 Control Rank	2012 Federal Research x $1000	2012 National Rank	2012 Control Rank	2011 Federal Research x $1000	2011 National Rank	2011 Control Rank
190,066	67	41	182,188	68	42	178,153	68	42
56,809	144	99	55,118	149	103	59,061	146	102
47,913	154	108	55,106	150	104	54,254	155	108
285,230	44	19	268,753	48	23	295,529	44	21
265,476	48	23	273,204	45	21	300,923	41	20
43,963	160	47	44,061	162	47	47,793	162	48
120,977	87	32	127,665	85	32	123,649	92	33
272,223	47	22	322,295	34	16	340,131	30	16
215,560	57	24	209,307	60	25	200,878	65	25
347,628	28	14	358,722	26	14	352,938	28	15
47,825	155	109	48,182	157	111	49,365	161	114
50,002	152	106	46,205	159	113	42,292	168	120
41,002	163	48	43,874	163	48	55,450	152	47
213,355	58	34	245,573	53	30	230,661	56	33
619,557	7	4	631,961	6	3	634,973	7	3
299,951	36	16	298,596	41	20	314,371	38	19
154,917	75	30	147,218	79	31	131,518	87	32
74,047	125	42	85,584	119	38	81,424	123	39
580,416	10	5	585,636	10	5	584,161	9	5
364,136	26	13	360,934	25	13	369,945	25	13
57,858	139	95	54,204	153	107	61,687	139	95
132,583	81	50	131,998	84	53	136,332	81	51
57,154	141	97	57,504	145	99	61,016	141	97
119,441	92	33	111,068	97	36	115,463	99	36
113,703	99	35	113,229	95	35	122,802	93	34
520,754	14	8	482,349	16	9	426,088	22	11
575,868	11	6	574,346	11	6	530,908	14	6
277,517	46	21	271,722	46	22	295,291	45	22
82,005	120	82	72,501	133	91	69,298	136	93
120,934	88	56	117,144	94	60	116,109	97	62
1,881,959	1	1	1,845,845	1	1	1,875,410	1	1
67,524	132	90	73,247	131	89	74,414	131	89
93,281	109	72	91,238	114	77	96,050	113	75
487,647	19	8	478,955	18	8	482,544	17	8
116,765	96	34	125,325	87	33	133,929	84	31
127,472	84	53	136,907	81	50	143,464	80	50
246,131	52	29	250,416	52	29	222,937	60	36
73,834	126	84	96,132	111	74	97,987	110	73
66,451	133	91	78,409	125	85	78,431	127	86
86,538	115	78	120,209	91	58	88,950	116	78
55,017	147	101	57,513	143	98	52,873	157	110
86,546	114	77	90,338	115	78	90,283	115	77
283,382	45	20	300,271	40	19	289,172	46	23
174,440	70	44	171,464	72	44	152,790	78	48
82,587	119	38	75,733	129	42	65,757	138	44
389,757	25	12	385,377	24	12	393,449	24	12
425,547	22	13	416,304	23	12	471,331	18	10
244,867	53	30	242,219	55	32	268,777	49	26
148,174	78	48	155,667	78	48	146,069	79	49

Federal Research

	Institutions with Over $40 Million in Federal Research, Alphabetically	2015 Federal Research x $1000	2015 National Rank	2015 Control Rank	2014 Federal Research x $1000	2014 National Rank	2014 Control Rank
Public	Penn. State Univ. - Hershey Med. Ctr.	59,933	135	92	54,404	142	97
Public	Pennsylvania State Univ. - Univ. Park	447,956	19	11	461,896	18	10
Private	Princeton University	157,867	75	29	163,805	72	28
Public	Purdue University - West Lafayette	209,005	56	33	227,857	53	30
Private	Rensselaer Polytechnic Institute	59,417	136	44	58,940	136	44
Private	Rice University	73,817	122	42	73,782	124	42
Private	Rockefeller University	81,949	114	39	81,820	114	38
Private	Rush University	52,193	142	46	53,501	144	46
Public	Rutgers University - New Brunswick	320,311	35	20	355,116	25	13
Public	San Diego State University	43,526	154	106	44,807	154	107
Private	Scripps Research Institute	274,097	42	19	292,268	38	18
Private	Stanford University	645,633	4	2	608,342	4	2
Public	Stony Brook University	115,031	93	59	111,386	97	63
Public	Temple University	119,945	89	55	118,892	89	56
Public	Texas A&M Univ. - College Station	291,714	38	22	298,489	37	20
Private	Thomas Jefferson University	58,536	137	45	54,676	141	45
Private	Tufts University	120,181	88	34	115,046	92	34
Private	Tulane University	84,143	109	37	94,287	104	37
Public	Uniformed Services Univ. of the HS	299,007	37	21	213,389	55	32
Public	University at Albany	78,824	118	79	104,861	99	64
Public	University at Buffalo	174,146	70	44	185,144	66	40
Public	University of Alabama - Birmingham	325,008	33	18	276,112	45	25
Public	University of Alabama - Huntsville	66,564	129	86	73,913	123	82
Public	University of Alaska - Fairbanks	78,985	117	78	83,483	113	76
Public	University of Arizona	265,878	46	26	286,595	39	21
Public	Univ. of Arkansas for Med. Sciences	50,603	143	97	55,556	139	95
Public	University of California - Berkeley	342,042	26	13	309,305	33	18
Public	University of California - Davis	322,919	34	19	327,697	30	16
Public	University of California - Irvine	170,622	72	45	180,431	69	43
Public	University of California - Los Angeles	482,771	16	9	458,157	19	11
Public	University of California - Riverside	62,642	133	90	56,327	137	93
Public	University of California - San Diego	601,184	5	3	597,270	7	4
Public	Univ. of California - San Francisco	535,457	12	7	544,697	12	6
Public	Univ. of California - Santa Barbara	114,596	94	60	119,816	87	54
Public	University of California - Santa Cruz	91,249	104	69	89,206	110	73
Public	University of Central Florida	81,788	115	76	64,323	130	88
Private	University of Chicago	290,776	39	17	276,237	44	20
Public	University of Cincinnati - Cincinnati	250,457	51	28	243,705	51	28
Public	University of Colorado - Boulder	341,828	27	14	302,877	34	19
Public	U. of Colorado - Denv.Anschutz Med.	266,147	45	25	277,209	42	24
Public	University of Connecticut - Health Center	43,512	155	107	59,277	135	92
Public	University of Connecticut - Storrs	91,837	103	68	80,317	115	77
Private	University of Dayton	74,548	121	41	63,881	131	43
Public	University of Delaware	109,258	97	62	111,933	96	62
Public	University of Florida	281,317	40	23	279,920	41	23
Public	University of Georgia	127,825	84	51	122,145	85	52
Public	University of Hawaii - Manoa	199,818	58	35	202,574	59	35
Public	University of Houston - Univ. Park	54,516	140	95	55,574	138	94
Public	University of Idaho	49,591	147	101	49,423	150	104

2013 Federal Research x $1000	2013 National Rank	2013 Control Rank	2012 Federal Research x $1000	2012 National Rank	2012 Control Rank	2011 Federal Research x $1000	2011 National Rank	2011 Control Rank
55,619	146	100	56,615	146	100	59,039	147	103
500,567	16	9	469,597	19	11	400,294	23	12
156,070	73	29	160,985	75	30	162,491	73	29
258,596	49	26	255,691	51	28	246,116	51	28
60,765	137	44	62,063	139	45	58,951	148	45
79,742	123	40	76,431	128	41	78,249	128	42
80,384	122	39	84,616	121	39	97,710	111	38
57,063	142	45	57,512	144	46	57,978	149	46
288,374	41	23	273,498	44	24	235,178	54	31
45,175	157	111	51,690	155	109	59,769	143	99
308,628	33	15	309,471	36	17	317,201	36	18
625,144	5	2	607,578	8	4	633,287	8	4
118,432	94	61	123,198	89	56	124,938	89	57
124,764	85	54	85,062	120	82	84,581	119	81
302,356	35	20	290,245	43	23	314,468	37	19
56,247	145	46	68,976	136	43	80,027	124	40
112,495	100	36	120,042	93	34	120,864	95	35
97,873	107	37	101,130	108	37	110,222	104	37
119,647	91	59	110,276	101	65	117,781	96	61
113,736	98	64	112,161	96	61	124,848	90	58
200,212	62	37	186,747	67	41	176,923	69	43
286,873	42	24	303,677	39	21	340,342	29	14
83,396	118	81	75,715	130	88	70,197	134	92
92,602	111	74	97,472	110	73	100,638	108	71
334,680	31	17	328,369	33	18	324,751	35	18
64,856	135	92	69,883	135	93	75,924	130	88
305,932	34	19	333,179	30	16	326,120	34	17
344,632	29	15	356,540	27	13	359,704	27	13
196,256	65	40	204,062	62	37	204,134	63	39
489,820	17	10	527,899	14	8	545,882	13	8
57,032	143	98	61,304	141	96	59,351	145	101
630,009	4	3	653,549	5	3	635,223	6	4
566,117	12	6	559,329	12	6	570,116	10	5
131,392	82	51	134,984	82	51	132,490	86	55
88,600	112	75	91,409	113	76	95,015	114	76
68,691	131	89	72,620	132	90	66,736	137	94
294,862	39	18	329,119	31	15	365,824	26	14
256,816	50	27	266,507	49	26	286,003	47	24
309,072	32	18	319,019	35	19	313,531	39	20
290,443	40	22	308,023	37	20	299,230	42	22
59,929	138	94	61,568	140	95	56,351	151	105
86,471	116	79	88,834	116	79	84,901	118	80
66,396	134	43	64,369	138	44	69,847	135	43
114,048	97	63	110,760	98	62	112,523	103	67
285,778	43	25	295,745	42	22	296,950	43	23
127,487	83	52	133,525	83	52	134,273	83	53
225,263	55	32	193,722	66	40	201,700	64	40
57,569	140	96	54,657	151	105	57,090	150	104
52,430	149	103	53,765	154	108	52,812	158	111

Federal Research

Institutions with Over $40 Million in Federal Research, Alphabetically		2015 Federal Research x $1000	2015 National Rank	2015 Control Rank	2014 Federal Research x $1000	2014 National Rank	2014 Control Rank
Public	University of Illinois - Chicago	192,930	61	38	201,646	60	36
Public	Univ. of Illinois - Urbana-Champaign	330,479	30	17	336,172	26	14
Public	University of Iowa	223,730	53	30	234,122	52	29
Public	University of Kansas - Lawrence	85,862	107	71	88,725	111	74
Public	University of Kansas Medical Center	42,512	156	108	42,461	157	110
Public	University of Kentucky	145,097	80	49	140,450	80	50
Public	University of Louisville	66,100	130	87	63,258	132	89
Public	University of Maryland - Baltimore	211,773	55	32	220,700	54	31
Public	Univ. of Maryland - Baltimore County	47,591	150	103	46,993	152	106
Public	University of Maryland - College Park	332,079	28	15	328,828	28	15
Public	Univ. of Massachusetts - Amherst	97,206	101	66	102,682	101	66
Public	Univ. of Mass. Med. Sch. - Worcester	183,588	68	43	183,582	68	42
Private	University of Miami	192,691	62	24	202,818	58	24
Public	University of Michigan - Ann Arbor	728,712	3	2	733,779	3	2
Public	University of Minnesota - Twin Cities	468,482	18	10	483,542	15	9
Public	University of Missouri - Columbia	102,852	99	64	102,784	100	65
Public	University of Nebraska - Lincoln	94,763	102	67	93,190	106	69
Public	University of Nebraska Medical Ctr.	71,918	124	82	76,195	121	81
Public	University of Nevada - Reno	49,977	146	100	50,904	147	101
Public	Univ. of New Hampshire - Durham	83,106	111	74	89,640	107	70
Public	Univ. of New Mexico - Albuquerque	151,619	76	47	151,082	75	46
Public	Univ. of North Carolina - Chapel Hill	577,574	8	4	601,933	6	3
Private	University of Notre Dame	82,615	112	38	79,192	119	39
Public	University of Oklahoma - HSC	65,463	131	88	55,133	140	96
Public	University of Oklahoma - Norman	57,455	138	93	53,223	145	99
Public	University of Oregon	56,448	139	94	62,824	133	90
Private	University of Pennsylvania	597,791	6	3	606,115	5	3
Public	University of Pittsburgh - Pittsburgh	554,658	10	5	565,409	9	5
Public	University of Rhode Island	61,085	134	91	61,836	134	91
Private	University of Rochester	261,023	47	21	265,686	46	21
Public	Univ. of South Carolina - Columbia	84,723	108	72	87,844	112	75
Public	University of South Florida - Tampa	196,215	59	36	205,155	57	34
Private	University of Southern California	408,105	21	10	421,887	20	9
Public	University of Tennessee - Knoxville	116,928	92	58	122,120	86	53
Public	University of Texas - Austin	331,388	29	16	313,955	32	17
Public	University of Texas - El Paso	40,334	158	110	34,528	166	118
Public	University of Texas HSC - Houston	125,890	85	52	136,145	83	51
Public	Univ. of Texas HSC - San Antonio	85,940	106	70	89,303	108	71
Public	U. of Texas MD Anderson Cancer Ctr.	161,171	74	46	158,986	73	45
Public	U. of Texas Med. Branch - Galveston	98,050	100	65	101,761	102	67
Public	Univ. of Texas SW Med. Ctr. - Dallas	183,787	67	42	185,137	67	41
Public	University of Utah	270,311	43	24	284,125	40	22
Public	University of Vermont	83,733	110	73	79,727	118	80
Public	University of Virginia	186,676	66	41	192,907	63	38
Public	University of Washington - Seattle	851,573	2	1	849,713	2	1
Public	University of Wisconsin - Madison	506,910	14	8	522,251	13	7
Public	University of Wyoming	47,232	151	104	39,778	162	114
Public	Utah State University	119,811	90	56	114,075	93	59
Private	Vanderbilt University	390,701	23	11	408,743	23	11

2013 Federal Research x $1000	2013 National Rank	2013 Control Rank	2012 Federal Research x $1000	2012 National Rank	2012 Control Rank	2011 Federal Research x $1000	2011 National Rank	2011 Control Rank
219,473	56	33	243,622	54	31	245,323	52	29
459,791	20	12	348,536	28	14	312,796	40	21
252,161	51	28	265,780	50	27	280,989	48	25
99,374	105	69	99,034	109	72	78,884	126	85
48,183	153	107	48,018	158	112	71,840	132	90
148,758	77	47	157,813	77	47	175,801	70	44
72,047	128	86	79,252	124	84	84,557	120	82
237,749	54	31	229,858	56	33	228,637	57	34
44,257	158	112	44,669	161	115	61,110	140	96
341,942	30	16	340,180	29	15	333,879	33	16
103,233	104	68	106,470	105	69	106,315	105	68
189,159	68	42	202,149	63	38	208,244	62	38
204,315	61	25	222,535	58	24	223,870	59	24
802,114	3	2	773,766	3	2	801,194	3	2
489,318	18	11	480,531	17	10	482,639	16	9
108,305	101	65	110,446	100	64	113,072	101	65
96,177	108	71	103,294	107	71	104,240	106	69
80,750	121	83	84,196	122	83	86,295	117	79
53,898	148	102	55,150	148	102	55,374	153	106
92,778	110	73	109,728	103	67	96,552	112	74
155,684	74	45	159,302	76	46	161,950	74	45
614,627	8	4	597,629	9	5	559,620	12	7
79,268	124	41	82,244	123	40	79,003	125	41
50,860	151	105	59,704	142	97	42,654	167	119
68,902	130	88	64,427	137	94	46,027	164	116
61,856	136	93	71,157	134	92	71,344	133	91
623,939	6	3	656,425	4	2	689,571	4	2
601,358	9	5	620,070	7	4	647,060	5	3
70,900	129	87	78,194	126	86	77,668	129	87
298,781	37	17	307,390	38	18	337,312	31	17
87,562	113	76	93,237	112	75	100,045	109	72
207,441	60	36	218,772	59	35	220,931	61	37
423,708	23	10	433,136	20	9	443,458	20	10
122,051	86	55	120,933	90	57	115,224	100	64
352,788	27	14	328,560	32	17	334,240	32	15
37,741	165	117	39,274	167	119	34,765	180	130
144,235	80	49	146,424	80	49	156,790	76	46
99,198	106	70	106,177	106	70	121,200	94	60
182,971	69	43	196,753	65	39	236,400	53	30
108,287	102	66	109,867	102	66	128,098	88	56
198,114	63	38	207,513	61	36	231,639	55	32
297,099	38	21	271,629	47	25	263,623	50	27
85,028	117	80	87,843	117	80	101,465	107	70
212,051	59	35	225,558	57	34	227,937	58	35
869,623	2	1	876,941	2	1	921,399	2	1
533,220	13	7	557,688	13	7	568,389	11	6
52,296	150	104	55,663	147	101	47,782	163	115
106,074	103	67	107,054	104	68	112,611	102	66
432,752	21	9	430,445	22	11	434,213	21	11

Federal Research

	Institutions with Over $40 Million in Federal Research, Alphabetically	2015 Federal Research x $1000	2015 National Rank	2015 Control Rank	2014 Federal Research x $1000	2014 National Rank	2014 Control Rank
Public	Virginia Commonwealth University	123,665	86	53	119,507	88	55
Public	Virginia Polytechnic Inst. and St. U.	191,080	63	39	198,092	62	37
Private	Wake Forest University	148,084	78	30	153,069	74	29
Public	Washington State Univ. - Pullman	121,627	87	54	112,568	95	61
Private	Washington University in St. Louis	424,723	20	9	410,115	22	10
Public	Wayne State University	108,221	98	63	112,608	94	60
Private	Weill Cornell Medical College	168,103	73	28	139,514	81	31
Public	West Virginia University	66,608	128	85	67,450	127	85
Private	Woods Hole Oceanographic Inst.	172,995	71	27	177,616	71	27
Private	Yale University	471,381	17	8	475,585	17	8
Private	Yeshiva University	180,791	69	26	186,885	64	26

2013 Federal Research x $1000	2013 National Rank	2013 Control Rank	2012 Federal Research x $1000	2012 National Rank	2012 Control Rank	2011 Federal Research x $1000	2011 National Rank	2011 Control Rank
119,293	93	60	124,836	88	55	134,431	82	52
197,462	64	39	181,371	69	43	187,269	67	41
156,506	72	28	172,779	70	27	173,004	71	27
119,921	90	58	120,146	92	59	115,775	98	63
402,702	24	11	432,434	21	10	460,282	19	9
118,217	95	62	125,965	86	54	133,925	85	54
144,352	79	31	172,428	71	28	161,792	75	30
72,677	127	85	77,981	127	87	84,061	121	83
158,672	71	27	161,115	74	29	165,819	72	28
502,439	15	7	517,072	15	7	518,195	15	7
193,831	66	26	201,397	64	26	192,241	66	26

Research by Major Discipline	2015 Total Research by Major Discipline					
Institutions with Over $40 Million in Federal Research, Alphabetically	Percent Life Science	Percent Physical Science	Percent Enviro Science	Percent Eng Science	Percent Computer Science	Percent Math
Public	Arizona State University	19.3%	5.0%	9.7%	28.9%	3.8%	1.2%
Public	Auburn University	57.0%	3.5%	2.6%	30.3%	0.0%	0.2%
Public	Augusta University	100.0%	0.0%	0.0%	0.0%	0.0%	0.0%
Private	Baylor College of Medicine	100.0%	0.0%	0.0%	0.0%	0.0%	0.0%
Private	Boston University	67.6%	9.0%	2.0%	14.0%	1.2%	1.1%
Private	Brandeis University	44.6%	13.2%	0.0%	0.0%	3.5%	1.0%
Private	Brown University	47.2%	8.9%	2.3%	12.8%	5.4%	8.4%
Private	California Institute of Technology	18.2%	46.8%	8.3%	23.8%	0.0%	2.9%
Private	Carnegie Mellon University	4.6%	5.9%	0.1%	36.8%	42.7%	2.4%
Private	Case Western Reserve University	85.0%	2.4%	0.2%	10.9%	0.0%	0.2%
Public	Clemson University	32.8%	7.5%	0.0%	48.3%	4.6%	2.1%
Public	Cleveland State University	74.3%	1.6%	0.0%	18.5%	0.0%	0.6%
Private	Cold Spring Harbor Laboratory	100.0%	0.0%	0.0%	0.0%	0.0%	0.0%
Public	Colorado State University - Fort Collins	39.7%	4.2%	38.9%	10.6%	1.2%	1.1%
Private	Columbia University	69.4%	5.6%	13.6%	6.8%	2.7%	0.4%
Private	Cornell University	50.6%	16.6%	3.9%	16.4%	3.1%	0.5%
Private	Dartmouth College	76.0%	4.4%	1.5%	12.3%	2.2%	0.5%
Private	Drexel University	57.3%	1.9%	3.5%	28.1%	4.6%	0.4%
Private	Duke University	83.2%	1.8%	1.7%	8.3%	0.6%	1.2%
Private	Emory University	92.4%	4.5%	0.2%	1.0%	0.0%	0.4%
Public	Florida International University	33.5%	6.7%	5.4%	30.2%	9.8%	0.9%
Public	Florida State University	14.3%	27.1%	9.1%	18.1%	2.7%	1.8%
Public	George Mason University	20.5%	4.3%	10.9%	11.3%	14.2%	2.2%
Private	George Washington University	70.4%	1.9%	0.5%	5.9%	2.9%	0.5%
Private	Georgetown University	81.7%	3.7%	0.0%	0.0%	1.4%	0.2%
Public	Georgia Institute of Technology	2.6%	6.2%	2.5%	70.4%	14.1%	0.9%
Private	Harvard University	55.8%	7.6%	3.3%	7.7%	0.6%	1.1%
Private	Icahn School of Medicine at Mount Sinai	100.0%	0.0%	0.0%	0.0%	0.0%	0.0%
Public	Indiana University - Bloomington	71.6%	7.7%	0.9%	0.0%	6.1%	0.5%
Public	Iowa State University	50.5%	7.0%	1.0%	28.5%	1.5%	4.7%
Private	Johns Hopkins University	37.7%	7.3%	1.4%	43.1%	5.4%	2.1%
Public	Kansas State University	68.1%	5.0%	0.7%	13.3%	2.7%	0.6%
Public	Louisiana State University - Baton Rouge	56.5%	8.0%	12.3%	14.1%	1.1%	0.8%
Private	Massachusetts Institute of Technology	15.0%	13.9%	6.9%	48.5%	8.9%	1.1%
Private	Medical College of Wisconsin	100.0%	0.0%	0.0%	0.0%	0.0%	0.0%
Public	Medical University of South Carolina	100.0%	0.0%	0.0%	0.0%	0.0%	0.0%
Public	Michigan State University	49.9%	25.4%	0.5%	8.5%	2.2%	1.7%
Public	Mississippi State University	53.2%	3.5%	2.0%	20.4%	4.4%	0.6%
Public	Montana State University - Bozeman	42.1%	15.9%	10.2%	20.2%	0.5%	0.8%
Public	Naval Postgraduate School	0.3%	15.1%	15.2%	38.2%	6.6%	4.2%
Public	New Jersey Institute of Technology	3.1%	7.9%	0.2%	61.6%	5.9%	4.8%
Public	New Mexico State University - Las Cruces	30.1%	13.0%	1.4%	50.8%	1.4%	0.2%
Private	New York University	80.7%	3.0%	0.2%	2.0%	2.6%	2.3%
Public	North Carolina State University	45.2%	4.5%	5.4%	31.0%	3.1%	4.6%
Private	Northeastern University	29.5%	15.1%	2.8%	33.9%	8.7%	0.6%
Private	Northwestern University	72.0%	6.9%	0.3%	12.4%	0.0%	0.4%
Public	Ohio State University - Columbus	63.6%	5.5%	1.4%	19.4%	2.9%	0.9%
Public	Oregon Health & Science University	91.1%	0.0%	2.3%	3.4%	0.0%	0.0%
Public	Oregon State University	50.5%	1.2%	18.0%	17.7%	3.2%	0.6%

			2015 Federal Research by Major Discipline								
Percent Psychology	Percent Social Science	Percent Other Science	Percent Life Science	Percent Physical Science	Percent Enviro Science	Percent Eng Science	Percent Computer Science	Percent Math	Percent Psychology	Percent Social Science	Percent Other Science
4.1%	15.5%	12.4%	24.3%	6.0%	15.1%	28.6%	5.5%	1.8%	5.9%	9.4%	3.3%
0.3%	2.1%	4.0%	39.4%	7.1%	4.9%	41.6%	0.0%	0.5%	0.4%	4.9%	1.2%
0.0%	0.0%	0.0%	100.0%	0.0%	0.0%	0.0%	0.0%	0.0%	0.0%	0.0%	0.0%
0.0%	0.0%	0.0%	100.0%	0.0%	0.0%	0.0%	0.0%	0.0%	0.0%	0.0%	0.0%
3.7%	1.0%	0.4%	69.9%	8.8%	2.2%	12.2%	1.3%	1.1%	4.1%	0.4%	0.1%
4.5%	33.3%	0.0%	46.9%	14.0%	0.0%	0.0%	4.2%	1.0%	5.4%	28.5%	0.0%
3.1%	8.8%	3.2%	50.6%	9.1%	2.1%	12.7%	4.4%	9.5%	4.6%	2.4%	4.5%
0.0%	0.0%	0.0%	17.8%	55.8%	8.8%	14.6%	0.0%	3.1%	0.0%	0.0%	0.0%
3.2%	2.8%	1.4%	4.0%	6.6%	0.1%	35.0%	44.3%	2.2%	3.8%	2.6%	1.5%
0.5%	0.6%	0.2%	86.3%	2.2%	0.3%	10.0%	0.1%	0.2%	0.4%	0.6%	0.0%
0.6%	4.1%	0.0%	17.3%	10.3%	0.0%	57.4%	6.2%	1.7%	1.3%	5.9%	0.0%
0.4%	4.5%	0.0%	81.1%	0.5%	0.0%	16.6%	0.0%	0.7%	0.1%	1.1%	0.0%
0.0%	0.0%	0.0%	100.0%	0.0%	0.0%	0.0%	0.0%	0.0%	0.0%	0.0%	0.0%
1.0%	2.2%	1.1%	33.7%	4.0%	47.8%	9.0%	1.5%	1.3%	1.1%	1.7%	0.0%
0.5%	1.1%	0.0%	68.1%	6.3%	13.5%	7.2%	3.2%	0.4%	0.6%	0.6%	0.0%
2.2%	6.5%	0.3%	31.5%	30.5%	3.3%	21.8%	4.9%	0.9%	1.8%	5.0%	0.1%
1.6%	1.0%	0.6%	73.8%	5.2%	1.7%	13.0%	2.7%	0.6%	2.0%	0.4%	0.7%
3.4%	0.6%	0.2%	51.1%	1.5%	1.7%	34.3%	6.0%	0.6%	4.6%	0.2%	0.0%
0.8%	2.5%	0.0%	75.8%	2.7%	2.1%	12.3%	0.9%	2.0%	1.1%	3.1%	0.0%
0.4%	0.6%	0.4%	93.4%	3.5%	0.3%	1.4%	0.0%	0.4%	0.5%	0.5%	0.0%
7.8%	5.7%	0.0%	35.2%	6.8%	4.8%	35.3%	7.9%	0.2%	8.6%	1.2%	0.0%
16.3%	5.9%	4.7%	15.0%	24.1%	6.5%	22.9%	2.2%	2.1%	20.0%	3.2%	4.0%
8.4%	28.2%	0.0%	20.0%	5.8%	14.3%	15.8%	21.6%	2.4%	10.0%	10.1%	0.0%
1.5%	9.1%	7.3%	79.8%	2.1%	0.3%	4.8%	2.9%	0.5%	1.8%	4.5%	3.2%
0.8%	12.1%	0.0%	89.0%	4.0%	0.0%	0.0%	1.3%	0.3%	1.0%	4.4%	0.0%
1.0%	1.2%	1.0%	2.0%	6.3%	2.6%	71.2%	14.7%	0.5%	1.1%	0.9%	0.7%
0.7%	10.2%	12.9%	59.6%	9.0%	4.3%	7.2%	0.9%	1.7%	0.9%	3.0%	13.3%
0.0%	0.0%	0.0%	100.0%	0.0%	0.0%	0.0%	0.0%	0.0%	0.0%	0.0%	0.0%
3.4%	7.1%	2.6%	73.0%	8.5%	0.8%	0.0%	9.7%	0.6%	4.3%	3.0%	0.1%
0.9%	4.0%	1.9%	48.0%	5.8%	1.0%	30.8%	1.2%	5.7%	0.7%	4.1%	2.7%
0.2%	0.5%	2.4%	31.2%	7.8%	1.5%	48.0%	5.9%	2.3%	0.2%	0.5%	2.7%
2.2%	3.9%	3.5%	59.2%	10.4%	1.5%	14.0%	4.7%	0.9%	3.9%	5.0%	0.4%
0.2%	2.6%	4.4%	55.3%	14.0%	10.4%	12.1%	1.9%	1.7%	0.5%	3.2%	0.7%
0.2%	2.8%	2.7%	14.6%	20.0%	8.0%	44.7%	9.5%	1.4%	0.1%	0.5%	1.1%
0.0%	0.0%	0.0%	100.0%	0.0%	0.0%	0.0%	0.0%	0.0%	0.0%	0.0%	0.0%
0.0%	0.0%	0.0%	100.0%	0.0%	0.0%	0.0%	0.0%	0.0%	0.0%	0.0%	0.0%
1.9%	7.5%	2.2%	42.3%	33.9%	0.4%	9.2%	2.5%	2.1%	2.0%	7.1%	0.6%
0.6%	11.6%	3.8%	40.8%	3.0%	3.4%	30.4%	7.9%	0.3%	0.3%	9.6%	4.3%
0.7%	2.2%	7.3%	33.3%	19.5%	14.5%	18.7%	0.7%	1.1%	0.9%	1.4%	9.9%
0.0%	10.3%	10.1%	0.3%	15.4%	15.3%	38.2%	6.3%	4.1%	0.0%	10.1%	10.2%
0.0%	0.1%	16.5%	1.9%	4.9%	0.3%	72.1%	2.3%	3.6%	0.0%	0.1%	14.7%
0.1%	0.1%	2.9%	19.4%	12.4%	1.5%	64.2%	1.8%	0.3%	0.0%	0.1%	0.4%
5.2%	4.0%	0.0%	81.1%	3.8%	0.0%	1.4%	3.0%	3.0%	6.6%	1.2%	0.0%
0.7%	2.8%	2.7%	31.1%	7.1%	7.8%	34.4%	5.9%	6.1%	1.0%	2.6%	4.1%
3.9%	5.5%	0.1%	23.7%	15.6%	2.1%	36.9%	11.0%	0.7%	4.4%	5.7%	0.0%
0.6%	3.2%	4.2%	71.6%	7.6%	0.3%	12.8%	0.0%	0.4%	0.7%	2.6%	4.1%
1.0%	2.7%	2.7%	64.3%	6.8%	1.5%	16.4%	2.2%	1.4%	1.4%	3.7%	2.3%
0.9%	0.0%	2.2%	90.3%	0.0%	2.8%	3.2%	0.0%	0.0%	1.2%	0.0%	2.5%
0.0%	2.1%	6.6%	38.3%	1.4%	26.2%	19.6%	4.4%	0.5%	0.0%	1.5%	8.1%

Research by Major Discipline	2015 Total Research by Major Discipline					
Institutions with Over $40 Million in Federal Research, Alphabetically	Percent Life Science	Percent Physical Science	Percent Enviro Science	Percent Eng Science	Percent Computer Science	Percent Math
Public Penn. State University - Hershey Med. Ctr.	100.0%	0.0%	0.0%	0.0%	0.0%	0.0%
Public Pennsylvania State University - Univ. Park	21.9%	7.6%	8.0%	43.4%	8.1%	1.8%
Private Princeton University	15.2%	25.5%	8.8%	27.8%	4.2%	2.9%
Public Purdue University - West Lafayette	42.1%	6.2%	0.9%	39.0%	4.0%	1.4%
Private Rensselaer Polytechnic Institute	5.5%	9.5%	2.2%	68.1%	10.2%	1.7%
Private Rice University	8.3%	24.4%	4.2%	43.5%	6.8%	4.7%
Private Rockefeller University	94.0%	2.9%	0.2%	0.0%	2.4%	0.4%
Private Rush University	94.7%	0.0%	0.0%	0.0%	0.0%	0.0%
Public Rutgers University - New Brunswick	60.3%	7.2%	6.9%	11.8%	1.5%	2.7%
Public San Diego State University	44.9%	10.8%	2.6%	8.4%	3.7%	4.5%
Private Scripps Research Institute	100.0%	0.0%	0.0%	0.0%	0.0%	0.0%
Private Stanford University	66.8%	9.9%	3.4%	13.8%	2.1%	0.8%
Public Stony Brook University	40.4%	14.6%	14.0%	10.5%	4.7%	3.5%
Public Temple University	80.3%	6.1%	0.4%	3.0%	1.8%	0.5%
Public Texas A&M University - College Station	38.3%	6.4%	13.5%	35.7%	1.4%	1.1%
Private Thomas Jefferson University	100.0%	0.0%	0.0%	0.0%	0.0%	0.0%
Private Tufts University	68.2%	4.0%	0.1%	12.0%	1.9%	1.6%
Private Tulane University	84.1%	3.5%	0.4%	5.0%	0.0%	1.5%
Public Uniformed Services University of the HS	99.8%	0.0%	0.0%	0.0%	0.0%	0.0%
Public University at Albany	68.6%	4.1%	8.5%	0.0%	6.9%	0.1%
Public University at Buffalo	65.0%	3.7%	0.8%	24.1%	3.6%	0.2%
Public University of Alabama - Birmingham	89.4%	0.6%	1.6%	7.3%	0.2%	0.0%
Public University of Alabama - Huntsville	1.5%	10.7%	13.9%	42.1%	28.8%	0.6%
Public University of Alaska - Fairbanks	15.3%	9.3%	45.3%	15.7%	1.3%	0.0%
Public University of Arizona	48.9%	28.3%	5.7%	9.6%	1.2%	0.5%
Public University of Arkansas for Medical Sciences	100.0%	0.0%	0.0%	0.0%	0.0%	0.0%
Public University of California - Berkeley	28.2%	22.6%	1.3%	24.7%	0.9%	1.0%
Public University of California - Davis	72.6%	5.0%	3.9%	11.8%	1.1%	0.5%
Public University of California - Irvine	62.3%	11.4%	2.7%	12.9%	4.2%	1.5%
Public University of California - Los Angeles	72.4%	5.9%	2.9%	8.3%	1.7%	1.1%
Public University of California - Riverside	55.4%	10.8%	6.0%	17.1%	3.5%	0.5%
Public University of California - San Diego	58.7%	6.5%	15.5%	10.7%	3.6%	0.5%
Public University of California - San Francisco	95.5%	4.5%	0.0%	0.0%	0.0%	0.0%
Public University of California - Santa Barbara	11.3%	17.8%	15.0%	41.9%	4.7%	0.6%
Public University of California - Santa Cruz	15.4%	20.5%	15.1%	41.2%	2.3%	0.4%
Public University of Central Florida	15.8%	20.8%	5.6%	29.7%	11.8%	2.3%
Private University of Chicago	67.7%	12.8%	2.1%	1.8%	5.5%	1.5%
Public University of Cincinnati - Cincinnati	85.0%	1.7%	0.3%	9.6%	0.0%	0.4%
Public University of Colorado - Boulder	6.6%	20.3%	31.8%	27.1%	1.9%	0.5%
Public U. of Colorado - Denver/Anschutz Medical	97.3%	0.2%	0.0%	2.0%	0.0%	0.1%
Public University of Connecticut - Health Center	100.0%	0.0%	0.0%	0.0%	0.0%	0.0%
Public University of Connecticut - Storrs	36.7%	6.4%	6.1%	26.0%	2.2%	0.9%
Private University of Dayton	0.9%	1.8%	0.1%	93.4%	2.7%	0.0%
Public University of Delaware	34.7%	9.5%	11.1%	28.5%	2.9%	1.1%
Public University of Florida	77.1%	3.8%	2.1%	12.5%	1.2%	0.2%
Public University of Georgia	70.4%	3.5%	5.5%	3.0%	1.3%	1.8%
Public University of Hawaii - Manoa	38.9%	8.9%	28.6%	7.7%	7.0%	0.0%
Public University of Houston - University Park	19.3%	20.0%	4.5%	37.8%	4.5%	1.9%
Public University of Idaho	66.0%	2.6%	5.5%	13.6%	2.5%	0.3%

Percent Psychology	Percent Social Science	Percent Other Science	2015 Federal Research by Major Discipline								
			Percent Life Science	Percent Physical Science	Percent Enviro Science	Percent Eng Science	Percent Computer Science	Percent Math	Percent Psychology	Percent Social Science	Percent Other Science
0.0%	0.0%	0.0%	100.0%	0.0%	0.0%	0.0%	0.0%	0.0%	0.0%	0.0%	0.0%
3.6%	5.5%	0.0%	9.9%	5.1%	5.1%	31.6%	7.2%	1.3%	2.6%	2.9%	0.0%
6.5%	9.0%	0.1%	17.2%	26.9%	8.8%	29.3%	4.4%	3.6%	5.5%	4.2%	0.1%
0.8%	4.9%	0.9%	30.6%	9.2%	1.5%	45.6%	6.6%	2.0%	1.1%	3.5%	0.0%
2.3%	0.6%	0.0%	3.5%	10.5%	2.3%	65.6%	11.9%	2.2%	3.7%	0.3%	0.0%
0.9%	6.2%	0.8%	10.1%	22.9%	4.2%	43.8%	10.8%	5.4%	0.7%	1.2%	0.9%
0.0%	0.0%	0.0%	94.2%	5.3%	0.4%	0.0%	0.0%	0.1%	0.0%	0.0%	0.0%
5.3%	0.0%	0.0%	92.9%	0.0%	0.0%	0.0%	0.0%	0.0%	7.1%	0.0%	0.0%
2.2%	6.4%	1.1%	60.7%	9.2%	6.3%	11.4%	1.9%	3.6%	2.4%	4.3%	0.1%
16.2%	6.7%	2.3%	55.3%	2.8%	3.2%	7.0%	4.2%	2.7%	19.4%	4.3%	1.0%
0.0%	0.0%	0.0%	100.0%	0.0%	0.0%	0.0%	0.0%	0.0%	0.0%	0.0%	0.0%
1.6%	1.7%	0.0%	66.6%	11.3%	1.6%	14.6%	2.7%	1.0%	1.4%	0.9%	0.0%
2.4%	0.8%	9.2%	45.1%	18.0%	12.2%	11.3%	5.6%	3.8%	1.9%	0.3%	1.9%
5.7%	1.4%	0.7%	78.8%	6.7%	0.4%	1.9%	2.4%	0.7%	7.2%	1.5%	0.4%
0.4%	2.4%	0.7%	36.6%	6.7%	28.3%	22.4%	2.5%	1.6%	0.4%	1.3%	0.2%
0.0%	0.0%	0.0%	100.0%	0.0%	0.0%	0.0%	0.0%	0.0%	0.0%	0.0%	0.0%
5.3%	6.9%	0.0%	67.1%	4.7%	0.1%	12.8%	2.5%	2.0%	2.6%	8.2%	0.0%
0.6%	4.9%	0.0%	89.1%	3.8%	0.4%	3.0%	0.0%	1.6%	0.8%	1.2%	0.0%
0.2%	0.0%	0.0%	99.8%	0.0%	0.0%	0.0%	0.0%	0.0%	0.2%	0.0%	0.0%
2.4%	9.4%	0.0%	78.2%	2.6%	5.4%	0.0%	7.2%	0.1%	1.7%	4.8%	0.0%
1.1%	1.2%	0.2%	59.6%	4.6%	1.0%	28.3%	3.5%	0.3%	1.6%	1.0%	0.0%
0.8%	0.1%	0.0%	87.1%	0.8%	0.7%	10.0%	0.2%	0.0%	1.1%	0.1%	0.0%
0.3%	2.0%	0.0%	0.7%	8.8%	13.5%	41.8%	34.1%	0.1%	0.2%	0.9%	0.0%
0.0%	1.5%	11.4%	15.6%	8.1%	58.3%	4.7%	0.8%	0.0%	0.0%	2.0%	10.4%
0.7%	3.8%	1.2%	44.8%	30.4%	6.3%	10.4%	2.4%	0.7%	0.8%	3.0%	1.2%
0.0%	0.0%	0.0%	100.0%	0.0%	0.0%	0.0%	0.0%	0.0%	0.0%	0.0%	0.0%
1.5%	7.0%	12.6%	28.4%	32.8%	2.0%	20.5%	0.0%	1.8%	1.6%	4.4%	8.6%
0.5%	3.8%	0.9%	74.2%	5.8%	2.8%	10.3%	2.0%	0.8%	0.7%	3.3%	0.1%
1.4%	3.7%	0.0%	60.9%	14.6%	3.3%	12.3%	4.3%	1.7%	1.5%	1.4%	0.0%
1.8%	3.6%	2.2%	68.5%	8.4%	3.8%	9.4%	2.0%	2.0%	2.3%	1.4%	2.3%
2.0%	3.7%	1.0%	46.7%	18.5%	6.4%	16.4%	5.0%	0.9%	3.1%	3.1%	0.0%
1.7%	1.6%	1.1%	57.7%	8.3%	15.0%	10.4%	4.2%	0.7%	2.2%	1.0%	0.4%
0.0%	0.0%	0.0%	93.6%	6.4%	0.0%	0.0%	0.0%	0.0%	0.0%	0.0%	0.0%
2.5%	5.9%	0.3%	7.9%	21.3%	12.5%	42.5%	6.4%	1.1%	3.1%	5.2%	0.0%
0.4%	2.5%	2.2%	17.9%	14.2%	13.5%	49.7%	2.0%	0.5%	0.3%	1.7%	0.1%
2.7%	9.4%	1.7%	10.6%	24.9%	6.1%	32.4%	20.5%	0.6%	2.6%	2.4%	0.0%
2.9%	5.8%	0.0%	68.5%	13.9%	2.5%	2.0%	6.7%	1.7%	2.6%	2.1%	0.0%
0.6%	2.1%	0.3%	93.4%	1.5%	0.2%	3.4%	0.0%	0.3%	0.6%	0.6%	0.0%
3.5%	3.4%	4.8%	5.9%	20.8%	36.0%	23.2%	2.1%	0.6%	4.0%	1.9%	5.5%
0.2%	0.1%	0.0%	97.1%	0.2%	0.0%	2.1%	0.0%	0.2%	0.3%	0.0%	0.0%
0.0%	0.0%	0.0%	100.0%	0.0%	0.0%	0.0%	0.0%	0.0%	0.0%	0.0%	0.0%
11.0%	4.0%	6.7%	42.1%	8.3%	7.1%	23.3%	3.0%	1.0%	11.4%	3.4%	0.5%
0.1%	0.2%	0.9%	0.9%	1.9%	0.1%	94.6%	2.1%	0.0%	0.0%	0.1%	0.2%
2.4%	9.5%	0.3%	27.7%	12.0%	11.9%	33.3%	3.9%	1.5%	3.0%	6.5%	0.1%
0.7%	2.3%	0.1%	69.9%	5.2%	3.0%	16.6%	1.8%	0.3%	1.3%	2.0%	0.0%
5.0%	5.9%	3.5%	74.4%	4.0%	6.2%	2.7%	1.4%	1.3%	6.6%	3.4%	0.0%
0.1%	1.0%	7.7%	35.5%	8.8%	29.3%	8.6%	10.4%	0.0%	0.1%	0.6%	6.6%
8.9%	3.1%	0.1%	23.4%	8.7%	1.9%	41.8%	4.5%	3.1%	13.5%	3.1%	0.0%
0.2%	3.2%	6.1%	59.3%	2.9%	5.8%	15.6%	3.5%	0.5%	0.2%	2.6%	9.5%

Research by Major Discipline		2015 Total Research by Major Discipline					
Institutions with Over $40 Million in Federal Research, Alphabetically		Percent Life Science	Percent Physical Science	Percent Enviro Science	Percent Eng Science	Percent Computer Science	Percent Math
Public	University of Illinois - Chicago	74.9%	3.3%	0.6%	6.3%	3.0%	1.3%
Public	University of Illinois - Urbana-Champaign	35.8%	10.9%	1.2%	26.3%	17.9%	0.8%
Public	University of Iowa	76.0%	5.0%	0.7%	11.9%	0.4%	0.2%
Public	University of Kansas - Lawrence	62.4%	9.1%	10.6%	11.6%	1.0%	1.0%
Public	University of Kansas Medical Center	100.0%	0.0%	0.0%	0.0%	0.0%	0.0%
Public	University of Kentucky	71.5%	2.2%	0.7%	15.0%	0.7%	0.3%
Public	University of Louisville	84.9%	1.3%	0.1%	11.7%	0.3%	0.1%
Public	University of Maryland - Baltimore	97.9%	0.0%	0.4%	1.7%	0.0%	0.0%
Public	University of Maryland - Baltimore County	17.2%	9.7%	23.2%	18.4%	11.2%	1.6%
Public	University of Maryland - College Park	23.0%	18.3%	8.0%	24.7%	7.9%	1.4%
Public	University of Massachusetts - Amherst	41.2%	16.1%	2.4%	21.0%	9.8%	1.3%
Public	Univ. of Mass. Med. Sch. - Worcester	100.0%	0.0%	0.0%	0.0%	0.0%	0.0%
Private	University of Miami	74.3%	2.4%	17.3%	1.5%	0.5%	0.2%
Public	University of Michigan - Ann Arbor	60.0%	4.0%	1.1%	19.6%	0.6%	1.4%
Public	University of Minnesota - Twin Cities	68.9%	4.8%	1.8%	13.6%	1.8%	1.7%
Public	University of Missouri - Columbia	74.6%	2.6%	0.6%	14.6%	1.1%	0.9%
Public	University of Nebraska - Lincoln	53.9%	9.5%	1.4%	16.3%	2.8%	2.3%
Public	University of Nebraska Medical Center	100.0%	0.0%	0.0%	0.0%	0.0%	0.0%
Public	University of Nevada - Reno	54.2%	7.6%	16.2%	16.9%	1.6%	0.7%
Public	University of New Hampshire - Durham	29.0%	1.8%	41.0%	19.2%	1.1%	0.2%
Public	University of New Mexico - Albuquerque	63.2%	3.9%	2.5%	15.4%	1.9%	0.6%
Public	University of North Carolina - Chapel Hill	76.3%	3.0%	3.1%	0.5%	1.8%	0.9%
Private	University of Notre Dame	15.8%	23.1%	1.0%	39.3%	4.6%	2.4%
Public	University of Oklahoma - HSC	100.0%	0.0%	0.0%	0.0%	0.0%	0.0%
Public	University of Oklahoma - Norman	0.0%	12.9%	41.8%	26.2%	1.5%	0.4%
Public	University of Oregon	46.6%	19.8%	5.7%	1.3%	6.2%	1.1%
Private	University of Pennsylvania	82.1%	3.5%	0.2%	5.6%	1.7%	0.4%
Public	University of Pittsburgh - Pittsburgh	86.1%	3.2%	1.6%	4.4%	0.8%	0.3%
Public	University of Rhode Island	24.8%	6.6%	46.8%	6.8%	0.5%	0.1%
Private	University of Rochester	67.0%	3.1%	0.6%	24.3%	0.9%	0.1%
Public	University of South Carolina - Columbia	61.1%	8.3%	2.4%	18.5%	0.7%	1.2%
Public	University of South Florida - Tampa	70.3%	2.4%	4.8%	11.4%	1.6%	0.5%
Private	University of Southern California	63.3%	2.6%	3.1%	10.7%	14.2%	0.3%
Public	University of Tennessee - Knoxville	30.3%	7.1%	2.6%	32.6%	9.5%	0.4%
Public	University of Texas - Austin	13.4%	15.2%	13.0%	39.3%	12.5%	1.5%
Public	University of Texas - El Paso	32.4%	9.0%	6.9%	31.6%	7.9%	1.1%
Public	University of Texas HSC - Houston	100.0%	0.0%	0.0%	0.0%	0.0%	0.0%
Public	University of Texas HSC - San Antonio	100.0%	0.0%	0.0%	0.0%	0.0%	0.0%
Public	Univ. of Texas MD Anderson Cancer Ctr.	92.9%	1.9%	0.0%	0.0%	0.0%	2.1%
Public	Univ. of Texas Medical Branch - Galveston	98.2%	0.0%	0.0%	1.8%	0.0%	0.0%
Public	Univ. of Texas SW Medical Center - Dallas	100.0%	0.0%	0.0%	0.0%	0.0%	0.0%
Public	University of Utah	64.1%	3.8%	2.5%	20.5%	6.0%	1.2%
Public	University of Vermont	82.1%	0.9%	0.9%	7.5%	0.5%	0.7%
Public	University of Virginia	67.0%	6.4%	1.7%	17.2%	1.9%	0.5%
Public	University of Washington - Seattle	69.4%	4.3%	10.1%	11.8%	1.7%	0.5%
Public	University of Wisconsin - Madison	62.8%	7.8%	5.3%	14.4%	2.4%	0.7%
Public	University of Wyoming	35.6%	7.4%	38.9%	10.1%	0.5%	2.5%
Public	Utah State University	34.1%	2.5%	1.2%	53.4%	1.3%	0.3%
Private	Vanderbilt University	79.0%	6.8%	0.7%	9.8%	0.0%	0.2%

Percent Psychology	Percent Social Science	Percent Other Science	2015 Federal Research by Major Discipline								
			Percent Life Science	Percent Physical Science	Percent Enviro Science	Percent Eng Science	Percent Computer Science	Percent Math	Percent Psychology	Percent Social Science	Percent Other Science
3.1%	4.1%	3.5%	78.7%	4.0%	0.4%	4.5%	3.1%	1.2%	3.4%	2.8%	1.9%
2.8%	3.5%	0.8%	25.7%	13.7%	1.8%	28.7%	23.8%	1.0%	2.6%	2.7%	0.1%
1.8%	3.0%	1.0%	77.5%	7.2%	0.4%	10.6%	0.5%	0.3%	2.5%	0.9%	0.0%
1.0%	2.1%	1.3%	54.7%	14.4%	11.8%	10.3%	1.8%	1.8%	1.5%	2.2%	1.6%
0.0%	0.0%	0.0%	100.0%	0.0%	0.0%	0.0%	0.0%	0.0%	0.0%	0.0%	0.0%
3.2%	2.5%	3.8%	69.7%	3.6%	0.7%	14.7%	0.9%	0.6%	5.9%	1.2%	2.8%
1.1%	0.5%	0.0%	86.4%	2.5%	0.1%	8.7%	0.5%	0.2%	1.5%	0.1%	0.0%
0.0%	0.0%	0.0%	98.3%	0.0%	0.2%	1.6%	0.0%	0.0%	0.0%	0.0%	0.0%
3.0%	15.1%	0.5%	5.1%	10.2%	28.9%	21.0%	13.8%	1.9%	2.9%	15.7%	0.4%
1.4%	15.3%	0.0%	19.8%	21.3%	11.3%	20.9%	7.7%	1.4%	1.4%	16.2%	0.0%
3.4%	2.8%	2.0%	33.3%	20.2%	3.1%	21.8%	13.8%	1.7%	3.9%	1.4%	0.9%
0.0%	0.0%	0.0%	100.0%	0.0%	0.0%	0.0%	0.0%	0.0%	0.0%	0.0%	0.0%
3.6%	0.2%	0.0%	68.4%	2.8%	22.2%	1.4%	0.6%	0.3%	4.2%	0.1%	0.0%
1.7%	11.5%	0.1%	56.3%	4.6%	1.0%	24.4%	0.6%	1.0%	1.6%	10.3%	0.1%
3.0%	4.2%	0.1%	66.0%	6.0%	1.6%	13.6%	2.3%	2.3%	4.1%	4.0%	0.0%
0.8%	4.9%	0.0%	73.7%	5.4%	1.2%	8.9%	2.2%	1.9%	1.6%	5.2%	0.0%
4.7%	5.0%	4.0%	43.3%	17.1%	2.1%	18.3%	4.2%	2.2%	6.0%	3.4%	3.4%
0.0%	0.0%	0.0%	100.0%	0.0%	0.0%	0.0%	0.0%	0.0%	0.0%	0.0%	0.0%
1.6%	0.9%	0.3%	52.8%	9.1%	14.7%	17.5%	1.8%	0.9%	2.1%	1.0%	0.2%
0.3%	5.1%	2.4%	25.7%	2.6%	51.2%	14.6%	1.6%	0.2%	0.0%	4.1%	0.0%
3.7%	4.2%	4.6%	62.3%	5.2%	3.1%	17.0%	1.7%	0.7%	4.2%	2.3%	3.4%
5.0%	9.4%	0.0%	73.9%	3.3%	3.0%	0.6%	2.5%	1.1%	4.7%	10.9%	0.0%
3.4%	4.9%	5.6%	14.5%	30.2%	0.0%	41.6%	4.5%	2.9%	4.1%	0.9%	1.2%
0.0%	0.0%	0.0%	100.0%	0.0%	0.0%	0.0%	0.0%	0.0%	0.0%	0.0%	0.0%
1.7%	15.5%	0.0%	0.0%	16.5%	39.6%	23.3%	2.5%	0.6%	2.3%	15.2%	0.0%
15.6%	3.8%	0.0%	47.0%	19.6%	5.1%	0.5%	6.7%	1.1%	16.7%	3.2%	0.0%
2.7%	3.1%	0.8%	80.4%	4.2%	0.2%	6.6%	2.0%	0.5%	3.1%	2.9%	0.1%
2.0%	0.4%	1.2%	85.8%	2.8%	1.7%	4.3%	0.8%	0.3%	2.7%	0.4%	1.1%
1.8%	5.4%	7.1%	27.3%	8.0%	43.3%	5.3%	0.6%	0.1%	1.9%	5.1%	8.4%
3.5%	0.0%	0.6%	60.8%	3.5%	0.5%	30.1%	0.9%	0.1%	3.8%	0.0%	0.2%
4.2%	2.5%	1.1%	57.2%	9.2%	2.3%	17.5%	1.3%	2.0%	6.8%	1.5%	2.1%
2.5%	6.2%	0.4%	69.3%	2.3%	4.5%	13.1%	0.7%	0.3%	3.2%	6.5%	0.2%
1.5%	4.3%	0.1%	58.1%	2.0%	3.8%	10.6%	20.7%	0.3%	1.6%	3.0%	0.1%
0.6%	3.7%	13.3%	17.5%	9.8%	3.2%	34.3%	14.7%	0.7%	0.6%	4.1%	15.1%
1.8%	2.6%	0.6%	15.1%	16.6%	6.7%	37.4%	18.3%	1.3%	2.3%	2.0%	0.2%
5.5%	5.3%	0.2%	29.4%	10.4%	6.4%	28.2%	11.5%	1.3%	5.0%	7.8%	0.0%
0.0%	0.0%	0.0%	100.0%	0.0%	0.0%	0.0%	0.0%	0.0%	0.0%	0.0%	0.0%
0.0%	0.0%	0.0%	100.0%	0.0%	0.0%	0.0%	0.0%	0.0%	0.0%	0.0%	0.0%
2.1%	0.9%	0.0%	87.1%	4.8%	0.0%	0.0%	0.0%	3.0%	4.1%	1.0%	0.0%
0.0%	0.0%	0.0%	98.5%	0.0%	0.0%	1.5%	0.0%	0.0%	0.0%	0.0%	0.0%
0.0%	0.0%	0.0%	100.0%	0.0%	0.0%	0.0%	0.0%	0.0%	0.0%	0.0%	0.0%
0.7%	1.2%	0.0%	70.1%	5.0%	3.0%	10.1%	8.1%	1.4%	0.8%	1.4%	0.0%
1.9%	0.3%	5.3%	80.4%	1.0%	0.6%	8.1%	0.3%	0.6%	2.2%	0.2%	6.6%
1.5%	2.0%	1.7%	65.3%	8.3%	1.8%	18.3%	2.8%	0.5%	1.9%	0.4%	0.7%
0.8%	1.3%	0.0%	68.1%	4.9%	11.3%	11.5%	1.5%	0.6%	0.9%	1.1%	0.0%
0.7%	4.8%	1.0%	56.6%	9.8%	7.2%	17.0%	3.2%	0.9%	0.8%	4.0%	0.5%
0.1%	4.7%	0.1%	36.2%	7.0%	40.0%	8.6%	0.4%	2.8%	0.0%	5.0%	0.0%
6.0%	1.0%	0.3%	22.9%	2.5%	1.6%	65.4%	1.0%	0.3%	5.8%	0.6%	0.0%
2.0%	1.1%	0.4%	77.9%	6.8%	0.8%	10.8%	0.0%	0.3%	2.1%	1.0%	0.3%

Research by Major Discipline	2015 Total Research by Major Discipline					
Institutions with Over $40 Million in Federal Research, Alphabetically	Percent Life Science	Percent Physical Science	Percent Enviro Science	Percent Eng Science	Percent Computer Science	Percent Math
Public Virginia Commonwealth University	83.6%	3.2%	0.5%	6.3%	0.2%	0.7%
Public Virginia Polytechnic Institute and St. Univ.	42.3%	2.8%	1.2%	45.6%	5.0%	0.6%
Private Wake Forest University	97.7%	1.9%	0.0%	0.0%	0.1%	0.1%
Public Washington State University - Pullman	54.3%	14.2%	3.5%	17.8%	1.7%	0.3%
Private Washington University in St. Louis	90.8%	2.1%	0.9%	4.0%	0.6%	0.1%
Public Wayne State University	75.6%	8.3%	0.3%	9.1%	1.6%	0.5%
Private Weill Cornell Medical College	100.0%	0.0%	0.0%	0.0%	0.0%	0.0%
Public West Virginia University	59.9%	6.2%	6.3%	21.2%	0.5%	0.4%
Private Woods Hole Oceanographic Institution	0.0%	0.0%	60.2%	39.8%	0.0%	0.0%
Private Yale University	83.9%	5.7%	1.0%	4.9%	1.0%	0.3%
Private Yeshiva University	100.0%	0.0%	0.0%	0.0%	0.0%	0.0%

			2015 Federal Research by Major Discipline									
Percent Psychology	Percent Social Science	Percent Other Science	Percent Life Science	Percent Physical Science	Percent Enviro Science	Percent Eng Science	Percent Computer Science	Percent Math	Percent Psychology	Percent Social Science	Percent Other Science
4.5%	1.0%	0.0%	83.0%	4.7%	0.4%	4.5%	0.3%	1.0%	6.0%	0.1%	0.0%
0.9%	1.4%	0.2%	38.5%	3.7%	1.6%	46.1%	7.1%	0.6%	1.4%	0.6%	0.4%
0.2%	0.0%	0.0%	97.9%	1.8%	0.0%	0.0%	0.1%	0.1%	0.2%	0.0%	0.0%
0.7%	6.6%	1.0%	55.5%	17.6%	3.5%	15.1%	2.1%	0.5%	0.7%	4.6%	0.4%
0.9%	0.2%	0.4%	88.5%	2.7%	1.3%	5.0%	0.9%	0.1%	0.9%	0.1%	0.5%
2.1%	1.7%	0.9%	77.1%	8.3%	0.3%	8.6%	1.8%	0.6%	2.7%	0.6%	0.0%
0.0%	0.0%	0.0%	100.0%	0.0%	0.0%	0.0%	0.0%	0.0%	0.0%	0.0%	0.0%
0.5%	4.8%	0.2%	53.7%	9.3%	8.3%	25.4%	1.0%	0.6%	0.3%	1.2%	0.3%
0.0%	0.0%	0.0%	0.0%	0.0%	56.3%	43.7%	0.0%	0.0%	0.0%	0.0%	0.0%
1.5%	1.2%	0.3%	85.2%	5.5%	0.6%	5.4%	1.1%	0.4%	0.9%	0.6%	0.3%
0.0%	0.0%	0.0%	100.0%	0.0%	0.0%	0.0%	0.0%	0.0%	0.0%	0.0%	0.0%

Endowment Assets

	Institutions with Over $40 Million in Federal Research, Alphabetically	2016 Endowment Assets x $1000	2016 National Rank	2016 Control Rank	2015 Endowment Assets x $1000	2015 National Rank	2015 Control Rank
Public	Arizona State University	612,590	148	53	643,188	143	51
Public	Auburn University	646,624	141	51	641,993	144	52
Public	Augusta University	210,595	294	121	210,595	297	120
Private	Baylor College of Medicine	1,063,678	81	52	1,095,326	80	53
Private	Boston University	1,654,531	52	34	1,644,117	53	36
Private	Brandeis University	866,778	100	61	915,087	93	58
Private	Brown University	2,963,366	31	21	3,073,349	31	21
Private	California Institute of Technology	2,106,724	39	24	2,198,887	39	25
Private	Carnegie Mellon University	1,708,618	49	32	1,739,474	52	35
Private	Case Western Reserve University	1,662,739	51	33	1,775,999	51	34
Public	Clemson University	621,294	145	52	648,611	141	50
Public	Cleveland State University	72,700	612	218	74,900	570	200
Private	Cold Spring Harbor Laboratory						
Public	Colorado State Univ. - Fort Collins	286,348	247	99	281,355	252	99
Private	Columbia University	9,041,027	11	8	9,639,065	11	8
Private	Cornell University	4,524,419	20	16	4,760,560	19	15
Private	Dartmouth College	4,474,404	21	17	4,663,491	21	17
Private	Drexel University	650,252	140	90	668,386	138	90
Private	Duke University	6,839,780	14	11	7,296,545	14	11
Private	Emory University	6,401,650	16	13	6,684,305	16	13
Public	Florida International University	174,061	340	135	178,750	340	133
Public	Florida State University	584,529	153	56	605,275	150	56
Public	George Mason University	71,566	622	220	72,245	586	206
Private	George Washington University	1,570,278	56	38	1,616,357	56	37
Private	Georgetown University	1,483,502	60	40	1,528,869	60	39
Public	Georgia Institute of Technology	1,843,764	46	17	1,858,977	46	16
Private	Harvard University	34,541,893	1	1	36,448,817	1	1
Private	Icahn School of Med. at Mount Sinai	659,261	138	89	717,372	128	82
Public	Indiana University - Bloomington	991,134	89	33	960,625	90	33
Public	Iowa State University	760,461	115	44	786,205	113	43
Private	Johns Hopkins University	3,381,281	28	20	3,412,617	28	20
Public	Kansas State University	475,617	178	70	488,936	172	67
Public	Louisiana State Univ. - Baton Rouge	416,717	196	80	427,852	194	78
Private	Massachusetts Institute of Tech.	13,181,515	5	5	13,474,743	5	5
Private	Medical College of Wisconsin	748,862	118	72	778,315	115	72
Public	Medical University of South Carolina	312,002	231	92	322,644	227	91
Public	Michigan State University	2,585,841	34	13	2,672,822	34	13
Public	Mississippi State University	444,485	190	76	449,106	183	74
Public	Montana State University - Bozeman	138,207	407	154	142,661	394	149
Public	Naval Postgraduate School	5,184	1387	605	5,086	1136	479
Public	New Jersey Institute of Technology	98,006	495	177	99,257	476	171
Public	New Mexico State Univ. - Las Cruces	214,778	291	120	221,005	286	117
Private	New York University	3,487,702	27	19	3,576,180	26	19
Public	North Carolina State University	998,600	87	32	983,979	88	32
Private	Northeastern University	693,025	128	81	729,400	124	79
Private	Northwestern University	9,648,497	10	7	10,193,037	7	6
Public	Ohio State University - Columbus	3,578,562	25	7	3,633,887	24	6
Public	Oregon Health & Science University	570,485	156	58	571,341	153	58
Public	Oregon State University	492,546	172	66	505,369	168	65

2014 Endowment Assets x $1000	2014 National Rank	2014 Control Rank	2013 Endowment Assets x $1000	2013 National Rank	2013 Control Rank	2012 Endowment Assets x $1000	2012 National Rank	2012 Control Rank
625,833	143	51	552,789	141	51	500,667	138	50
621,106	147	55	522,145	147	56	461,727	148	57
212,697	293	119	142,208	354	139	117,426	382	145
1,021,458	84	56	873,721	85	57	789,997	86	58
1,616,004	53	35	1,403,061	54	36	1,157,075	59	40
861,152	99	63	766,205	99	62	674,522	97	64
2,999,749	30	21	2,699,948	29	21	2,460,131	28	21
2,093,842	41	27	1,849,880	38	24	1,746,526	37	24
1,599,900	54	36	1,371,365	56	38	987,054	68	46
1,758,570	49	33	1,595,300	47	31	1,600,013	44	29
623,262	146	54	528,697	146	55	482,866	142	53
72,300	575	202	61,707	588	208	54,300	605	215
284,495	242	97	245,887	243	97	225,362	244	95
9,223,047	11	8	8,197,880	8	6	7,654,152	8	6
4,646,134	19	15	4,133,842	19	15	3,850,426	19	15
4,468,219	21	17	3,733,596	21	17	3,486,383	21	17
660,150	136	87	586,938	137	89	555,381	131	84
7,036,776	14	11	6,040,973	14	11	5,555,196	14	11
6,681,479	15	12	5,816,046	15	12	5,461,158	15	12
176,500	339	133	149,384	344	132	132,554	351	137
624,557	145	53	548,095	143	52	497,709	139	51
69,554	594	213	59,261	605	217	55,165	599	212
1,576,508	56	38	1,375,202	55	37	1,305,892	53	36
1,461,276	62	41	1,286,323	61	40	1,140,486	60	41
1,889,014	45	16	1,714,876	45	16	1,608,248	43	15
35,883,891	1	1	32,334,293	1	1	30,435,375	1	1
691,221	131	84	630,518	128	81	594,968	120	77
961,054	89	31	835,123	89	30	772,185	88	29
777,018	112	43	673,515	115	44	604,897	115	43
3,451,947	26	19	2,987,298	25	19	2,678,721	25	20
473,987	170	66	364,675	191	78	329,240	193	78
425,417	186	73	383,443	183	73	357,602	178	70
12,425,131	5	5	10,857,976	5	5	10,308,274	5	5
748,637	122	75	597,865	134	86	470,510	146	91
312,580	227	91	272,319	227	89	239,472	229	89
2,548,913	34	13	1,997,985	36	14	1,721,100	38	14
456,610	176	69	394,925	178	70	343,857	184	73
141,066	388	148	121,755	395	149	119,821	376	143
5,182	1019	417	4,461	1008	406	4,466	1129	470
98,117	471	171	82,965	486	174	74,248	495	175
222,581	283	114	197,387	282	113	181,134	282	114
3,422,227	27	20	2,949,000	27	20	2,755,000	24	19
885,055	93	34	769,404	97	37	635,326	107	39
713,200	127	80	616,618	130	83	566,767	128	82
9,778,112	8	6	7,883,323	10	7	7,118,595	9	7
3,547,566	24	6	3,149,169	24	6	2,366,033	30	9
522,384	160	60	463,969	156	60	433,288	154	60
511,427	162	62	443,826	164	64	403,606	165	67

Endowment Assets

	Institutions with Over $40 Million in Federal Research, Alphabetically	2016 Endowment Assets x $1000	2016 National Rank	2016 Control Rank	2015 Endowment Assets x $1000	2015 National Rank	2015 Control Rank
Public	Penn. State Univ. - Hershey Med. Ctr.	449,943	185	74	436,288	190	75
Public	Pennsylvania State Univ. - Univ. Park	1,912,254	45	16	1,854,222	47	17
Private	Princeton University	22,152,580	4	4	22,723,473	3	3
Public	Purdue University - West Lafayette	2,254,541	36	14	2,397,902	35	14
Private	Rensselaer Polytechnic Institute	634,916	143	92	676,546	137	89
Private	Rice University	5,324,289	18	14	5,557,479	18	14
Private	Rockefeller University	1,927,404	44	29	1,987,027	44	29
Private	Rush University	538,823	160	102	555,610	156	98
Public	Rutgers University - New Brunswick	865,867	101	40	710,802	129	47
Public	San Diego State University	219,994	289	118	209,372	299	122
Private	Scripps Research Institute						
Private	Stanford University	22,398,130	3	3	22,222,957	4	4
Public	Stony Brook University	262,191	265	104	247,397	274	108
Public	Temple University	494,187	171	65	386,230	206	84
Public	Texas A&M Univ. - College Station	9,944,936	8	2	9,856,983	10	3
Private	Thomas Jefferson University	500,943	168	105	437,750	188	114
Private	Tufts University	1,562,968	57	39	1,593,019	57	38
Private	Tulane University	1,171,314	71	46	1,220,464	68	45
Public	Uniformed Services Univ. of the HS						
Public	University at Albany	59,273	689	249	54,810	678	244
Public	University at Buffalo	600,961	151	54	619,296	148	54
Public	University of Alabama - Birmingham	431,459	193	79	388,405	205	83
Public	University of Alabama - Huntsville	71,053	626	222	65,978	622	224
Public	University of Alaska - Fairbanks	173,372	342	136	189,476	323	129
Public	University of Arizona	754,651	117	46	767,940	117	44
Public	Univ. of Arkansas for Med. Sciences	31,733	939	347	32,632	845	309
Public	University of California - Berkeley	3,845,281	23	6	4,045,451	23	5
Public	University of California - Davis	965,805	90	34	1,013,936	86	30
Public	University of California - Irvine	498,171	169	64	512,904	166	63
Public	University of California - Los Angeles	3,849,133	22	5	3,493,903	27	8
Public	University of California - Riverside	191,420	318	127	185,335	331	131
Public	University of California - San Diego	1,176,581	70	25	951,367	91	34
Public	Univ. of California - San Francisco	2,112,014	38	15	2,124,970	41	15
Public	Univ. of California - Santa Barbara	273,679	253	101	265,930	260	104
Public	University of California - Santa Cruz	162,211	361	143	164,331	359	140
Public	University of Central Florida	146,416	386	148	150,627	377	145
Private	University of Chicago	7,001,204	13	10	7,549,710	13	10
Public	University of Cincinnati - Cincinnati	1,165,522	72	26	1,195,899	71	25
Public	University of Colorado - Boulder	583,190	154	57	598,355	152	57
Public	U. of Colorado - Denv./Anschutz Med.	479,474	176	69	491,942	171	66
Public	Univ. of Connecticut - Health Center	83,260	552	196	103,450	461	168
Public	University of Connecticut - Storrs	275,335	252	100	279,699	255	102
Private	University of Dayton	473,122	179	109	500,407	169	104
Public	University of Delaware	1,261,790	66	22	1,341,373	65	22
Public	University of Florida	1,461,347	62	21	1,555,703	58	20
Public	University of Georgia	1,016,732	84	30	1,004,987	87	31
Public	University of Hawaii - Manoa	271,180	257	102	280,210	254	101
Public	University of Houston - Univ. Park	665,001	134	49	707,437	130	48
Public	University of Idaho	237,528	279	110	239,603	276	109

2014 Endowment Assets x $1000	2014 National Rank	2014 Control Rank	2013 Endowment Assets x $1000	2013 National Rank	2013 Control Rank	2012 Endowment Assets x $1000	2012 National Rank	2012 Control Rank
381,158	206	85	309,312	215	85	284,793	212	82
1,739,032	51	17	1,411,236	53	18	1,299,369	54	18
20,995,518	4	4	18,200,433	4	4	16,954,128	4	4
2,443,494	35	14	2,182,171	34	13	1,916,968	34	13
659,035	137	88	616,836	129	82	583,350	124	80
5,527,693	18	14	4,836,728	18	14	4,418,595	18	14
1,985,942	44	29	1,772,394	42	28	1,692,300	39	25
554,269	152	95	500,797	150	93	457,217	150	93
763,561	116	45	729,431	102	39	645,556	103	37
190,608	324	129	158,406	333	128	136,408	345	134
21,446,006	3	3	18,688,868	3	3	17,035,804	3	3
214,446	288	116	180,716	298	119	155,172	320	124
374,758	210	86	323,837	210	83	277,479	214	83
10,540,226	7	2	8,072,055	9	3	7,034,588	10	3
375,697	208	123	336,658	205	124	314,152	200	121
1,590,045	55	37	1,440,527	52	35	1,351,166	52	35
1,183,924	70	46	1,047,813	73	49	960,972	72	48
49,522	686	249	40,522	713	258	35,190	743	267
624,791	144	52	554,392	140	50	511,020	137	49
406,098	195	80	374,260	188	76	349,290	181	72
70,419	590	211	65,986	567	199	61,788	562	192
194,276	318	127	211,332	270	109	192,485	273	111
760,679	117	46	611,746	131	48	563,655	129	47
32,764	803	299	29,496	796	289	27,388	818	302
3,913,416	23	5	3,330,553	23	5	3,031,896	23	5
946,302	90	32	790,060	91	32	713,180	92	33
387,157	204	84	330,104	208	82	300,220	206	81
3,226,030	28	8	2,626,965	30	9	2,449,838	29	8
179,669	337	131	148,777	345	133	138,816	341	130
752,079	120	47	642,605	122	46	567,772	127	46
1,993,470	43	15	1,716,203	44	15	1,541,415	46	16
257,987	264	103	226,034	261	104	206,032	257	102
152,855	365	144	124,926	384	147	116,800	385	146
154,595	362	143	135,475	364	143	122,609	367	142
7,545,544	13	10	6,668,974	13	10	6,570,875	12	9
1,183,922	71	25	1,045,606	74	25	976,814	70	24
510,646	164	63	495,900	151	58	431,593	155	61
419,832	188	75	389,636	179	71	339,727	186	75
103,885	453	165	92,927	456	164	84,059	460	164
280,876	247	99	251,247	240	95	227,272	240	93
510,107	165	102	442,252	165	101	397,794	168	101
1,310,133	64	22	1,171,166	65	22	1,087,870	63	21
1,519,522	57	19	1,359,643	57	19	1,263,277	55	19
975,890	87	30	786,171	93	34	674,164	98	34
272,280	255	101	235,383	253	99	211,970	250	98
683,950	132	48	637,475	125	47	579,264	126	45
240,980	272	108	209,398	272	110	188,511	277	112

Endowment Assets

	Institutions with Over $40 Million in Federal Research, Alphabetically	2016 Endowment Assets x $1000	2016 National Rank	2016 Control Rank	2015 Endowment Assets x $1000	2015 National Rank	2015 Control Rank
Public	University of Illinois - Chicago	287,188	245	98	302,121	239	97
Public	Univ. of Illinois - Urbana-Champaign	1,489,991	59	20	1,530,658	59	21
Public	University of Iowa	1,259,309	67	23	1,263,043	67	23
Public	University of Kansas - Lawrence	1,150,623	75	27	1,170,313	73	26
Public	University of Kansas Medical Center	345,852	218	87	330,089	224	89
Public	University of Kentucky	1,117,852	78	28	1,142,722	77	27
Public	University of Louisville	715,689	124	47	844,288	103	39
Public	University of Maryland - Baltimore	254,733	267	106	256,008	269	105
Public	Univ. of Maryland - Baltimore County	78,101	585	203	75,752	567	198
Public	University of Maryland - College Park	466,075	183	72	482,628	173	68
Public	Univ. of Massachusetts - Amherst	287,213	244	97	303,984	238	96
Public	Univ. of Mass. Med. Sch. - Worcester	183,435	327	130	194,251	319	127
Private	University of Miami	844,643	102	62	887,329	96	60
Public	University of Michigan - Ann Arbor	9,743,461	9	3	9,952,113	9	2
Public	University of Minnesota - Twin Cities	3,280,681	29	9	3,297,460	29	9
Public	University of Missouri - Columbia	869,566	99	39	857,471	100	38
Public	University of Nebraska - Lincoln	869,874	98	38	906,156	94	36
Public	University of Nebraska Medical Ctr.	223,753	286	116	226,077	282	114
Public	University of Nevada - Reno	302,698	239	95	306,587	235	94
Public	Univ. of New Hampshire - Durham	330,131	223	90	346,926	217	87
Public	Univ. of New Mexico - Albuquerque	393,240	202	83	403,670	202	81
Public	Univ. of North Carolina - Chapel Hill	2,889,679	32	11	2,988,806	32	11
Private	University of Notre Dame	8,374,083	12	9	8,566,952	12	9
Public	University of Oklahoma - HSC	516,920	166	62	456,907	179	72
Public	University of Oklahoma - Norman	1,003,434	85	31	1,066,117	82	28
Public	University of Oregon	758,692	116	45	719,111	127	46
Private	University of Pennsylvania	10,715,364	7	6	10,133,569	8	7
Public	University of Pittsburgh - Pittsburgh	3,524,904	26	8	3,588,775	25	7
Public	University of Rhode Island	124,629	432	160	131,655	408	153
Private	University of Rochester	1,927,573	43	28	2,050,199	43	28
Public	Univ. of South Carolina - Columbia	655,469	139	50	625,186	147	53
Public	University of South Florida - Tampa	395,324	201	82	417,415	196	80
Private	University of Southern California	4,608,714	19	15	4,709,511	20	16
Public	University of Tennessee - Knoxville	597,475	152	55	608,873	149	55
Public	University of Texas - Austin	10,935,781	6	1	10,507,795	6	1
Public	University of Texas - El Paso	218,880	290	119	217,286	290	118
Public	University of Texas HSC - Houston	336,086	222	89	306,094	236	95
Public	Univ. of Texas HSC - San Antonio	486,652	173	67	476,632	175	70
Public	U. of Texas MD Anderson Cancer Ctr.	1,212,099	69	24	1,200,742	70	24
Public	U. of Texas Med. Branch - Galveston	533,972	163	60	531,562	163	61
Public	Univ. of Texas SW Med. Ctr. - Dallas	1,684,130	50	18	1,620,501	55	19
Public	University of Utah	1,076,649	80	29	1,023,004	85	29
Public	University of Vermont	467,702	181	71	453,653	181	73
Public	University of Virginia	5,852,309	17	4	6,180,515	17	4
Public	University of Washington - Seattle	2,968,013	30	10	3,076,226	30	10
Public	University of Wisconsin - Madison	2,739,728	33	12	2,792,622	33	12
Public	University of Wyoming	458,486	184	73	481,469	174	69
Public	Utah State University	325,287	226	91	314,668	231	92
Private	Vanderbilt University	3,822,187	24	18	4,133,542	22	18

2014 Endowment Assets x $1000	2014 National Rank	2014 Control Rank	2013 Endowment Assets x $1000	2013 National Rank	2013 Control Rank	2012 Endowment Assets x $1000	2012 National Rank	2012 Control Rank
299,522	235	94	245,900	242	96	217,195	246	96
1,488,828	59	21	1,310,300	60	21	1,137,035	61	20
1,251,356	65	23	1,094,803	69	24	981,104	69	23
1,147,213	76	26	1,005,416	78	26	922,220	75	25
323,573	222	89	283,579	220	87	260,113	220	87
1,136,833	78	27	995,295	79	27	900,158	78	26
876,825	94	35	788,529	92	33	726,244	91	32
250,194	269	106	230,006	258	102	206,582	256	101
73,012	571	201	66,825	561	194	59,996	572	198
471,391	171	67	433,821	167	65	408,984	162	66
307,098	232	93	272,087	228	90	233,317	235	92
211,880	295	120	171,437	314	124	144,846	333	125
865,435	98	62	777,947	94	60	678,694	95	62
9,731,460	9	3	8,382,311	7	2	7,691,052	7	2
3,176,456	29	9	2,757,476	28	8	2,494,050	27	7
804,003	106	40	692,853	112	43	622,209	113	42
1,005,716	86	29	870,173	86	29	790,011	85	28
232,088	277	110	200,809	278	111	182,310	281	113
295,334	237	95	259,775	232	92	238,286	231	90
333,203	220	88	231,504	255	100	214,879	249	97
412,772	192	79	371,362	189	77	343,321	185	74
2,695,663	33	12	2,381,151	31	10	2,179,177	31	10
8,039,756	12	9	6,856,301	12	9	6,329,866	13	10
448,040	179	71	397,294	174	69	351,739	179	71
1,045,426	82	28	927,019	83	28	820,724	82	27
627,004	142	50	558,437	139	49	477,599	144	54
9,582,335	10	7	7,741,396	11	8	6,754,658	11	8
3,492,839	25	7	2,975,896	26	7	2,618,436	26	6
132,234	405	152	102,885	430	158	93,659	433	156
2,015,283	42	28	1,730,829	43	29	1,581,773	45	30
596,379	148	56	544,399	145	54	513,936	135	48
417,335	189	76	363,924	192	79	334,132	190	77
4,593,014	20	16	3,868,355	20	16	3,488,933	20	16
854,073	101	37	726,483	104	40	647,826	100	36
11,340,760	6	1	9,145,142	6	1	8,209,163	6	1
221,019	286	115	196,458	283	114	178,973	285	115
256,097	267	104	227,043	260	103	201,989	264	106
485,459	169	65	432,031	168	66	412,085	160	64
1,236,742	67	24	1,111,653	67	23	1,056,878	64	22
549,315	154	58	495,887	152	59	473,427	145	55
1,661,474	52	18	1,450,655	51	17	1,465,375	48	17
844,761	103	38	745,553	101	38	670,411	99	35
394,454	202	82	374,316	187	75	325,555	195	79
5,945,952	17	4	5,166,660	17	4	4,788,852	17	4
2,832,753	31	10	2,346,693	32	11	2,111,332	32	11
2,699,253	32	11	2,334,560	33	12	2,082,181	33	12
455,105	177	70	404,074	172	68	358,530	177	69
282,465	245	98	242,025	246	98	209,188	252	99
4,086,040	22	18	3,673,434	22	18	3,399,293	22	18

Endowment Assets

	Institutions with Over $40 Million in Federal Research, Alphabetically	2016 Endowment Assets x $1000	2016 National Rank	2016 Control Rank	2015 Endowment Assets x $1000	2015 National Rank	2015 Control Rank
Public	Virginia Commonwealth University	1,559,874	58	19	1,638,147	54	18
Public	Virginia Polytechnic Inst. and St. U.	842,991	103	41	817,759	106	41
Private	Wake Forest University	1,141,211	77	50	1,167,400	75	49
Public	Washington State Univ. - Pullman	907,828	96	36	885,777	97	37
Private	Washington University in St. Louis	6,461,717	15	12	6,818,748	15	12
Public	Wayne State University	301,470	241	96	307,569	234	93
Private	Weill Cornell Medical College	1,233,303	68	45	1,276,986	66	44
Public	West Virginia University	511,384	167	63	533,599	162	60
Private	Woods Hole Oceanographic Inst.						
Private	Yale University	25,408,600	2	2	25,572,100	2	2
Private	Yeshiva University	632,856	144	93	680,327	136	88

2014 Endowment Assets x $1000	2014 National Rank	2014 Control Rank	2013 Endowment Assets x $1000	2013 National Rank	2013 Control Rank	2012 Endowment Assets x $1000	2012 National Rank	2012 Control Rank
1,509,431	58	20	1,326,915	59	20	438,140	153	59
796,437	109	42	660,340	119	45	594,776	121	44
1,148,026	75	50	1,061,639	70	46	1,000,133	67	45
868,091	96	36	777,628	95	35	737,409	89	30
6,643,379	16	13	5,651,860	16	13	5,225,992	16	13
311,337	228	92	276,234	225	88	247,111	226	88
1,243,814	66	43	1,138,386	66	44	1,096,528	62	42
533,627	158	59	460,640	158	61	417,504	159	63
23,894,800	2	2	20,780,000	2	2	19,345,000	2	2
1,094,558	79	52	1,183,499	64	43	1,054,052	65	43

Annual Giving

	Institutions with Over $40 Million in Federal Research, Alphabetically	2016 Annual Giving x $1000	2016 National Rank	2016 Control Rank	2015 Annual Giving x $1000	2015 National Rank	2015 Control Rank
Public	Arizona State University	140,417	60	34	130,775	61	32
Public	Auburn University	118,477	70	42	106,353	82	48
Public	Augusta University	11,544	375	185	12,151	348	164
Private	Baylor College of Medicine	77,605	100	38	61,656	119	44
Private	Boston University	156,941	50	23	140,393	56	26
Private	Brandeis University	57,593	130	48	60,196	120	45
Private	Brown University	207,725	34	19	187,754	37	21
Private	California Institute of Technology	182,869	41	21	161,929	47	23
Private	Carnegie Mellon University	155,302	51	24	139,563	57	27
Private	Case Western Reserve University	158,323	48	22	132,826	58	28
Public	Clemson University	90,623	91	57	81,861	103	63
Public	Cleveland State University	11,802	370	182	17,732	266	130
Private	Cold Spring Harbor Laboratory						
Public	Colorado State Univ. - Fort Collins	42,798	155	92	41,342	154	92
Private	Columbia University	584,809	6	5	552,682	6	5
Private	Cornell University	427,089	15	11	434,465	17	14
Private	Dartmouth College	227,038	32	18	218,832	32	19
Private	Drexel University	60,905	122	44	88,916	95	38
Private	Duke University	506,441	10	8	472,008	11	9
Private	Emory University	192,700	38	20	228,034	31	18
Public	Florida International University	27,820	202	113	23,312	212	110
Public	Florida State University	75,413	103	65	68,634	112	70
Public	George Mason University	67,940	113	73	53,164	128	80
Private	George Washington University	101,391	77	32	248,030	28	16
Private	Georgetown University	153,384	52	25	172,452	43	22
Public	Georgia Institute of Technology	129,304	64	38	119,118	73	42
Private	Harvard University	1,187,530	1	1	1,045,872	2	2
Private	Icahn School of Med. at Mount Sinai	120,327	68	28	109,733	78	33
Public	Indiana University - Bloomington	195,908	37	18	211,471	34	15
Public	Iowa State University	90,148	93	58	105,512	83	49
Private	Johns Hopkins University	657,293	4	4	582,675	5	4
Public	Kansas State University	96,626	86	52	98,094	88	53
Public	Louisiana State Univ. - Baton Rouge	147,998	55	30	130,763	62	33
Private	Massachusetts Inst. of Technology	419,752	16	12	439,404	16	13
Private	Medical College of Wisconsin	19,028	267	132	20,907	230	112
Public	Medical University of South Carolina	44,310	154	91	31,498	178	103
Public	Michigan State University	176,131	43	22	131,499	60	31
Public	Mississippi State University	69,763	108	68	56,857	125	78
Public	Montana State University - Bozeman	21,161	249	130	13,299	331	161
Public	Naval Postgraduate School						
Public	New Jersey Institute of Technology				8,821	443	199
Public	New Mexico State Univ. - Las Cruces	16,539	306	155	16,568	282	142
Private	New York University	461,150	12	9	439,662	15	12
Public	North Carolina State University	129,948	63	37	119,150	72	41
Private	Northeastern University	56,292	134	51	59,857	122	46
Private	Northwestern University	401,679	17	13	536,831	8	7
Public	Ohio State University - Columbus	386,112	18	5	359,798	21	6
Public	Oregon Health & Science University	156,961	49	27	141,018	55	30
Public	Oregon State University	97,101	85	51	99,318	87	52

2014 Annual Giving x $1000	2014 National Rank	2014 Control Rank	2013 Annual Giving x $1000	2013 National Rank	2013 Control Rank	2012 Annual Giving x $1000	2012 National Rank	2012 Control Rank
99,212	78	44	108,011	65	38	98,844	66	41
86,579	88	50	67,911	105	64	63,712	106	68
61,007	123	76	33,894	165	95	4,664	593	242
84,211	93	39	100,540	74	29	80,736	83	30
132,583	55	27	116,562	58	26	86,181	76	27
56,905	126	49	54,556	123	48	60,768	108	39
201,731	33	20	176,416	35	19	178,065	32	18
113,370	71	33	103,446	72	28	99,983	65	25
137,573	50	24	112,164	60	27	79,141	85	32
124,509	62	30	94,238	79	31	90,584	73	26
61,721	121	75	75,666	98	60	71,304	96	62
14,179	309	156	6,163	515	220	5,265	556	230
143,239	47	24	112,473	59	33	29,925	166	98
469,969	9	7	646,663	4	4	490,311	5	5
341,851	19	13	326,497	16	11	263,358	19	11
254,944	27	17	160,165	41	20	170,847	34	19
89,966	86	38	64,953	108	42	67,459	103	37
437,382	12	9	423,658	9	9	350,944	11	10
268,926	26	16	204,171	32	17	211,589	26	15
21,459	226	121	24,706	197	111	15,267	269	138
55,725	128	78	61,270	115	72	54,942	116	74
48,467	139	83	44,617	134	80	44,111	133	82
98,515	79	35	84,436	85	34	73,070	94	34
134,685	52	25	131,044	47	23	113,721	52	22
141,888	48	25	102,717	73	45	118,429	50	29
1,155,610	1	1	792,256	2	2	650,243	2	2
150,420	45	23	127,027	51	24	103,111	60	23
190,593	35	15	160,548	40	21	122,489	46	25
64,854	116	71	62,288	114	71	60,716	109	70
614,606	5	5	518,571	5	5	479,654	6	6
156,335	42	20	108,060	64	37	75,373	88	56
110,644	73	40	96,895	78	48	105,784	55	33
375,031	18	12	403,539	11	10	379,058	10	9
16,704	270	131	13,263	322	161	19,197	218	101
38,853	156	90	43,841	138	82	40,197	139	85
117,566	65	34	130,964	48	25	122,883	45	24
66,002	114	70	65,925	106	65	51,332	122	78
12,185	337	165	16,659	263	138	10,602	358	171
8,918	420	195	10,023	384	179	8,442	418	190
13,928	313	157	12,499	335	165	12,060	321	158
455,718	10	8	449,344	7	7	395,510	9	8
117,535	66	35	131,378	46	24	100,324	64	40
39,543	154	65	46,828	130	53	34,512	151	61
616,351	4	4	295,601	18	12	233,746	25	14
332,627	20	7	290,595	20	8	334,509	13	3
153,281	43	21	121,027	56	31	91,560	72	47
97,217	81	46	81,027	88	54	101,634	62	39

Annual Giving

	Institutions with Over $40 Million in Federal Research, Alphabetically	2016 Annual Giving x $1000	2016 National Rank	2016 Control Rank	2015 Annual Giving x $1000	2015 National Rank	2015 Control Rank
Public	Penn. State Univ. - Hershey Med. Ctr.	35,472	173	99	35,023	171	100
Public	Pennsylvania State Univ. - Univ. Park	147,570	56	31	155,658	50	26
Private	Princeton University	267,876	27	16	549,840	7	6
Public	Purdue University - West Lafayette	151,217	53	28	172,219	44	22
Private	Rensselaer Polytechnic Institute	37,798	167	72	38,364	164	68
Private	Rice University	102,977	76	31	122,186	67	30
Private	Rockefeller University	67,659	115	41	18,562	262	133
Private	Rush University	3,070	727	424	3,689	681	402
Public	Rutgers University - New Brunswick	118,493	69	41	127,846	63	34
Public	San Diego State University	79,781	98	61	76,036	107	66
Private	Scripps Research Institute						
Private	Stanford University	951,149	2	2	1,625,036	1	1
Public	Stony Brook University	76,704	101	63	86,687	98	59
Public	Temple University	62,254	119	77	58,792	124	77
Public	Texas A&M Univ. - College Station	276,475	25	11	255,179	26	11
Private	Thomas Jefferson University	56,821	133	50	38,809	162	67
Private	Tufts University	60,405	124	45	62,131	118	43
Private	Tulane University	98,919	81	33	88,422	96	39
Public	Uniformed Services Univ. of the HS						
Public	University at Albany	9,122	432	200	9,439	419	191
Public	University at Buffalo	36,219	170	97	30,565	184	105
Public	University of Alabama - Birmingham	88,043	95	59	76,612	106	65
Public	University of Alabama - Huntsville	2,297	792	342	2,032	803	348
Public	University of Alaska - Fairbanks	27,865	201	112	26,959	195	107
Public	University of Arizona	186,870	40	20	190,184	36	16
Public	Univ. of Arkansas for Med. Sciences	24,655	220	119	16,815	273	134
Public	University of California - Berkeley	348,865	20	6	366,116	20	5
Public	University of California - Davis	129,224	65	39	185,840	38	17
Public	University of California - Irvine	73,657	106	67	66,617	114	72
Public	University of California - Los Angeles	498,800	11	3	473,205	10	2
Public	University of California - Riverside	24,369	224	120	16,985	272	133
Public	University of California - San Diego	206,873	35	16	171,059	46	24
Public	Univ. of California - San Francisco	595,940	5	1	608,580	4	1
Public	Univ. of California - Santa Barbara	101,177	78	46	63,413	116	74
Public	University of California - Santa Cruz	69,052	112	72	24,831	202	109
Public	University of Central Florida	22,427	237	128	32,779	176	102
Private	University of Chicago	443,305	13	10	443,792	13	10
Public	University of Cincinnati - Cincinnati	162,076	45	24	119,700	71	40
Public	University of Colorado - Boulder	160,445	46	25	151,553	52	27
Public	U. of Colorado - Denv./Anschutz Med.	106,963	73	44	171,102	45	23
Public	Univ. of Connecticut - Health Center	6,747	519	228	8,475	451	202
Public	University of Connecticut - Storrs	65,620	117	76	40,751	156	94
Private	University of Dayton	21,668	246	117	28,219	189	84
Public	University of Delaware	56,843	132	83	44,896	147	89
Public	University of Florida	243,666	30	14	215,580	33	14
Public	University of Georgia	133,881	62	36	104,108	84	50
Public	University of Hawaii - Manoa	42,209	157	93	90,650	93	56
Public	University of Houston - Univ. Park	98,449	83	50	95,602	91	55
Public	University of Idaho	16,842	305	154	19,358	254	126

2014 Annual Giving x $1000	2014 National Rank	2014 Control Rank	2013 Annual Giving x $1000	2013 National Rank	2013 Control Rank	2012 Annual Giving x $1000	2012 National Rank	2012 Control Rank
38,772	157	91	39,174	150	84	32,677	158	94
172,319	39	18	174,105	36	17	145,186	38	18
240,931	29	18	242,551	25	15	246,035	23	13
129,490	59	30	121,592	55	30	170,449	35	16
53,230	133	53	41,814	143	61	32,058	159	65
104,113	76	34	122,673	53	25	80,676	84	31
13,457	321	163	37,562	156	68	28,192	173	73
3,960	659	390				7,474	455	254
105,811	74	41	90,313	80	49	69,238	99	64
79,854	98	58	72,452	102	61	60,561	110	71
928,458	2	2	931,569	1	1	1,034,849	1	1
78,655	102	60	97,892	77	47	82,276	81	52
60,787	124	77	63,014	112	69	36,757	147	88
317,549	22	8	254,628	23	10	180,886	30	13
29,305	188	82	31,469	176	75	30,299	164	68
69,847	107	43	52,260	124	49	48,937	126	47
78,768	100	42	77,824	95	37	53,572	119	43
9,948	391	182	8,389	430	195	18,928	220	118
33,300	172	100	28,700	185	106	68,104	101	66
80,004	97	57	63,762	110	67	70,130	97	63
3,329	701	291	2,435	788	329	7,227	463	203
20,328	233	123	14,461	295	148	17,829	232	124
186,192	37	16	151,363	42	22	180,317	31	14
25,062	201	111	27,370	190	109	20,608	206	116
389,935	17	6	340,919	15	5	405,435	8	1
133,393	54	28	104,743	69	42	93,977	69	44
97,241	80	45	77,210	97	59	77,236	87	55
430,276	15	5	419,647	10	1	344,201	12	2
22,692	214	116	25,450	193	110	33,837	153	91
150,446	44	22	167,404	38	19	135,543	40	20
444,938	11	3	385,745	12	2	329,477	14	4
67,505	110	67	60,999	116	73	105,362	57	35
40,855	151	89	23,684	202	114	22,766	194	109
23,116	213	115	38,839	152	86	14,858	277	141
405,350	16	11	289,447	21	13	255,764	21	12
140,645	49	26	105,037	67	40	105,168	58	36
67,726	109	66	63,377	111	68	86,295	75	49
66,852	111	68	51,596	125	76	133,993	42	22
5,395	567	238	6,879	484	210	6,242	497	211
30,570	183	104	38,982	151	85	35,371	149	90
20,199	237	113	18,071	243	113	17,308	239	114
48,905	136	82	46,844	129	77	45,796	131	81
215,184	30	12	210,951	31	15	173,385	33	15
96,088	82	47	85,814	84	51	81,568	82	53
92,519	84	48	62,465	113	70	50,267	124	79
85,269	91	53	84,201	86	52	72,850	95	61
26,912	193	108	17,759	248	133	16,534	250	130

Annual Giving

	Institutions with Over $40 Million in Federal Research, Alphabetically	2016 Annual Giving x $1000	2016 National Rank	2016 Control Rank	2015 Annual Giving x $1000	2015 National Rank	2015 Control Rank
Public	University of Illinois - Chicago	53,815	137	85	62,590	117	75
Public	Univ. of Illinois - Urbana-Champaign	159,693	47	26	177,235	40	19
Public	University of Iowa	192,262	39	19	159,532	48	25
Public	University of Kansas - Lawrence	149,771	54	29	176,704	42	21
Public	University of Kansas Medical Center	37,443	168	96	44,176	148	90
Public	University of Kentucky	163,919	44	23	118,190	74	43
Public	University of Louisville	85,186	97	60	86,309	100	61
Public	University of Maryland - Baltimore	57,911	129	82	69,153	109	67
Public	Univ. of Maryland - Baltimore County	13,788	340	167	7,663	476	212
Public	Univ. of Maryland - College Park	146,044	57	32	122,694	66	37
Public	Univ. of Massachusetts - Amherst	32,805	183	106	35,327	170	99
Public	Univ. of Mass. Med. Sch. - Worcester	7,550	487	216	8,328	458	204
Private	University of Miami	236,334	31	17	193,809	35	20
Public	University of Michigan - Ann Arbor	433,776	14	4	394,310	18	4
Public	University of Minnesota - Twin Cities	332,851	22	8	344,303	22	7
Public	University of Missouri - Columbia	113,079	71	43	108,689	79	46
Public	University of Nebraska - Lincoln	100,542	79	47	177,321	39	18
Public	University of Nebraska Medical Ctr.	91,702	89	55	89,054	94	57
Public	University of Nevada - Reno	69,521	109	69	100,048	85	51
Public	Univ. of New Hampshire - Durham	14,372	332	163	9,605	413	188
Public	Univ. of New Mexico - Albuquerque	66,077	116	75	68,992	110	68
Public	Univ. of North Carolina - Chapel Hill	308,694	24	10	301,177	25	10
Private	University of Notre Dame	371,762	19	14	379,869	19	15
Public	University of Oklahoma - HSC	69,440	110	70	64,872	115	73
Public	University of Oklahoma - Norman	252,996	28	12	252,475	27	12
Public	University of Oregon	136,295	61	35	145,109	54	29
Private	University of Pennsylvania	542,851	7	6	517,198	9	8
Public	University of Pittsburgh - Pittsburgh	127,155	66	40	124,602	65	36
Public	University of Rhode Island	15,788	318	159	17,563	267	131
Private	University of Rochester	107,297	72	29	108,217	80	34
Public	Univ. of South Carolina - Columbia	94,103	87	53	113,506	76	44
Public	University of South Florida - Tampa	45,583	152	89	59,903	121	76
Private	University of Southern California	666,641	3	3	653,025	3	3
Public	University of Tennessee - Knoxville	91,456	90	56	119,749	70	39
Public	University of Texas - Austin	345,992	21	7	310,212	24	9
Public	University of Texas - El Paso	19,194	265	135	16,668	279	140
Public	University of Texas HSC - Houston	55,453	135	84	46,346	144	87
Public	Univ. of Texas HSC - San Antonio	40,458	160	94	42,764	151	91
Public	U. of Texas MD Anderson Cancer Ctr.	208,482	33	15	176,908	41	20
Public	U. of Texas Med. Branch - Galveston	44,659	153	90	41,039	155	93
Public	U. of Texas SW Med. Ctr. - Dallas	181,153	42	21	149,243	53	28
Public	University of Utah	201,854	36	17	126,244	64	35
Public	University of Vermont	61,407	121	78	40,458	157	95
Public	University of Virginia	245,392	29	13	233,218	30	13
Public	University of Washington - Seattle	541,444	8	2	447,021	12	3
Public	University of Wisconsin - Madison	318,828	23	9	330,454	23	8
Public	University of Wyoming	49,374	141	86	48,390	140	83
Public	Utah State University	34,359	180	104	52,076	130	81
Private	Vanderbilt University	143,605	58	26	121,909	69	31

2014 Annual Giving x $1000	2014 National Rank	2014 Control Rank	2013 Annual Giving x $1000	2013 National Rank	2013 Control Rank	2012 Annual Giving x $1000	2012 National Rank	2012 Control Rank
66,508	112	69	55,700	121	75	59,017	114	72
177,193	38	17	169,548	37	18	137,059	39	19
146,748	46	23	122,102	54	29	104,392	59	37
129,794	57	29	135,754	45	23	121,186	47	26
32,448	177	102	33,938	163	94	30,296	165	97
105,565	75	42	78,903	93	57	73,788	91	58
85,065	92	54	123,415	52	28	73,547	92	59
62,004	120	74	109,647	63	36	77,984	86	54
9,143	411	192	21,057	220	120	11,776	325	159
81,788	95	56	79,118	92	56	93,736	71	46
33,918	169	99	31,914	174	100	32,017	160	95
4,855	600	247	10,158	379	175	3,584	672	270
186,528	36	21	180,538	34	18	163,978	37	20
432,596	13	4	351,552	14	4	291,335	17	7
287,361	24	10	219,905	28	12	254,855	22	10
118,745	64	33	103,979	71	44	88,689	74	48
116,724	68	37	120,093	57	32	109,388	54	32
83,219	94	55	70,505	103	62	62,028	107	69
38,414	158	92	28,426	186	107	23,554	192	108
18,350	257	134	20,880	221	121	16,501	251	131
73,517	106	64	65,919	107	66	64,063	105	67
298,804	23	9	272,767	22	9	286,710	18	8
320,316	21	14	247,928	24	14	203,250	28	17
34,274	167	97	32,210	172	99	23,801	191	107
126,639	61	32	162,048	39	20	115,172	51	30
68,221	108	65	185,648	33	16	109,529	53	31
483,569	7	6	506,607	6	6	440,603	7	7
117,068	67	36	127,859	49	26	118,700	49	28
14,627	299	151	12,649	334	164	12,719	311	153
120,038	63	31	90,023	81	32	85,415	79	29
115,683	69	38	107,008	66	39	85,566	78	50
37,419	160	93	36,520	158	90	43,613	135	83
731,933	3	3	674,512	3	3	491,854	4	4
111,303	72	39	104,164	70	43	124,196	44	23
529,391	6	1	290,987	19	7	258,308	20	9
18,502	251	131	27,502	189	108	26,991	180	104
37,179	161	94	39,323	149	83	48,552	127	80
44,606	143	85	37,617	155	88	36,599	148	89
163,188	40	19	212,506	30	14	186,667	29	12
40,965	150	88	29,682	180	104	55,947	115	73
127,930	60	31	104,866	68	41	120,844	48	27
194,893	34	14	213,984	29	13	134,011	41	21
37,119	162	95	37,003	157	89	21,728	200	114
214,412	31	13	224,541	27	11	237,221	24	11
478,072	8	2	322,231	17	6	295,564	16	6
249,661	28	11	360,689	13	3	315,278	15	5
28,541	189	107	43,884	137	81	26,503	182	105
33,941	168	98	32,488	170	97	27,664	177	102
157,510	41	22	145,433	44	22	126,367	43	21

Annual Giving

	Institutions with Over $40 Million in Federal Research, Alphabetically	2016 Annual Giving x $1000	2016 National Rank	2016 Control Rank	2015 Annual Giving x $1000	2015 National Rank	2015 Control Rank
Public	Virginia Commonwealth University	69,180	111	71	67,256	113	71
Public	Virginia Polytechnic Inst. and St. U.	100,057	80	48	86,391	99	60
Private	Wake Forest University	88,787	94	36	99,763	86	35
Public	Washington State Univ. - Pullman	103,845	75	45	106,370	81	47
Private	Washington University in St. Louis	269,877	26	15	246,714	29	17
Public	Wayne State University	60,708	123	79	47,983	141	84
Private	Weill Cornell Medical College	85,207	96	37	156,176	49	24
Public	West Virginia University	74,882	105	66	110,384	77	45
Private	Woods Hole Oceanographic Inst.						
Private	Yale University	519,146	9	7	440,807	14	11
Private	Yeshiva University	39,298	165	71	59,420	123	47

2014 Annual Giving x $1000	2014 National Rank	2014 Control Rank	2013 Annual Giving x $1000	2013 National Rank	2013 Control Rank	2012 Annual Giving x $1000	2012 National Rank	2012 Control Rank
64,190	117	72	59,238	117	74	101,716	61	38
78,141	103	61	86,970	83	50	75,120	89	57
91,772	85	37	79,631	90	35	73,797	90	33
85,672	89	51	45,336	132	78	105,469	56	34
274,498	25	15	233,019	26	16	205,687	27	16
						53,761	118	76
204,237	32	19	148,460	43	21	67,578	102	36
85,323	90	52	99,034	76	46	83,933	80	51
430,309	14	10	444,171	8	8	543,905	3	3
63,153	118	46	75,591	99	39	86,032	77	28

National Academy Membership

	Institutions with Over $40 Million in Federal Research, Alphabetically	2016 National Academy Membership	2016 National Rank	2016 Control Rank	2015 National Academy Membership	2015 National Rank	2015 Control Rank
Public	Arizona State University	22	53	28	22	55	29
Public	Auburn University	1	162	98	1	162	99
Public	Augusta University	0	224	137	0	220	135
Private	Baylor College of Medicine	25	50	24	24	50	24
Private	Boston University	19	61	30	20	58	28
Private	Brandeis University	11	71	35	11	70	34
Private	Brown University	21	56	28	22	55	27
Private	California Institute of Technology	114	11	8	112	12	8
Private	Carnegie Mellon University	43	28	17	39	31	18
Private	Case Western Reserve University	22	53	26	20	58	28
Public	Clemson University	2	136	81	2	141	86
Public	Cleveland State University	0	224	137	0	220	135
Private	Cold Spring Harbor Laboratory	5	103	42	5	104	43
Public	Colorado State Univ. - Fort Collins	8	87	50	9	77	41
Private	Columbia University	136	5	4	134	6	4
Private	Cornell University	63	20	12	62	20	12
Private	Dartmouth College	16	62	31	15	62	31
Private	Drexel University	8	87	38	7	92	39
Private	Duke University	67	19	11	66	19	11
Private	Emory University	31	38	20	32	35	20
Public	Florida International University	2	136	81	1	162	99
Public	Florida State University	8	87	50	7	92	54
Public	George Mason University	2	136	81	2	141	86
Private	George Washington University	11	71	35	12	68	33
Private	Georgetown University	9	78	37	9	77	37
Public	Georgia Institute of Technology	31	38	19	31	38	18
Private	Harvard University	382	1	1	371	1	1
Private	Icahn School of Med. at Mount Sinai	20	59	29	17	61	30
Public	Indiana University - Bloomington	13	67	36	8	84	47
Public	Iowa State University	9	78	42	8	84	47
Private	Johns Hopkins University	101	14	9	97	15	9
Public	Kansas State University	1	162	98	1	162	99
Public	Louisiana State Univ. - Baton Rouge	2	136	81	3	119	73
Private	Massachusetts Institute of Tech.	267	3	3	268	3	3
Private	Medical College of Wisconsin	3	120	48	3	119	47
Public	Medical University of South Carolina	2	136	81	3	119	73
Public	Michigan State University	14	63	32	13	65	34
Public	Mississippi State University	1	162	98	1	162	99
Public	Montana State University - Bozeman	1	162	98	0	220	135
Public	Naval Postgraduate School	3	120	73	3	119	73
Public	New Jersey Institute of Technology	1	162	98	1	162	99
Public	New Mexico State Univ. - Las Cruces	0	224	137	0	220	135
Private	New York University	56	22	13	59	21	13
Public	North Carolina State University	21	56	29	20	58	31
Private	Northeastern University	3	120	48	3	119	47
Private	Northwestern University	42	29	18	43	28	17
Public	Ohio State University - Columbus	33	35	16	32	35	16
Public	Oregon Health & Science University	10	74	38	10	73	37
Public	Oregon State University	5	103	62	5	104	62

The Center for Measuring University Performance

2014 National Academy Membership	2014 National Rank	2014 Control Rank	2013 National Academy Membership	2013 National Rank	2013 Control Rank	2012 National Academy Membership	2012 National Rank	2012 Control Rank
22	53	28	21	54	29	20	54	29
1	164	101	1	164	100	1	162	98
0	221	136	0	219	136	0	219	135
24	51	25	22	52	25	21	52	25
21	55	26	20	56	27	19	56	27
11	68	33	12	67	33	12	66	32
19	60	29	18	58	29	17	60	29
113	11	7	111	10	7	110	9	6
37	32	18	37	31	18	32	33	18
20	57	28	19	57	28	18	58	28
2	139	84	2	136	81	2	135	80
0	221	136	0	219	136	0	219	135
4	108	44	4	105	44	4	105	44
8	81	44	5	101	59	5	100	58
131	6	4	125	6	4	120	6	4
61	20	12	61	20	12	61	19	11
13	66	32	14	64	31	15	62	30
7	89	39	6	95	41	7	88	40
65	19	11	63	18	10	62	18	10
28	41	20	27	41	20	27	43	21
1	164	101	1	164	100	1	162	98
6	96	55	6	95	55	7	88	49
2	139	84	2	136	81	2	135	80
10	72	35	10	69	35	11	68	34
10	72	35	10	69	35	11	68	34
26	47	25	26	43	22	30	36	18
370	1	1	356	1	1	355	1	1
16	61	30	16	61	30	14	63	31
8	81	44	8	83	46	10	70	35
5	103	61	7	90	51	7	88	49
95	15	9	91	15	9	90	15	9
1	164	101	1	164	100	0	219	135
3	117	72	3	115	69	2	135	80
265	3	3	270	3	3	269	3	3
3	117	46	3	115	47	3	113	49
3	117	72	3	115	69	3	113	65
12	67	35	10	69	35	9	73	37
2	139	84	2	136	81	1	162	98
0	221	136	0	219	136	0	219	135
3	117	72	3	115	69	3	113	65
2	139	84	2	136	81	2	135	80
0	221	136	0	219	136	0	219	135
53	23	13	52	23	13	45	25	15
20	57	30	18	58	30	19	56	30
3	117	46	3	115	47	3	113	49
43	28	17	43	28	17	42	27	17
32	36	17	32	34	16	30	36	18
10	72	38	9	74	37	9	73	37
4	108	65	4	105	62	3	113	65

National Academy Membership

	Institutions with Over $40 Million in Federal Research, Alphabetically	2016 National Academy Membership	2016 National Rank	2016 Control Rank	2015 National Academy Membership	2015 National Rank	2015 Control Rank
Public	Penn. State Univ. - Hershey Med. Ctr.	2	136	81	2	141	86
Public	Pennsylvania State Univ. - Univ. Park	28	43	23	27	44	23
Private	Princeton University	126	7	5	120	7	5
Public	Purdue University - West Lafayette	28	43	23	27	44	23
Private	Rensselaer Polytechnic Institute	7	94	39	7	92	39
Private	Rice University	24	51	25	25	48	23
Private	Rockefeller University	51	24	14	51	24	14
Private	Rush University	3	120	48	2	141	56
Public	Rutgers University - New Brunswick	36	32	14	39	31	14
Public	San Diego State University	0	224	137	0	220	135
Private	Scripps Research Institute	27	46	22	26	46	22
Private	Stanford University	340	2	2	320	2	2
Public	Stony Brook University	14	63	32	14	63	32
Public	Temple University	5	103	62	4	111	68
Public	Texas A&M Univ. - College Station	32	36	17	30	41	21
Private	Thomas Jefferson University	4	111	44	4	111	44
Private	Tufts University	12	70	34	11	70	34
Private	Tulane University	2	136	56	1	162	64
Public	Uniformed Services Univ. of the HS	4	111	68	4	111	68
Public	University at Albany	1	162	98	2	141	86
Public	University at Buffalo	8	87	50	8	84	47
Public	University of Alabama - Birmingham	7	94	56	8	84	47
Public	University of Alabama - Huntsville	1	162	98	0	220	135
Public	University of Alaska - Fairbanks	2	136	81	2	141	86
Public	University of Arizona	29	41	21	31	38	18
Public	Univ. of Arkansas for Med. Sciences	1	162	98	1	162	99
Public	University of California - Berkeley	230	4	1	230	4	1
Public	University of California - Davis	46	27	11	45	27	11
Public	University of California - Irvine	30	40	20	31	38	18
Public	University of California - Los Angeles	100	15	6	101	14	6
Public	University of California - Riverside	9	78	42	8	84	47
Public	University of California - San Diego	119	8	3	117	8	3
Public	Univ. of California - San Francisco	133	6	2	135	5	2
Public	Univ. of California - Santa Barbara	58	21	9	56	22	9
Public	University of California - Santa Cruz	9	78	42	10	73	37
Public	University of Central Florida	1	162	98	1	162	99
Private	University of Chicago	70	17	10	69	17	10
Public	University of Cincinnati - Cincinnati	8	87	50	8	84	47
Public	University of Colorado - Boulder	29	41	21	30	41	21
Public	U. of Colorado - Denv./Anschutz Med.	14	63	32	14	63	32
Public	Univ. of Connecticut - Health Center	4	111	68	4	111	68
Public	University of Connecticut - Storrs	1	162	98	1	162	99
Private	University of Dayton	0	224	88	0	220	86
Public	University of Delaware	8	87	50	7	92	54
Public	University of Florida	26	49	26	25	48	26
Public	University of Georgia	7	94	56	6	99	58
Public	University of Hawaii - Manoa	10	74	38	10	73	37
Public	University of Houston - Univ. Park	10	74	38	9	77	41
Public	University of Idaho	0	224	137	0	220	135

2014 National Academy Membership	2014 National Rank	2014 Control Rank	2013 National Academy Membership	2013 National Rank	2013 Control Rank	2012 National Academy Membership	2012 National Rank	2012 Control Rank
2	139	84	2	136	81	1	162	98
27	43	22	26	43	22	24	48	26
124	7	5	120	7	5	117	7	5
27	43	22	25	47	25	26	45	24
7	89	39	8	83	38	8	83	38
25	49	24	25	47	23	23	50	23
47	25	15	46	26	16	46	24	14
2	139	56	2	136	56	2	135	56
36	33	15	37	31	14	34	32	15
0	221	136	0	219	136	0	219	135
28	41	20	26	43	22	26	45	22
316	2	2	310	2	2	297	2	2
15	63	33	14	64	34	14	63	33
3	117	72	3	115	69	2	135	80
27	43	22	25	47	25	26	45	24
3	117	46	3	115	47	4	105	44
11	68	33	11	68	34	10	70	36
1	164	64	1	164	65	2	135	56
4	108	65	4	105	62	4	105	62
2	139	84	2	136	81	2	135	80
7	89	51	7	90	51	7	88	49
8	81	44	7	90	51	7	88	49
0	221	136	0	219	136	1	162	98
1	164	101	1	164	100	1	162	98
30	37	18	28	40	21	28	40	22
1	164	101	1	164	100	1	162	98
230	4	1	227	4	1	230	4	1
46	27	11	44	27	11	41	28	11
30	37	18	30	38	19	31	35	17
100	14	6	95	14	6	94	14	6
8	81	44	8	83	46	7	88	49
118	8	3	117	8	3	115	8	3
132	5	2	129	5	2	125	5	2
58	21	9	57	21	9	60	20	9
11	68	36	9	74	37	9	73	37
1	164	101	1	164	100	1	162	98
67	18	10	63	18	10	60	20	12
8	81	44	9	74	37	9	73	37
30	37	18	30	38	19	29	39	21
15	63	33	15	62	32	16	61	32
4	108	65	4	105	62	4	105	62
1	164	101	1	164	100	1	162	98
0	221	86	0	219	84	0	219	85
7	89	51	7	90	51	8	83	46
25	49	34	24	50	27	24	48	26
6	96	55	6	95	55	6	96	55
8	81	44	9	74	37	9	73	37
9	78	41	9	74	37	9	73	37
0	221	136	0	219	136	0	219	135

National Academy Membership

	Institutions with Over $40 Million in Federal Research, Alphabetically	2016 National Academy Membership	2016 National Rank	2016 Control Rank	2015 National Academy Membership	2015 National Rank	2015 Control Rank
Public	University of Illinois - Chicago	6	99	59	6	99	58
Public	Univ. of Illinois - Urbana-Champaign	56	22	10	56	22	9
Public	University of Iowa	20	59	31	22	55	29
Public	University of Kansas - Lawrence	5	103	62	5	104	62
Public	University of Kansas Medical Center	2	136	81	3	119	73
Public	University of Kentucky	2	136	81	3	119	73
Public	University of Louisville	2	136	81	2	141	86
Public	University of Maryland - Baltimore	9	78	42	9	77	41
Public	Univ. of Maryland - Baltimore County	1	162	98	0	220	135
Public	University of Maryland - College Park	27	46	25	26	46	25
Public	Univ. of Massachusetts - Amherst	9	78	42	7	92	54
Public	Univ. of Mass. Med. Sch. - Worcester	7	94	56	7	92	54
Private	University of Miami	13	67	32	11	70	34
Public	University of Michigan - Ann Arbor	113	12	4	108	13	5
Public	University of Minnesota - Twin Cities	41	30	12	41	29	12
Public	University of Missouri - Columbia	9	78	42	9	77	41
Public	University of Nebraska - Lincoln	3	120	73	3	119	73
Public	Univ. of Nebraska Medical Center	1	162	98	1	162	99
Public	University of Nevada - Reno	2	136	81	2	141	86
Public	Univ. of New Hampshire - Durham	0	224	137	0	220	135
Public	Univ. of New Mexico - Albuquerque	5	103	62	5	104	62
Public	Univ. of North Carolina - Chapel Hill	38	31	13	38	33	15
Private	University of Notre Dame	4	111	44	4	111	44
Public	University of Oklahoma - HSC	1	162	98	1	162	99
Public	University of Oklahoma - Norman	1	162	98	1	162	99
Public	University of Oregon	9	78	42	9	77	41
Private	University of Pennsylvania	118	9	6	117	8	6
Public	University of Pittsburgh - Pittsburgh	32	36	17	32	35	16
Public	University of Rhode Island	2	136	81	2	141	86
Private	University of Rochester	22	53	26	24	50	24
Public	Univ. of South Carolina - Columbia	0	224	137	1	162	99
Public	University of South Florida - Tampa	8	87	50	8	84	47
Private	University of Southern California	48	25	15	50	25	15
Public	University of Tennessee - Knoxville	6	99	59	5	104	62
Public	University of Texas - Austin	70	17	8	69	17	8
Public	University of Texas - El Paso	0	224	137	0	220	135
Public	University of Texas HSC - Houston	4	111	68	3	119	73
Public	Univ. of Texas HSC - San Antonio	5	103	62	5	104	62
Public	U. of Texas MD Anderson Cancer Ctr.	11	71	37	12	68	36
Public	U. of Texas Med. Branch - Galveston	3	120	73	3	119	73
Public	Univ. of Texas SW Med. Ctr. - Dallas	36	32	14	40	30	13
Public	University of Utah	21	56	29	23	54	28
Public	University of Vermont	2	136	81	2	141	86
Public	University of Virginia	23	52	27	24	50	27
Public	University of Washington - Seattle	110	13	5	115	10	4
Public	University of Wisconsin - Madison	77	16	7	77	16	7
Public	University of Wyoming	2	136	81	2	141	86
Public	Utah State University	0	224	137	0	220	135
Private	Vanderbilt University	34	34	19	36	34	19

2014 National Academy Membership	2014 National Rank	2014 Control Rank	2013 National Academy Membership	2013 National Rank	2013 Control Rank	2012 National Academy Membership	2012 National Rank	2012 Control Rank
7	89	51	8	83	46	8	83	46
55	22	10	57	21	9	55	22	10
22	53	28	22	52	28	21	52	28
5	103	61	5	101	59	6	96	55
3	117	72	2	136	81	2	135	80
3	117	72	3	115	69	3	113	65
2	139	84	2	136	81	2	135	80
9	78	41	9	74	37	9	73	37
0	221	136	0	219	136	0	219	135
30	37	18	31	36	18	30	36	18
7	89	51	8	83	46	8	83	46
6	96	55	5	101	59	5	100	58
10	72	35	10	69	35	9	73	37
106	13	5	100	13	5	95	13	5
40	29	12	39	29	12	38	29	12
8	81	44	8	83	46	7	88	49
2	139	84	2	136	81	3	113	65
1	164	101	1	164	100	1	162	98
2	139	84	2	136	81	3	113	65
0	221	136	0	219	136	0	219	135
4	108	65	3	115	69	3	113	65
38	30	13	34	33	15	35	31	14
3	117	46	4	105	44	4	105	44
1	164	101	1	164	100	1	162	98
1	164	101	1	164	100	1	162	98
10	72	38	9	74	37	9	73	37
114	10	6	114	9	6	110	9	6
33	35	16	32	34	16	32	33	16
2	139	84	2	136	81	2	135	80
26	47	23	27	41	20	28	40	19
2	139	84	2	136	81	2	135	80
6	96	55	3	115	69	3	113	65
51	24	14	50	24	14	50	23	13
5	103	61	4	105	62	3	113	65
72	17	8	69	17	8	67	17	8
0	221	136	0	219	136	0	219	135
3	117	72	3	115	69	3	113	65
4	108	65	4	105	62	3	113	65
11	68	36	9	74	37	5	100	58
3	117	72	3	115	69	2	135	80
38	30	13	38	30	13	37	30	13
20	57	30	17	60	31	18	58	31
2	139	84	2	136	81	2	135	80
24	51	27	26	43	22	27	43	23
116	9	4	110	12	4	109	12	4
75	16	7	70	16	7	68	16	7
2	139	84	2	136	81	2	135	80
0	221	136	0	219	136	0	219	135
34	34	19	31	36	19	28	40	19

National Academy Membership

	Institutions with Over $40 Million in Federal Research, Alphabetically	2016 National Academy Membership	2016 National Rank	2016 Control Rank	2015 National Academy Membership	2015 National Rank	2015 Control Rank
Public	Virginia Commonwealth University	6	99	59	6	99	58
Public	Virginia Polytechnic Inst. and St. U.	14	63	32	13	65	34
Private	Wake Forest University	6	99	41	7	92	39
Public	Washington State Univ. - Pullman	9	78	42	9	77	41
Private	Washington University in St. Louis	48	25	15	46	26	16
Public	Wayne State University	3	120	73	3	119	73
Private	Weill Cornell Medical College	28	43	21	28	43	21
Public	West Virginia University	2	136	81	2	141	86
Private	Woods Hole Oceanographic Inst.	3	120	48	3	119	47
Private	Yale University	117	10	7	114	11	7
Private	Yeshiva University	13	67	32	13	65	32

2014 National Academy Membership	2014 National Rank	2014 Control Rank	2013 National Academy Membership	2013 National Rank	2013 Control Rank	2012 National Academy Membership	2012 National Rank	2012 Control Rank
6	96	55	6	95	55	5	100	58
16	61	32	15	62	32	14	63	33
6	96	42	5	101	43	5	100	43
9	78	41	9	74	37	9	73	37
47	25	15	48	25	15	44	26	16
3	117	72	2	136	81	2	135	80
27	43	22	24	50	24	20	54	26
1	164	101	1	164	100	1	162	98
3	117	46	3	115	47	3	113	49
111	12	8	111	10	7	110	9	6
14	65	31	13	66	32	12	66	32

Faculty Awards

	Institutions with Over $40 Million in Federal Research, Alphabetically	2016 Faculty Awards	2016 National Rank	2016 Control Rank	2015 Faculty Awards	2015 National Rank	2015 Control Rank
Public	Arizona State University	19	28	15	23	24	10
Public	Auburn University	5	101	66	3	144	92
Public	Augusta University	0	461	273	0	473	285
Private	Baylor College of Medicine	4	121	44	6	98	33
Private	Boston University	10	58	22	16	40	18
Private	Brandeis University	7	81	31	9	76	29
Private	Brown University	16	35	16	20	29	16
Private	California Institute of Technology	8	69	27	16	40	18
Private	Carnegie Mellon University	16	35	16	13	49	24
Private	Case Western Reserve University	12	51	21	11	58	26
Public	Clemson University	5	101	66	3	144	92
Public	Cleveland State University	0	461	273	2	178	115
Private	Cold Spring Harbor Laboratory	1	245	157	2	178	115
Public	Colorado State Univ. - Fort Collins	4	121	78	11	58	33
Private	Columbia University	25	15	6	34	8	4
Private	Cornell University	20	25	12	30	12	7
Private	Dartmouth College	9	63	25	6	98	33
Private	Drexel University	5	101	36	5	110	39
Private	Duke University	25	15	6	30	12	7
Private	Emory University	18	30	14	19	33	17
Public	Florida International University	3	142	93	13	49	26
Public	Florida State University	9	63	39	9	76	48
Public	George Mason University	3	142	93	5	110	72
Private	George Washington University	8	69	27	14	45	21
Private	Georgetown University	2	178	64	4	127	45
Public	Georgia Institute of Technology	19	28	15	21	27	12
Private	Harvard University	66	1	1	84	1	1
Private	Icahn School of Med. at Mount Sinai	5	101	36	6	98	33
Public	Indiana University - Bloomington	16	35	20	15	42	23
Public	Iowa State University	7	81	51	6	98	66
Private	Johns Hopkins University	21	21	9	33	9	5
Public	Kansas State University	7	81	51	2	178	115
Public	Louisiana State Univ. - Baton Rouge	3	142	93	5	110	72
Private	Massachusetts Institute of Tech.	33	8	4	41	5	3
Private	Medical College of Wisconsin	0	461	188	0	473	189
Public	Medical University of South Carolina	1	245	157	1	263	167
Public	Michigan State University	12	51	31	11	58	33
Public	Mississippi State University	1	245	157	4	127	83
Public	Montana State University - Bozeman	3	142	93	2	178	115
Public	Naval Postgraduate School	1	245	157	0	473	285
Public	New Jersey Institute of Technology	3	142	93	0	473	285
Public	New Mexico State Univ. - Las Cruces	2	178	115	6	98	66
Private	New York University	18	30	14	27	22	13
Public	North Carolina State University	20	25	14	11	58	33
Private	Northeastern University	9	63	25	14	45	21
Private	Northwestern University	25	15	6	33	9	5
Public	Ohio State University - Columbus	21	21	13	17	38	21
Public	Oregon Health & Science University	4	121	78	8	85	56
Public	Oregon State University	10	58	37	5	110	72

2014 Faculty Awards	2014 National Rank	2014 Control Rank	2013 Faculty Awards	2013 National Rank	2013 Control Rank	2012 Faculty Awards	2012 National Rank	2012 Control Rank
9	62	38	5	119	76	14	45	26
2	195	126	1	264	168	3	156	101
0	473	281	1	264	168	0	550	313
3	153	53	5	119	44	4	129	46
16	34	18	21	22	11	23	24	13
4	126	42	11	58	23	7	97	36
17	30	16	16	36	18	11	56	22
12	48	22	10	67	25	16	37	19
10	58	24	10	67	25	12	50	21
4	126	42	11	58	23	8	84	31
5	109	71	4	135	86	6	101	64
1	259	163	0	523	306	4	129	84
4	126	85	2	194	128	2	189	122
7	78	50	8	75	46	5	117	73
25	19	11	32	9	4	37	7	4
24	20	12	19	28	14	21	30	15
6	91	34	12	51	21	6	101	38
4	126	42	7	88	32	8	84	31
33	7	4	20	25	12	30	13	6
26	17	10	18	31	16	22	26	14
5	109	71	4	135	86	8	84	54
7	78	50	2	194	128	7	97	62
5	109	71	3	156	100	2	189	122
11	54	23	12	51	21	13	47	20
7	78	29	4	135	50	10	67	26
16	34	17	15	39	20	22	26	13
90	1	1	87	1	1	93	1	1
8	68	27	7	88	32	6	101	38
18	29	14	17	33	17	12	50	30
6	91	58	10	67	43	11	56	35
32	11	7	24	19	8	27	17	8
4	126	85	3	156	100	2	189	122
4	126	85	5	119	76	5	117	73
42	3	3	29	12	5	29	14	7
0	473	193	1	264	97	1	271	98
1	259	163	1	264	168	3	156	101
13	42	23	16	36	19	13	47	28
1	259	163	1	264	168	3	156	101
1	259	163	4	135	86	2	189	122
1	259	163	0	523	306	1	271	174
0	473	281	4	135	86	0	550	313
2	195	126	1	264	168	5	117	73
29	13	8	25	18	7	25	19	10
12	48	27	14	44	24	12	50	30
9	62	25	8	75	30	8	84	31
28	15	9	22	21	10	25	19	10
13	42	23	29	12	8	11	56	35
5	109	71	7	88	57	10	67	42
6	91	58	8	75	46	15	40	21

Faculty Awards

	Institutions with Over $40 Million in Federal Research, Alphabetically	2016 Faculty Awards	2016 National Rank	2016 Control Rank	2015 Faculty Awards	2015 National Rank	2015 Control Rank
Public	Penn. State Univ. - Hershey Med. Ctr.	2	178	115	2	178	115
Public	Pennsylvania State Univ. - Univ. Park	22	19	11	19	33	17
Private	Princeton University	20	25	12	22	26	15
Public	Purdue University - West Lafayette	27	12	7	19	33	17
Private	Rensselaer Polytechnic Institute	4	121	44	5	110	39
Private	Rice University	8	69	27	6	98	33
Private	Rockefeller University	7	81	31	7	90	31
Private	Rush University	0	461	188	0	473	189
Public	Rutgers University - New Brunswick	12	51	31	20	29	14
Public	San Diego State University	3	142	93	3	144	92
Private	Scripps Research Institute	10	58	22	8	85	30
Private	Stanford University	48	2	2	56	2	2
Public	Stony Brook University	8	69	43	10	67	40
Public	Temple University	5	101	66	10	67	40
Public	Texas A&M Univ. - College Station	8	69	43	14	45	25
Private	Thomas Jefferson University	0	461	188	1	263	97
Private	Tufts University	8	69	27	6	98	33
Private	Tulane University	6	92	34	4	127	45
Public	Uniformed Services Univ. of the HS	2	178	115	2	178	115
Public	University at Albany	2	178	115	4	127	83
Public	University at Buffalo	6	92	59	6	98	66
Public	University of Alabama - Birmingham	3	142	93	0	473	285
Public	University of Alabama - Huntsville	0	461	273	2	178	115
Public	University of Alaska - Fairbanks	0	461	273	2	178	115
Public	University of Arizona	13	46	27	9	76	48
Public	Univ. of Arkansas for Med. Sciences	0	461	273	0	473	285
Public	University of California - Berkeley	36	5	3	45	3	1
Public	University of California - Davis	14	45	26	12	54	30
Public	University of California - Irvine	15	41	22	20	29	14
Public	University of California - Los Angeles	22	19	11	29	19	8
Public	University of California - Riverside	12	51	31	7	90	60
Public	University of California - San Diego	25	15	10	29	19	8
Public	Univ. of California - San Francisco	28	9	5	31	11	5
Public	Univ. of California - Santa Barbara	8	69	43	12	54	30
Public	University of California - Santa Cruz	8	69	43	8	85	56
Public	University of Central Florida	8	69	43	7	90	60
Private	University of Chicago	21	21	9	25	23	14
Public	University of Cincinnati - Cincinnati	13	46	27	10	67	40
Public	University of Colorado - Boulder	16	35	20	21	27	12
Public	U. of Colorado - Denv./Anschutz Med.	7	81	51	5	110	72
Public	Univ. of Connecticut - Health Center	2	178	115	3	144	92
Public	University of Connecticut - Storrs	15	41	22	9	76	48
Private	University of Dayton	0	461	188	0	473	189
Public	University of Delaware	4	121	78	9	76	48
Public	University of Florida	15	41	22	23	24	10
Public	University of Georgia	9	63	39	6	98	66
Public	University of Hawaii - Manoa	5	101	66	4	127	83
Public	University of Houston - Univ. Park	7	81	51	4	127	83
Public	University of Idaho	3	142	93	2	178	115

2014 Faculty Awards	2014 National Rank	2014 Control Rank	2013 Faculty Awards	2013 National Rank	2013 Control Rank	2012 Faculty Awards	2012 National Rank	2012 Control Rank
2	195	126	2	194	128	3	156	101
14	38	20	21	22	12	20	32	16
24	20	12	17	33	17	21	30	15
15	36	18	14	44	24	22	26	13
5	109	39	7	88	32	8	84	31
7	78	29	6	102	39	9	70	27
7	78	29	7	88	32	11	56	22
0	473	193	0	523	218	0	550	236
21	26	11	20	25	14	16	37	19
3	153	101	5	119	76	6	101	64
13	42	20	10	67	25	11	56	22
46	2	2	48	3	2	44	2	2
11	54	32	11	58	36	4	129	84
8	68	42	8	75	46	8	84	54
7	78	50	18	31	16	23	24	12
1	259	97	1	264	97	1	271	98
6	91	34	8	75	30	4	129	46
3	153	53	3	156	57	5	117	45
2	195	126	2	194	128	2	189	122
5	109	71	2	194	128	4	129	84
6	91	58	13	47	27	8	84	54
4	126	85	1	264	168	0	550	313
1	259	163	1	264	168	1	271	174
3	153	101	3	156	100	5	117	73
10	58	35	12	51	31	15	40	21
1	259	163	1	264	168	1	271	174
42	3	1	32	9	6	40	5	2
8	68	42	14	44	24	14	45	26
15	36	18	15	39	20	13	47	28
28	15	7	33	8	5	28	16	9
9	62	38	9	72	44	11	56	35
19	28	13	35	7	4	35	8	4
33	7	4	40	4	2	32	11	6
10	58	35	11	58	36	11	56	35
5	109	71	4	135	86	2	189	122
7	78	50	6	102	64	7	97	62
24	20	12	24	19	8	26	18	9
9	62	38	11	58	36	10	67	42
12	48	27	19	28	15	12	50	30
8	68	42	6	102	64	9	70	44
3	153	101	3	156	100	1	271	174
5	109	71	8	75	46	6	101	64
0	473	193	0	523	218	0	550	236
12	48	27	6	102	64	11	56	35
21	26	11	15	39	20	20	32	16
17	30	15	8	75	46	12	50	30
5	109	71	11	58	36	5	117	73
7	78	50	5	119	76	15	40	21
0	473	281	4	135	86	1	271	174

Faculty Awards

	Institutions with Over $40 Million in Federal Research, Alphabetically	2016 Faculty Awards	2016 National Rank	2016 Control Rank	2015 Faculty Awards	2015 National Rank	2015 Control Rank
Public	University of Illinois - Chicago	11	56	35	11	58	33
Public	Univ. of Illinois - Urbana-Champaign	38	4	2	30	12	6
Public	University of Iowa	9	63	39	10	67	40
Public	University of Kansas - Lawrence	4	121	78	11	58	33
Public	University of Kansas Medical Center	0	461	273	0	473	285
Public	University of Kentucky	7	81	51	10	67	40
Public	University of Louisville	1	245	157	5	110	72
Public	University of Maryland - Baltimore	2	178	115	3	144	92
Public	Univ. of Maryland - Baltimore County	3	142	93	2	178	115
Public	University of Maryland - College Park	13	46	27	20	29	14
Public	Univ. of Massachusetts - Amherst	8	69	43	17	38	21
Public	Univ. of Mass. Med. Sch. - Worcester	11	56	35	12	54	30
Private	University of Miami	5	101	36	7	90	31
Public	University of Michigan - Ann Arbor	48	2	1	42	4	2
Public	University of Minnesota - Twin Cities	27	12	7	35	7	4
Public	University of Missouri - Columbia	7	81	51	9	76	48
Public	University of Nebraska - Lincoln	8	69	43	3	144	92
Public	Univ. of Nebraska Medical Center	0	461	273	0	473	285
Public	University of Nevada - Reno	2	178	115	0	473	285
Public	Univ. of New Hampshire - Durham	6	92	59	3	144	92
Public	Univ. of New Mexico - Albuquerque	9	63	39	10	67	40
Public	Univ. of North Carolina - Chapel Hill	28	9	5	19	33	17
Private	University of Notre Dame	16	35	16	14	45	21
Public	University of Oklahoma - HSC	1	245	157	0	473	285
Public	University of Oklahoma - Norman	4	121	78	9	76	48
Public	University of Oregon	8	69	43	11	58	33
Private	University of Pennsylvania	34	7	3	30	12	7
Public	University of Pittsburgh - Pittsburgh	17	33	18	13	49	26
Public	University of Rhode Island	3	142	93	2	178	115
Private	University of Rochester	5	101	36	12	54	25
Public	Univ. of South Carolina - Columbia	5	101	66	9	76	48
Public	University of South Florida - Tampa	13	46	27	13	49	26
Private	University of Southern California	21	21	9	30	12	7
Public	University of Tennessee - Knoxville	17	33	18	8	85	56
Public	University of Texas - Austin	18	30	17	19	33	17
Public	University of Texas - El Paso	0	461	273	1	263	167
Public	University of Texas HSC - Houston	1	245	157	2	178	115
Public	Univ. of Texas HSC - San Antonio	0	461	273	0	473	285
Public	U. of Texas MD Anderson Cancer Ctr.	2	178	115	3	144	92
Public	U. of Texas Med. Branch - Galveston	0	461	273	0	473	285
Public	U. of Texas SW Med. Ctr. - Dallas	12	51	31	13	49	26
Public	University of Utah	15	41	22	10	67	40
Public	University of Vermont	5	101	66	5	110	72
Public	University of Virginia	7	81	51	15	42	23
Public	University of Washington - Seattle	35	6	4	39	6	3
Public	University of Wisconsin - Madison	27	12	7	30	12	6
Public	University of Wyoming	1	245	157	3	144	92
Public	Utah State University	7	81	51	3	144	92
Private	Vanderbilt University	13	46	20	15	42	20

2014 Faculty Awards	2014 National Rank	2014 Control Rank	2013 Faculty Awards	2013 National Rank	2013 Control Rank	2012 Faculty Awards	2012 National Rank	2012 Control Rank
12	48	27	8	75	46	11	56	35
35	5	2	29	12	8	24	23	11
11	54	32	12	51	31	15	40	21
14	38	20	8	75	46	11	56	35
1	259	163	2	194	128	1	271	174
9	62	38	12	51	31	8	84	54
3	153	101	5	119	76	9	70	44
4	126	85	6	102	64	6	101	64
4	126	85	3	156	100	3	156	101
14	38	20	11	58	36	16	37	19
10	58	35	12	51	31	8	84	54
12	48	27	13	47	27	15	40	21
8	68	27	7	88	32	7	97	36
34	6	3	50	2	1	40	5	2
26	17	8	32	9	6	33	10	5
7	78	50	6	102	64	9	70	44
4	126	85	9	72	44	6	101	64
0	473	281	0	523	306	0	550	313
3	153	101	6	102	64	4	129	84
6	91	58	2	194	128	5	117	73
8	68	42	7	88	57	6	101	64
24	20	9	21	22	12	25	19	10
14	38	19	15	39	20	9	70	27
0	473	281	0	523	306	0	550	313
6	91	58	3	156	100	5	117	73
6	91	58	7	88	57	9	70	44
33	7	4	29	12	5	35	8	5
24	20	9	28	16	10	22	26	13
2	195	126	4	135	86	4	129	84
3	153	53	6	102	39	6	101	38
6	91	58	8	75	46	9	70	44
8	68	42	7	88	57	5	117	73
23	25	15	19	28	14	25	19	10
7	78	50	11	58	36	9	70	44
17	30	15	17	33	17	31	12	7
3	153	101	1	264	168	2	189	122
5	109	71	1	264	168	2	189	122
1	259	163	1	264	168	2	189	122
2	195	126	1	264	168	1	271	174
0	473	281	1	264	168	2	189	122
13	42	23	15	39	20	17	36	18
13	42	23	13	47	27	12	50	30
6	91	58	6	102	64	9	70	44
11	54	32	11	58	36	8	84	54
30	12	5	39	5	3	42	4	1
29	13	6	26	17	11	29	14	8
6	91	58	3	156	100	3	156	101
4	126	85	7	88	57	2	189	122
13	42	20	16	36	18	19	34	17

Faculty Awards

	Institutions with Over $40 Million in Federal Research, Alphabetically	2016 Faculty Awards	2016 National Rank	2016 Control Rank	2015 Faculty Awards	2015 National Rank	2015 Control Rank
Public	Virginia Commonwealth University	2	178	115	6	98	66
Public	Virginia Polytechnic Inst. and St. U.	6	92	59	10	67	40
Private	Wake Forest University	3	142	50	3	144	53
Public	Washington State Univ. - Pullman	10	58	37	7	90	60
Private	Washington University in St. Louis	16	35	16	29	19	12
Public	Wayne State University	3	142	93	5	110	72
Private	Weill Cornell Medical College	10	58	22	10	67	28
Public	West Virginia University	5	101	66	8	85	56
Private	Woods Hole Oceanographic Inst.	0	461	188	1	263	97
Private	Yale University	28	9	5	30	12	7
Private	Yeshiva University	4	121	44	5	110	39

2014 Faculty Awards	2014 National Rank	2014 Control Rank	2013 Faculty Awards	2013 National Rank	2013 Control Rank	2012 Faculty Awards	2012 National Rank	2012 Control Rank
6	91	58	13	47	27	9	70	44
8	68	42	7	88	57	8	84	54
6	91	34	7	88	32	9	70	27
6	91	58	8	75	46	9	70	44
17	30	16	20	25	12	18	35	18
8	68	42	6	102	64	4	129	84
9	62	25	9	72	29	8	84	31
5	109	71	8	75	46	6	101	64
1	259	97	2	194	67	1	271	98
33	7	4	37	6	3	44	2	2
7	78	29	7	88	32	9	70	27

Doctorates Awarded

	Institutions with Over $40 Million in Federal Research, Alphabetically	2016 Doctorates	2016 National Rank	2016 Control Rank	2015 Doctorates	2015 National Rank	2015 Control Rank
Public	Arizona State University	674	14	11	687	14	12
Public	Auburn University	272	79	59	257	80	58
Public	Augusta University	20	375	213	29	314	191
Private	Baylor College of Medicine	94	179	59	111	157	50
Private	Boston University	579	22	7	484	36	11
Private	Brandeis University	83	192	64	100	170	55
Private	Brown University	235	88	24	215	94	26
Private	California Institute of Technology	190	105	32	182	110	32
Private	Carnegie Mellon University	323	60	18	333	62	19
Private	Case Western Reserve University	230	90	25	197	101	30
Public	Clemson University	233	89	65	237	88	64
Public	Cleveland State University	54	238	154	59	232	154
Private	Cold Spring Harbor Laboratory	0	626	343	0	621	335
Public	Colorado State Univ. - Fort Collins	249	85	62	251	81	59
Private	Columbia University	587	21	6	564	24	7
Private	Cornell University	497	35	11	487	34	9
Private	Dartmouth College	87	185	62	85	192	65
Private	Drexel University	214	95	28	213	96	27
Private	Duke University	537	26	9	485	35	10
Private	Emory University	251	84	23	264	78	22
Public	Florida International University	151	123	86	189	108	77
Public	Florida State University	386	48	33	424	46	31
Public	George Mason University	322	62	44	249	82	60
Private	George Washington University	264	81	22	222	91	25
Private	Georgetown University	124	146	49	114	154	48
Public	Georgia Institute of Technology	531	28	19	526	29	21
Private	Harvard University	713	12	3	745	10	1
Private	Icahn School of Med. at Mount Sinai	23	350	153	28	320	127
Public	Indiana University - Bloomington	485	38	26	538	26	19
Public	Iowa State University	327	59	42	336	60	42
Private	Johns Hopkins University	528	30	10	535	27	8
Public	Kansas State University	179	110	76	190	107	76
Public	Louisiana State Univ. - Baton Rouge	344	56	39	331	63	44
Private	Massachusetts Institute of Tech.	646	17	5	606	20	5
Private	Medical College of Wisconsin	24	343	148	26	330	134
Public	Medical University of South Carolina	181	109	75	191	106	75
Public	Michigan State University	533	27	18	577	22	17
Public	Mississippi State University	153	121	85	146	127	91
Public	Montana State University - Bozeman	52	248	159	79	204	136
Public	Naval Postgraduate School	15	417	230	15	394	224
Public	New Jersey Institute of Technology	57	232	151	65	224	149
Public	New Mexico State Univ. - Las Cruces	105	167	113	131	138	97
Private	New York University	489	37	12	438	39	12
Public	North Carolina State University	518	33	23	512	31	23
Private	Northeastern University	186	107	33	157	121	35
Private	Northwestern University	467	40	13	438	39	12
Public	Ohio State University - Columbus	807	4	4	832	4	4
Public	Oregon Health & Science University	44	272	174	43	268	171
Public	Oregon State University	214	95	68	215	94	69

2014 Doctorates	2014 National Rank	2014 Control Rank	2013 Doctorates	2013 National Rank	2013 Control Rank	2012 Doctorates	2012 National Rank	2012 Control Rank
596	20	16	611	19	15	545	21	16
249	83	59	237	80	59	247	74	53
28	314	193	22	339	198	23	320	191
105	166	52	85	179	61	83	174	59
513	27	9	488	31	11	507	24	7
97	172	54	93	168	56	82	177	60
227	91	26	205	96	29	232	81	24
181	107	33	236	81	22	172	107	31
341	57	18	295	67	19	284	62	18
199	98	28	168	109	33	186	101	29
216	92	66	187	103	73	220	87	62
38	282	177	44	251	163	35	272	172
0	612	329	8	458	212	5	481	233
230	90	65	232	83	61	235	80	57
636	16	3	627	18	4	558	20	5
505	28	10	490	29	10	501	25	8
95	176	55	91	172	57	73	187	66
183	106	32	207	94	28	163	112	32
557	23	7	495	28	9	450	36	11
271	74	22	227	87	24	243	78	23
159	120	83	156	115	80	151	118	86
410	47	32	370	52	36	428	42	30
256	81	58	249	77	56	212	90	65
238	87	25	228	86	23	224	86	25
133	133	41	131	136	41	116	143	46
553	25	18	488	31	21	483	29	20
746	10	1	686	14	2	691	12	2
45	260	91	35	277	103	41	250	91
458	40	28	479	36	24	468	33	23
347	55	38	363	53	37	376	49	34
477	35	11	530	24	7	479	30	10
166	118	81	158	113	78	162	113	81
345	56	39	305	65	47	322	58	41
594	21	5	587	20	5	573	18	4
47	254	87	40	263	96	38	262	96
174	110	76	137	128	90	130	135	95
602	19	15	499	27	19	491	27	19
138	129	90	131	136	96	135	131	93
56	231	152	49	236	155	53	227	147
30	302	185	19	357	207	12	392	221
52	241	160	67	201	135	65	201	130
114	152	106	132	135	95	102	154	106
476	36	12	440	40	13	448	37	12
494	31	21	488	31	21	446	38	26
186	103	31	177	105	32	125	139	43
446	42	13	481	35	12	378	48	15
747	9	9	807	5	5	756	7	6
46	256	169	41	259	167	57	220	144
186	103	73	215	91	65	197	98	71

Doctorates Awarded

	Institutions with Over $40 Million in Federal Research, Alphabetically	2016 Doctorates	2016 National Rank	2016 Control Rank	2015 Doctorates	2015 National Rank	2015 Control Rank
Public	Penn. State Univ. - Hershey Med. Ctr.	24	343	196	26	330	197
Public	Pennsylvania State Univ. - Univ. Park	659	16	12	673	17	14
Private	Princeton University	373	50	17	371	51	17
Public	Purdue University - West Lafayette	727	8	7	717	12	11
Private	Rensselaer Polytechnic Institute	142	132	41	164	119	34
Private	Rice University	211	97	29	176	113	33
Private	Rockefeller University	31	315	129	28	320	127
Private	Rush University	20	375	163	17	381	162
Public	Rutgers University - New Brunswick	620	19	14	597	21	16
Public	San Diego State University	85	191	128	140	129	92
Private	Scripps Research Institute						
Private	Stanford University	763	7	1	688	13	2
Public	Stony Brook University	350	53	36	347	57	40
Public	Temple University	256	82	60	197	101	72
Public	Texas A&M Univ. - College Station	705	13	10	758	8	8
Private	Thomas Jefferson University	13	427	196	21	352	143
Private	Tufts University	135	136	43	116	153	47
Private	Tulane University	135	136	43	123	147	45
Public	Uniformed Services Univ. of the HS						
Public	University at Albany	193	104	73	164	119	86
Public	University at Buffalo	340	57	40	342	58	41
Public	University of Alabama - Birmingham	149	127	89	170	115	82
Public	University of Alabama - Huntsville	34	304	184	33	294	181
Public	University of Alaska - Fairbanks	47	263	168	40	273	173
Public	University of Arizona	524	32	22	528	28	20
Public	Univ. of Arkansas for Med. Sciences	48	257	165	38	281	176
Public	University of California - Berkeley	576	23	16	826	6	6
Public	University of California - Davis	513	34	24	553	25	18
Public	University of California - Irvine	393	47	32	390	49	33
Public	University of California - Los Angeles	775	6	6	774	7	7
Public	University of California - Riverside	239	87	64	272	75	55
Public	University of California - San Diego	529	29	20	505	32	24
Public	Univ. of California - San Francisco	123	149	100	130	139	98
Public	Univ. of California - Santa Barbara	346	54	37	349	56	39
Public	University of California - Santa Cruz	174	114	79	151	124	88
Public	University of Central Florida	299	75	55	286	72	52
Private	University of Chicago	396	46	15	392	48	16
Public	University of Cincinnati - Cincinnati	284	77	57	213	96	70
Public	University of Colorado - Boulder	410	45	31	434	43	30
Public	U. of Colorado - Denv./Anschutz Med.	123	149	100	103	168	114
Public	Univ. of Connecticut - Health Center	16	406	225	16	388	221
Public	University of Connecticut - Storrs	320	65	46	323	66	47
Private	University of Dayton	39	290	110	34	290	110
Public	University of Delaware	283	78	58	237	88	64
Public	University of Florida	723	10	9	754	9	9
Public	University of Georgia	526	31	21	467	37	26
Public	University of Hawaii - Manoa	204	101	71	239	87	63
Public	University of Houston - Univ. Park	358	51	34	326	64	45
Public	University of Idaho	69	210	139	80	201	134

2014 Doctorates	2014 National Rank	2014 Control Rank	2013 Doctorates	2013 National Rank	2013 Control Rank	2012 Doctorates	2012 National Rank	2012 Control Rank
22	347	206	20	352	203	32	280	177
638	15	13	662	17	14	629	17	14
389	50	17	319	61	17	351	51	16
732	12	11	684	15	13	649	14	12
135	131	40	150	119	36	136	129	38
191	101	30	178	104	31	190	100	28
23	339	138	17	373	164	40	253	93
9	443	203	12	410	182	7	450	208
369	52	35	417	45	31	414	43	31
80	189	129	82	184	122	48	234	153
729	13	2	764	9	1	764	6	1
301	67	48	309	64	46	263	70	50
238	87	63	208	93	66	216	89	64
744	11	10	728	12	11	675	13	11
27	320	124	24	319	128	17	352	149
128	136	42	121	146	47	143	125	36
110	159	50	130	140	44	120	140	44
186	103	73	154	118	83	158	116	84
360	53	36	335	55	39	305	60	43
166	118	81	147	123	86	174	106	76
30	302	185	28	302	182	37	266	169
49	249	166	52	226	149	50	230	150
460	39	27	441	39	27	446	38	26
40	278	174	29	299	180	32	280	177
937	1	1	937	1	1	892	1	1
504	29	19	580	21	16	566	19	15
414	44	31	435	42	29	413	44	32
795	7	7	784	6	6	725	9	8
264	78	56	255	75	55	263	70	50
487	34	24	489	30	20	523	22	17
138	129	90	136	129	91	134	132	94
360	53	36	387	50	34	346	52	36
179	108	75	160	111	77	172	107	77
266	76	54	238	78	57	229	82	58
401	48	16	413	46	15	401	45	13
265	77	55	230	84	62	242	79	56
380	51	34	386	51	35	344	53	37
120	146	101	122	145	99	107	151	103
28	314	193	23	327	194	29	291	180
274	73	52	272	72	52	265	68	49
27	320	124	30	294	115	23	320	130
207	96	70	202	97	68	228	84	60
796	6	6	742	11	10	696	11	10
463	38	26	440	40	28	453	35	25
194	100	71	229	85	63	196	99	72
275	72	51	317	62	45	301	61	44
87	184	125	95	164	110	58	216	141

Doctorates Awarded

	Institutions with Over $40 Million in Federal Research, Alphabetically	2016 Doctorates	2016 National Rank	2016 Control Rank	2015 Doctorates	2015 National Rank	2015 Control Rank
Public	University of Illinois - Chicago	346	54	37	314	68	49
Public	Univ. of Illinois - Urbana-Champaign	726	9	8	829	5	5
Public	University of Iowa	468	39	27	453	38	27
Public	University of Kansas - Lawrence	314	68	49	365	53	36
Public	University of Kansas Medical Center	22	359	205	25	336	199
Public	University of Kentucky	313	70	51	295	69	50
Public	University of Louisville	147	128	90	170	115	82
Public	University of Maryland - Baltimore	67	213	141	81	199	132
Public	Univ. of Maryland - Baltimore County	82	193	129	100	170	116
Public	University of Maryland - College Park	592	20	15	654	18	15
Public	Univ. of Massachusetts - Amherst	298	76	56	268	76	56
Public	Univ. of Mass. Med. Sch. - Worcester	64	220	145	61	230	152
Private	University of Miami	216	93	26	208	98	28
Public	University of Michigan - Ann Arbor	848	3	3	882	2	2
Public	University of Minnesota - Twin Cities	804	5	5	725	11	10
Public	University of Missouri - Columbia	416	43	30	435	42	29
Public	University of Nebraska - Lincoln	307	71	52	325	65	46
Public	University of Nebraska Medical Ctr.	86	187	125	81	199	132
Public	University of Nevada - Reno	130	140	96	109	158	108
Public	Univ. of New Hampshire - Durham	66	214	142	75	211	140
Public	Univ. of New Mexico - Albuquerque	200	103	72	222	91	67
Public	Univ. of North Carolina - Chapel Hill	542	24	17	519	30	22
Private	University of Notre Dame	216	93	26	244	83	23
Public	University of Oklahoma - HSC	29	324	189	29	314	191
Public	University of Oklahoma - Norman	210	98	69	218	93	68
Public	University of Oregon	159	118	83	199	100	71
Private	University of Pennsylvania	540	25	8	566	23	6
Public	University of Pittsburgh - Pittsburgh	461	41	28	438	39	28
Public	University of Rhode Island	97	175	118	93	181	122
Private	University of Rochester	301	74	20	267	77	21
Public	Univ. of South Carolina - Columbia	317	66	47	358	54	37
Public	University of South Florida - Tampa	314	68	49	321	67	48
Private	University of Southern California	714	11	2	685	16	3
Public	University of Tennessee - Knoxville	356	52	35	353	55	38
Public	University of Texas - Austin	896	1	1	899	1	1
Public	University of Texas - El Paso	78	198	132	124	144	100
Public	University of Texas HSC - Houston	113	161	110	153	123	87
Public	Univ. of Texas HSC - San Antonio	59	227	148	66	223	148
Public	U. of Texas MD Anderson Cancer Ctr.						
Public	U. of Texas Med. Branch - Galveston	52	248	159	39	278	174
Public	Univ. of Texas SW Med. Ctr. - Dallas	98	173	117	88	186	124
Public	University of Utah	331	58	41	384	50	34
Public	University of Vermont	78	198	132	79	204	136
Public	University of Virginia	315	67	48	366	52	35
Public	University of Washington - Seattle	632	18	13	687	14	12
Public	University of Wisconsin - Madison	870	2	2	857	3	3
Public	University of Wyoming	99	171	116	93	181	122
Public	Utah State University	94	179	121	102	169	115
Private	Vanderbilt University	322	62	19	340	59	18

2014 Doctorates	2014 National Rank	2014 Control Rank	2013 Doctorates	2013 National Rank	2013 Control Rank	2012 Doctorates	2012 National Rank	2012 Control Rank
328	61	43	352	54	38	342	55	38
804	5	5	809	4	4	869	2	2
490	33	23	538	23	17	437	40	28
290	68	49	325	57	41	273	64	46
38	282	177	37	270	172	29	291	180
328	61	43	305	65	47	322	58	41
148	126	87	138	127	89	185	102	73
63	215	141	81	186	124	75	183	120
102	170	117	95	164	110	72	188	122
620	17	14	696	13	12	632	16	13
287	70	50	295	67	49	268	67	48
58	228	150	52	226	149	66	199	128
173	111	35	163	110	34	181	104	30
881	3	3	885	2	2	857	4	4
778	8	8	772	7	7	734	8	7
390	49	33	411	47	32	367	50	35
313	65	46	325	57	41	246	75	54
52	241	160	42	255	165	40	253	161
118	147	102	125	143	98	111	147	100
75	197	131	64	204	137	58	216	141
231	89	64	202	97	68	202	97	70
557	23	17	530	24	18	495	26	18
206	97	27	214	92	27	210	92	26
33	295	182	24	319	192	24	316	189
210	95	69	206	95	67	218	88	63
155	123	84	169	107	75	170	109	78
535	26	8	527	26	8	514	23	6
496	30	20	435	42	29	479	30	21
101	171	118	97	162	109	89	167	113
281	71	21	290	70	20	265	68	20
325	63	45	334	56	40	279	63	45
330	58	40	295	67	49	270	66	47
594	21	5	663	16	3	634	15	3
458	40	28	484	34	23	461	34	24
892	2	2	849	3	3	867	3	3
118	147	102	103	156	107	59	212	137
141	128	89	117	148	100	127	137	96
54	237	157	51	230	153	56	223	145
45	260	170	52	226	149	40	253	161
92	179	122	89	175	117	98	158	108
330	58	40	324	59	43	339	56	39
71	203	136	84	180	119	62	207	135
424	43	30	399	48	33	393	46	33
663	14	12	763	10	9	708	10	9
813	4	4	772	7	7	813	5	5
107	162	111	81	186	124	72	188	122
109	161	110	105	155	106	94	161	111
318	64	19	310	63	18	273	64	19

Doctorates Awarded

	Institutions with Over $40 Million in Federal Research, Alphabetically	2016 Doctorates	2016 National Rank	2016 Control Rank	2015 Doctorates	2015 National Rank	2015 Control Rank
Public	Virginia Commonwealth University	306	72	53	282	73	53
Public	Virginia Polytechnic Inst. and St. U.	492	36	25	488	33	25
Private	Wake Forest University	58	229	80	53	248	89
Public	Washington State Univ. - Pullman	322	62	44	281	74	54
Private	Washington University in St. Louis	266	80	21	292	70	20
Public	Wayne State University	222	92	67	242	84	61
Private	Weill Cornell Medical College	58	229	80	68	220	74
Public	West Virginia University	210	98	69	183	109	78
Private	Woods Hole Oceanographic Inst.						
Private	Yale University	411	44	14	426	45	15
Private	Yeshiva University	152	122	37	96	177	59

2014 Doctorates	2014 National Rank	2014 Control Rank	2013 Doctorates	2013 National Rank	2013 Control Rank	2012 Doctorates	2012 National Rank	2012 Control Rank
329	60	42	324	59	43	333	57	40
494	31	21	479	36	24	469	32	22
53	239	81	50	233	79	57	220	77
260	80	57	268	74	54	203	95	68
261	79	23	255	75	21	251	73	21
244	84	60	223	88	64	229	82	58
70	205	68	73	196	64	57	220	77
155	123	84	158	113	78	162	113	81
413	45	14	398	49	16	390	47	14
124	138	44	131	136	41	129	136	41

Postdoctoral Appointees

	Institutions with Over $40 Million in Federal Research, Alphabetically	2015 Postdocs	2015 National Rank	2015 Control Rank	2014 Postdocs	2014 National Rank	2014 Control Rank
Public	Arizona State University	257	71	42	253	68	42
Public	Auburn University	40	175	121	40	174	120
Public	Augusta University	159	98	64	188	91	57
Private	Baylor College of Medicine	537	37	19	594	31	16
Private	Boston University	421	46	23	444	46	23
Private	Brandeis University	95	128	45	102	127	45
Private	Brown University	252	74	30	244	71	27
Private	California Institute of Technology	552	35	18	552	34	18
Private	Carnegie Mellon University	193	90	33	215	81	30
Private	Case Western Reserve University	271	66	27	190	90	34
Public	Clemson University	77	139	91	65	143	94
Public	Cleveland State University	3	310	207	3	313	209
Private	Cold Spring Harbor Laboratory	143	105	36	153	104	38
Public	Colorado State Univ. - Fort Collins	254	73	44	297	63	37
Private	Columbia University	1,249	7	5	1,274	6	5
Private	Cornell University	502	39	21	466	40	21
Private	Dartmouth College	204	87	32	222	78	28
Private	Drexel University	93	129	46	74	139	49
Private	Duke University	584	31	15	656	23	11
Private	Emory University	642	24	11	674	20	9
Public	Florida International University	75	141	93	64	145	96
Public	Florida State University	202	88	56	211	83	53
Public	George Mason University	44	168	115	33	185	129
Private	George Washington University	111	117	42	94	132	47
Private	Georgetown University	109	118	43	127	116	40
Public	Georgia Institute of Technology	237	77	47	217	80	51
Private	Harvard University	5,674	1	1	5,761	1	1
Private	Icahn School of Med. at Mount Sinai	643	23	10	670	21	10
Public	Indiana University - Bloomington	365	51	28	144	108	69
Public	Iowa State University	299	59	35	331	55	32
Private	Johns Hopkins University	1,679	3	3	1,715	3	3
Public	Kansas State University	146	102	67	142	111	72
Public	Louisiana State Univ. - Baton Rouge	148	101	66	141	112	73
Private	Massachusetts Institute of Tech.	1,493	4	4	1,516	4	4
Private	Medical College of Wisconsin	66	145	49	175	94	35
Public	Medical University of South Carolina	178	93	59	173	95	60
Public	Michigan State University	471	44	22	450	44	22
Public	Mississippi State University	51	157	106	46	165	113
Public	Montana State University - Bozeman	51	157	106	38	177	123
Public	Naval Postgraduate School	22	219	153	16	226	158
Public	New Jersey Institute of Technology	42	171	117	24	201	141
Public	New Mexico State Univ. - Las Cruces	24	212	147	28	194	136
Private	New York University	680	20	9	596	30	15
Public	North Carolina State University	497	40	19	473	39	19
Private	Northeastern University	114	116	41	117	121	43
Private	Northwestern University	746	19	8	708	18	8
Public	Ohio State University - Columbus	619	27	15	629	28	15
Public	Oregon Health & Science University	292	61	37	270	65	39
Public	Oregon State University	212	84	53	201	85	54

2013 Postdocs	2013 National Rank	2013 Control Rank	2012 Postdocs	2012 National Rank	2012 Control Rank	2011 Postdocs	2011 National Rank	2011 Control Rank
257	69	42	221	77	50	204	83	53
36	175	124	45	161	112	42	168	116
139	107	71	143	107	71	156	104	68
596	29	14	588	29	14	572	31	14
464	39	20	530	35	17	600	28	12
116	118	40	128	118	40	102	122	40
259	68	27	274	67	26	279	65	27
579	31	16	623	25	12	573	30	13
194	87	31	241	72	27	234	73	28
224	81	29	219	78	28	194	87	32
42	165	115	45	161	112	44	165	113
8	263	184	9	261	183	12	246	172
0	335	112	0	341	113	0	339	111
290	60	34	313	57	34	233	74	46
1,232	7	5	1,283	6	5	1,276	7	6
437	42	21	386	45	21	487	38	19
228	76	28	208	83	31	199	86	31
69	139	45	63	140	46	54	150	48
732	19	8	747	19	8	784	19	9
712	21	10	678	22	11	691	23	11
49	155	107	55	149	103	51	153	105
212	85	56	235	73	46	218	78	49
32	187	133	31	182	127	31	186	131
80	134	44	98	125	42	68	137	44
115	119	41	131	117	39	112	119	39
267	65	39	307	60	36	295	62	36
5,809	1	1	6,019	1	1	6,120	1	1
621	26	12	579	31	15	536	35	17
117	117	78	316	56	33	125	113	76
299	59	33	158	99	65	152	105	69
1,693	3	3	1,775	3	3	1,649	3	3
136	109	73	112	121	81	103	121	82
149	102	66	138	110	73	158	102	66
1,406	4	4	1,398	5	4	1,345	4	4
122	112	38	133	114	38	136	111	37
179	91	57	186	90	57	194	87	56
446	41	21	429	40	20	455	40	20
41	168	118	35	176	123	41	170	118
42	165	115	41	168	118	56	146	100
24	201	144	0	341	229	0	339	229
39	169	119	17	231	166	36	176	122
24	201	144	29	187	131	24	200	143
593	30	15	623	25	12	493	37	18
490	36	18	371	49	27	318	55	30
105	125	42	96	129	43	100	123	41
716	20	9	742	20	9	813	17	8
625	25	14	616	28	15	617	27	16
280	64	38	303	62	38	298	60	34
237	70	43	214	81	52	189	91	58

Postdoctoral Appointees

	Institutions with Over $40 Million in Federal Research, Alphabetically	2015 Postdocs	2015 National Rank	2015 Control Rank	2014 Postdocs	2014 National Rank	2014 Control Rank
Public	Penn. State Univ. - Hershey Med. Ctr.	70	142	94	91	133	86
Public	Pennsylvania State Univ. - Univ. Park	366	50	27	365	50	27
Private	Princeton University	526	38	20	464	42	22
Public	Purdue University - West Lafayette	389	48	25	358	51	28
Private	Rensselaer Polytechnic Institute	83	134	48	82	136	48
Private	Rice University	263	68	28	206	84	31
Private	Rockefeller University	292	61	25	298	62	26
Private	Rush University	28	197	60	33	185	57
Public	Rutgers University - New Brunswick	306	56	32	345	54	31
Public	San Diego State University	33	182	126	32	187	130
Private	Scripps Research Institute	573	33	17	648	24	12
Private	Stanford University	2,264	2	2	2,048	2	2
Public	Stony Brook University	263	68	41	224	77	50
Public	Temple University	167	95	61	192	89	56
Public	Texas A&M Univ. - College Station	615	28	16	508	37	18
Private	Thomas Jefferson University	117	115	40	119	120	42
Private	Tufts University	182	92	34	194	88	33
Private	Tulane University	133	107	37	124	117	41
Public	Uniformed Services Univ. of the HS	33	182	126	36	180	126
Public	University at Albany	86	132	85	69	140	91
Public	University at Buffalo	256	72	43	301	60	35
Public	University of Alabama - Birmingham	252	74	45	228	75	48
Public	University of Alabama - Huntsville	13	246	173	19	216	150
Public	University of Alaska - Fairbanks	37	178	124	47	162	110
Public	University of Arizona	471	44	22	451	43	21
Public	Univ. of Arkansas for Med. Sciences	23	216	151	57	149	99
Public	University of California - Berkeley	1,184	9	4	1,148	10	4
Public	University of California - Davis	833	15	8	765	17	10
Public	University of California - Irvine	297	60	36	315	57	33
Public	University of California - Los Angeles	1,016	12	6	1,088	11	5
Public	University of California - Riverside	190	91	58	141	112	73
Public	University of California - San Diego	1,250	6	2	1,338	5	1
Public	Univ. of California - San Francisco	1,041	11	5	1,051	12	6
Public	Univ. of California - Santa Barbara	306	56	32	285	64	38
Public	University of California - Santa Cruz	125	111	74	120	119	78
Public	University of Central Florida	51	157	106	47	162	110
Private	University of Chicago	586	30	14	583	32	17
Public	University of Cincinnati - Cincinnati	303	58	34	466	40	20
Public	University of Colorado - Boulder	911	13	7	879	14	7
Public	U. of Colorado - Denv./Anschutz Med.	288	63	38	267	66	40
Public	Univ. of Connecticut - Health Center	104	123	80	104	126	82
Public	University of Connecticut - Storrs	109	118	76	121	118	77
Private	University of Dayton	9	264	81	10	264	82
Public	University of Delaware	132	109	72	166	100	63
Public	University of Florida	679	21	12	644	25	13
Public	University of Georgia	250	76	46	231	74	47
Public	University of Hawaii - Manoa	234	79	49	243	72	45
Public	University of Houston - Univ. Park	264	67	40	258	67	41
Public	University of Idaho	51	157	106	56	153	102

2013 Postdocs	2013 National Rank	2013 Control Rank	2012 Postdocs	2012 National Rank	2012 Control Rank	2011 Postdocs	2011 National Rank	2011 Control Rank
95	126	84	100	124	83	88	127	85
380	45	24	401	42	22	380	48	25
527	34	17	457	39	20	471	39	20
289	61	35	306	61	37	297	61	35
85	130	43	80	135	44	77	133	43
182	90	34	158	99	35	165	99	35
303	57	26	309	58	24	318	55	26
33	185	54	36	175	53	51	153	49
237	70	43	243	71	45	240	70	43
30	191	137	31	182	127	46	160	110
0	335	112	0	341	113	0	339	111
1,976	2	2	1,887	2	2	1,798	2	2
236	72	45	222	76	49	202	84	54
156	100	64	159	98	64	110	120	81
448	40	20	422	41	21	417	43	22
134	110	37	145	104	36	163	100	36
194	87	31	201	85	32	205	82	30
162	96	36	143	107	37	124	116	38
42	165	115	71	136	92	71	135	92
80	134	91	92	130	87	86	128	86
266	66	40	264	68	42	299	59	33
226	78	50	226	74	47	245	69	42
14	235	167	8	266	185	15	236	167
50	154	106	58	147	101	52	152	104
303	57	32	308	59	35	270	67	40
54	147	99	41	168	118	33	182	128
1,255	6	2	1,533	4	1	1,286	6	1
779	15	8	757	18	11	819	15	8
325	53	29	379	46	25	369	49	26
1,084	11	5	1,009	12	6	1,062	12	6
143	104	68	133	114	77	167	98	64
1,275	5	1	1,219	8	2	1,260	8	2
1,047	12	6	1,066	11	5	1,091	11	5
281	63	37	300	63	39	291	63	37
122	112	75	141	109	72	150	106	70
52	149	101	55	149	103	65	141	97
598	28	13	565	33	16	562	32	15
468	38	19	465	38	19	410	46	23
836	14	7	776	17	10	770	20	11
285	62	36	300	63	39	284	64	38
122	112	75	125	119	79	116	118	80
115	119	79	134	111	74	125	113	76
7	268	81	11	253	74	14	239	72
131	111	74	133	114	77	124	116	79
677	23	12	674	23	12	625	26	15
228	76	49	245	70	44	279	65	39
265	67	41	339	54	31	238	72	45
219	82	53	198	87	55	213	79	50
51	152	104	43	164	115	50	155	106

Postdoctoral Appointees

	Institutions with Over $40 Million in Federal Research, Alphabetically	2015 Postdocs	2015 National Rank	2015 Control Rank	2014 Postdocs	2014 National Rank	2014 Control Rank
Public	University of Illinois - Chicago	214	83	52	238	73	46
Public	Univ. of Illinois - Urbana-Champaign	542	36	18	525	35	17
Public	University of Iowa	346	54	30	355	53	30
Public	University of Kansas - Lawrence	149	100	65	154	103	66
Public	University of Kansas Medical Center	100	126	83	111	124	80
Public	University of Kentucky	221	82	51	155	102	65
Public	University of Louisville	107	121	78	97	129	84
Public	University of Maryland - Baltimore	325	55	31	358	51	28
Public	Univ. of Maryland - Baltimore County	67	144	96	63	146	97
Public	University of Maryland - College Park	496	41	20	437	47	24
Public	Univ. of Massachusetts - Amherst	144	104	69	153	104	67
Public	Univ. of Mass. Med. Sch. - Worcester	348	53	29	315	57	33
Private	University of Miami	258	70	29	198	87	32
Public	University of Michigan - Ann Arbor	1,299	5	1	1,238	7	2
Public	University of Minnesota - Twin Cities	752	18	11	679	19	11
Public	University of Missouri - Columbia	165	97	63	184	93	59
Public	University of Nebraska - Lincoln	205	86	55	201	85	54
Public	University of Nebraska Medical Ctr.	108	120	77	110	125	81
Public	University of Nevada - Reno	78	138	90	65	143	94
Public	Univ. of New Hampshire - Durham	46	165	113	45	167	114
Public	Univ. of New Mexico - Albuquerque	124	112	75	139	114	75
Public	Univ. of North Carolina - Chapel Hill	803	16	9	802	15	8
Private	University of Notre Dame	124	112	38	171	96	36
Public	University of Oklahoma - HSC	83	134	87	89	134	87
Public	University of Oklahoma - Norman	133	107	71	145	107	68
Public	University of Oregon	105	122	79	85	135	88
Private	University of Pennsylvania	901	14	7	919	13	7
Public	University of Pittsburgh - Pittsburgh	664	22	13	659	22	12
Public	University of Rhode Island	32	185	129	27	196	138
Private	University of Rochester	233	80	31	222	78	28
Public	Univ. of South Carolina - Columbia	129	110	73	144	108	69
Public	University of South Florida - Tampa	282	65	39	300	61	36
Private	University of Southern California	475	43	22	480	38	20
Public	University of Tennessee - Knoxville	136	106	70	143	110	71
Public	University of Texas - Austin	370	49	26	370	49	26
Public	University of Texas - El Paso	58	151	101	12	252	174
Public	University of Texas HSC - Houston	237	77	47	212	82	52
Public	Univ. of Texas HSC - San Antonio	167	95	61	165	101	64
Public	U. of Texas MD Anderson Cancer Ctr.	637	25	14	640	26	14
Public	U. of Texas Med. Branch - Galveston	102	125	82	131	115	76
Public	Univ. of Texas SW Med. Ctr. - Dallas	562	34	17	571	33	16
Public	University of Utah	487	42	21	429	48	25
Public	University of Vermont	86	132	85	95	131	85
Public	University of Virginia	420	47	24	447	45	23
Public	University of Washington - Seattle	1,205	8	3	1,184	9	3
Public	University of Wisconsin - Madison	765	17	10	767	16	9
Public	University of Wyoming	54	154	104	55	154	103
Public	Utah State University	42	171	117	47	162	110
Private	Vanderbilt University	629	26	12	634	27	13

2013 Postdocs	2013 National Rank	2013 Control Rank	2012 Postdocs	2012 National Rank	2012 Control Rank	2011 Postdocs	2011 National Rank	2011 Control Rank
232	74	47	251	69	43	257	68	41
562	32	16	558	34	18	548	34	18
352	49	27	363	50	28	368	51	28
155	101	65	184	91	58	172	95	61
113	121	80	134	111	74	125	113	76
217	84	55	344	53	30	303	58	32
92	127	85	114	120	80	135	112	75
352	49	27	350	51	29	343	53	29
58	145	97	45	161	112	36	176	122
379	46	25	399	43	23	431	42	21
165	94	60	165	94	60	209	80	51
315	56	31	324	55	32	386	47	24
202	86	30	219	78	28	227	76	29
1,227	8	3	1,080	10	4	1,121	10	4
660	24	13	580	30	16	640	25	14
225	79	51	199	86	54	219	77	48
157	99	63	163	96	62	159	101	65
112	122	81	145	104	69	148	108	72
80	134	91	53	152	105	66	140	96
34	180	128	48	157	109	46	160	110
83	133	90	70	138	94	193	89	57
778	16	9	850	14	7	878	14	7
186	89	33	182	92	34	182	93	34
84	132	89	90	131	88	81	131	89
142	105	69	134	111	74	80	132	90
89	129	87	90	131	88	67	139	95
947	13	7	956	13	7	978	13	7
741	17	10	841	15	8	818	16	9
36	175	124	50	155	107	50	155	106
325	53	25	214	81	30	413	44	22
119	116	77	97	126	84	144	109	73
321	55	30	289	66	41	304	57	31
486	37	19	506	36	18	447	41	21
149	102	66	145	104	69	171	96	62
361	48	26	372	48	26	369	49	26
31	190	136	26	193	136	24	200	143
229	75	48	224	75	48	209	80	51
169	92	58	173	93	59	171	96	62
604	27	15	621	27	14	509	36	19
137	108	72	150	102	67	157	103	67
552	33	17	572	32	17	582	29	17
384	43	22	389	44	24	732	21	12
85	130	88	85	134	91	68	137	94
384	43	22	658	24	13	643	24	13
1,187	10	4	1,190	9	3	1,186	9	3
738	18	11	798	16	9	797	18	10
66	140	95	61	142	96	55	149	102
45	159	110	22	207	150	22	211	152
678	22	11	711	21	10	720	22	10

Postdoctoral Appointees

	Institutions with Over $40 Million in Federal Research, Alphabetically	2015 Postdocs	2015 National Rank	2015 Control Rank	2014 Postdocs	2014 National Rank	2014 Control Rank
Public	Virginia Commonwealth University	194	89	57	249	69	43
Public	Virginia Polytechnic Inst. and St. U.	225	81	50	226	76	49
Private	Wake Forest University	87	130	47	152	106	39
Public	Washington State Univ. - Pullman	175	94	60	169	97	61
Private	Washington University in St. Louis	615	28	13	625	29	14
Public	Wayne State University	146	102	67	185	92	58
Private	Weill Cornell Medical College	354	52	24	322	56	24
Public	West Virginia University	51	157	106	67	142	93
Private	Woods Hole Oceanographic Inst.	99	127	44	97	129	46
Private	Yale University	1,157	10	6	1,201	8	6
Private	Yeshiva University	283	64	26	303	59	25

2013 Postdocs	2013 National Rank	2013 Control Rank	2012 Postdocs	2012 National Rank	2012 Control Rank	2011 Postdocs	2011 National Rank	2011 Control Rank
225	79	51	217	80	51	232	75	47
235	73	46	202	84	53	202	84	54
164	95	35	188	89	33	192	90	33
166	93	59	190	88	56	184	92	59
350	51	23	374	47	22	559	33	16
158	98	62	164	95	61	138	110	74
334	52	24	347	52	23	344	52	24
38	171	120	46	160	111	93	126	84
120	115	39	107	122	41	99	124	42
1,214	9	6	1,256	7	6	1,307	5	5
365	47	22	293	65	25	321	54	25

SAT Scores

Institutions with Over $40 Million in Federal Research, Alphabetically		2015 Median SAT	2015 National Rank	2015 Control Rank	2014 Median SAT	2014 National Rank	2014 Control Rank
Public	Arizona State University	1170	210	68	1145	273	92
Public	Auburn University	1220	138	38	1220	143	38
Public	Augusta University	1035	630	238	1030	673	237
Private	Baylor College of Medicine						
Private	Boston University	1305	81	69	1300	82	71
Private	Brandeis University	1360	51	48	1365	51	47
Private	Brown University	1465	13	13	1440	23	23
Private	California Institute of Technology	1550	1	1	1550	1	1
Private	Carnegie Mellon University	1450	20	20	1440	23	23
Private	Case Western Reserve University	1400	35	34	1370	46	44
Public	Clemson University	1250	115	28	1245	114	27
Public	Cleveland State University	1030	641	239	1010	790	288
Private	Cold Spring Harbor Laboratory						
Public	Colorado State Univ. - Fort Collins	1150	246	83	1130	286	98
Private	Columbia University	1475	11	11	1480	8	8
Private	Cornell University	1430	30	30	1420	28	28
Private	Dartmouth College	1445	21	21	1455	18	18
Private	Drexel University	1203	179	123	1200	174	122
Private	Duke University	1455	19	19	1460	13	13
Private	Emory University	1380	45	43	1370	46	44
Public	Florida International University	1080	451	165	1080	475	166
Public	Florida State University	1220	138	38	1240	118	29
Public	George Mason University	1145	275	96	1150	252	80
Private	George Washington University	1290	90	76	1295	93	80
Private	Georgetown University	1410	32	32	1420	28	28
Public	Georgia Institute of Technology	1405	34	1	1400	35	1
Private	Harvard University	1500	6	6	1505	3	3
Private	Icahn School of Med. at Mount Sinai						
Public	Indiana University - Bloomington	1175	206	65	1175	213	65
Public	Iowa State University	1150	246	83	1150	252	80
Private	Johns Hopkins University	1445	21	21	1435	26	26
Public	Kansas State University						
Public	Louisiana State Univ. - Baton Rouge	1170	210	68	1170	215	66
Private	Massachusetts Institute of Tech.	1505	5	5	1495	6	6
Private	Medical College of Wisconsin						
Public	Medical University of South Carolina						
Public	Michigan State University	1170	210	68	1170	215	66
Public	Mississippi State University	1150	246	83	1130	286	98
Public	Montana State University - Bozeman	1130	288	100	1130	286	98
Public	Naval Postgraduate School						
Public	New Jersey Institute of Technology	1210	152	46	1165	234	72
Public	New Mexico State Univ. - Las Cruces	990	854	330	990	899	333
Private	New York University	1360	51	48	1345	59	54
Public	North Carolina State University	1245	117	29	1245	114	27
Private	Northeastern University	1440	25	25	1420	28	28
Private	Northwestern University	1440	25	25	1475	10	10
Public	Ohio State University - Columbus	1300	83	13	1300	82	12
Public	Oregon Health & Science University						
Public	Oregon State University	1105	378	131	1105	393	132

2013 Median SAT	2013 National Rank	2013 Control Rank	2012 Median SAT	2012 National Rank	2012 Control Rank	2011 Median SAT	2011 National Rank	2011 Control Rank
1145	309	93	1105	421	127	1095	439	130
1220	155	38	1220	152	35	1220	154	35
1015	841	286						
1285	94	82	1275	104	89	1275	101	87
1350	58	53	1340	63	58	1340	60	56
1435	24	24	1425	24	24	1390	35	35
1545	1	1	1525	1	1	1525	1	1
1435	24	24	1420	27	27	1410	26	26
1375	42	42	1370	45	45	1340	60	56
1245	125	28	1235	136	26	1235	138	27
1030	727	233	1010	859	285	990	972	342
1130	324	97	1130	322	97	1130	316	93
1480	8	8	1485	9	9	1480	8	8
1420	29	29	1415	29	29	1400	29	29
1455	17	17	1455	13	13	1465	10	10
1190	201	146	1220	152	118	1205	176	133
1455	17	17	1440	18	18	1440	16	16
1365	46	46	1375	43	43	1405	28	28
1150	276	80	1140	310	91	1070	531	168
1220	155	38	1220	152	35	1205	176	44
1150	276	80	1150	284	81	1150	277	79
1295	91	79	1295	87	75	1300	81	73
1405	33	33	1390	35	35	1395	32	32
1360	50	2	1355	55	4	1335	65	6
1505	3	3	1500	2	2	1490	5	5
1175	225	64	1165	262	75	1165	256	74
1150	276	80	1150	284	81	1150	277	79
1415	30	30	1405	32	32	1400	29	29
1170	231	66	1170	229	64	1170	234	64
1500	5	5	1490	7	7	1490	5	5
1170	231	66	1170	229	64	1170	234	64
1110	367	109	1090	451	140	1090	449	134
1110	367	109	1110	381	112	1130	316	93
1140	316	94	1140	310	91	1120	355	102
990	972	339	990	969	344	990	972	342
1355	54	51	1350	59	54	1360	49	48
1225	151	36	1185	216	57	1185	220	57
1390	35	35	1370	45	45	1340	60	56
1470	11	11	1440	18	18	1455	14	14
1300	82	10	1260	111	20	1260	110	18
1100	435	131	1090	451	140	1090	449	134

SAT Scores

	Institutions with Over $40 Million in Federal Research, Alphabetically	2015 Median SAT	2015 National Rank	2015 Control Rank	2014 Median SAT	2014 National Rank	2014 Control Rank
Public	Penn. State Univ. - Hershey Med. Ctr.						
Public	Pennsylvania State Univ. - Univ. Park	1195	183	59	1190	184	56
Private	Princeton University	1490	7	7	1500	5	5
Public	Purdue University - West Lafayette	1205	160	50	1205	164	49
Private	Rensselaer Polytechnic Institute	1385	41	39	1395	37	36
Private	Rice University	1475	11	11	1470	12	12
Private	Rockefeller University						
Private	Rush University						
Public	Rutgers University - New Brunswick	1225	136	36	1215	157	43
Public	San Diego State University	1120	327	110	1110	347	115
Private	Scripps Research Institute						
Private	Stanford University	1485	8	8	1475	10	10
Public	Stony Brook University	1265	104	21	1250	112	26
Public	Temple University				1120	335	111
Public	Texas A&M Univ. - College Station	1190	190	63	1195	179	53
Private	Thomas Jefferson University						
Private	Tufts University	1445	21	21	1440	23	23
Private	Tulane University	1360	51	48	1360	54	50
Public	Uniformed Services Univ. of the HS						
Public	University at Albany	1085	440	160	1095	416	142
Public	University at Buffalo	1160	238	78	1150	252	80
Public	University of Alabama - Birmingham	1150	246	83	1110	347	115
Public	University of Alabama - Huntsville	1220	138	38	1220	143	38
Public	University of Alaska - Fairbanks	1030	641	239			
Public	University of Arizona						
Public	Univ. of Arkansas for Med. Sciences						
Public	University of California - Berkeley	1380	45	3	1370	46	3
Public	University of California - Davis	1205	160	50	1205	164	49
Public	University of California - Irvine	1160	238	78	1160	240	73
Public	University of California - Los Angeles	1325	71	10	1325	66	8
Public	University of California - Riverside	1095	395	138	1130	286	98
Public	University of California - San Diego	1335	68	9	1310	79	11
Public	Univ. of California - San Francisco						
Public	Univ. of California - Santa Barbara	1225	136	36	1235	133	33
Public	University of California - Santa Cruz	1175	206	65	1130	286	98
Public	University of Central Florida	1175	206	65	1185	209	62
Private	University of Chicago	1520	2	2	1518	2	2
Public	University of Cincinnati - Cincinnati	1170	210	68	1170	215	66
Public	University of Colorado - Boulder	1220	138	38	1220	143	38
Public	U. of Colorado - Denv./Anschutz Med.	1050	548	201	1050	560	192
Public	Univ. of Connecticut - Health Center						
Public	University of Connecticut - Storrs	1235	129	33	1240	118	29
Private	University of Dayton	1205	160	111	1205	164	116
Public	University of Delaware	1195	183	59	1190	184	56
Public	University of Florida	1260	109	25	1265	104	22
Public	University of Georgia	1240	120	31	1235	133	33
Public	University of Hawaii - Manoa	1080	451	165	1085	466	161
Public	University of Houston - Univ. Park	1150	246	83	1145	273	92
Public	University of Idaho	1055	534	196	1040	650	229

2013 Median SAT	2013 National Rank	2013 Control Rank	2012 Median SAT	2012 National Rank	2012 Control Rank	2011 Median SAT	2011 National Rank	2011 Control Rank
1195	193	51	1195	194	49	1195	197	51
1505	3	3	1500	2	2	1500	2	2
1200	192	50	1180	221	61	1170	234	64
1389	38	38	1365	49	48	1375	45	44
1460	12	12	1445	15	15	1430	20	20
1210	172	43	1195	194	49	1195	197	51
1090	455	140	1085	504	155	1085	498	156
1475	10	10	1475	11	11	1455	14	14
1250	122	27	1235	136	26	1230	143	28
1120	351	106	1110	381	112	1110	372	107
1180	221	62	1195	194	49	1210	169	39
1445	20	20	1435	21	21	1430	20	20
1360	50	49	1360	50	49	1325	67	61
1100	435	131	1105	421	127	1115	368	105
1155	270	77	1155	276	78	1155	269	77
1150	276	80	1110	381	112	1110	372	107
1190	201	56	1170	229	64	1170	234	64
1107	421	124	1095	440	135	1100	427	122
1355	54	4	1370	45	1	1360	49	2
1195	193	51	1210	173	42	1210	169	39
1130	324	97	1160	267	77	1185	220	57
1300	82	10	1300	77	8	1300	81	9
1090	455	140	1080	513	157	1050	625	201
1280	99	16	1235	136	26	1270	104	15
1215	167	41	1215	167	37	1205	176	44
1095	448	138	1140	310	91	1135	312	90
1180	221	62	1180	221	61	1185	220	57
1515	2	2	1485	9	9	1485	7	7
1130	324	97	1130	322	97	1140	303	87
1205	179	46	1170	229	64	1190	200	53
1070	532	174	1070	531	163	1050	625	201
1230	147	34	1230	141	31	1220	154	35
1205	179	134	1205	179	136	1205	176	133
1170	231	66	1185	216	57	1205	176	44
1265	110	20	1265	109	18	1260	110	18
1235	142	32	1215	167	37	1225	145	30
1085	503	159	1080	513	157	1090	449	134
1140	316	94	1130	322	97	1110	372	107
1070	532	174	1070	531	163	1070	531	168

SAT Scores

	Institutions with Over $40 Million in Federal Research, Alphabetically	2015 Median SAT	2015 National Rank	2015 Control Rank	2014 Median SAT	2014 National Rank	2014 Control Rank
Public	University of Illinois - Chicago	1090	402	143	1130	286	98
Public	Univ. of Illinois - Urbana-Champaign	1280	94	16	1300	82	12
Public	University of Iowa	1170	210	68	1170	215	66
Public	University of Kansas - Lawrence	1150	246	83	1150	252	80
Public	University of Kansas Medical Center						
Public	University of Kentucky	1150	246	83	1150	252	80
Public	University of Louisville	1170	210	68	1150	252	80
Public	University of Maryland - Baltimore						
Public	Univ. of Maryland - Baltimore County	1210	152	46	1210	162	47
Public	University of Maryland - College Park	1315	78	11	1315	77	10
Public	Univ. of Massachusetts - Amherst	1220	138	38	1215	157	43
Public	Univ. of Mass. Med. Sch. - Worcester						
Private	University of Miami	1340	64	57	1320	70	62
Public	University of Michigan - Ann Arbor	1390	38	2	1390	38	2
Public	University of Minnesota - Twin Cities	1280	94	16	1260	107	23
Public	University of Missouri - Columbia	1205	160	50	1170	215	66
Public	University of Nebraska - Lincoln	1150	246	83	1150	252	80
Public	University of Nebraska Medical Ctr.						
Public	University of Nevada - Reno	1080	451	165	1075	481	168
Public	Univ. of New Hampshire - Durham	1105	378	131	1100	403	138
Public	Univ. of New Mexico - Albuquerque	1030	641	239	1050	560	192
Public	Univ. of North Carolina - Chapel Hill	1360	51	4	1320	70	9
Private	University of Notre Dame	1460	15	15	1460	13	13
Public	University of Oklahoma - HSC						
Public	University of Oklahoma - Norman	1205	160	50	1190	184	56
Public	University of Oregon	1115	332	114	1110	347	115
Private	University of Pennsylvania	1465	13	13	1455	18	18
Public	University of Pittsburgh - Pittsburgh	1265	104	21	1270	103	21
Public	University of Rhode Island	1070	461	170	1070	491	172
Private	University of Rochester						
Public	Univ. of South Carolina - Columbia	1200	180	57	1210	162	47
Public	University of South Florida - Tampa	1170	210	68	1160	240	73
Private	University of Southern California	1385	41	39	1380	43	41
Public	University of Tennessee - Knoxville	1220	138	38	1205	164	49
Public	University of Texas - Austin	1290	90	15	1290	94	14
Public	University of Texas - El Paso	935	1073	427	935	1114	427
Public	University of Texas HSC - Houston						
Public	Univ. of Texas HSC - San Antonio						
Public	U. of Texas MD Anderson Cancer Ctr.						
Public	U. of Texas Med. Branch - Galveston						
Public	U. of Texas SW Medical Ctr. - Dallas						
Public	University of Utah	1130	288	100	1130	286	98
Public	University of Vermont	1195	183	59	1185	209	62
Public	University of Virginia	1355	58	7	1355	56	5
Public	University of Washington - Seattle	1245	117	29	1230	137	36
Public	University of Wisconsin - Madison	1300	83	13	1280	97	17
Public	University of Wyoming	1130	288	100	1130	286	98
Public	Utah State University	1090	402	143	1070	491	172
Private	Vanderbilt University	1485	8	8	1460	13	13

2013 Median SAT	2013 National Rank	2013 Control Rank	2012 Median SAT	2012 National Rank	2012 Control Rank	2011 Median SAT	2011 National Rank	2011 Control Rank
1090	455	140	1090	451	140	1090	449	134
1280	99	16	1280	95	14	1280	96	14
1205	179	46	1150	284	81	1170	234	64
1150	276	80	1150	284	81	1150	277	79
1150	276	80	1170	229	64	1150	277	79
1150	276	80	1130	322	97	1110	372	107
1210	172	43	1225	149	34	1210	169	39
1310	75	7	1300	77	8	1290	88	11
1210	172	43	1190	202	53	1185	220	57
1325	67	61	1325	68	62	1315	73	67
1340	61	6	1340	63	6	1390	35	1
1260	111	21	1240	125	24	1240	125	25
1170	231	66	1170	229	64	1170	234	64
1150	276	80	1170	229	64	1150	277	79
1075	521	168	1065	582	183	1055	611	198
1100	435	131	1095	440	135	1100	427	122
1030	727	233	1030	729	242	1030	707	228
1305	78	8	1300	77	8	1305	79	8
1460	12	12	1440	18	18	1460	11	11
1190	201	56	1190	202	53	1190	200	53
1105	423	125	1108	420	126	1105	417	118
1450	19	19	1445	15	15	1440	16	16
1255	118	26	1275	104	16	1270	104	15
1070	532	174	1055	611	194	1060	596	195
1350	58	53	1340	63	58	1345	56	53
1195	193	51	1195	194	49	1185	220	57
1170	231	66	1170	229	64	1155	269	77
1380	41	41	1375	43	43	1385	41	40
1205	179	46	1205	179	44	1205	176	44
1260	111	21	1255	119	23	1250	117	23
920	1253	465	915	1258	470	925	1238	467
1110	367	109	1110	381	112	1110	372	107
1185	218	61	1185	216	57	1185	220	57
1355	54	4	1360	50	2	1350	53	3
1230	147	34	1215	167	37	1225	145	30
1260	111	21	1260	111	20	1260	110	18
1130	324	97	1130	322	97	1110	372	107
1090	455	140	1070	531	163	1090	449	134
1460	12	12	1460	12	12	1440	16	16

SAT Scores

	Institutions with Over $40 Million in Federal Research, Alphabetically	2015 Median SAT	2015 National Rank	2015 Control Rank	2014 Median SAT	2014 National Rank	2014 Control Rank
Public	Virginia Commonwealth University	1095	395	138	1105	393	132
Public	Virginia Polytechnic Inst. and St. U.	1210	152	46	1215	157	43
Private	Wake Forest University						
Public	Washington State Univ. - Pullman	1030	641	239	1030	673	237
Private	Washington University in St. Louis	1460	15	15	1460	13	13
Public	Wayne State University	1070	461	170	1070	491	172
Private	Weill Cornell Medical College						
Public	West Virginia University	1110	338	117	1090	420	144
Private	Woods Hole Oceanographic Inst.						
Private	Yale University	1515	4	4	1505	3	3
Private	Yeshiva University	1250	115	88	1240	118	90

2013 Median SAT	2013 National Rank	2013 Control Rank	2012 Median SAT	2012 National Rank	2012 Control Rank	2011 Median SAT	2011 National Rank	2011 Control Rank
1105	423	125	1105	421	127	1080	505	158
1220	155	38	1215	167	37	1210	169	39
1030	727	233	1050	627	201	1065	582	188
1460	12	12	1490	7	7	1460	11	11
1050	616	203	1030	729	242	1010	831	277
1035	714	227	1055	611	194	1090	449	134
1500	5	5	1495	4	4	1500	2	2
1235	142	111	1220	152	118	1225	145	116

National Merit and Achievement Scholars

	Institutions with Over $40 Million in Federal Research, Alphabetically	2016 National Merit Scholars	2016 National Rank	2016 Control Rank	2015 National Merit Scholars	2015 National Rank	2015 Control Rank
Public	Arizona State University	109	19	9	112	17	7
Public	Auburn University	60	32	13	64	30	14
Public	Augusta University	2	209	96	3	193	87
Private	Baylor College of Medicine	0	331	187	0	326	188
Private	Boston University	56	34	20	35	60	31
Private	Brandeis University	11	115	56	12	114	59
Private	Brown University	100	21	12	76	24	14
Private	California Institute of Technology	44	46	27	45	48	27
Private	Carnegie Mellon University	55	35	21	51	44	25
Private	Case Western Reserve University	72	28	16	60	34	19
Public	Clemson University	43	47	20	55	41	19
Public	Cleveland State University	0	331	145	1	247	107
Private	Cold Spring Harbor Laboratory	0	331	187	0	326	188
Public	Colorado State Univ. - Fort Collins	9	127	66	4	173	80
Private	Columbia University	67	30	18	78	23	13
Private	Cornell University	81	23	13	72	26	16
Private	Dartmouth College	49	43	25	64	30	17
Private	Drexel University	4	169	91	7	143	77
Private	Duke University	106	20	11	108	19	11
Private	Emory University	54	38	22	58	38	21
Public	Florida International University	0	331	145	0	326	139
Public	Florida State University	22	80	41	22	84	41
Public	George Mason University	1	243	108	1	247	107
Private	George Washington University	17	92	43	17	96	48
Private	Georgetown University	33	63	33	32	68	36
Public	Georgia Institute of Technology	55	35	15	59	36	17
Private	Harvard University	233	3	2	209	4	3
Private	Icahn School of Med. at Mount Sinai	0	331	187	0	326	188
Public	Indiana University - Bloomington	52	39	17	68	28	12
Public	Iowa State University	35	60	28	33	64	31
Private	Johns Hopkins University	47	44	26	47	45	26
Public	Kansas State University	6	148	74	9	128	60
Public	Louisiana State Univ. - Baton Rouge	25	73	36	27	74	34
Private	Massachusetts Institute of Tech.	154	11	7	139	14	9
Private	Medical College of Wisconsin	0	331	187	0	326	188
Public	Medical University of South Carolina	0	331	145	0	326	139
Public	Michigan State University	34	62	30	43	51	23
Public	Mississippi State University	37	56	25	37	56	27
Public	Montana State University - Bozeman	12	112	58	7	143	67
Public	Naval Postgraduate School	0	331	145	0	326	139
Public	New Jersey Institute of Technology	2	209	96	0	326	139
Public	New Mexico State Univ. - Las Cruces	0	331	145	0	326	139
Private	New York University	15	100	47	12	114	59
Public	North Carolina State University	8	134	68	5	158	73
Private	Northeastern University	81	23	13	85	22	12
Private	Northwestern University	168	7	6	206	5	4
Public	Ohio State University - Columbus	19	85	45	18	93	46
Public	Oregon Health & Science University	0	331	145	0	326	139
Public	Oregon State University	8	134	68	4	173	80

2014 National Merit Scholars	2014 National Rank	2014 Control Rank	2013 National Merit Scholars	2013 National Rank	2013 Control Rank	2012 National Merit Scholars	2012 National Rank	2012 Control Rank
118	17	5	120	19	6	99	24	8
74	27	10	70	33	13	62	39	18
0	343	146	0	355	147	0	369	144
0	343	198	0	355	209	0	369	226
36	61	34	34	59	31	44	52	29
15	107	55	17	100	52	7	156	86
104	22	14	101	22	15	101	23	16
43	51	30	43	51	30	51	47	26
38	58	32	32	64	34	38	61	35
51	42	26	66	37	23	59	41	22
43	51	22	39	55	25	43	54	24
0	343	146	0	355	147	0	369	144
0	343	198	0	355	209	0	369	226
5	170	76	9	137	60	6	166	74
103	23	15	103	21	14	128	20	14
92	24	16	87	26	16	66	33	20
63	33	20	70	33	21	79	28	18
5	170	95	4	187	103	5	178	101
127	16	12	167	13	11	135	19	13
54	39	23	53	47	28	53	45	25
1	257	111	2	229	96	1	257	107
14	110	54	16	105	51	14	112	52
1	257	111	1	258	108	1	257	107
20	94	48	17	100	52	19	94	51
35	62	35	28	74	40	39	59	33
57	36	15	176	11	1	127	21	7
309	3	2	321	2	2	322	1	1
0	343	198	0	355	209	0	369	226
48	47	19	67	36	14	65	35	15
43	51	22	38	58	28	36	66	30
43	51	30	33	62	33	32	71	39
6	159	68	8	146	64	12	120	55
25	84	42	43	51	22	38	61	27
185	10	9	212	9	9	191	12	10
0	343	198	0	355	209	0	369	226
0	343	146	0	355	147	0	369	144
45	48	20	39	55	25	40	58	26
41	55	24	32	64	31	17	101	46
8	144	66	10	130	57	11	131	63
0	343	146	0	355	147	0	369	144
1	257	111	1	258	108	0	369	144
0	343	146	1	258	108	0	369	144
20	94	48	26	80	43	28	76	42
11	124	59	10	130	57	12	120	55
114	18	13	151	16	13	105	22	15
228	8	7	259	4	4	240	7	6
16	103	51	22	87	42	62	39	18
0	343	146	0	355	147	0	369	144
13	115	57	5	173	79	11	131	63

National Merit and Achievement Scholars

	Institutions with Over $40 Million in Federal Research, Alphabetically	2016 National Merit Scholars	2016 National Rank	2016 Control Rank	2015 National Merit Scholars	2015 National Rank	2015 Control Rank
Public	Penn. State Univ. - Hershey Med. Ctr.	0	331	145	0	326	139
Public	Pennsylvania State Univ. - Univ. Park	16	97	52	21	85	42
Private	Princeton University	117	18	10	146	11	8
Public	Purdue University - West Lafayette	125	15	6	94	21	10
Private	Rensselaer Polytechnic Institute	25	73	38	19	90	46
Private	Rice University	67	30	18	59	36	20
Private	Rockefeller University	0	331	187	0	326	188
Private	Rush University	0	331	187	0	326	188
Public	Rutgers University - New Brunswick	35	60	28	35	60	30
Public	San Diego State University	0	331	145	0	326	139
Private	Scripps Research Institute	0	331	187	0	326	188
Private	Stanford University	179	6	5	176	7	6
Public	Stony Brook University	24	77	39	25	77	37
Public	Temple University	0	331	145	1	247	107
Public	Texas A&M Univ. - College Station	122	16	7	142	13	5
Private	Thomas Jefferson University	0	331	187	0	326	188
Private	Tufts University	50	40	23	55	41	23
Private	Tulane University	39	54	31	33	64	34
Public	Uniformed Services Univ. of the HS	0	331	145	0	326	139
Public	University at Albany	0	331	145	0	326	139
Public	University at Buffalo	1	243	108	1	247	107
Public	University of Alabama - Birmingham	22	80	41	24	79	38
Public	University of Alabama - Huntsville	1	243	108	2	217	91
Public	University of Alaska - Fairbanks	0	331	145	0	326	139
Public	University of Arizona	43	47	20	65	29	13
Public	Univ. of Arkansas for Med. Sciences	0	331	145	0	326	139
Public	University of California - Berkeley	161	8	2	129	16	6
Public	University of California - Davis	4	169	79	3	193	87
Public	University of California - Irvine	3	190	86	2	217	91
Public	University of California - Los Angeles	43	47	20	43	51	23
Public	University of California - Riverside	1	243	108	1	247	107
Public	University of California - San Diego	19	85	45	18	93	46
Public	Univ. of California - San Francisco	0	331	145	0	326	139
Public	Univ. of California - Santa Barbara	3	190	86	4	173	80
Public	University of California - Santa Cruz	0	331	145	0	326	139
Public	University of Central Florida	77	26	11	69	27	11
Private	University of Chicago	277	2	1	294	1	1
Public	University of Cincinnati - Cincinnati	50	40	18	44	49	22
Public	University of Colorado - Boulder	10	120	61	5	158	73
Public	U. of Colorado - Denv./Anschutz Med.	0	331	145	0	326	139
Public	Univ. of Connecticut - Health Center	0	331	145	0	326	139
Public	University of Connecticut - Storrs	2	209	96	2	217	91
Private	University of Dayton	1	243	136	4	173	94
Public	University of Delaware	3	190	86	3	193	87
Public	University of Florida	158	9	3	146	11	4
Public	University of Georgia	39	54	24	42	54	25
Public	University of Hawaii - Manoa	0	331	145	0	326	139
Public	University of Houston - Univ. Park	25	73	36	29	72	33
Public	University of Idaho	17	92	50	23	80	39

2014 National Merit Scholars	2014 National Rank	2014 Control Rank	2013 National Merit Scholars	2013 National Rank	2013 Control Rank	2012 National Merit Scholars	2012 National Rank	2012 Control Rank
0	343	146	0	355	147	0	369	144
24	87	44	16	105	51	23	84	39
179	11	10	192	10	10	216	9	8
28	75	36	20	93	45	16	103	48
32	67	37	29	71	38	21	87	47
64	31	18	74	29	19	162	13	11
0	343	198	0	355	209	0	369	226
0	343	198	0	355	209	0	369	226
35	62	28	24	85	40	24	83	38
0	343	146	0	355	147	0	369	144
0	343	198	0	355	209	0	369	226
249	5	4	219	8	8	242	6	5
11	124	59	14	114	55	12	120	55
1	257	111	0	355	147	0	369	144
165	12	2	158	14	3	137	18	6
0	343	198	0	355	209	0	369	226
64	31	18	69	35	22	51	47	26
44	50	29	30	69	37	39	59	33
0	343	146	0	355	147	0	369	144
0	343	146	0	355	147	0	369	144
2	223	98	1	258	108	1	257	107
21	92	46	27	77	36	12	120	55
1	257	111	2	229	96	1	257	107
1	257	111	0	355	147	0	369	144
71	28	11	72	31	12	85	26	10
0	343	146	0	355	147	0	369	144
114	18	6	111	20	7	92	25	9
1	257	111	3	204	90	2	231	97
4	183	82	0	355	147	2	231	97
32	67	31	18	98	48	27	78	35
0	343	146	0	355	147	0	369	144
14	110	54	15	110	54	12	120	55
0	343	146	0	355	147	0	369	144
3	203	92	1	258	108	4	188	83
0	343	146	1	258	108	0	369	144
84	26	9	64	38	15	68	32	13
315	1	1	333	1	1	316	2	2
49	45	17	30	69	33	38	61	27
6	159	68	6	160	72	6	166	74
0	343	146	0	355	147	0	369	144
0	343	146	0	355	147	0	369	144
1	257	111	5	173	79	1	257	107
3	203	112	2	229	134	4	188	106
4	183	82	2	229	96	2	231	97
32	67	31	23	86	41	147	15	3
45	48	20	61	43	19	56	43	20
0	343	146	0	355	147	0	369	144
33	64	29	26	80	38	30	74	33
23	88	45	25	84	39	12	120	55

National Merit and Achievement Scholars

	Institutions with Over $40 Million in Federal Research, Alphabetically	2016 National Merit Scholars	2016 National Rank	2016 Control Rank	2015 National Merit Scholars	2015 National Rank	2015 Control Rank
Public	University of Illinois - Chicago	2	209	96	1	247	107
Public	Univ. of Illinois - Urbana-Champaign	29	67	32	26	75	35
Public	University of Iowa	26	70	35	20	87	43
Public	University of Kansas - Lawrence	18	91	49	26	75	35
Public	University of Kansas Medical Center	0	331	145	0	326	139
Public	University of Kentucky	99	22	10	111	18	8
Public	University of Louisville	20	83	43	19	90	45
Public	University of Maryland - Baltimore	0	331	145	0	326	139
Public	Univ. of Maryland - Baltimore County	3	190	86	2	217	91
Public	University of Maryland - College Park	55	35	15	61	33	15
Public	Univ. of Massachusetts - Amherst	1	243	108	1	247	107
Public	Univ. of Mass. Med. Sch. - Worcester	0	331	145	0	326	139
Private	University of Miami	36	57	32	35	60	31
Public	University of Michigan - Ann Arbor	60	32	13	56	40	18
Public	University of Minnesota - Twin Cities	150	12	5	147	10	3
Public	University of Missouri - Columbia	13	108	56	18	93	46
Public	University of Nebraska - Lincoln	36	57	26	47	45	20
Public	University of Nebraska Medical Ctr.	0	331	145	0	326	139
Public	University of Nevada - Reno	10	120	61	16	98	50
Public	Univ. of New Hampshire - Durham	0	331	145	0	326	139
Public	Univ. of New Mexico - Albuquerque	20	83	43	14	106	55
Public	Univ. of North Carolina - Chapel Hill	28	69	34	20	87	43
Private	University of Notre Dame	43	47	28	57	39	22
Public	University of Oklahoma - HSC	0	331	145	0	326	139
Public	University of Oklahoma - Norman	279	1	1	288	2	1
Public	University of Oregon	9	127	66	6	152	69
Private	University of Pennsylvania	134	14	9	139	14	9
Public	University of Pittsburgh - Pittsburgh	25	73	36	16	98	50
Public	University of Rhode Island	0	331	145	0	326	139
Private	University of Rochester	24	77	39	37	56	30
Public	Univ of South Carolina - Columbia	36	57	26	46	47	21
Public	University of South Florida - Tampa	12	112	58	9	128	60
Private	University of Southern California	230	4	3	226	3	2
Public	University of Tennessee - Knoxville	19	85	45	23	80	39
Public	University of Texas - Austin	74	27	12	60	34	16
Public	University of Texas - El Paso	0	331	145	0	326	139
Public	University of Texas HSC - Houston	0	331	145	0	326	139
Public	Univ. of Texas HSC - San Antonio	0	331	145	0	326	139
Public	U. of Texas MD Anderson Cancer Ctr.	0	331	145	0	326	139
Public	U. of Texas Med. Branch - Galveston	0	331	145	0	326	139
Public	Univ. of Texas SW Med. Ctr. - Dallas	0	331	145	0	326	139
Public	University of Utah	33	63	31	33	64	31
Public	University of Vermont	10	120	61	10	120	57
Public	University of Virginia	29	67	32	36	59	29
Public	University of Washington - Seattle	23	79	40	12	114	56
Public	University of Wisconsin - Madison	17	92	50	15	102	53
Public	University of Wyoming	2	209	96	5	158	73
Public	Utah State University	0	331	145	1	247	107
Private	Vanderbilt University	220	5	4	206	5	4

2014 National Merit Scholars	2014 National Rank	2014 Control Rank	2013 National Merit Scholars	2013 National Rank	2013 Control Rank	2012 National Merit Scholars	2012 National Rank	2012 Control Rank
3	203	92	3	204	90	3	213	91
39	57	26	88	25	10	70	31	12
26	81	40	16	105	51	23	84	39
30	73	34	28	74	35	37	65	29
0	343	146	0	355	147	0	369	144
109	20	7	97	23	8	71	30	11
18	98	48	17	100	49	19	94	44
0	343	146	0	355	147	0	369	144
9	136	63	9	137	60	5	178	78
63	33	14	62	40	17	66	33	14
3	203	92	1	258	108	1	257	107
0	343	146	0	355	147	0	369	144
50	44	28	62	40	24	41	56	32
66	30	13	63	39	16	53	45	21
141	15	4	135	17	4	143	17	5
30	73	34	12	122	56	29	75	34
33	64	29	51	48	20	46	50	22
0	343	146	0	355	147	0	369	144
14	110	54	8	146	64	16	103	48
0	343	146	0	355	147	0	369	144
19	97	47	21	89	43	16	103	48
49	45	17	47	50	21	147	15	3
51	42	26	56	45	26	57	42	23
0	343	146	0	355	147	0	369	144
313	2	1	176	11	1	196	11	2
10	132	61	10	130	57	8	147	68
143	13	11	152	15	12	153	14	12
28	75	36	29	71	34	27	78	35
0	343	146	0	355	147	0	369	144
28	75	40	26	80	43	31	72	40
56	38	16	62	40	17	46	50	22
9	136	63	8	146	64	25	82	37
240	6	5	250	5	5	270	3	3
31	71	33	41	54	24	21	87	41
71	28	11	74	29	11	63	38	17
0	343	146	0	355	147	0	369	144
0	343	146	0	355	147	0	369	144
0	343	146	0	355	147	0	369	144
0	343	146	0	355	147	0	369	144
0	343	146	0	355	147	0	369	144
0	343	146	0	355	147	0	369	144
26	81	40	33	62	30	21	87	41
10	132	61	9	137	60	7	156	71
38	58	27	39	55	25	35	69	32
18	98	48	19	96	47	13	116	54
16	103	51	20	93	45	21	87	41
4	183	82	6	160	72	3	213	91
1	257	111	0	355	147	0	369	144
260	4	3	285	3	3	207	10	9

National Merit and Achievement Scholars

	Institutions with Over $40 Million in Federal Research, Alphabetically	2016 National Merit Scholars	2016 National Rank	2016 Control Rank	2015 National Merit Scholars	2015 National Rank	2015 Control Rank
Public	Virginia Commonwealth University	10	120	61	0	326	139
Public	Virginia Polytechnic Inst. and St. U.	0	331	145	4	173	80
Private	Wake Forest University	2	209	114	0	326	188
Public	Washington State Univ. - Pullman	2	209	96	5	158	73
Private	Washington University in St. Louis	33	63	33	32	68	36
Public	Wayne State University	10	120	61	7	143	67
Private	Weill Cornell Medical College	0	331	187	0	326	188
Public	West Virginia University	19	85	45	10	120	57
Private	Woods Hole Oceanographic Inst.	0	331	187	0	326	188
Private	Yale University	147	13	8	166	8	7
Private	Yeshiva University	3	190	105	0	326	188

2014 National Merit Scholars	2014 National Rank	2014 Control Rank	2013 National Merit Scholars	2013 National Rank	2013 Control Rank	2012 National Merit Scholars	2012 National Rank	2012 Control Rank
5	170	76	1	258	108	1	257	107
4	183	82	17	100	49	17	101	46
9	136	74	9	137	78	4	188	106
6	159	68	3	204	90	4	188	83
223	9	8	223	7	7	234	8	7
9	136	63	8	146	64	8	147	68
0	343	198	0	355	209	0	369	226
27	80	39	21	89	43	16	103	48
0	343	198	0	355	209	0	369	226
237	7	6	224	6	6	249	5	4
2	223	126	3	204	115	1	257	151

Change: Research		Total Research in Constant 1983 Dollars					
Institutions with Over $40 Million in Federal Research, Alphabetically		2015 Total Research x $1000	2006 Total Research x $1000	Net Change in Constant Dollars	Percent Change in Constant Dollars	Net Change in National Rank	Net Change in Control Rank
Public	Arizona State University	128,864	79,792	49,071	61.5%	30	20
Public	Auburn University	42,444	49,989	-7,545	-15.1%	-13	-7
Public	Augusta University	21,621	24,170	-2,549	-10.5%	-4	-2
Private	Baylor College of Medicine	166,054	182,684	-16,630	-9.1%	-12	-7
Private	Boston University	118,828	100,993	17,834	17.7%	5	2
Private	Brandeis University	21,926	22,527	-602	-2.7%	4	-1
Private	Brown University	91,397	62,397	29,001	46.5%	20	4
Private	California Institute of Technology	111,986	106,783	5,203	4.9%	0	0
Private	Carnegie Mellon University	77,192	83,961	-6,769	-8.1%	-7	-4
Private	Case Western Reserve University	127,733	145,896	-18,163	-12.4%	-18	-4
Public	Clemson University	38,578	71,055	-32,477	-45.7%	-42	-32
Public	Cleveland State University	18,093	5,727	12,366	215.9%	83	63
Private	Cold Spring Harbor Laboratory	27,021					
Public	Colorado State Univ. - Fort Collins	98,564	100,352	-1,788	-1.8%	-9	-6
Private	Columbia University	263,662	209,381	54,281	25.9%	4	0
Private	Cornell University	203,459	175,377	28,083	16.0%	1	1
Private	Dartmouth College	65,008	79,129	-14,121	-17.8%	-16	-5
Private	Drexel University	39,059	38,201	858	2.2%	3	-1
Private	Duke University	328,518	259,612	68,906	26.5%	4	2
Private	Emory University	183,371	136,700	46,671	34.1%	9	4
Public	Florida International University	39,782	25,115	14,667	58.4%	28	22
Public	Florida State University	75,787	73,344	2,443	3.3%	1	1
Public	George Mason University	28,679	19,906	8,773	44.1%	25	23
Private	George Washington University	72,181	45,034	27,147	60.3%	33	7
Private	Georgetown University	50,213	46,842	3,370	7.2%	2	-2
Public	Georgia Institute of Technology	241,671	174,199	67,473	38.7%	11	7
Private	Harvard University	304,915	179,042	125,873	70.3%	18	6
Private	Icahn School of Med. at Mount Sinai	162,266	107,948	54,319	50.3%	19	5
Public	Indiana University - Bloomington	144,121	56,105	88,016	156.9%	59	43
Public	Iowa State University	94,367	87,711	6,655	7.6%	-4	0
Private	Johns Hopkins University	733,859	592,641	141,218	23.8%	0	0
Public	Kansas State University	57,482	48,892	8,590	17.6%	11	11
Public	Louisiana State Univ. - Baton Rouge	87,461	99,216	-11,754	-11.8%	-14	-9
Private	Massachusetts Institute of Tech.	274,166	237,356	36,811	15.5%	0	0
Private	Medical College of Wisconsin	63,611	58,135	5,476	9.4%	5	-1
Public	Medical University of South Carolina	77,736	69,559	8,177	11.8%	10	8
Public	Michigan State University	165,982	141,484	24,498	17.3%	3	1
Public	Mississippi State University	69,208	75,036	-5,828	-7.8%	-9	-6
Public	Montana State University - Bozeman	31,431	44,420	-12,990	-29.2%	-17	-11
Public	Naval Postgraduate School	23,714	22,434	1,281	5.7%	7	7
Public	New Jersey Institute of Technology	30,766	30,653	113	0.4%	3	5
Public	New Mexico State Univ. - Las Cruces	40,538	65,189	-24,651	-37.8%	-32	-23
Private	New York University	161,219	112,273	48,945	43.6%	15	3
Public	North Carolina State University	147,581	130,753	16,828	12.9%	2	1
Private	Northeastern University	36,920	26,272	10,648	40.5%	20	3
Private	Northwestern University	200,241	165,936	34,304	20.7%	4	1
Public	Ohio State University - Columbus	237,880	257,735	-19,855	-7.7%	-11	-7
Public	Oregon Health & Science University	103,826	107,536	-3,710	-3.5%	-8	-5
Public	Oregon State University	77,525	74,913	2,612	3.5%	0	1

Federal Research in Constant 1983 Dollars						Non-Federal Research in Constant 1983 Dollars					
2015 Federal Research x $1000	2006 Federal Research x $1000	Net Change in Constant Dollars	Percent Change in Constant Dollars	Net Change in National Rank	Net Change in Control Rank	2015 Non-Federal Research x $1000	2006 Non-Federal Research x $1000	Net Change in Constant Dollars	Percent Change in Constant Dollars	Net Change in National Rank	Net Change in Control Rank
59,655	43,419	16,237	37.4%	18	13	69,208	36,374	32,835	90.3%	18	20
15,302	17,993	-2,691	-15.0%	-5	-1	27,142	31,996	-4,854	-15.2%	-35	-20
16,147	16,418	-272	-1.7%	10	9	5,475	7,751	-2,277	-29.4%	-29	-19
82,001	113,662	-31,661	-27.9%	-22	-9	84,053	69,022	15,031	21.8%	-3	-3
81,895	94,255	-12,360	-13.1%	-8	-2	36,933	6,738	30,195	448.1%	104	22
14,927	16,272	-1,345	-8.3%	5	0	6,999	6,256	743	11.9%	-7	-3
40,821	38,294	2,527	6.6%	12	0	50,576	24,103	26,473	109.8%	31	4
85,915	98,218	-12,304	-12.5%	-7	0	26,071	8,565	17,506	204.4%	58	10
59,773	73,247	-13,474	-18.4%	-9	-1	17,419	10,714	6,705	62.6%	18	-2
98,301	121,288	-22,987	-19.0%	-14	-5	29,432	24,608	4,824	19.6%	-2	-5
14,457	22,231	-7,774	-35.0%	-25	-18	24,121	48,823	-24,703	-50.6%	-62	-39
13,317	2,038	11,279	553.3%	148	111	4,776	3,689	1,087	29.5%	9	12
15,661						11,360					
68,208	72,164	-3,956	-5.5%	2	1	30,356	28,188	2,168	7.7%	-13	-5
184,444	178,264	6,180	3.5%	4	1	79,218	31,117	48,101	154.6%	34	6
88,470	100,070	-11,599	-11.6%	-6	0	114,989	75,307	39,682	52.7%	8	0
46,542	55,484	-8,942	-16.1%	-11	-4	18,467	23,646	-5,179	-21.9%	-33	-12
21,459	27,064	-5,605	-20.7%	-8	-3	17,601	11,137	6,464	58.0%	13	-2
178,294	163,737	14,557	8.9%	4	1	150,224	95,875	54,349	56.7%	6	0
110,614	105,845	4,769	4.5%	5	3	72,758	30,855	41,902	135.8%	26	1
21,480	18,133	3,347	18.5%	18	17	18,302	6,983	11,320	162.1%	47	40
42,635	43,602	-967	-2.2%	0	2	33,151	29,741	3,410	11.5%	-12	-4
17,273	14,188	3,084	21.7%	24	20	11,406	5,717	5,689	99.5%	31	26
43,305	29,715	13,590	45.7%	33	7	28,876	15,319	13,557	88.5%	28	2
27,856	36,455	-8,599	-23.6%	-3	0	22,357	10,387	11,970	115.2%	35	5
174,942	101,837	73,104	71.8%	22	11	66,730	72,361	-5,632	-7.8%	-21	-9
169,298	159,406	9,892	6.2%	2	2	135,617	19,636	115,981	590.7%	100	24
105,221	88,862	16,359	18.4%	11	8	57,045	19,085	37,960	198.9%	55	10
65,839	26,967	38,872	144.1%	62	45	78,282	29,138	49,144	168.7%	37	29
36,211	41,309	-5,098	-12.3%	-10	-6	58,156	46,403	11,753	25.3%	-4	2
634,887	516,575	118,312	22.9%	0	0	98,972	76,066	22,906	30.1%	2	-4
21,269	20,802	467	2.2%	6	6	36,213	28,090	8,123	28.9%	0	6
26,262	31,277	-5,014	-16.0%	-2	-2	61,199	67,939	-6,740	-9.9%	-22	-11
155,339	188,211	-32,872	-17.5%	-7	-3	118,828	49,145	69,683	141.8%	32	6
34,966	39,561	-4,595	-11.6%	-4	-3	28,645	18,574	10,071	54.2%	18	-1
37,428	41,113	-3,685	-9.0%	-5	-1	40,308	28,446	11,862	41.7%	4	7
81,788	66,818	14,970	22.4%	10	9	84,194	74,666	9,528	12.8%	-4	-1
25,275	37,168	-11,894	-32.0%	-17	-12	43,933	37,868	6,065	16.0%	-7	0
20,054	29,776	-9,721	-32.6%	-19	-14	11,376	14,645	-3,268	-22.3%	-30	-18
22,978	21,544	1,434	6.7%	7	7	736	890	-154	-17.3%	-36	-18
16,137	14,022	2,115	15.1%	21	18	14,630	16,631	-2,002	-12.0%	-22	-12
24,978	40,241	-15,262	-37.9%	-31	-21	15,560	24,949	-9,389	-37.6%	-46	-27
104,280	74,783	29,497	39.4%	21	8	56,939	37,490	19,449	51.9%	5	-4
62,582	51,862	10,720	20.7%	12	6	84,999	78,891	6,108	7.7%	-7	-1
25,019	14,252	10,767	75.5%	45	9	11,901	12,021	-119	-1.0%	-17	-9
123,169	98,767	24,402	24.7%	12	7	77,071	67,169	9,903	14.7%	-7	-7
129,896	124,818	5,078	4.1%	-1	-1	107,984	132,918	-24,933	-18.8%	-15	-11
77,845	88,188	-10,343	-11.7%	-8	-7	25,980	19,348	6,632	34.3%	3	9
48,080	46,063	2,016	4.4%	3	2	29,446	28,850	596	2.1%	-18	-10

Change: Research		Total Research in Constant 1983 Dollars					
Institutions with Over $40 Million in Federal Research, Alphabetically		2015 Total Research x $1000	2006 Total Research x $1000	Net Change in Constant Dollars	Percent Change in Constant Dollars	Net Change in National Rank	Net Change in Control Rank
Public	Penn. State Univ. - Hershey Med. Ctr.	29,169	30,278	-1,109	-3.7%	-1	2
Public	Pennsylvania State Univ. - Univ. Park	218,015	224,239	-6,224	-2.8%	-9	-6
Private	Princeton University	86,943	74,344	12,599	16.9%	7	1
Public	Purdue University - West Lafayette	159,245	147,356	11,889	8.1%	-7	-4
Private	Rensselaer Polytechnic Institute	32,597	27,885	4,713	16.9%	13	-1
Private	Rice University	45,306	26,299	19,006	72.3%	36	6
Private	Rockefeller University	103,399	85,111	18,288	21.5%	6	-1
Private	Rush University	25,232	32,870	-7,638	-23.2%	-16	-6
Public	Rutgers University - New Brunswick	193,836	111,021	82,816	74.6%	25	18
Public	San Diego State University	24,301	29,149	-4,848	-16.6%	-9	-4
Private	Scripps Research Institute	122,624	145,150	-22,526	-15.5%	-18	-4
Private	Stanford University	309,510	268,350	41,160	15.3%	0	-1
Public	Stony Brook University	70,060	92,704	-22,645	-24.4%	-21	-13
Public	Temple University	67,150	31,504	35,647	113.2%	46	37
Public	Texas A&M Univ. - College Station	266,931	224,837	42,094	18.7%	0	0
Private	Thomas Jefferson University	38,186	42,270	-4,084	-9.7%	-7	-3
Private	Tufts University	51,873	50,954	919	1.8%	-3	-3
Private	Tulane University	44,726	45,198	-473	-1.0%	0	-3
Public	Uniformed Services Univ. of the HS	115,286	26,755	88,532	330.9%	95	72
Public	University at Albany	35,203	108,397	-73,195	-67.5%	-81	-58
Public	University at Buffalo	117,189	117,704	-515	-0.4%	-6	-4
Public	University of Alabama - Birmingham	162,660	130,950	31,709	24.2%	8	5
Public	University of Alabama - Huntsville	27,051	23,402	3,648	15.6%	12	11
Public	University of Alaska - Fairbanks	44,562	60,636	-16,074	-26.5%	-21	-13
Public	University of Arizona	189,245	211,713	-22,468	-10.6%	-13	-6
Public	Univ. of Arkansas for Med. Sciences	42,278	42,620	-341	-0.8%	2	4
Public	University of California - Berkeley	238,806	215,738	23,068	10.7%	-2	0
Public	University of California - Davis	225,383	226,393	-1,010	-0.4%	-9	-6
Public	University of California - Irvine	100,164	118,620	-18,456	-15.6%	-18	-12
Public	University of California - Los Angeles	316,649	320,621	-3,972	-1.2%	-4	-3
Public	University of California - Riverside	43,569	49,316	-5,748	-11.7%	-10	-4
Public	University of California - San Diego	349,136	298,208	50,928	17.1%	2	2
Public	Univ. of California - San Francisco	359,617	314,558	45,059	14.3%	2	2
Public	Univ. of California - Santa Barbara	68,161	68,917	-756	-1.1%	0	1
Public	University of California - Santa Cruz	47,088	45,091	1,997	4.4%	4	5
Public	University of Central Florida	54,191	42,669	11,521	27.0%	16	14
Private	University of Chicago	128,566	120,624	7,942	6.6%	-2	1
Public	University of Cincinnati - Cincinnati	130,365	116,219	14,146	12.2%	4	2
Public	University of Colorado - Boulder	128,846	98,876	29,971	30.3%	14	8
Public	U. of Colorado - Denv./Anschutz Med.	127,844	101,948	25,897	25.4%	8	4
Public	Univ. of Connecticut - Health Center	25,820	42,950	-17,130	-39.9%	-29	-21
Public	University of Connecticut - Storrs	54,497	42,069	12,428	29.5%	21	18
Private	University of Dayton	29,787	27,294	2,494	9.1%	10	-1
Public	University of Delaware	53,595	45,431	8,164	18.0%	8	8
Public	University of Florida	223,360	223,425	-65	0.0%	-7	-4
Public	University of Georgia	105,423	127,950	-22,527	-17.6%	-16	-11
Public	University of Hawaii - Manoa	99,924	98,631	1,293	1.3%	-4	-2
Public	University of Houston - Univ. Park	40,211	29,894	10,317	34.5%	16	14
Public	University of Idaho	30,471	34,320	-3,849	-11.2%	-4	0

Federal Research in Constant 1983 Dollars						Non-Federal Research in Constant 1983 Dollars					
2015 Federal Research x $1000	2006 Federal Research x $1000	Net Change in Constant Dollars	Percent Change in Constant Dollars	Net Change in National Rank	Net Change in Control Rank	2015 Non-Federal Research x $1000	2006 Non-Federal Research x $1000	Net Change in Constant Dollars	Percent Change in Constant Dollars	Net Change in National Rank	Net Change in Control Rank
19,131	18,553	578	3.1%	5	5	10,038	11,725	-1,687	-14.4%	-27	-17
142,988	126,534	16,454	13.0%	1	-1	75,027	97,705	-22,678	-23.2%	-28	-15
50,391	46,561	3,831	8.2%	4	1	36,552	27,783	8,769	31.6%	3	-5
66,714	62,204	4,511	7.3%	5	4	92,530	85,152	7,378	8.7%	-6	0
18,966	17,657	1,309	7.4%	13	2	13,631	10,228	3,404	33.3%	7	-2
23,562	21,288	2,274	10.7%	9	1	21,743	5,011	16,732	333.9%	78	15
26,158	37,037	-10,879	-29.4%	-14	-4	77,241	48,074	29,167	60.7%	11	-2
16,660	17,797	-1,137	-6.4%	5	-1	8,572	15,073	-6,501	-43.1%	-48	-15
102,243	46,911	55,332	118.0%	42	28	91,593	64,110	27,483	42.9%	7	8
13,893	13,967	-74	-0.5%	13	12	10,408	15,182	-4,775	-31.4%	-38	-24
87,492	106,097	-18,606	-17.5%	-13	-4	35,132	39,052	-3,920	-10.0%	-20	-13
206,086	213,381	-7,295	-3.4%	0	0	103,424	54,969	48,455	88.1%	18	3
36,718	44,636	-7,918	-17.7%	-12	-8	33,342	48,069	-14,727	-30.6%	-33	-17
38,286	20,112	18,174	90.4%	47	38	28,864	11,392	17,472	153.4%	45	38
93,115	95,399	-2,284	-2.4%	2	-2	173,816	129,438	44,378	34.3%	1	1
18,685	32,616	-13,931	-42.7%	-31	-7	19,502	9,654	9,847	102.0%	32	5
38,362	37,915	446	1.2%	9	0	13,511	13,039	473	3.6%	-12	-9
26,858	33,209	-6,350	-19.1%	-4	0	17,867	11,989	5,878	49.0%	9	-2
95,443	15,591	79,852	512.2%	121	89	19,843	11,164	8,680	77.8%	22	21
25,161	41,025	-15,865	-38.7%	-31	-22	10,042	67,372	-57,330	-85.1%	-135	-95
55,587	60,510	-4,923	-8.1%	-6	-5	61,601	57,193	4,408	7.7%	-16	-6
103,743	115,749	-12,007	-10.4%	-8	-5	58,917	15,201	43,716	287.6%	70	56
21,247	17,636	3,612	20.5%	21	18	5,803	5,766	37	0.6%	-11	-6
25,212	38,850	-13,638	-35.1%	-24	-17	19,350	21,786	-2,436	-11.2%	-26	-15
84,868	119,170	-34,301	-28.8%	-23	-14	104,377	92,543	11,834	12.8%	-3	0
16,152	26,127	-9,974	-38.2%	-21	-15	26,126	16,493	9,633	58.4%	13	15
109,180	103,405	5,775	5.6%	6	3	129,626	112,334	17,293	15.4%	-2	0
103,076	98,060	5,016	5.1%	5	0	122,307	128,333	-6,026	-4.7%	-6	-4
54,463	67,160	-12,698	-18.9%	-13	-10	45,702	51,460	-5,758	-11.2%	-24	-13
154,101	191,178	-37,078	-19.4%	-10	-5	162,549	129,443	33,106	25.6%	-1	-1
19,995	22,925	-2,930	-12.8%	-8	-5	23,573	26,391	-2,818	-10.7%	-28	-16
191,898	183,250	8,648	4.7%	5	3	157,238	114,958	42,280	36.8%	2	2
170,918	183,587	-12,669	-6.9%	-3	-2	188,699	130,971	57,728	44.1%	1	1
36,579	41,947	-5,368	-12.8%	-10	-6	31,582	26,970	4,612	17.1%	-7	0
29,127	26,231	2,896	11.0%	17	12	17,961	18,860	-899	-4.8%	-16	-7
26,107	15,004	11,103	74.0%	46	37	28,084	27,666	418	1.5%	-20	-9
92,816	100,146	-7,331	-7.3%	-5	0	35,751	20,478	15,273	74.6%	26	0
79,946	79,708	238	0.3%	0	1	50,419	36,510	13,909	38.1%	1	6
109,111	88,370	20,741	23.5%	16	7	19,735	10,505	9,230	87.9%	29	26
84,954	87,402	-2,448	-2.8%	0	-2	42,890	14,546	28,344	194.9%	58	48
13,889	22,878	-8,989	-39.3%	-29	-21	11,931	20,072	-8,140	-40.6%	-44	-27
29,314	26,445	2,870	10.9%	17	12	25,183	15,624	9,558	61.2%	12	15
23,796	22,433	1,362	6.1%	6	0	5,992	4,860	1,132	23.3%	5	-1
34,875	31,466	3,409	10.8%	13	10	18,720	13,965	4,755	34.0%	8	11
89,796	98,112	-8,316	-8.5%	-2	-5	133,564	125,313	8,250	6.6%	-3	-1
40,802	36,607	4,195	11.5%	17	15	64,621	91,344	-26,722	-29.3%	-32	-17
63,782	79,976	-16,194	-20.2%	-8	-7	36,142	18,655	17,487	93.7%	35	32
17,402	15,235	2,167	14.2%	20	17	22,809	14,659	8,150	55.6%	11	12
15,829	18,577	-2,747	-14.8%	-8	-5	14,641	15,743	-1,102	-7.0%	-19	-9

Change: Research		Total Research in Constant 1983 Dollars					
Institutions with Over $40 Million in Federal Research, Alphabetically		2015 Total Research x $1000	2006 Total Research x $1000	Net Change in Constant Dollars	Percent Change in Constant Dollars	Net Change in National Rank	Net Change in Control Rank
Public	University of Illinois - Chicago	110,002	131,243	-21,240	-16.2%	-18	-13
Public	Univ. of Illinois - Urbana-Champaign	195,992	188,146	7,846	4.2%	-8	-2
Public	University of Iowa	135,190	136,846	-1,656	-1.2%	-6	-6
Public	University of Kansas - Lawrence	55,032	51,835	3,197	6.2%	3	4
Public	University of Kansas Medical Center	27,247	25,584	1,663	6.5%	9	8
Public	University of Kentucky	103,918	127,996	-24,078	-18.8%	-19	-13
Public	University of Louisville	51,136	53,683	-2,548	-4.7%	-8	-4
Public	University of Maryland - Baltimore	121,125	160,118	-38,993	-24.4%	-23	-16
Public	Univ. of Maryland - Baltimore County	21,688	25,965	-4,277	-16.5%	-6	-4
Public	University of Maryland - College Park	160,675	139,962	20,713	14.8%	-1	-1
Public	Univ. of Massachusetts - Amherst	62,941	53,446	9,495	17.8%	8	9
Public	Univ. of Mass. Med. Sch. - Worcester	79,908	61,814	18,094	29.3%	17	14
Private	University of Miami	104,724	84,360	20,364	24.1%	11	1
Public	University of Michigan - Ann Arbor	415,069	316,273	98,796	31.2%	2	2
Public	University of Minnesota - Twin Cities	269,410	235,036	34,374	14.6%	-1	-1
Public	University of Missouri - Columbia	77,703	85,041	-7,338	-8.6%	-8	-3
Public	University of Nebraska - Lincoln	83,041	85,282	-2,242	-2.6%	-7	-1
Public	University of Nebraska Medical Ctr.	46,287	42,676	3,611	8.5%	7	7
Public	University of Nevada - Reno	26,616	39,082	-12,466	-31.9%	-18	-11
Public	Univ. of New Hampshire - Durham	41,719	45,483	-3,763	-8.3%	-8	-4
Public	Univ. of New Mexico - Albuquerque	71,603	71,601	2	0.0%	-1	-1
Public	Univ. of North Carolina - Chapel Hill	299,809	175,341	124,468	71.0%	20	12
Private	University of Notre Dame	54,630	31,036	23,594	76.0%	35	6
Public	University of Oklahoma - HSC	43,249	30,701	12,549	40.9%	20	18
Public	University of Oklahoma - Norman	29,390	39,911	-10,521	-26.4%	-14	-8
Public	University of Oregon	20,820	22,581	-1,761	-7.8%	-3	-1
Private	University of Pennsylvania	264,505	267,108	-2,603	-1.0%	-8	-3
Public	University of Pittsburgh - Pittsburgh	272,065	209,467	62,598	29.9%	8	7
Public	University of Rhode Island	27,496	27,932	-436	-1.6%	3	6
Private	University of Rochester	110,099	144,867	-34,768	-24.0%	-23	-6
Public	Univ. of South Carolina - Columbia	58,012	60,741	-2,729	-4.5%	-2	0
Public	University of South Florida - Tampa	134,065	112,975	21,089	18.7%	6	4
Private	University of Southern California	207,626	177,863	29,763	16.7%	1	1
Public	University of Tennessee - Knoxville	74,581	66,482	8,099	12.2%	7	6
Public	University of Texas - Austin	176,088	170,445	5,643	3.3%	-3	-1
Public	University of Texas - El Paso	24,743	12,707	12,036	94.7%	48	38
Public	University of Texas HSC - Houston	74,788	69,203	5,585	8.1%	6	5
Public	Univ. of Texas HSC - San Antonio	54,352	59,281	-4,928	-8.3%	-8	-4
Public	U. of Texas MD Anderson Cancer Ctr.	266,023	180,836	85,188	47.1%	10	6
Public	U. of Texas Med. Branch - Galveston	55,383	71,084	-15,701	-22.1%	-14	-11
Public	Univ. of Texas SW Med. Ctr. - Dallas	140,073	131,662	8,411	6.4%	-3	-4
Public	University of Utah	162,603	98,051	64,552	65.8%	29	21
Public	University of Vermont	36,418	48,139	-11,722	-24.3%	-21	-13
Public	University of Virginia	108,468	94,332	14,137	15.0%	6	6
Public	University of Washington - Seattle	351,464	307,446	44,018	14.3%	2	2
Public	University of Wisconsin - Madison	299,526	328,682	-29,155	-8.9%	-9	-6
Public	University of Wyoming	17,533	35,327	-17,794	-50.4%	-41	-33
Public	Utah State University	55,492	54,789	704	1.3%	2	3
Private	Vanderbilt University	197,861	148,910	48,951	32.9%	5	1

Federal Research in Constant 1983 Dollars						Non-Federal Research in Constant 1983 Dollars					
2015 Federal Research x $1000	2006 Federal Research x $1000	Net Change in Constant Dollars	Percent Change in Constant Dollars	Net Change in National Rank	Net Change in Control Rank	2015 Non-Federal Research x $1000	2006 Non-Federal Research x $1000	Net Change in Constant Dollars	Percent Change in Constant Dollars	Net Change in National Rank	Net Change in Control Rank
61,583	80,551	-18,968	-23.5%	-13	-12	48,419	50,692	-2,273	-4.5%	-21	-10
105,489	104,561	928	0.9%	1	-2	90,503	83,585	6,919	8.3%	-7	-1
71,415	85,547	-14,133	-16.5%	-7	-6	63,776	51,298	12,477	24.3%	-7	1
27,407	29,278	-1,871	-6.4%	8	5	27,625	22,557	5,068	22.5%	-4	2
13,570	16,364	-2,794	-17.1%	-1	0	13,677	9,219	4,458	48.4%	14	14
46,315	59,754	-13,439	-22.5%	-15	-9	57,603	68,242	-10,639	-15.6%	-27	-16
21,099	27,847	-6,748	-24.2%	-14	-10	30,036	25,836	4,200	16.3%	-5	1
67,598	73,552	-5,954	-8.1%	-1	-1	53,527	86,566	-33,039	-38.2%	-42	-25
15,191	17,712	-2,521	-14.2%	-2	0	6,497	8,253	-1,756	-21.3%	-26	-19
106,000	82,878	23,122	27.9%	19	10	54,675	57,084	-2,409	-4.2%	-23	-11
31,028	27,331	3,697	13.5%	16	12	31,913	26,115	5,798	22.2%	-1	5
58,601	53,789	4,812	8.9%	3	-1	21,307	8,025	13,282	165.5%	48	40
61,507	59,426	2,081	3.5%	4	2	43,217	24,934	18,283	73.3%	20	0
232,605	223,523	9,081	4.1%	0	0	182,464	92,749	89,714	96.7%	11	10
149,539	128,870	20,670	16.0%	1	-1	119,870	106,166	13,704	12.9%	-2	0
32,830	40,194	-7,364	-18.3%	-9	-4	44,872	44,847	25	0.1%	-13	-4
30,248	31,897	-1,648	-5.2%	7	4	52,792	53,386	-593	-1.1%	-21	-11
22,956	21,260	1,697	8.0%	8	7	23,331	21,416	1,915	8.9%	-11	-3
15,953	25,474	-9,522	-37.4%	-23	-17	10,664	13,608	-2,944	-21.6%	-25	-13
26,527	34,143	-7,616	-22.3%	-7	-6	15,192	11,340	3,852	34.0%	4	8
48,397	50,536	-2,139	-4.2%	-3	-3	23,206	21,065	2,141	10.2%	-12	-4
184,362	130,073	54,289	41.7%	10	4	115,448	45,269	70,179	155.0%	38	30
26,371	22,011	4,360	19.8%	17	4	28,260	9,025	19,234	213.1%	64	11
20,896	16,685	4,210	25.2%	22	18	22,354	14,015	8,338	59.5%	15	16
18,340	19,221	-882	-4.6%	-1	1	11,051	20,690	-9,639	-46.6%	-56	-36
18,018	18,405	-387	-2.1%	3	5	2,802	4,176	-1,374	-32.9%	-42	-31
190,815	189,163	1,652	0.9%	1	0	73,690	77,945	-4,255	-5.5%	-19	-12
177,047	166,857	10,190	6.1%	2	2	95,018	42,610	52,408	123.0%	34	29
19,498	18,529	969	5.2%	7	7	7,997	9,403	-1,405	-14.9%	-19	-13
83,319	109,995	-26,677	-24.3%	-20	-7	26,780	34,871	-8,091	-23.2%	-38	-16
27,044	35,280	-8,236	-23.3%	-5	-5	30,968	25,461	5,507	21.6%	-2	4
62,632	60,741	1,890	3.1%	4	2	71,433	52,234	19,199	36.8%	-4	4
130,267	131,718	-1,451	-1.1%	-4	0	77,359	46,146	31,213	67.6%	15	0
37,323	30,981	6,342	20.5%	20	16	37,258	35,501	1,757	4.9%	-8	0
105,779	107,920	-2,141	-2.0%	-1	-2	70,309	62,525	7,784	12.4%	-12	-2
12,875	7,638	5,237	68.6%	47	37	11,868	5,069	6,799	134.1%	40	35
40,184	48,546	-8,362	-17.2%	-11	-7	34,604	20,657	13,947	67.5%	23	25
27,432	37,578	-10,146	-27.0%	-8	-6	26,920	21,703	5,218	24.0%	-4	2
51,446	71,919	-20,473	-28.5%	-17	-13	214,577	108,916	105,661	97.0%	9	9
31,298	47,573	-16,276	-34.2%	-25	-19	24,086	23,511	574	2.4%	-16	-8
58,665	77,685	-19,020	-24.5%	-15	-12	81,408	53,977	27,431	50.8%	6	7
86,283	69,098	17,185	24.9%	15	10	76,320	28,953	47,367	163.6%	34	29
26,728	32,603	-5,876	-18.0%	-3	-4	9,690	15,536	-5,846	-37.6%	-46	-30
59,587	80,513	-20,926	-26.0%	-17	-14	48,881	13,819	35,062	253.7%	71	58
271,822	256,971	14,851	5.8%	0	0	79,642	50,476	29,166	57.8%	12	13
161,806	194,314	-32,508	-16.7%	-9	-5	137,721	134,368	3,353	2.5%	-7	-6
15,076	10,211	4,865	47.6%	33	26	2,457	25,117	-22,660	-90.2%	-183	-129
38,244	38,025	218	0.6%	6	7	17,249	16,763	485	2.9%	-17	-7
124,712	118,697	6,015	5.1%	1	1	73,149	30,213	42,936	142.1%	28	3

Change: Research	Total Research in Constant 1983 Dollars					
Institutions with Over $40 Million in Federal Research, Alphabetically	2015 Total Research x $1000	2006 Total Research x $1000	Net Change in Constant Dollars	Percent Change in Constant Dollars	Net Change in National Rank	Net Change in Control Rank
Public Virginia Commonwealth University	62,695	58,971	3,724	6.3%	2	4
Public Virginia Polytechnic Inst. and St. U.	158,164	127,112	31,052	24.4%	6	5
Private Wake Forest University	54,755	72,354	-17,599	-24.3%	-18	-4
Public Washington State Univ. - Pullman	97,991	77,594	20,397	26.3%	9	7
Private Washington University in St. Louis	217,104	216,386	718	0.3%	-8	-3
Public Wayne State University	66,339	87,211	-20,871	-23.9%	-24	-15
Private Weill Cornell Medical College	98,638	80,965	17,673	21.8%	8	1
Public West Virginia University	51,251	48,255	2,996	6.2%	1	4
Private Woods Hole Oceanographic Inst.	69,136	48,158	20,978	43.6%	22	3
Private Yale University	253,111	181,776	71,335	39.2%	6	1
Private Yeshiva University	97,731	74,838	22,892	30.6%	11	2

Federal Research in Constant 1983 Dollars						Non-Federal Research in Constant 1983 Dollars					
2015 Federal Research x $1000	2006 Federal Research x $1000	Net Change in Constant Dollars	Percent Change in Constant Dollars	Net Change in National Rank	Net Change in Control Rank	2015 Non-Federal Research x $1000	2006 Non-Federal Research x $1000	Net Change in Constant Dollars	Percent Change in Constant Dollars	Net Change in National Rank	Net Change in Control Rank
39,474	38,552	922	2.4%	8	9	23,221	20,419	2,802	13.7%	-6	1
60,993	47,410	13,583	28.7%	13	8	97,172	79,703	17,469	21.9%	-2	4
47,268	55,136	-7,867	-14.3%	-9	-2	7,487	17,218	-9,732	-56.5%	-68	-18
38,823	32,131	6,692	20.8%	21	16	59,168	45,463	13,705	30.1%	0	5
135,572	161,360	-25,788	-16.0%	-6	-2	81,532	55,026	26,506	48.2%	5	-2
34,544	46,638	-12,094	-25.9%	-20	-14	31,795	40,572	-8,777	-21.6%	-27	-13
53,658	54,036	-378	-0.7%	-3	1	44,979	26,929	18,050	67.0%	15	0
21,261	25,193	-3,932	-15.6%	-4	-1	29,989	23,062	6,927	30.0%	4	6
55,220	40,154	15,066	37.5%	20	4	13,916	8,004	5,913	73.9%	27	3
150,465	137,692	12,772	9.3%	-1	1	102,646	44,083	58,562	132.8%	35	6
57,708	60,760	-3,052	-5.0%	-7	-1	40,022	14,078	25,944	184.3%	59	10

Change: Private Support & Doctorates	Endowment Assets in Constant 1998 Dollars					
Institutions with Over $40 Million in Federal Research, Alphabetically	2016 Endowment Assets x $1000	2007 Endowment Assets x $1000	Net Change in Constant Dollars	Percent Change in Constant Dollars	Net Change in National Rank	Net Change in Control Rank
Public Arizona State University	354,690	339,462	15,228	4.5%	-7	-3
Public Auburn University	374,395	272,567	101,829	37.4%	28	16
Public Augusta University	121,935	95,066	26,869	28.3%	59	6
Private Baylor College of Medicine	615,870	906,877	-291,007	-32.1%	-26	-14
Private Boston University	957,973	781,544	176,430	22.6%	14	11
Private Brandeis University	501,864	490,596	11,268	2.3%	1	8
Private Brown University	1,715,789	1,973,254	-257,465	-13.0%	-5	-1
Private California Institute of Technology	1,219,793	1,319,893	-100,100	-7.6%	-3	0
Private Carnegie Mellon University	989,290	791,729	197,561	25.0%	14	10
Private Case Western Reserve University	962,726	1,306,540	-343,814	-26.3%	-14	-8
Public Clemson University	359,729	305,142	54,587	17.9%	9	6
Public Cleveland State University	42,093	24,216	17,877	73.8%	84	25
Private Cold Spring Harbor Laboratory						
Public Colorado State Univ. - Fort Collins	165,795	132,315	33,481	25.3%	45	10
Private Columbia University	5,234,755	5,073,500	161,254	3.2%	-4	-2
Private Cornell University	2,619,639	3,156,500	-536,861	-17.0%	-2	-1
Private Dartmouth College	2,590,680	2,668,262	-77,582	-2.9%	-1	-1
Private Drexel University	376,496	445,960	-69,464	-15.6%	-27	-12
Private Duke University	3,960,233	4,193,935	-233,702	-5.6%	0	0
Private Emory University	3,706,555	3,946,613	-240,057	-6.1%	0	0
Public Florida International University	100,781	65,195	35,586	54.6%	84	12
Public Florida State University	338,442	389,566	-51,124	-13.1%	-25	-12
Public George Mason University	41,437	38,832	2,605	6.7%	-54	-23
Private George Washington University	909,191	814,231	94,960	11.7%	6	3
Private Georgetown University	858,948	751,710	107,238	14.3%	10	8
Public Georgia Institute of Technology	1,067,539	1,141,521	-73,981	-6.5%	0	-3
Private Harvard University	19,999,756	24,576,929	-4,577,173	-18.6%	0	0
Private Icahn School of Med. at Mount Sinai	381,712					
Public Indiana University - Bloomington	573,867	655,968	-82,102	-12.5%	-9	-7
Public Iowa State University	440,307	420,344	19,963	4.7%	6	-6
Private Johns Hopkins University	1,957,762	1,987,148	-29,386	-1.5%	-3	-1
Public Kansas State University	275,382	245,777	29,605	12.0%	10	0
Public Louisiana State Univ. - Baton Rouge	241,279	248,686	-7,407	-3.0%	-10	-11
Private Massachusetts Institute of Tech.	7,632,097	7,082,099	549,998	7.8%	0	0
Private Medical College of Wisconsin	433,591	359,813	73,778	20.5%	19	17
Public Medical University of South Carolina	180,649	106,661	73,988	69.4%	100	29
Public Michigan State University	1,497,202	885,377	611,825	69.1%	23	5
Public Mississippi State University	257,357	198,936	58,420	29.4%	21	3
Public Montana State University - Bozeman	80,022	78,310	1,712	2.2%	-14	-15
Public Naval Postgraduate School	3,002					
Public New Jersey Institute of Technology	56,745	50,129	6,616	13.2%	-5	-12
Public New Mexico State Univ. - Las Cruces	124,356	124,665	-308	-0.2%	12	-6
Private New York University	2,019,379	1,534,013	485,366	31.6%	5	2
Public North Carolina State University	578,189	379,638	198,551	52.3%	44	13
Private Northeastern University	401,261	482,475	-81,214	-16.8%	-25	-10
Private Northwestern University	5,586,480	4,614,736	971,744	21.1%	0	1
Public Ohio State University - Columbus	2,071,987	1,659,118	412,870	24.9%	3	1
Public Oregon Health & Science University	330,311	316,931	13,379	4.2%	-8	-4
Public Oregon State University	285,184	313,097	-27,913	-8.9%	-22	-11

Annual Giving in Constant 1998 Dollars						Doctorates Awarded					
2016 Annual Giving x $1000	2007 Annual Giving x $1000	Net Change in Constant Dollars	Percent Change in Constant Dollars	Net Change in National Rank	Net Change in Control Rank	2016 Doctorates Awarded	2007 Doctorates Awarded	Net Change in Doctorates	Percent Change in Doctorates	Net Change in National Rank	Net Change in Control Rank
81,301	73,806	7,495	10.2%	-6	-5	674	389	285	73.3%	23	14
68,598	54,270	14,328	26.4%	7	4	272	204	68	33.3%	5	-2
6,684	4,517	2,167	48.0%	145	29	20	26	-6	-23.1%	-22	-26
44,933	45,484	-551	-1.2%	-8	4	94	65	29	44.6%	32	25
90,869	59,720	31,149	52.2%	21	6	579	540	39	7.2%	-1	0
33,346	61,236	-27,890	-45.5%	-64	-21	83	93	-10	-10.8%	-24	0
120,273	128,879	-8,606	-6.7%	-4	-2	235	170	65	38.2%	11	7
105,881	130,039	-24,158	-18.6%	-13	-5	190	206	-16	-7.8%	-23	-6
89,920	53,019	36,901	69.6%	27	8	323	205	118	57.6%	23	9
91,669	49,241	42,428	86.2%	34	11	230	232	-2	-0.9%	-15	-1
52,471	67,105	-14,634	-21.8%	-30	-21	233	138	95	68.8%	36	16
6,833	5,739	1,095	19.1%	74	9	54	57	-3	-5.3%	-10	-16
24,780	25,089	-308	-1.2%	-7	-6	249	211	38	18.0%	-4	-6
338,604	300,763	37,841	12.6%	-1	0	587	568	19	3.3%	-1	0
247,285	202,128	45,156	22.3%	2	1	497	485	12	2.5%	-11	-3
131,455	111,126	20,329	18.3%	5	2	87	73	14	19.2%	9	13
35,264	31,335	3,929	12.5%	10	10	214	134	80	59.7%	33	17
293,229	264,204	29,025	11.0%	-2	0	537	277	260	93.9%	38	10
111,573	110,774	799	0.7%	0	1	251	217	34	15.7%	-6	2
16,108	7,715	8,392	108.8%	146	51	151	100	51	51.0%	39	16
43,664	40,429	3,235	8.0%	-3	-9	386	350	36	10.3%	-1	-1
39,337	15,607	23,730	152.0%	100	39	322	181	141	77.9%	32	20
58,705	42,089	16,617	39.5%	19	11	264	264	0	0.0%	-12	0
88,809	74,810	14,000	18.7%	1	0	124	99	25	25.3%	17	12
74,867	84,765	-9,898	-11.7%	-16	-13	531	459	72	15.7%	1	0
687,580	435,684	251,896	57.8%	1	1	713	683	30	4.4%	0	1
69,669						23	24	-1	-4.2%	11	19
113,431	120,376	-6,945	-5.8%	-5	-4	485	370	115	31.1%	4	3
52,196	49,639	2,556	5.1%	-13	-10	327	296	31	10.5%	1	0
380,573	305,451	75,122	24.6%	0	0	528	397	131	33.0%	4	2
55,946	33,399	22,547	67.5%	34	18	179	152	27	17.8%	4	-1
85,691	54,696	30,995	56.7%	21	15	344	274	70	25.5%	10	7
243,036	233,571	9,466	4.1%	-6	-3	646	601	45	7.5%	2	0
11,017						24	21	3	14.3%	37	36
25,655	19,381	6,275	32.4%	28	9	181	43	138	320.9%	158	85
101,980	82,267	19,713	24.0%	6	4	533	493	40	8.1%	-4	-2
40,393	32,301	8,092	25.1%	19	7	153	107	46	43.0%	30	9
12,252						52	56	-4	-7.1%	-17	-18
						15					
	5,647					57	52	5	9.6%	10	-6
9,576	26,411	-16,835	-63.7%	-162	-72	105	85	20	23.5%	6	-6
267,006	204,072	62,934	30.8%	4	2	489	377	112	29.7%	3	1
75,240	115,205	-39,965	-34.7%	-28	-20	518	411	107	26.0%	-2	-3
32,593	20,807	11,786	56.6%	35	23	186	167	19	11.4%	-5	-1
232,572	133,352	99,220	74.4%	10	2	467	462	5	1.1%	-13	-3
223,559	160,056	63,503	39.7%	6	6	807	667	140	21.0%	9	5
90,880						44	41	3	7.3%	2	-10
56,22138,83017,391		44.8%	21	9	214	179	35	19.6%	0	-3	

Change: Private Support & Doctorates	Endowment Assets in Constant 1998 Dollars					
Institutions with Over $40 Million in Federal Research, Alphabetically	2016 Endowment Assets x $1000	2007 Endowment Assets x $1000	Net Change in Constant Dollars	Percent Change in Constant Dollars	Net Change in National Rank	Net Change in Control Rank
Public Penn. State Univ. - Hershey Med. Ctr.	260,517	169,240	91,277	53.9%	51	12
Public Pennsylvania State Univ. - Univ. Park	1,107,195	832,659	274,536	33.0%	16	5
Private Princeton University	12,826,344	11,202,597	1,623,747	14.5%	0	0
Public Purdue University - West Lafayette	1,305,379	1,267,766	37,614	3.0%	2	-1
Private Rensselaer Polytechnic Institute	367,616	576,902	-209,286	-36.3%	-56	-33
Private Rice University	3,082,763	3,313,508	-230,745	-7.0%	-1	0
Private Rockefeller University	1,115,967	1,522,236	-406,269	-26.7%	-11	-7
Private Rush University	311,979	314,705	-2,727	-0.9%	-11	-7
Public Rutgers University - New Brunswick	501,337	427,072	74,265	17.4%	16	-3
Public San Diego State University	127,377	83,296	44,080	52.9%	87	15
Private Scripps Research Institute						
Private Stanford University	12,968,517	12,180,168	788,350	6.5%	0	0
Public Stony Brook University	151,809	74,206	77,603	104.6%	136	38
Public Temple University	286,134	167,971	118,163	70.3%	66	22
Public Texas A&M Univ. - College Station	5,758,118	4,363,901	1,394,217	31.9%	4	1
Private Thomas Jefferson University	290,046	435,934	-145,888	-33.5%	-53	-25
Private Tufts University	904,958	1,030,380	-125,422	-12.2%	-10	-6
Private Tulane University	678,191	716,078	-37,887	-5.3%	1	4
Public Uniformed Services Univ. of the HS						
Public University at Albany	34,319	18,966	15,353	80.9%	75	22
Public University at Buffalo	347,956	401,890	-53,934	-13.4%	-28	-14
Public University of Alabama - Birmingham	249,815	271,323	-21,508	-7.9%	-22	-11
Public University of Alabama - Huntsville	41,140	40,658	482	1.2%	-71	-32
Public University of Alaska - Fairbanks	100,383	145,560	-45,177	-31.0%	-76	-40
Public University of Arizona	436,943	377,756	59,187	15.7%	15	0
Public Univ. of Arkansas for Med. Sciences	18,373	21,998	-3,624	-16.5%	-215	-93
Public University of California - Berkeley	2,226,418	2,054,244	172,174	8.4%	0	-1
Public University of California - Davis	559,201	461,730	97,471	21.1%	20	0
Public University of California - Irvine	288,441	160,893	127,548	79.3%	79	28
Public University of California - Los Angeles	2,228,648	1,904,476	324,172	17.0%	5	2
Public University of California - Riverside	110,832	85,536	25,296	29.6%	50	3
Public University of California - San Diego	681,240	371,009	310,232	83.6%	66	23
Public Univ. of California - San Francisco	1,222,856	966,941	255,915	26.5%	14	2
Public Univ. of California - Santa Barbara	158,460	134,851	23,609	17.5%	34	4
Public University of California - Santa Cruz	93,920	83,572	10,348	12.4%	14	-11
Public University of Central Florida	84,775	82,520	2,255	2.7%	-7	-13
Private University of Chicago	4,053,697	4,402,493	-348,795	-7.9%	-2	-1
Public University of Cincinnati - Cincinnati	674,837	841,160	-166,323	-19.8%	-12	-6
Public University of Colorado - Boulder	337,667	287,138	50,529	17.6%	9	6
Public U. of Colorado - Denv./Anschutz Med.	277,615	209,587	68,028	32.5%	30	9
Public Univ. of Connecticut - Health Center	48,208	79,136	-30,928	-39.1%	-161	-58
Public University of Connecticut - Storrs	159,419	160,670	-1,251	-0.8%	-3	-7
Private University of Dayton	273,938	291,188	-17,250	-5.9%	-22	-11
Public University of Delaware	730,576	991,660	-261,084	-26.3%	-15	-6
Public University of Florida	846,120	865,021	-18,901	-2.2%	-4	-2
Public University of Georgia	588,688	500,492	88,196	17.6%	13	2
Public University of Hawaii - Manoa	157,013	163,964	-6,951	-4.2%	-11	-11
Public University of Houston - Univ. Park	385,036	285,432	99,603	34.9%	30	15
Public University of Idaho	137,529	133,884	3,645	2.7%	11	-3

Annual Giving in Constant 1998 Dollars						Doctorates Awarded					
2016 Annual Giving x $1000	2007 Annual Giving x $1000	Net Change in Constant Dollars	Percent Change in Constant Dollars	Net Change in National Rank	Net Change in Control Rank	2016 Doctorates Awarded	2007 Doctorates Awarded	Net Change in Doctorates	Percent Change in Doctorates	Net Change in National Rank	Net Change in Control Rank
20,538	23,356	-2,818	-12.1%	-17	-8	24	27	-3	-11.1%	5	-12
85,443	92,127	-6,684	-7.3%	-12	-9	659	646	13	2.0%	-1	-1
155,100	163,614	-8,514	-5.2%	-5	-3	373	332	41	12.3%	3	0
87,555	142,405	-54,850	-38.5%	-27	-16	727	613	114	18.6%	10	7
21,885	33,741	-11,856	-35.1%	-49	-22	142	163	-21	-12.9%	-27	-6
59,624	48,088	11,536	24.0%	10	6	211	143	68	47.6%	24	13
39,175	55,633	-16,459	-29.6%	-40	-10	31	28	3	10.7%	26	29
1,777						20	35	-15	-42.9%	-72	-35
68,608	62,683	5,924	9.5%	-4	-2	620	406	214	52.7%	14	8
46,193	33,179	13,014	39.2%	23	10	85	46	39	84.8%	67	27
550,715	590,632	-39,917	-6.8%	-1	-1	763	720	43	6.0%	2	1
44,412	17,899	26,513	148.1%	96	43	350	364	-14	-3.8%	-10	-6
36,045	34,121	1,924	5.6%	-3	-9	256	392	-136	-34.7%	-46	-36
160,079	119,551	40,528	33.9%	8	4	705	620	85	13.7%	4	3
32,899	20,420	12,479	61.1%	39	26	13	15	-2	-13.3%	-3	23
34,974	59,916	-24,941	-41.6%	-54	-17	135	101	34	33.7%	22	16
57,274	47,980	9,294	19.4%	7	5	135	155	-20	-12.9%	-23	-4
5,282	23,810	-18,528	-77.8%	-278	-111	193	163	30	18.4%	1	-2
20,971	19,088	1,883	9.9%	15	4	340	394	-54	-13.7%	-22	-17
50,977	68,841	-17,864	-25.9%	-37	-26	149	192	-43	-22.4%	-39	-29
1,330	2,671	-1,341	-50.2%	-108	-81	34	30	4	13.3%	24	-4
16,134	5,812	10,322	177.6%	238	75	47	33	14	42.4%	48	9
108,198	102,152	6,046	5.9%	-1	-2	524	460	64	13.9%	-4	-4
14,275						48	21	27	128.6%	123	32
201,993	172,150	29,842	17.3%	1	3	576	903	-327	-36.2%	-21	-15
74,821	67,220	7,600	11.3%	-5	-4	513	474	39	8.2%	-8	-7
42,647	52,679	-10,031	-19.0%	-27	-20	393	298	95	31.9%	12	9
288,805	258,848	29,957	11.6%	-2	-2	775	734	41	5.6%	2	1
14,110	13,259	851	6.4%	10	-1	239	177	62	35.0%	9	2
119,779	95,153	24,626	25.9%	7	4	529	387	142	36.7%	10	7
345,049	178,780	166,269	93.0%	14	6	123	145	-22	-15.2%	-30	-22
58,581	36,373	22,208	61.1%	32	17	346	310	36	11.6%	3	2
39,981	20,664	19,318	93.5%	58	24	174	132	42	31.8%	17	6
12,985	38,019	-25,034	-65.8%	-129	-67	299	212	87	41.0%	5	0
256,674	232,982	23,692	10.2%	-2	0	396	357	39	10.9%	-1	0
93,842	49,307	44,535	90.3%	36	25	284	261	23	8.8%	-7	-9
92,898	32,635	60,263	184.7%	78	48	410	319	91	28.5%	9	6
61,932	35,082	26,850	76.5%	40	22	123	163	-40	-24.5%	-44	-29
3,906	5,758	-1,852	-32.2%	-78	-39	16					
37,994	23,034	14,960	65.0%	42	17	320	339	-19	-5.6%	-13	-10
12,546	10,398	2,147	20.7%	40	35	39	30	9	30.0%	38	39
32,912	25,359	7,553	29.8%	15	2	283	224	59	26.3%	-1	-5
141,083	129,585	11,498	8.9%	-1	-1	723	794	-71	-8.9%	-6	-6
77,517	62,753	14,764	23.5%	2	2	526	388	138	35.6%	7	5
24,439	27,984	-3,545	-12.7%	-21	-14	204	149	55	36.9%	15	5
57,002	27,681	29,320	105.9%	55	30	358	239	119	49.8%	22	17
9,752	7,994	1,758	22.0%	35	5	69	105	-36	-34.3%	-57	-43

Change: Private Support & Doctorates	Endowment Assets in Constant 1998 Dollars					
Institutions with Over $40 Million in Federal Research, Alphabetically	2016 Endowment Assets x $1000	2007 Endowment Assets x $1000	Net Change in Constant Dollars	Percent Change in Constant Dollars	Net Change in National Rank	Net Change in Control Rank
Public University of Illinois - Chicago	166,282	138,159	28,123	20.4%	29	2
Public Univ. of Illinois - Urbana-Champaign	862,705	780,560	82,145	10.5%	8	2
Public University of Iowa	729,140	697,131	32,009	4.6%	7	0
Public University of Kansas - Lawrence	666,211	685,603	-19,392	-2.8%	1	-3
Public University of Kansas Medical Center	200,248	184,585	15,663	8.5%	9	-4
Public University of Kentucky	647,236	679,519	-32,282	-4.8%	0	-3
Public University of Louisville	414,384	565,418	-151,034	-26.7%	-36	-18
Public University of Maryland - Baltimore	147,490	140,310	7,180	5.1%	6	-7
Public Univ. of Maryland - Baltimore County	45,220	39,621	5,600	14.1%	-24	-11
Public University of Maryland - College Park	269,857	316,941	-47,084	-14.9%	-36	-19
Public Univ. of Massachusetts - Amherst	166,296	101,891	64,406	63.2%	95	27
Public Univ. of Mass. Med. Sch. - Worcester	106,209	47,217	58,992	124.9%	184	44
Private University of Miami	489,048	526,085	-37,036	-7.0%	-10	-1
Public University of Michigan - Ann Arbor	5,641,464	5,030,943	610,521	12.1%	-1	-1
Public University of Minnesota - Twin Cities	1,899,514	1,990,049	-90,535	-4.5%	-5	-3
Public University of Missouri - Columbia	503,479	456,359	47,119	10.3%	12	-4
Public University of Nebraska - Lincoln	503,657	589,082	-85,424	-14.5%	-14	-10
Public University of Nebraska Medical Ctr.	129,553	135,942	-6,388	-4.7%	-4	-14
Public University of Nevada - Reno	175,262	170,537	4,725	2.8%	-4	-10
Public Univ. of New Hampshire - Durham	191,146	190,347	799	0.4%	1	-9
Public Univ. of New Mexico - Albuquerque	227,686	227,214	472	0.2%	-3	-9
Public Univ. of North Carolina - Chapel Hill	1,673,124	1,535,889	137,235	8.9%	-1	0
Private University of Notre Dame	4,848,594	4,241,260	607,334	14.3%	1	1
Public University of Oklahoma - HSC	299,297	228,495	70,801	31.0%	31	11
Public University of Oklahoma - Norman	580,988	562,301	18,687	3.3%	4	-1
Public University of Oregon	439,283	323,282	116,001	35.9%	29	7
Private University of Pennsylvania	6,204,196	4,708,329	1,495,867	31.8%	2	1
Public University of Pittsburgh - Pittsburgh	2,040,919	1,599,707	441,212	27.6%	3	1
Public University of Rhode Island	72,160	67,461	4,699	7.0%	-14	-15
Private University of Rochester	1,116,065	1,224,995	-108,930	-8.9%	-3	-1
Public Univ. of South Carolina - Columbia	379,517	311,170	68,347	22.0%	13	6
Public University of South Florida - Tampa	228,893	275,691	-46,798	-17.0%	-33	-16
Private University of Southern California	2,668,445	2,636,357	32,088	1.2%	2	2
Public University of Tennessee - Knoxville	345,938	526,907	-180,969	-34.3%	-61	-24
Public University of Texas - Austin	6,331,817	5,102,121	1,229,697	24.1%	0	0
Public University of Texas - El Paso	126,732	112,098	14,633	13.1%	34	1
Public University of Texas HSC - Houston	194,594	133,010	61,584	46.3%	69	19
Public Univ. of Texas HSC - San Antonio	281,772	287,514	-5,742	-2.0%	-12	-5
Public U. of Texas MD Anderson Cancer Ctr.	701,805	400,573	301,233	75.2%	55	17
Public U. of Texas Med. Branch - Galveston	309,170	352,583	-43,413	-12.3%	-25	-11
Public Univ. of Texas SW Med. Ctr. - Dallas	975,111	1,017,964	-42,853	-4.2%	-1	-3
Public University of Utah	623,380	433,189	190,191	43.9%	36	7
Public University of Vermont	270,799	238,683	32,116	13.5%	12	0
Public University of Virginia	3,388,487	3,101,100	287,387	9.3%	2	0
Public University of Washington - Seattle	1,718,480	1,550,032	168,448	10.9%	0	0
Public University of Wisconsin - Madison	1,586,303	1,360,091	226,211	16.6%	1	0
Public University of Wyoming	265,463	215,839	49,624	23.0%	20	4
Public Utah State University	188,341	92,634	95,707	103.3%	131	37
Private Vanderbilt University	2,213,046	2,474,730	-261,684	-10.6%	-2	0

Annual Giving in Constant 1998 Dollars						Doctorates Awarded					
2016 Annual Giving x $1000	2007 Annual Giving x $1000	Net Change in Constant Dollars	Percent Change in Constant Dollars	Net Change in National Rank	Net Change in Control Rank	2016 Doctorates Awarded	2007 Doctorates Awarded	Net Change Doctorates	Percent Change Doctorates	Net Change in National Rank	Net Change in Control Rank
31,159	32,262	-1,103	-3.4%	-8	-8	346	317	29	9.1%	1	1
92,462	94,558	-2,096	-2.2%	-4	-5	726	698	28	4.0%	1	0
111,320	81,947	29,372	35.8%	11	8	468	376	92	24.5%	2	1
86,718	56,046	30,671	54.7%	20	15	314	260	54	20.8%	3	0
21,679	14,189	7,490	52.8%	60	20	22	67	-45	-67.2%	-152	-79
94,909	39,038	55,871	143.1%	61	36	313	292	21	7.2%	-7	-6
49,323	41,959	7,364	17.6%	0	-6	147	135	12	8.9%	-1	-7
33,530	32,753	777	2.4%	-6	-10	67	128	-61	-47.7%	-79	-55
7,983	9,399	-1,415	-15.1%	-37	-23	82	81	1	1.2%	-10	-16
84,559	60,724	23,835	39.3%	12	10	592	653	-61	-9.3%	-6	-5
18,994	18,047	948	5.3%	12	-1	298	293	5	1.7%	-15	-13
4,371						64	35	29	82.9%	83	31
136,837	127,746	9,091	7.1%	0	1	216	187	29	15.5%	-2	3
251,156	208,199	42,958	20.6%	0	0	848	789	59	7.5%	2	1
192,721	204,897	-12,176	-5.9%	-7	-3	804	819	-15	-1.8%	-2	-3
65,473	63,348	2,125	3.4%	-8	-6	416	293	123	42.0%	18	13
58,214	43,621	14,593	33.5%	15	5	307	274	33	12.0%	-5	-6
53,095	23,794	29,302	123.1%	66	35	86	75	11	14.7%	2	-9
40,253	22,768	17,485	76.8%	53	25	130	75	55	73.3%	49	20
8,321	8,962	-641	-7.2%	-19	-17	66	59	7	11.9%	8	-6
38,259	42,311	-4,053	-9.6%	-21	-22	200	185	15	8.1%	-11	-9
178,734	175,175	3,559	2.0%	-4	-2	542	512	30	5.9%	-2	-2
215,250	147,342	67,908	46.1%	6	0	216	159	57	35.8%	17	10
40,206	19,714	20,492	103.9%	69	28	29	27	2	7.4%	24	-5
146,485	78,857	67,628	85.8%	23	16	210	174	36	20.7%	0	-1
78,915	71,848	7,067	9.8%	-6	-5	159	170	-11	-6.5%	-19	-14
314,311	278,462	35,849	12.9%	-1	0	540	483	57	11.8%	0	1
73,623	85,959	-12,336	-14.4%	-19	-16	461	410	51	12.4%	-9	-7
9,141	8,954	188	2.1%	-4	-12	97	85	12	14.1%	-2	-11
62,125	57,437	4,688	8.2%	1	1	301	239	62	25.9%	-1	3
54,486	33,434	21,051	63.0%	32	16	317	244	73	29.9%	6	3
26,393	40,324	-13,931	-34.5%	-51	-32	314	229	85	37.1%	8	3
385,985	333,262	52,724	15.8%	0	0	714	691	23	3.3%	0	1
52,953	60,932	-7,979	-13.1%	-22	-15	356	347	9	2.6%	-3	-1
200,329	162,327	38,002	23.4%	2	3	896	779	117	15.0%	5	4
11,113	11,877	-764	-6.4%	-9	-7	78	39	39	100.0%	82	35
32,107	26,724	5,384	20.1%	7	-2	113	118	-5	-4.2%	-24	-22
23,425	39,173	-15,748	-40.2%	-56	-36	59	38	21	55.3%	61	22
120,711	100,985	19,726	19.5%	7	4						
25,858	35,669	-9,811	-27.5%	-41	-25	52	53	-1	-1.9%	-7	-15
104,888	118,025	-13,137	-11.1%	-8	-5	98	84	14	16.7%	6	-7
116,873						331	345	-14	-4.1%	-7	-6
35,555	20,345	15,210	74.8%	52	19	78	57	21	36.8%	30	6
142,082	200,541	-58,459	-29.2%	-11	-7	315	348	-33	-9.5%	-19	-15
313,496	213,022	100,474	47.2%	5	1	632	631	1	0.2%	-2	-1
184,601	230,859	-46,258	-20.0%	-11	-7	870	775	95	12.3%	5	4
28,588	27,551	1,037	3.8%	-2	-5	99	61	38	62.3%	47	17
19,894	18,437	1,457	7.9%	14	0	94	85	9	10.6%	-6	-14
83,147	97,409	-14,262	-14.6%	-17	-4	322	274	48	17.5%	4	2

Change: Private Support & Doctorates		Endowment Assets in Constant 1998 Dollars					
Institutions with Over $40 Million in Federal Research, Alphabetically		2016 Endowment Assets x $1000	2007 Endowment Assets x $1000	Net Change in Constant Dollars	Percent Change in Constant Dollars	Net Change in National Rank	Net Change in Control Rank
Public	Virginia Commonwealth University	903,167	233,600	669,567	286.6%	137	53
Public	Virginia Polytechnic Inst. and St. U.	488,092	372,349	115,743	31.1%	30	6
Private	Wake Forest University	660,761	886,074	-225,313	-25.4%	-21	-11
Public	Washington State Univ. - Pullman	525,632	461,881	63,752	13.8%	13	-3
Private	Washington University in St. Louis	3,741,334	3,950,941	-209,607	-5.3%	0	0
Public	Wayne State University	174,551	167,933	6,618	3.9%	-3	-8
Private	Weill Cornell Medical College	714,082	692,890	21,192	3.1%	7	7
Public	West Virginia University	296,091	310,046	-13,955	-4.5%	-14	-6
Private	Woods Hole Oceanographic Inst.		272,061				
Private	Yale University	14,711,579	15,987,430	-1,275,851	-8.0%	0	0
Private	Yeshiva University	366,424	1,000,235	-633,812	-63.4%	-94	-58

Annual Giving in Constant 1998 Dollars						Doctorates Awarded					
2016 Annual Giving x $1000	2007 Annual Giving x $1000	Net Change in Constant Dollars	Percent Change in Constant Dollars	Net Change in National Rank	Net Change in Control Rank	2016 Doctorates Awarded	2007 Doctorates Awarded	Net Change in Doctorates	Percent Change in Doctorates	Net Change in National Rank	Net Change in Control Rank
40,055	37,754	2,301	6.1%	-2	-9	306	191	115	60.2%	18	9
57,933	57,904	29	0.0%	-8	-5	492	356	136	38.2%	10	6
51,408	49,137	2,271	4.6%	-11	-2	58	35	23	65.7%	74	48
60,126	44,795	15,331	34.2%	18	6	322	175	147	84.0%	35	23
156,259	112,268	43,991	39.2%	10	4	266	347	-81	-23.3%	-31	-5
35,150	68,513	-33,363	-48.7%	-64	-45	222	213	9	4.2%	-13	-13
49,335	86,627	-37,292	-43.0%	-50	-14	58	41	17	41.5%	45	31
43,357	61,180	-17,823	-29.1%	-38	-26	210	148	62	41.9%	19	8
300,586	277,677	22,908	8.3%	-2	0	411	360	51	14.2%	0	0
22,754						152	128	24	18.8%	12	12

Change: Students		SAT Scores					
Institutions with Over $40 Million in Federal Research, Alphabetically		2015 Median SAT	2006 Median SAT	Net Change in SAT	Percent Change in SAT	Net Change in National Rank	Net Change in Control Rank
Public	Arizona State University	1170	1095	75	6.8%	246	56
Public	Auburn University	1220	1130	90	8.0%	177	39
Public	Augusta University	1035					
Private	Baylor College of Medicine						
Private	Boston University	1305	1275	30	2.4%	11	12
Private	Brandeis University	1360	1355	5	0.4%	-7	-4
Private	Brown University	1465	1440	25	1.7%	0	0
Private	California Institute of Technology	1550	1520	30	2.0%	0	0
Private	Carnegie Mellon University	1450	1395	55	3.9%	5	5
Private	Case Western Reserve University	1400	1330	70	5.3%	21	19
Public	Clemson University	1250	1215	35	2.9%	42	2
Public	Cleveland State University	1030	910	120	13.2%	634	216
Private	Cold Spring Harbor Laboratory						
Public	Colorado State Univ. - Fort Collins	1150	1110	40	3.6%	141	15
Private	Columbia University	1475	1440	35	2.4%	2	2
Private	Cornell University	1430	1385	45	3.2%	2	2
Private	Dartmouth College	1445	1450	-5	-0.3%	-11	-11
Private	Drexel University	1203	1120	83	7.4%	177	147
Private	Duke University	1455	1470	-15	-1.0%	-13	-13
Private	Emory University	1380	1385	-5	-0.4%	-13	-11
Public	Florida International University	1080	1100	-20	-1.8%	-5	-47
Public	Florida State University	1220	1160	60	5.2%	130	23
Public	George Mason University	1145	1110	35	3.2%	112	2
Private	George Washington University	1290	1295	-5	-0.4%	-13	-6
Private	Georgetown University	1410	1390	20	1.4%	-2	-2
Public	Georgia Institute of Technology	1405	1315	90	6.8%	34	4
Private	Harvard University	1500	1490	10	0.7%	-3	-3
Private	Icahn School of Med. at Mount Sinai						
Public	Indiana University - Bloomington	1175	1120	55	4.9%	150	22
Public	Iowa State University	1150	1130	20	1.8%	69	-6
Private	Johns Hopkins University	1445	1380	65	4.7%	14	14
Public	Kansas State University	0	1090	-1090	-100.0%	-813	-387
Public	Louisiana State Univ. - Baton Rouge	1170	1150	20	1.7%	72	-2
Private	Massachusetts Institute of Tech.	1505	1470	35	2.4%	1	1
Private	Medical College of Wisconsin						
Public	Medical University of South Carolina						
Public	Michigan State University	1170	1130	40	3.5%	105	9
Public	Mississippi State University	1150	1090	60	5.5%	215	42
Public	Montana State University - Bozeman	1130	1070	60	5.6%	246	55
Public	Naval Postgraduate School						
Public	New Jersey Institute of Technology	1210	1110	100	9.0%	235	52
Public	New Mexico State Univ. - Las Cruces	990	950	40	4.2%	308	71
Private	New York University	1360	1310	50	3.8%	18	16
Public	North Carolina State University	1245	1185	60	5.1%	93	20
Private	Northeastern University	1440	1240	200	16.1%	93	72
Private	Northwestern University	1440	1410	30	2.1%	-5	-5
Public	Ohio State University - Columbus	1300	1205	95	7.9%	84	21
Public	Oregon Health & Science University						
Public	Oregon State University	1105	1080	25	2.3%	133	11

National Merit and Achievement Scholars						Headcount Enrollment			
2016 National Merit Scholars	2007 National Merit Scholars	Net Change in Merit Scholars	Percent Change in Merit Scholars	Net Change in National Rank	Net Change in Control Rank	Fall 2015 Total Student Headcount	Fall 2006 Total Student Headcount	Net Change in Enrollment	Percent Change in Enrollment
109	154	-45	-29.2%	-1	-3	90,906	51,234	39,672	77.4%
60	28	32	114.3%	45	24	27,287	23,547	3,740	15.9%
2	0	2		191	61	8,333			
						1,572	1,358	214	15.8%
56	47	9	19.1%	14	8	32,158	31,574	584	1.8%
11	31	-20	-64.5%	-45	-18	5,752	5,313	439	8.3%
100	94	6	6.4%	4	4	9,458	8,125	1,333	16.4%
44	36	8	22.2%	15	6	2,255	2,086	169	8.1%
55	32	23	71.9%	29	14	12,963	9,999	2,964	29.6%
72	41	31	75.6%	28	15	11,340	9,592	1,748	18.2%
43	53	-10	-18.9%	-3	-2	22,698	17,309	5,389	31.1%
0	0					16,915	14,807	2,108	14.2%
9	17	-8	-47.1%	-22	-17	30,614	27,636	2,978	10.8%
67	87	-20	-23.0%	-2	-1	28,086	22,317	5,769	25.9%
81	63	18	28.6%	15	10	21,904	19,639	2,265	11.5%
49	55	-6	-10.9%	-1	0	6,350	5,753	597	10.4%
4	3	1	33.3%	58	46	25,595	19,860	5,735	28.9%
106	106	0	0.0%	2	3	15,984	13,373	2,611	19.5%
54	73	-19	-26.0%	-6	-2	13,788	12,338	1,450	11.8%
0	1	-1	-100.0%	-48	-37	49,782	37,997	11,785	31.0%
22	16	6	37.5%	28	9	40,830	39,973	857	2.1%
1	0	1		157	49	33,929	29,889	4,040	13.5%
17	11	6	54.5%	39	32	26,212	24,531	1,681	6.9%
33	43	-10	-23.3%	-12	-4	18,459	14,148	4,311	30.5%
55	117	-62	-53.0%	-14	-7	25,034	17,936	7,098	39.6%
233	359	-126	-35.1%	-2	-1	29,652	25,778	3,874	15.0%
						1,150	696	454	65.2%
52	63	-11	-17.5%	-1	-1	48,514	38,247	10,267	26.8%
35	45	-10	-22.2%	-11	-7	35,714	25,462	10,252	40.3%
47	27	20	74.1%	35	16	22,686	19,708	2,978	15.1%
6	8	-2	-25.0%	8	-10	24,146	23,141	1,005	4.3%
25	43	-18	-41.9%	-22	-13	31,524	29,925	1,599	5.3%
154	171	-17	-9.9%	4	3	11,331	10,253	1,078	10.5%
						1,217	1,319	-102	-7.7%
						2,992	2,498	494	19.8%
34	40	-6	-15.0%	-5	-4	50,538	45,520	5,018	11.0%
37	29	8	27.6%	19	10	20,873	16,206	4,667	28.8%
12	7	5	71.4%	52	9	15,236	12,052	3,184	26.4%
						2,665	2,627	38	1.4%
2	0	2		191	61	11,325	8,209	3,116	38.0%
0	1	-1	-100.0%	-48	-37	15,490	16,415	-925	-5.6%
15	167	-152	-91.0%	-84	-36	50,027	40,870	9,157	22.4%
8	7	1	14.3%	30	-1	34,015	31,130	2,885	9.3%
81	2	79	3950.0%	226	138	19,940	23,411	-3,471	-14.8%
168	254	-86	-33.9%	-4	-4	21,655	18,486	3,169	17.1%
19	128	-109	-85.2%	-65	-38	58,663	51,818	6,845	13.2%
						2,895	2,418	477	19.7%
8	5	3	60.0%	59	10	29,576	19,352	10,224	52.8%

Change: Students		SAT Scores					
Institutions with Over $40 Million in Federal Research, Alphabetically		2015 Median SAT	2006 Median SAT	Net Change in SAT	Percent Change in SAT	Net Change in National Rank	Net Change in Control Rank
Public	Penn. State Univ. - Hershey Med. Ctr.						
Public	Pennsylvania State Univ. - Univ. Park	1195	1200	-5	-0.4%	-6	-22
Private	Princeton University	1490	1480	10	0.7%	-2	-2
Public	Purdue University - West Lafayette	1205	1135	70	6.2%	149	25
Private	Rensselaer Polytechnic Institute	1385	1320	65	4.9%	21	19
Private	Rice University	1475	1430	45	3.1%	5	5
Private	Rockefeller University						
Private	Rush University						
Public	Rutgers University - New Brunswick	1225	1195	30	2.5%	50	5
Public	San Diego State University	1120	1080	40	3.7%	184	32
Private	Scripps Research Institute						
Private	Stanford University	1485	1440	45	3.1%	5	5
Public	Stony Brook University	1265	1180	85	7.2%	108	30
Public	Temple University		1090				
Public	Texas A&M Univ. - College Station	1190	1185	5	0.4%	20	-14
Private	Thomas Jefferson University						
Private	Tufts University	1445	1410	35	2.5%	-1	-1
Private	Tulane University	1360	1323	37	2.8%	10	9
Public	Uniformed Services Univ. of the HS						
Public	University at Albany	1085	1110	-25	-2.3%	-53	-62
Public	University at Buffalo	1160	1145	15	1.3%	65	-4
Public	University of Alabama - Birmingham	1150	1090	60	5.5%	215	42
Public	University of Alabama - Huntsville	1220	1110	110	9.9%	249	60
Public	University of Alaska - Fairbanks	1030	1050	-20	-1.9%	-26	-57
Public	University of Arizona		1110				
Public	Univ. of Arkansas for Med. Sciences						
Public	University of California - Berkeley	1380	1335	45	3.4%	9	0
Public	University of California - Davis	1205	1180	25	2.1%	52	1
Public	University of California - Irvine	1160	1200	-40	-3.3%	-61	-41
Public	University of California - Los Angeles	1325	1290	35	2.7%	10	-2
Public	University of California - Riverside	1095	1075	20	1.9%	129	12
Public	University of California - San Diego	1335	1260	75	6.0%	36	6
Public	Univ. of California - San Francisco						
Public	Univ. of California - Santa Barbara	1225	1200	25	2.1%	41	1
Public	University of California - Santa Cruz	1175	1160	15	1.3%	62	-4
Public	University of Central Florida	1175	1155	20	1.7%	73	0
Private	University of Chicago	1520	1465	55	3.8%	7	7
Public	University of Cincinnati - Cincinnati	1170	1110	60	5.4%	177	30
Public	University of Colorado - Boulder	1220	1170	50	4.3%	93	15
Public	U. of Colorado - Denv./Anschutz Med.	1050	1050	0	0.0%	67	-19
Public	Univ. of Connecticut - Health Center						
Public	University of Connecticut - Storrs	1235	1190	45	3.8%	66	12
Private	University of Dayton	1205	1170	35	3.0%	71	68
Public	University of Delaware	1195	1195	0	0.0%	3	-18
Public	University of Florida	1260	1250	10	0.8%	6	-5
Public	University of Georgia	1240	1230	10	0.8%	11	-6
Public	University of Hawaii - Manoa	1080	1100	-20	-1.8%	-5	-47
Public	University of Houston - Univ. Park	1150	1070	80	7.5%	288	72
Public	University of Idaho	1055	1070	-15	-1.4%	0	-41

National Merit and Achievement Scholars						Headcount Enrollment			
2016 National Merit Scholars	2007 National Merit Scholars	Net Change in Merit Scholars	Percent Change in Merit Scholars	Net Change in National Rank	Net Change in Control Rank	Fall 2015 Total Student Headcount	Fall 2006 Total Student Headcount	Net Change in Enrollment	Percent Change in Enrollment
						878	791	87	11.0%
16	15	1	6.7%	14	0	47,307	42,914	4,393	10.2%
117	211	-94	-44.5%	-11	-4	8,138	7,085	1,053	14.9%
125	88	37	42.0%	11	4	40,472	40,609	-137	-0.3%
25	21	4	19.0%	24	16	6,982	6,680	302	4.5%
67	167	-100	-59.9%	-14	-7	6,719	5,024	1,695	33.7%
						209	199	10	5.0%
						2,515	1,508	1,007	66.8%
35	26	9	34.6%	22	11	49,428	34,392	15,036	43.7%
0	0					34,254	33,441	813	2.4%
179	198	-19	-9.6%	3	3	16,980	17,747	-767	-4.3%
24	3	21	700.0%	150	52	25,272	22,522	2,750	12.2%
0	0					38,007	33,865	4,142	12.2%
122	180	-58	-32.2%	-3	-3	63,813	45,380	18,433	40.6%
0	0					3,717	2,867	850	29.6%
50	63	-13	-20.6%	-2	0	11,137	9,638	1,499	15.6%
39	24	15	62.5%	35	18	12,485	10,237	2,248	22.0%
0	0					17,178	17,434	-256	-1.5%
1	1	0	0.0%	40	0	29,796	27,823	1,973	7.1%
22	6	16	266.7%	101	31	18,333	16,561	1,772	10.7%
1	1	0	0.0%	40	0	7,866	7,091	775	10.9%
0	0					8,638	8,340	298	3.6%
43	71	-28	-39.4%	-13	-6	42,595	36,805	5,790	15.7%
						3,021	2,435	586	24.1%
161	63	98	155.6%	30	14	38,189	33,920	4,269	12.6%
4	6	-2	-33.3%	12	-7	35,186	29,628	5,558	18.8%
3	6	-3	-50.0%	-9	-14	30,836	25,230	5,606	22.2%
43	32	11	34.4%	17	10	41,908	36,611	5,297	14.5%
1	0	1		157	49	21,385	16,875	4,510	26.7%
19	15	4	26.7%	26	7	32,906	26,247	6,659	25.4%
						3,107	2,943	164	5.6%
3	1	2	200.0%	93	22	23,497	21,082	2,415	11.5%
0	1	-1	-100.0%	-48	-37	17,868	15,364	2,504	16.3%
77	45	32	71.1%	23	10	62,953	46,646	16,307	35.0%
277	205	72	35.1%	6	6	15,391	14,263	1,128	7.9%
50	27	23	85.2%	39	20	36,042	28,327	7,715	27.2%
10	7	3	42.9%	44	6	33,056	31,665	1,391	4.4%
0	0					23,671	20,162	3,509	17.4%
							487		
2	3	-1	-33.3%	18	-5	27,043	23,557	3,486	14.8%
1	13	-12	-92.3%	-125	-73	11,250	10,503	747	7.1%
3	19	-16	-84.2%	-89	-39	22,852	20,380	2,472	12.1%
158	196	-38	-19.4%	1	-1	50,645	50,912	-267	-0.5%
39	52	-13	-25.0%	-8	-4	36,130	33,959	2,171	6.4%
0	0					18,865	20,357	-1,492	-7.3%
25	8	17	212.5%	83	28	42,704	34,334	8,370	24.4%
17	14	3	21.4%	22	4	11,372	11,739	-367	-3.1%

Change: Students		SAT Scores					
Institutions with Over $40 Million in Federal Research, Alphabetically		2015 Median SAT	2006 Median SAT	Net Change in SAT	Percent Change in SAT	Net Change in National Rank	Net Change in Control Rank
Public	University of Illinois - Chicago	1090	1090	0	0.0%	59	-18
Public	Univ. of Illinois - Urbana-Champaign	1280	1280	0	0.0%	-7	-6
Public	University of Iowa	1170	1150	20	1.7%	72	-2
Public	University of Kansas - Lawrence	1150	1130	20	1.8%	69	-6
Public	University of Kansas Medical Center						
Public	University of Kentucky	1150	1130	20	1.8%	69	-6
Public	University of Louisville	1170	1110	60	5.4%	177	30
Public	University of Maryland - Baltimore						
Public	Univ. of Maryland - Baltimore County	1210	1190	20	1.7%	43	-1
Public	University of Maryland - College Park	1315	1280	35	2.7%	9	-1
Public	Univ. of Massachusetts - Amherst	1220	1150	70	6.1%	144	28
Public	U. of Mass. Med. Sch. - Worcester						
Private	University of Miami	1340	1270	70	5.5%	31	26
Public	University of Michigan - Ann Arbor	1390	1300	90	6.9%	35	4
Public	University of Minnesota - Twin Cities	1280	1170	110	9.4%	137	37
Public	University of Missouri - Columbia	1205	1170	35	3.0%	71	3
Public	University of Nebraska - Lincoln	1150	1150	0	0.0%	36	-17
Public	University of Nebraska Medical Ctr.						
Public	University of Nevada - Reno	1080	1040	40	3.8%	252	50
Public	Univ. of New Hampshire - Durham	1105	1120	-15	-1.3%	-22	-44
Public	Univ. of New Mexico - Albuquerque	1030	1030	0	0.0%	93	-7
Public	Univ. of North Carolina - Chapel Hill	1360	1300	60	4.6%	22	2
Private	University of Notre Dame	1460	1395	65	4.7%	10	10
Public	University of Oklahoma - HSC						
Public	University of Oklahoma - Norman	1205	1170	35	3.0%	71	3
Public	University of Oregon	1115	1120	-5	-0.4%	24	-27
Private	University of Pennsylvania	1465	1395	70	5.0%	12	12
Public	University of Pittsburgh - Pittsburgh	1265	1230	35	2.8%	27	4
Public	University of Rhode Island	1070	1065	5	0.5%	118	-1
Private	University of Rochester		1325				
Public	Univ. of South Carolina - Columbia	1200	1165	35	3.0%	82	3
Public	University of South Florida - Tampa	1170	1080	90	8.3%	301	74
Private	University of Southern California	1385	1370	15	1.1%	-1	1
Public	University of Tennessee - Knoxville	1220	1170	50	4.3%	93	15
Public	University of Texas - Austin	1290	1225	65	5.3%	49	12
Public	University of Texas - El Paso	935					
Public	University of Texas HSC - Houston						
Public	Univ. of Texas HSC - San Antonio						
Public	U. of Texas MD Anderson Cancer Ctr.						
Public	U. of Texas Med. Branch - Galveston						
Public	Univ. of Texas SW Med. Ctr. - Dallas						
Public	University of Utah	1130	1110	20	1.8%	99	-2
Public	University of Vermont	1195	1170	25	2.1%	48	-6
Public	University of Virginia	1355	1325	30	2.3%	-1	-3
Public	University of Washington - Seattle	1245	1210	35	2.9%	46	3
Public	University of Wisconsin - Madison	1300	1260	40	3.2%	21	2
Public	University of Wyoming	1130	1070	60	5.6%	246	55
Public	Utah State University	1090	1110	-20	-1.8%	-15	-45
Private	Vanderbilt University	1485	1370	115	8.4%	32	32

National Merit and Achievement Scholars						Headcount Enrollment			
2016 National Merit Scholars	2007 National Merit Scholars	Net Change in Merit Scholars	Percent Change in Merit Scholars	Net Change in National Rank	Net Change in Control Rank	Fall 2015 Total Student Headcount	Fall 2006 Total Student Headcount	Net Change in Enrollment	Percent Change in Enrollment
2	3	-1	-33.3%	18	-5	29,048	24,644	4,404	17.9%
29	88	-59	-67.0%	-41	-22	45,842	42,738	3,104	7.3%
26	22	4	18.2%	22	6	30,844	28,816	2,028	7.0%
18	36	-18	-50.0%	-30	-20	27,259	26,773	486	1.8%
							2,150		
99	30	69	230.0%	50	23	29,727	26,382	3,345	12.7%
20	22	-2	-9.1%	9	-2	21,294	20,785	509	2.4%
						6,329	5,636	693	12.3%
3	4	-1	-25.0%	20	-2	13,839	11,798	2,041	17.3%
55	53	2	3.8%	9	3	38,140	35,102	3,038	8.7%
1	1	0	0.0%	40	0	29,269	25,593	3,676	14.4%
						1,079	1,020	59	5.8%
36	31	5	16.1%	13	6	16,825	15,670	1,155	7.4%
60	72	-12	-16.7%	1	0	43,651	40,025	3,626	9.1%
150	100	50	50.0%	11	4	50,678	50,402	276	0.5%
13	20	-7	-35.0%	-8	-10	35,424	28,184	7,240	25.7%
36	66	-30	-45.5%	-20	-11	25,260	22,106	3,154	14.3%
						3,790	3,067	723	23.6%
10	4	6	150.0%	90	23	20,898	16,663	4,235	25.4%
0	2	-2	-100.0%	-82	-46	15,351	14,811	540	3.6%
20	1	19	1900.0%	200	65	27,285	25,721	1,564	6.1%
28	182	-154	-84.6%	-57	-31	29,084	27,717	1,367	4.9%
43	50	-7	-14.0%	0	-1	12,292	11,603	689	5.9%
						3,389	3,790	-401	-10.6%
279	176	103	58.5%	13	4	27,428	25,923	1,505	5.8%
9	7	2	28.6%	37	1	24,032	20,348	3,684	18.1%
134	145	-11	-7.6%	5	4	24,876	23,743	1,133	4.8%
25	30	-5	-16.7%	-1	-3	28,649	26,860	1,789	6.7%
0	1	-1	-100.0%	-48	-37	16,613	15,062	1,551	10.3%
24	32	-8	-25.0%	-13	-4	11,105	8,846	2,259	25.5%
36	39	-3	-7.7%	2	1	33,724	27,390	6,334	23.1%
12	12	0	0.0%	12	-2	42,067	43,636	-1,569	-3.6%
230	244	-14	-5.7%	0	0	43,401	33,389	10,012	30.0%
19	21	-2	-9.5%	12	-1	27,845	28,901	-1,056	-3.7%
74	291	-217	-74.6%	-25	-11	50,950	49,697	1,253	2.5%
0	0					23,397	19,842	3,555	17.9%
						4,795	3,651	1,144	31.3%
						3,130	2,874	256	8.9%
						320	108	212	196.3%
						3,169	2,255	914	40.5%
						2,295	2,434	-139	-5.7%
33	21	12	57.1%	34	13	31,592	30,511	1,081	3.5%
10	5	5	100.0%	73	17	12,815	11,870	945	8.0%
29	42	-13	-31.0%	-13	-8	23,883	24,068	-185	-0.8%
23	42	-19	-45.2%	-25	-16	45,408	39,524	5,884	14.9%
17	32	-15	-46.9%	-28	-20	42,716	41,028	1,688	4.1%
2	4	-2	-50.0%	1	-12	12,648	13,203	-555	-4.2%
0	0					28,622	14,444	14,178	98.2%
220	184	36	19.6%	6	5	12,567	11,607	960	8.3%

Change: Students		SAT Scores					
Institutions with Over $40 Million in Federal Research, Alphabetically		2015 Median SAT	2006 Median SAT	Net Change in SAT	Percent Change in SAT	Net Change in National Rank	Net Change in Control Rank
Public	Virginia Commonwealth University	1095	1060	35	3.3%	194	34
Public	Virginia Polytechnic Inst. and St. U.	1210	1195	15	1.3%	34	-5
Private	Wake Forest University		1320				
Public	Washington State Univ. - Pullman	1030	1090	-60	-5.5%	-180	-114
Private	Washington University in St. Louis	1460	1450	10	0.7%	-5	-5
Public	Wayne State University	1070	950	120	12.6%	701	231
Private	Weill Cornell Medical College						
Public	West Virginia University	1110	1045	65	6.2%	355	93
Private	Woods Hole Oceanographic Inst.						
Private	Yale University	1515	1490	25	1.7%	-1	-1
Private	Yeshiva University	1250	1215	35	2.9%	42	40

National Merit and Achievement Scholars						Headcount Enrollment			
2016 National Merit Scholars	2007 National Merit Scholars	Net Change in Merit Scholars	Percent Change in Merit Scholars	Net Change in National Rank	Net Change in Control Rank	Fall 2015 Total Student Headcount	Fall 2006 Total Student Headcount	Net Change in Enrollment	Percent Change in Enrollment
10	2	8	400.0%	129	38	30,918	30,189	729	2.4%
0	19	-19	-100.0%	-230	-98	32,663	28,470	4,193	14.7%
2	14	-12	-85.7%	-95	-53	7,837	6,739	1,098	16.3%
2	7	-5	-71.4%	-45	-29	29,686	23,655	6,031	25.5%
33	228	-195	-85.5%	-57	-28	14,688	13,355	1,333	10.0%
10	1	9	900.0%	163	47	27,140	32,061	-4,921	-15.3%
					57	1,037	848	189	22.3%
19	29	-10	-34.5%	-10	-10	28,776	27,115	1,661	6.1%
147	240	-93	-38.8%	-8	-4	12,385	11,415	970	8.5%
3	3	0	0.0%	37	32	6,194	6,211	-17	-0.3%

Institutional Characteristics

	Institutions with Over $40 Million in Federal Research, Alphabetically	State	Highest Degree Offered	Has a Medical School
Public	Arizona State University	AZ	Doctor's - Research/Scholar	
Public	Auburn University	AL	Doctor's - Res/Sch & Prof Prac	
Public	Augusta University	GA	Doctor's - Res/Sch & Prof Prac	Yes
Private	Baylor College of Medicine	TX	Doctor's - Res/Sch & Prof Prac	Yes
Private	Boston University	MA	Doctor's - Res/Sch & Prof Prac	Yes
Private	Brandeis University	MA	Doctor's - Research/Scholar	
Private	Brown University	RI	Doctor's - Res/Sch & Prof Prac	Yes
Private	California Institute of Technology	CA	Doctor's - Research/Scholar	
Private	Carnegie Mellon University	PA	Doctor's - Research/Scholar	
Private	Case Western Reserve University	OH	Doctor's - Res/Sch & Prof Prac	Yes
Public	Clemson University	SC	Doctor's - Research/Scholar	
Public	Cleveland State University	OH	Doctor's - Res/Sch & Prof Prac	
Private	Cold Spring Harbor Laboratory	NY	Doctor's - Research/Scholar	
Public	Colorado State University - Fort Collins	CO	Doctor's - Res/Sch & Prof Prac	
Private	Columbia University	NY	Doctor's - Res/Sch & Prof Prac	Yes
Private	Cornell University	NY	Doctor's - Res/Sch & Prof Prac	
Private	Dartmouth College	NH	Doctor's - Res/Sch & Prof Prac	Yes
Private	Drexel University	PA	Doctor's - Res/Sch & Prof Prac	Yes
Private	Duke University	NC	Doctor's - Res/Sch & Prof Prac	Yes
Private	Emory University	GA	Doctor's - Res/Sch & Prof Prac	Yes
Public	Florida International University	FL	Doctor's - Res/Sch & Prof Prac	Yes
Public	Florida State University	FL	Doctor's - Res/Sch & Prof Prac	Yes
Public	George Mason University	VA	Doctor's - Res/Sch & Prof Prac	
Private	George Washington University	DC	Doctor's - Res/Sch & Prof Prac	Yes
Private	Georgetown University	DC	Doctor's - Res/Sch & Prof Prac	Yes
Public	Georgia Institute of Technology	GA	Doctor's - Research/Scholar	
Private	Harvard University	MA	Doctor's - Res/Sch & Prof Prac	Yes
Private	Icahn School of Medicine at Mount Sinai	NY	Doctor's - Res/Sch & Prof Prac	Yes
Public	Indiana University - Bloomington	IN	Doctor's - Res/Sch & Prof Prac	Yes
Public	Iowa State University	IA	Doctor's - Res/Sch & Prof Prac	
Private	Johns Hopkins University	MD	Doctor's - Res/Sch & Prof Prac	Yes
Public	Kansas State University	KS	Doctor's - Res/Sch & Prof Prac	
Public	Louisiana State University - Baton Rouge	LA	Doctor's - Res/Sch & Prof Prac	
Private	Massachusetts Institute of Technology	MA	Doctor's - Research/Scholar	
Private	Medical College of Wisconsin	WI	Doctor's - Res/Sch & Prof Prac	Yes
Public	Medical University of South Carolina	SC	Doctor's - Res/Sch & Prof Prac	Yes
Public	Michigan State University	MI	Doctor's - Res/Sch & Prof Prac	Yes
Public	Mississippi State University	MS	Doctor's - Res/Sch & Prof Prac	
Public	Montana State University - Bozeman	MT	Doctor's - Res/Sch & Prof Prac	
Public	Naval Postgraduate School	CA	Doctor's - Research/Scholar	
Public	New Jersey Institute of Technology	NJ	Doctor's - Research/Scholar	
Public	New Mexico State University - Las Cruces	NM	Doctor's - Res/Sch & Prof Prac	
Private	New York University	NY	Doctor's - Res/Sch & Prof Prac	Yes
Public	North Carolina State University	NC	Doctor's - Res/Sch & Prof Prac	
Private	Northeastern University	MA	Doctor's - Res/Sch & Prof Prac	
Private	Northwestern University	IL	Doctor's - Res/Sch & Prof Prac	Yes
Public	Ohio State University - Columbus	OH	Doctor's - Res/Sch & Prof Prac	Yes
Public	Oregon Health & Science University	OR	Doctor's - Res/Sch & Prof Prac	Yes
Public	Oregon State University	OR	Doctor's - Res/Sch & Prof Prac	

Federal Land Grant Institution	Federal Research Focus	Total Student Enrollment Fall 2015
	Moderate Engineering	90,906
Yes	Moderate Engineering and Moderate Life Sciences	27,287
	All Life Sciences	8,333
	All Life Sciences	1,572
	Strong Life Sciences	32,158
	Moderate Social Sciences and Moderate Life Sciences	5,752
	Strong Life Sciences	9,458
	Strong Physical Sciences	2,255
	Moderate Computer Sciences and Moderate Engineering	12,963
	Heavy Life Sciences	11,340
Yes	Strong Engineering	22,698
	Heavy Life Sciences	16,915
	All Life Sciences	
Yes	Moderate Environmental Sciences and Moderate Life Sciences	30,614
	Strong Life Sciences	28,086
Yes	Strong Life Sciences	21,904
	Strong Life Sciences	6,350
	Strong Life Sciences and Moderate Engineering	25,595
	Heavy Life Sciences	15,984
	Heavy Life Sciences	13,788
	Moderate Engineering and Moderate Life Sciences	49,782
	Mixed	40,830
	Mixed	33,929
	Heavy Life Sciences	26,212
	Heavy Life Sciences	18,459
	Strong Engineering	25,034
	Strong Life Sciences	29,652
	All Life Sciences	1,150
	Strong Life Sciences	48,514
Yes	Moderate Engineering and Moderate Life Sciences	35,714
	Moderate Engineering and Moderate Life Sciences	22,686
Yes	Strong Life Sciences	24,146
Yes-System	Strong Life Sciences	31,524
	Moderate Engineering	11,331
	All Life Sciences	1,217
	All Life Sciences	2,992
Yes	Moderate Physical Sciences and Moderate Life Sciences	50,538
Yes	Moderate Engineering and Moderate Life Sciences	20,873
Yes	Moderate Life Sciences	15,236
	Moderate Engineering	2,665
	Strong Engineering	11,325
Yes	Strong Engineering	15,490
	Heavy Life Sciences	50,027
Yes	Moderate Engineering and Moderate Life Sciences	34,015
	Moderate Engineering	19,940
	Strong Life Sciences	21,655
Yes	Strong Life Sciences	58,663
	Heavy Life Sciences	2,895
Yes	Moderate Environmental Sciences and Moderate Life Sciences	29,576

Institutional Characteristics

	Institutions with Over $40 Million in Federal Research, Alphabetically	State	Highest Degree Offered	Has a Medical School
Public	Pennsylvania State University - Hershey Medical Ctr.	PA	Doctor's - Res/Sch & Prof Prac	Yes
Public	Pennsylvania State University - University Park	PA	Doctor's - Res/Sch & Prof Prac	
Private	Princeton University	NJ	Doctor's - Research/Scholar	
Public	Purdue University - West Lafayette	IN	Doctor's - Res/Sch & Prof Prac	
Private	Rensselaer Polytechnic Institute	NY	Doctor's - Research/Scholar	
Private	Rice University	TX	Doctor's - Research/Scholar	
Private	Rockefeller University	NY	Doctor's - Research/Scholar	
Private	Rush University	IL	Doctor's - Res/Sch & Prof Prac	Yes
Public	Rutgers University - New Brunswick	NJ	Doctor's - Res/Sch & Prof Prac	Yes
Public	San Diego State University	CA	Doctor's - Res/Sch & Prof Prac	
Private	Scripps Research Institute	CA	Doctor's - Research/Scholar	
Private	Stanford University	CA	Doctor's - Res/Sch & Prof Prac	Yes
Public	Stony Brook University	NY	Doctor's - Res/Sch & Prof Prac	Yes
Public	Temple University	PA	Doctor's - Res/Sch & Prof Prac	Yes
Public	Texas A&M University - College Station	TX	Doctor's - Res/Sch & Prof Prac	Yes
Private	Thomas Jefferson University	PA	Doctor's - Res/Sch & Prof Prac	Yes
Private	Tufts University	MA	Doctor's - Res/Sch & Prof Prac	Yes
Private	Tulane University	LA	Doctor's - Res/Sch & Prof Prac	Yes
Public	Uniformed Services University of the Health Sciences	MD	Doctor's - Res/Sch & Prof Prac	
Public	University at Albany	NY	Doctor's - Research/Scholar	
Public	University at Buffalo	NY	Doctor's - Res/Sch & Prof Prac	Yes
Public	University of Alabama - Birmingham	AL	Doctor's - Res/Sch & Prof Prac	Yes
Public	University of Alabama - Huntsville	AL	Doctor's - Res/Sch & Prof Prac	
Public	University of Alaska - Fairbanks	AK	Doctor's - Research/Scholar	
Public	University of Arizona	AZ	Doctor's - Res/Sch & Prof Prac	Yes
Public	University of Arkansas for Medical Sciences	AR	Doctor's - Res/Sch & Prof Prac	Yes
Public	University of California - Berkeley	CA	Doctor's - Res/Sch & Prof Prac	
Public	University of California - Davis	CA	Doctor's - Res/Sch & Prof Prac	Yes
Public	University of California - Irvine	CA	Doctor's - Res/Sch & Prof Prac	Yes
Public	University of California - Los Angeles	CA	Doctor's - Res/Sch & Prof Prac	Yes
Public	University of California - Riverside	CA	Doctor's - Res/Sch & Prof Prac	Yes
Public	University of California - San Diego	CA	Doctor's - Res/Sch & Prof Prac	Yes
Public	University of California - San Francisco	CA	Doctor's - Res/Sch & Prof Prac	Yes
Public	University of California - Santa Barbara	CA	Doctor's - Research/Scholar	
Public	University of California - Santa Cruz	CA	Doctor's - Research/Scholar	
Public	University of Central Florida	FL	Doctor's - Res/Sch & Prof Prac	Yes
Private	University of Chicago	IL	Doctor's - Res/Sch & Prof Prac	Yes
Public	University of Cincinnati - Cincinnati	OH	Doctor's - Res/Sch & Prof Prac	Yes
Public	University of Colorado - Boulder	CO	Doctor's - Res/Sch & Prof Prac	
Public	University of Colorado - Denver/Anschutz Medical	CO	Doctor's - Res/Sch & Prof Prac	Yes
Public	University of Connecticut - Health Center	CT	Doctor's - Res/Sch & Prof Prac	Yes
Public	University of Connecticut - Storrs	CT	Doctor's - Res/Sch & Prof Prac	
Private	University of Dayton	OH	Doctor's - Res/Sch & Prof Prac	
Public	University of Delaware	DE	Doctor's - Res/Sch & Prof Prac	
Public	University of Florida	FL	Doctor's - Res/Sch & Prof Prac	Yes
Public	University of Georgia	GA	Doctor's - Res/Sch & Prof Prac	
Public	University of Hawaii - Manoa	HI	Doctor's - Res/Sch & Prof Prac	Yes
Public	University of Houston - University Park	TX	Doctor's - Res/Sch & Prof Prac	
Public	University of Idaho	ID	Doctor's - Res/Sch & Prof Prac	Yes

Federal Land Grant Institution	Federal Research Focus	Total Student Enrollment Fall 2015
	All Life Sciences	878
Yes	Moderate Engineering	47,307
	Moderate Engineering and Moderate Physical Sciences	8,138
Yes	Moderate Engineering and Moderate Life Sciences	40,472
	Strong Engineering	6,982
	Moderate Engineering	6,719
	Heavy Life Sciences	209
	Heavy Life Sciences	2,515
Yes	Strong Life Sciences	49,428
	Strong Life Sciences	34,254
	All Life Sciences	
	Strong Life Sciences	16,980
	Moderate Life Sciences	25,272
	Heavy Life Sciences	38,007
Yes	Moderate Environmental Sciences and Moderate Life Sciences	63,813
	All Life Sciences	3,717
	Strong Life Sciences	11,137
	Heavy Life Sciences	12,485
	All Life Sciences	
	Heavy Life Sciences	17,178
	Strong Life Sciences and Moderate Engineering	29,796
	Heavy Life Sciences	18,333
	Moderate Computer Sciences and Moderate Engineering	7,866
Yes-System	Strong Environmental Sciences	8,638
Yes	Moderate Physical Sciences and Moderate Life Sciences	42,595
	All Life Sciences	3,021
Yes-System	Moderate Physical Sciences and Moderate Life Sciences	38,189
Yes-System	Strong Life Sciences	35,186
No-System	Strong Life Sciences	30,836
No-System	Strong Life Sciences	41,908
Yes-System	Moderate Life Sciences	21,385
No-System	Strong Life Sciences	32,906
No-System	Heavy Life Sciences	3,107
No-System	Moderate Engineering	23,497
No-System	Moderate Engineering	17,868
	Moderate Engineering	62,953
	Strong Life Sciences	15,391
	Heavy Life Sciences	36,042
	Moderate Environmental Sciences	33,056
	All Life Sciences	23,671
	All Life Sciences	
Yes	Moderate Engineering and Moderate Life Sciences	27,043
	Heavy Engineering	11,250
Yes	Moderate Engineering and Moderate Life Sciences	22,852
Yes	Strong Life Sciences	50,645
Yes	Strong Life Sciences	36,130
Yes	Moderate Environmental Sciences and Moderate Life Sciences	18,865
	Moderate Engineering	42,704
Yes	Strong Life Sciences	11,372

Institutional Characteristics

	Institutions with Over $40 Million in Federal Research, Alphabetically	State	Highest Degree Offered	Has a Medical School
Public	University of Illinois - Chicago	IL	Doctor's - Res/Sch & Prof Prac	Yes
Public	University of Illinois - Urbana-Champaign	IL	Doctor's - Res/Sch & Prof Prac	
Public	University of Iowa	IA	Doctor's - Res/Sch & Prof Prac	Yes
Public	University of Kansas - Lawrence	KS	Doctor's - Res/Sch & Prof Prac	
Public	University of Kansas Medical Center	KS	Doctor's - Res/Sch & Prof Prac	Yes
Public	University of Kentucky	KY	Doctor's - Res/Sch & Prof Prac	Yes
Public	University of Louisville	KY	Doctor's - Res/Sch & Prof Prac	Yes
Public	University of Maryland - Baltimore	MD	Doctor's - Res/Sch & Prof Prac	Yes
Public	University of Maryland - Baltimore County	MD	Doctor's - Research/Scholar	
Public	University of Maryland - College Park	MD	Doctor's - Res/Sch & Prof Prac	
Public	University of Massachusetts - Amherst	MA	Doctor's - Res/Sch & Prof Prac	
Public	University of Massachusetts Medical Sch. - Worcester	MA	Doctor's - Res/Sch & Prof Prac	Yes
Private	University of Miami	FL	Doctor's - Res/Sch & Prof Prac	Yes
Public	University of Michigan - Ann Arbor	MI	Doctor's - Res/Sch & Prof Prac	Yes
Public	University of Minnesota - Twin Cities	MN	Doctor's - Res/Sch & Prof Prac	Yes
Public	University of Missouri - Columbia	MO	Doctor's - Res/Sch & Prof Prac	Yes
Public	University of Nebraska - Lincoln	NE	Doctor's - Res/Sch & Prof Prac	
Public	University of Nebraska Medical Center	NE	Doctor's - Res/Sch & Prof Prac	Yes
Public	University of Nevada - Reno	NV	Doctor's - Res/Sch & Prof Prac	Yes
Public	University of New Hampshire - Durham	NH	Doctor's - Res/Sch & Prof Prac	
Public	University of New Mexico - Albuquerque	NM	Doctor's - Res/Sch & Prof Prac	Yes
Public	University of North Carolina - Chapel Hill	NC	Doctor's - Res/Sch & Prof Prac	Yes
Private	University of Notre Dame	IN	Doctor's - Res/Sch & Prof Prac	
Public	University of Oklahoma - Health Sciences Center	OK	Doctor's - Res/Sch & Prof Prac	Yes
Public	University of Oklahoma - Norman	OK	Doctor's - Res/Sch & Prof Prac	
Public	University of Oregon	OR	Doctor's - Res/Sch & Prof Prac	
Private	University of Pennsylvania	PA	Doctor's - Res/Sch & Prof Prac	Yes
Public	University of Pittsburgh - Pittsburgh	PA	Doctor's - Res/Sch & Prof Prac	Yes
Public	University of Rhode Island	RI	Doctor's - Res/Sch & Prof Prac	
Private	University of Rochester	NY	Doctor's - Res/Sch & Prof Prac	Yes
Public	University of South Carolina - Columbia	SC	Doctor's - Res/Sch & Prof Prac	Yes
Public	University of South Florida - Tampa	FL	Doctor's - Res/Sch & Prof Prac	Yes
Private	University of Southern California	CA	Doctor's - Res/Sch & Prof Prac	Yes
Public	University of Tennessee - Knoxville	TN	Doctor's - Res/Sch & Prof Prac	Yes
Public	University of Texas - Austin	TX	Doctor's - Res/Sch & Prof Prac	
Public	University of Texas - El Paso	TX	Doctor's - Res/Sch & Prof Prac	
Public	University of Texas Health Science Center - Houston	TX	Doctor's - Res/Sch & Prof Prac	Yes
Public	University of Texas Health Science Ctr. - San Antonio	TX	Doctor's - Res/Sch & Prof Prac	Yes
Public	University of Texas MD Anderson Cancer Center	TX	Master's	
Public	University of Texas Medical Branch - Galveston	TX	Doctor's - Res/Sch & Prof Prac	Yes
Public	University of Texas SW Medical Center - Dallas	TX	Doctor's - Res/Sch & Prof Prac	Yes
Public	University of Utah	UT	Doctor's - Res/Sch & Prof Prac	Yes
Public	University of Vermont	VT	Doctor's - Res/Sch & Prof Prac	Yes
Public	University of Virginia	VA	Doctor's - Res/Sch & Prof Prac	Yes
Public	University of Washington - Seattle	WA	Doctor's - Res/Sch & Prof Prac	Yes
Public	University of Wisconsin - Madison	WI	Doctor's - Res/Sch & Prof Prac	Yes
Public	University of Wyoming	WY	Doctor's - Res/Sch & Prof Prac	
Public	Utah State University	UT	Doctor's - Res/Sch & Prof Prac	
Private	Vanderbilt University	TN	Doctor's - Res/Sch & Prof Prac	Yes

Federal Land Grant Institution	Federal Research Focus	Total Student Enrollment Fall 2015
	Heavy Life Sciences	29,048
Yes	Moderate Engineering and Moderate Life Sciences	45,842
	Heavy Life Sciences	30,844
	Strong Life Sciences	27,259
Yes	Strong Life Sciences	29,727
	Heavy Life Sciences	21,294
	All Life Sciences	6,329
	Moderate Environmental Sciences	13,839
Yes	Mixed	38,140
Yes	Moderate Life Sciences	29,269
	All Life Sciences	1,079
	Strong Life Sciences	16,825
	Strong Life Sciences	43,651
Yes	Strong Life Sciences	50,678
Yes-System	Strong Life Sciences	35,424
Yes-System	Moderate Life Sciences	25,260
No-System	All Life Sciences	3,790
Yes	Strong Life Sciences	20,898
Yes	Strong Environmental Sciences and Moderate Life Sciences	15,351
	Strong Life Sciences	27,285
	Strong Life Sciences	29,084
	Moderate Engineering and Moderate Physical Sciences	12,292
	All Life Sciences	3,389
	Moderate Environmental Sciences and Moderate Life Sciences	27,428
	Moderate Life Sciences	24,032
	Heavy Life Sciences	24,876
	Heavy Life Sciences	28,649
Yes	Moderate Environmental Sciences and Moderate Life Sciences	16,613
	Strong Life Sciences and Moderate Engineering	11,105
	Strong Life Sciences	33,724
	Strong Life Sciences	42,067
	Strong Life Sciences	43,401
Yes	Moderate Engineering	27,845
	Moderate Engineering	50,950
	Moderate Engineering and Moderate Life Sciences	23,397
	All Life Sciences	4,795
	All Life Sciences	3,130
	Heavy Life Sciences	320
	All Life Sciences	3,169
	All Life Sciences	2,295
	Strong Life Sciences	31,592
Yes	Heavy Life Sciences	12,815
	Strong Life Sciences	23,883
	Strong Life Sciences	45,408
Yes	Strong Life Sciences	42,716
Yes	Moderate Environmental Sciences and Moderate Life Sciences	12,648
Yes	Strong Engineering	28,622
	Heavy Life Sciences	12,567

Institutional Characteristics

	Institutions with Over $40 Million in Federal Research, Alphabetically	State	Highest Degree Offered	Has a Medical School
Public	Virginia Commonwealth University	VA	Doctor's - Res/Sch & Prof Prac	Yes
Public	Virginia Polytechnic Institute and State University	VA	Doctor's - Res/Sch & Prof Prac	
Private	Wake Forest University	NC	Doctor's - Res/Sch & Prof Prac	Yes
Public	Washington State University - Pullman	WA	Doctor's - Res/Sch & Prof Prac	Yes
Private	Washington University in St. Louis	MO	Doctor's - Res/Sch & Prof Prac	Yes
Public	Wayne State University	MI	Doctor's - Res/Sch & Prof Prac	Yes
Private	Weill Cornell Medical College	NY	Doctor's - Res/Sch & Prof Prac	Yes
Public	West Virginia University	WV	Doctor's - Res/Sch & Prof Prac	Yes
Private	Woods Hole Oceanographic Institution	MA	Non-Degree Granting	
Private	Yale University	CT	Doctor's - Res/Sch & Prof Prac	Yes
Private	Yeshiva University	NY	Doctor's - Res/Sch & Prof Prac	Yes

Federal Land Grant Institution	Federal Research Focus	Total Student Enrollment Fall 2015
	Heavy Life Sciences	30,918
Yes	Moderate Engineering and Moderate Life Sciences	32,663
	All Life Sciences	7,837
Yes	Strong Life Sciences	29,686
	Heavy Life Sciences	14,688
	Heavy Life Sciences	27,140
	All Life Sciences	1,037
Yes	Strong Life Sciences and Moderate Engineering	28,776
	Strong Environmental Sciences and Moderate Engineering	
	Heavy Life Sciences	12,385
	All Life Sciences	6,194

Student Characteristics		Fall 2015 Headcount Enrollment						
Institutions with Over $40 Million in Federal Research, Alphabetically		Total Student Enrollment	Total Undergraduate Students	%	Total Graduate Students	%	First-time, Full-time Students	Full-time Transfer Students
Public	Arizona State University	90,906	74,139	81.6%	16,767	18.4%	11,557	6,866
Public	Auburn University	27,287	21,786	79.8%	5,501	20.2%	4,854	1,128
Public	Augusta University	8,333	4,976	59.7%	3,357	40.3%	779	443
Private	Baylor College of Medicine	1,572	0	0.0%	1,572	100.0%	0	0
Private	Boston University	32,158	17,932	55.8%	14,226	44.2%	3,630	480
Private	Brandeis University	5,752	3,621	63.0%	2,131	37.0%	802	52
Private	Brown University	9,458	6,652	70.3%	2,806	29.7%	1,613	100
Private	California Institute of Technology	2,255	1,001	44.4%	1,254	55.6%	241	6
Private	Carnegie Mellon University	12,963	6,049	46.7%	6,914	53.3%	1,575	60
Private	Case Western Reserve University	11,340	5,121	45.2%	6,219	54.8%	1,258	32
Public	Clemson University	22,698	18,016	79.4%	4,682	20.6%	3,439	1,288
Public	Cleveland State University	16,915	12,101	71.5%	4,814	28.5%	1,847	1,103
Private	Cold Spring Harbor Laboratory							
Public	Colorado State Univ. - Fort Collins	30,614	23,917	78.1%	6,697	21.9%	4,622	1,422
Private	Columbia University	28,086	8,102	28.8%	19,984	71.2%	1,456	475
Private	Cornell University	21,904	14,315	65.4%	7,589	34.6%	3,180	497
Private	Dartmouth College	6,350	4,307	67.8%	2,043	32.2%	1,112	17
Private	Drexel University	25,595	16,464	64.3%	9,131	35.7%	2,720	842
Private	Duke University	15,984	6,639	41.5%	9,345	58.5%	1,746	23
Private	Emory University	13,788	6,867	49.8%	6,921	50.2%	1,357	229
Public	Florida International University	49,782	41,032	82.4%	8,750	17.6%	3,768	3,271
Public	Florida State University	40,830	32,706	80.1%	8,124	19.9%	6,039	1,753
Public	George Mason University	33,929	23,066	68.0%	10,863	32.0%	3,154	1,711
Private	George Washington University	26,212	11,157	42.6%	15,055	57.4%	2,578	363
Private	Georgetown University	18,459	7,562	41.0%	10,897	59.0%	1,566	186
Public	Georgia Institute of Technology	25,034	15,142	60.5%	9,892	39.5%	3,087	458
Private	Harvard University	29,652	10,255	34.6%	19,397	65.4%	1,659	8
Private	Icahn School of Medi. at Mount Sinai	1,150	0	0.0%	1,150	100.0%	0	0
Public	Indiana University - Bloomington	48,514	38,364	79.1%	10,150	20.9%	7,846	855
Public	Iowa State University	35,714	30,034	84.1%	5,680	15.9%	6,202	1,867
Private	Johns Hopkins University	22,686	6,427	28.3%	16,259	71.7%	1,368	105
Public	Kansas State University	24,146	19,859	82.2%	4,287	17.8%	3,559	1,230
Public	Louisiana State Univ. - Baton Rouge	31,524	26,156	83.0%	5,368	17.0%	5,619	945
Private	Massachusetts Institute of Tech.	11,331	4,527	40.0%	6,804	60.0%	1,105	19
Private	Medical College of Wisconsin	1,217	0	0.0%	1,217	100.0%	0	0
Public	Medical University of South Carolina	2,992	324	10.8%	2,668	89.2%	0	147
Public	Michigan State University	50,538	39,143	77.5%	11,395	22.5%	7,991	1,513
Public	Mississippi State University	20,873	17,421	83.5%	3,452	16.5%	3,464	1,701
Public	Montana State University - Bozeman	15,236	13,633	89.5%	1,603	10.5%	2,546	686
Public	Naval Postgraduate School	2,665	0	0.0%	2,665	100.0%	0	0
Public	New Jersey Institute of Technology	11,325	8,008	70.7%	3,317	29.3%	1,000	576
Public	New Mexico State Univ. - Las Cruces	15,490	12,526	80.9%	2,964	19.1%	1,978	547
Private	New York University	50,027	25,722	51.4%	24,305	48.6%	5,886	769
Public	North Carolina State University	34,015	24,111	70.9%	9,904	29.1%	4,359	1,019
Private	Northeastern University	19,940	13,697	68.7%	6,243	31.3%	2,797	517
Private	Northwestern University	21,655	8,839	40.8%	12,816	59.2%	2,018	109
Public	Ohio State University - Columbus	58,663	45,289	77.2%	13,374	22.8%	7,023	2,642
Public	Oregon Health & Science University	2,895	827	28.6%	2,068	71.4%	0	168
Public	Oregon State University	29,576	24,612	83.2%	4,964	16.8%	3,340	1,398

Fall 2015 Part-Time Enrollment			2015-2016 Degrees Awarded				
Percentage of Total Students Enrolled Part Time	Percentage of Under-graduates Enrolled Part Time	Percentage of Graduates Enrolled Part Time	Associate's Degrees	Bachelor's Degrees	Master's Degrees	Doctorate Degrees	Professional Degrees
22.4%	19.0%	37.2%	0	15,297	5,508	674	198
16.0%	9.4%	42.2%	0	4,514	1,186	272	251
17.7%	19.9%	14.5%	10	909	462	20	377
0.2%	0.0%	0.2%	0	0	65	94	183
19.2%	7.5%	33.8%	0	4,495	4,435	579	637
9.6%	0.5%	24.9%	0	1,421	840	83	0
6.0%	5.0%	8.2%	0	1,902	626	235	116
0.0%	0.0%	0.0%	0	249	140	190	0
9.0%	3.2%	14.1%	0	1,577	2,947	323	0
10.0%	2.0%	16.5%	0	1,337	1,410	230	412
11.3%	4.3%	38.3%	0	4,025	1,258	233	0
32.6%	24.6%	52.9%	0	2,417	1,426	54	148
21.9%	13.2%	53.0%	0	5,176	1,774	249	130
16.2%	7.1%	19.9%	0	2,709	7,596	587	702
0.4%	0.1%	1.0%	0	4,092	2,510	497	281
1.8%	0.9%	3.6%	0	1,313	618	87	85
26.8%	14.4%	49.3%	29	4,013	2,455	214	488
5.0%	0.4%	8.3%	0	2,231	2,574	537	346
10.2%	1.7%	18.6%	0	2,403	1,518	251	486
36.1%	37.5%	29.3%	68	9,660	3,104	151	333
14.0%	10.8%	26.8%	192	9,800	2,064	386	330
33.4%	20.1%	61.7%	0	5,270	2,804	322	130
32.5%	8.9%	50.0%	192	2,811	4,109	264	841
20.2%	5.1%	30.7%	0	2,254	3,762	124	845
21.9%	9.7%	40.6%	0	3,419	2,296	531	0
30.6%	30.0%	31.0%	8	1,908	4,350	713	799
0.0%	0.0%	0.0%	0	0	91	23	141
21.7%	17.3%	38.2%	8	7,662	2,485	485	276
9.0%	4.2%	34.4%	0	6,541	1,054	327	141
39.1%	8.6%	51.2%	0	1,964	5,005	528	132
15.9%	9.7%	44.5%	22	3,982	990	179	115
11.7%	9.8%	21.1%	0	4,856	1,134	344	256
1.3%	0.8%	1.7%	0	1,285	1,754	646	0
15.4%	0.0%	15.4%	0	0	53	24	193
6.8%	0.3%	7.5%	0	226	303	181	312
12.9%	8.9%	26.5%	0	8,924	2,246	533	619
14.4%	8.0%	46.4%	0	3,302	716	153	83
20.0%	14.4%	67.2%	60	2,282	470	52	8
44.1%	0.0%	44.1%	0	0	1,258	15	0
27.3%	22.9%	38.0%	0	1,415	1,210	57	0
22.7%	16.8%	47.4%	27	2,749	746	105	15
18.5%	4.8%	32.9%	87	6,389	8,523	489	1,010
21.3%	12.8%	42.0%	120	5,669	2,519	518	98
4.6%	0.2%	14.2%	0	4,041	2,086	186	414
20.6%	6.7%	30.3%	0	2,880	4,923	467	502
13.1%	9.2%	26.3%	0	10,958	2,631	807	802
42.9%	75.1%	30.0%	0	427	278	44	234
25.3%	24.9%	27.6%	0	5,133	946	214	151

Student Characteristics		Fall 2015 Headcount Enrollment						
Institutions with Over $40 Million in Federal Research, Alphabetically		Total Student Enrollment	Total Undergraduate Students	%	Total Graduate Students	%	First-time, Full-time Students	Full-time Transfer Students
Public	Penn. State Univ. - Hershey Med. Ctr.	878	0	0.0%	878	100.0%	0	0
Public	Pennsylvania State Univ. - Univ. Park	47,307	40,742	86.1%	6,565	13.9%	7,600	421
Private	Princeton University	8,138	5,402	66.4%	2,736	33.6%	1,317	0
Public	Purdue University - West Lafayette	40,472	30,560	75.5%	9,912	24.5%	6,983	943
Private	Rensselaer Polytechnic Institute	6,982	5,864	84.0%	1,118	16.0%	1,379	147
Private	Rice University	6,719	3,910	58.2%	2,809	41.8%	967	42
Private	Rockefeller University	209	0	0.0%	209	100.0%	0	0
Private	Rush University	2,515	134	5.3%	2,381	94.7%	0	52
Public	Rutgers University - New Brunswick	49,428	35,484	71.8%	13,944	28.2%	6,602	2,579
Public	San Diego State University	34,254	29,253	85.4%	5,001	14.6%	4,955	3,113
Private	Scripps Research Institute							
Private	Stanford University	16,980	7,000	41.2%	9,980	58.8%	1,719	15
Public	Stony Brook University	25,272	16,831	66.6%	8,441	33.4%	2,836	1,521
Public	Temple University	38,007	28,609	75.3%	9,398	24.7%	4,892	2,135
Public	Texas A&M Univ. - College Station	63,813	48,959	76.7%	14,854	23.3%	9,028	2,526
Private	Thomas Jefferson University	3,717	875	23.5%	2,842	76.5%	0	434
Private	Tufts University	11,137	5,290	47.5%	5,847	52.5%	1,358	74
Private	Tulane University	12,485	7,841	62.8%	4,644	37.2%	1,719	132
Public	Uniformed Services Univ. of the HS							
Public	University at Albany	17,178	12,907	75.1%	4,271	24.9%	2,588	1,272
Public	University at Buffalo	29,796	19,953	67.0%	9,843	33.0%	3,607	1,768
Public	University of Alabama - Birmingham	18,333	11,511	62.8%	6,822	37.2%	1,593	837
Public	University of Alabama - Huntsville	7,866	6,013	76.4%	1,853	23.6%	1,027	605
Public	University of Alaska - Fairbanks	8,638	7,533	87.2%	1,105	12.8%	697	280
Public	University of Arizona	42,595	33,331	78.3%	9,264	21.7%	6,973	1,569
Public	Univ. of Arkansas for Med. Sciences	3,021	774	25.6%	2,247	74.4%	0	17
Public	University of California - Berkeley	38,189	27,496	72.0%	10,693	28.0%	5,510	2,116
Public	University of California - Davis	35,186	28,257	80.3%	6,929	19.7%	5,304	2,880
Public	University of California - Irvine	30,836	25,256	81.9%	5,580	18.1%	5,746	1,909
Public	University of California - Los Angeles	41,908	29,585	70.6%	12,323	29.4%	5,671	3,053
Public	University of California - Riverside	21,385	18,607	87.0%	2,778	13.0%	4,033	1,254
Public	University of California - San Diego	32,906	26,590	80.8%	6,316	19.2%	5,286	2,626
Public	Univ. of California - San Francisco	3,107	0	0.0%	3,107	100.0%	0	0
Public	Univ. of California - Santa Barbara	23,497	20,607	87.7%	2,890	12.3%	4,459	1,484
Public	University of California - Santa Cruz	17,868	16,231	90.8%	1,637	9.2%	3,607	1,105
Public	University of Central Florida	62,953	54,662	86.8%	8,291	13.2%	6,324	4,552
Private	University of Chicago	15,391	5,883	38.2%	9,508	61.8%	1,537	28
Public	University of Cincinnati - Cincinnati	36,042	25,009	69.4%	11,033	30.6%	4,394	839
Public	University of Colorado - Boulder	33,056	27,142	82.1%	5,914	17.9%	6,184	1,026
Public	U. of Colorado - Denv./Anschutz Med.	23,671	14,036	59.3%	9,635	40.7%	1,278	1,429
Public	Univ. of Connecticut - Health Center	581	0	0.0%	575	99.0%	0	0
Public	University of Connecticut - Storrs	26,462	18,826	71.1%	7,642	28.9%	3,766	839
Private	University of Dayton	11,250	8,665	77.0%	2,585	23.0%	2,138	113
Public	University of Delaware	22,852	19,100	83.6%	3,752	16.4%	4,478	329
Public	University of Florida	50,645	33,402	66.0%	17,243	34.0%	6,848	1,626
Public	University of Georgia	36,130	27,547	76.2%	8,583	23.8%	5,248	1,421
Public	University of Hawaii - Manoa	18,865	13,689	72.6%	5,176	27.4%	1,857	1,187
Public	University of Houston - Univ. Park	42,704	34,830	81.6%	7,874	18.4%	4,010	3,165
Public	University of Idaho	11,372	9,116	80.2%	2,256	19.8%	1,557	482

Fall 2015 Part-Time Enrollment			2015-2016 Degrees Awarded				
Percentage of Total Students Enrolled Part Time	Percentage of Under-graduates Enrolled Part Time	Percentage of Graduates Enrolled Part Time	Associate's Degrees	Bachelor's Degrees	Master's Degrees	Doctorate Degrees	Professional Degrees
4.9%	0.0%	4.9%	0	0	60	24	144
4.0%	3.0%	10.3%	12	10,984	1,396	659	96
1.5%	2.3%	0.0%	0	1,307	533	373	0
13.4%	6.1%	36.0%	63	7,317	1,879	727	232
1.6%	0.3%	8.4%	0	1,267	408	142	0
3.7%	1.2%	7.1%	0	1,217	739	211	0
0.0%	0.0%	0.0%	0	0	8	31	0
43.7%	26.1%	44.7%	0	58	450	20	300
14.8%	5.9%	37.3%	101	7,838	3,019	620	627
15.4%	11.1%	40.6%	0	7,058	1,790	85	33
7.1%	0.0%	12.0%	0	1,827	2,328	763	269
16.7%	6.6%	36.8%	0	4,414	1,920	350	280
15.0%	11.5%	25.7%	3	6,133	1,516	256	882
13.1%	11.1%	19.6%	0	10,762	3,213	705	718
28.3%	27.8%	28.5%	2	405	346	13	372
8.6%	1.4%	15.1%	0	1,798	1,286	135	484
17.9%	19.3%	15.6%	60	2,320	1,588	135	399
15.9%	5.3%	48.1%	0	3,364	1,216	193	0
16.6%	7.5%	35.0%	0	5,371	2,405	340	627
35.6%	27.9%	48.5%	0	2,294	1,618	149	360
30.3%	20.6%	61.8%	0	1,087	484	34	17
54.5%	54.9%	52.2%	334	572	227	47	0
14.1%	11.2%	24.3%	0	7,368	1,923	524	383
28.7%	25.7%	29.7%	51	314	238	48	293
5.8%	3.2%	12.7%	0	8,260	2,667	576	391
3.9%	2.8%	8.4%	0	8,185	1,225	513	375
2.5%	1.6%	6.8%	0	6,856	1,518	393	221
3.4%	2.0%	6.7%	0	8,552	3,035	775	598
2.2%	1.8%	4.9%	0	4,507	609	239	0
3.0%	2.5%	5.3%	0	6,477	1,325	529	200
0.0%	0.0%	0.0%	0	0	360	123	455
2.2%	1.8%	5.4%	0	5,721	610	346	0
2.7%	2.5%	4.2%	0	4,301	378	174	0
34.1%	31.1%	53.6%	469	13,002	2,218	299	141
15.7%	0.8%	24.9%	0	1,860	2,727	396	296
26.4%	16.0%	50.1%	42	5,596	3,092	284	476
16.8%	7.7%	58.8%	0	5,994	1,167	410	190
48.0%	42.5%	56.0%	0	2,212	2,162	123	555
0.0%	0.0%	0.0%	0	0	51	16	123
12.6%	3.7%	34.4%	24	5,568	1,743	320	286
10.9%	5.3%	29.7%	0	2,055	808	39	114
10.0%	8.1%	19.9%	288	4,465	889	283	32
15.8%	9.7%	27.6%	380	8,477	3,812	723	1,169
9.9%	6.0%	22.6%	0	7,475	1,620	526	441
24.8%	16.6%	46.3%	0	3,600	1,077	204	174
27.9%	28.5%	25.5%	0	6,802	1,911	358	453
23.6%	18.8%	42.8%	0	1,865	523	69	137

Student Characteristics		Fall 2015 Headcount Enrollment						
Institutions with Over $40 Million in Federal Research, Alphabetically		Total Student Enrollment	Total Undergraduate Students	%	Total Graduate Students	%	First-time, Full-time Students	Full-time Transfer Students
Public	University of Illinois - Chicago	29,048	17,575	60.5%	11,473	39.5%	3,462	1,383
Public	Univ. of Illinois - Urbana-Champaign	45,842	33,368	72.8%	12,474	27.2%	7,556	1,370
Public	University of Iowa	30,844	23,357	75.7%	7,487	24.3%	4,846	886
Public	University of Kansas - Lawrence	23,356	18,716	80.1%	4,578	19.6%	3,567	1,003
Public	University of Kansas Medical Center	3,903	529	13.6%	3,436	88.0%	465	28
Public	University of Kentucky	29,727	22,705	76.4%	7,022	23.6%	5,167	787
Public	University of Louisville	21,294	15,768	74.0%	5,526	26.0%	2,735	785
Public	University of Maryland - Baltimore	6,329	866	13.7%	5,463	86.3%	0	205
Public	Univ. of Maryland - Baltimore County	13,839	11,243	81.2%	2,596	18.8%	1,543	996
Public	University of Maryland - College Park	38,140	27,443	72.0%	10,697	28.0%	3,958	1,920
Public	Univ. of Massachusetts - Amherst	29,269	22,748	77.7%	6,521	22.3%	4,692	1,150
Public	U. of Mass. Med. Sch. - Worcester	1,079	0	0.0%	1,079	100.0%	0	0
Private	University of Miami	16,825	11,100	66.0%	5,725	34.0%	2,057	513
Public	University of Michigan - Ann Arbor	43,651	28,312	64.9%	15,339	35.1%	6,050	859
Public	University of Minnesota - Twin Cities	50,678	34,071	67.2%	16,607	32.8%	5,756	2,211
Public	University of Missouri - Columbia	35,424	27,791	78.5%	7,633	21.5%	6,035	974
Public	University of Nebraska - Lincoln	25,260	20,182	79.9%	5,078	20.1%	4,603	839
Public	University of Nebraska Medical Ctr.	3,790	885	23.4%	2,905	76.6%	0	354
Public	University of Nevada - Reno	20,898	17,770	85.0%	3,128	15.0%	3,818	970
Public	Univ. of New Hampshire - Durham	15,351	13,030	84.9%	2,321	15.1%	3,221	515
Public	Univ. of New Mexico - Albuquerque	27,285	21,347	78.2%	5,938	21.8%	3,289	811
Public	Univ. of North Carolina - Chapel Hill	29,084	18,415	63.3%	10,669	36.7%	4,073	833
Private	University of Notre Dame	12,292	8,462	68.8%	3,830	31.2%	2,007	125
Public	University of Oklahoma - HSC	3,389	835	24.6%	2,554	75.4%	0	456
Public	University of Oklahoma - Norman	27,428	21,297	77.6%	6,131	22.4%	3,915	857
Public	University of Oregon	24,032	20,538	85.5%	3,494	14.5%	4,047	1,239
Private	University of Pennsylvania	24,876	11,588	46.6%	13,288	53.4%	2,377	144
Public	University of Pittsburgh - Pittsburgh	28,649	18,908	66.0%	9,741	34.0%	4,010	748
Public	University of Rhode Island	16,613	13,641	82.1%	2,972	17.9%	2,989	523
Private	University of Rochester	11,105	6,304	56.8%	4,801	43.2%	1,400	140
Public	Univ. of South Carolina - Columbia	33,724	25,237	74.8%	8,487	25.2%	5,156	1,800
Public	University of South Florida - Tampa	42,067	31,111	74.0%	10,956	26.0%	4,085	2,453
Private	University of Southern California	43,401	18,810	43.3%	24,591	56.7%	2,948	1,495
Public	University of Tennessee - Knoxville	27,845	21,863	78.5%	5,982	21.5%	4,700	1,341
Public	University of Texas - Austin	50,950	39,619	77.8%	11,331	22.2%	7,566	2,355
Public	University of Texas - El Paso	23,397	20,220	86.4%	3,177	13.6%	3,061	1,041
Public	University of Texas HSC - Houston	4,795	677	14.1%	4,118	85.9%	0	100
Public	Univ. of Texas HSC - San Antonio	3,130	793	25.3%	2,337	74.7%	0	203
Public	U. of Texas MD Anderson Cancer Ctr.	320	304	95.0%	16	5.0%	0	104
Public	U. of Texas Med. Branch - Galveston	3,169	745	23.5%	2,424	76.5%	0	245
Public	Univ. of Texas SW Med. Ctr. - Dallas	2,295	0	0.0%	2,295	100.0%	0	0
Public	University of Utah	31,592	23,794	75.3%	7,798	24.7%	3,086	1,408
Public	University of Vermont	12,815	10,973	85.6%	1,842	14.4%	2,387	514
Public	University of Virginia	23,883	16,736	70.1%	7,147	29.9%	3,672	585
Public	University of Washington - Seattle	45,408	31,063	68.4%	14,345	31.6%	6,731	1,597
Public	University of Wisconsin - Madison	42,716	30,991	72.6%	11,725	27.4%	6,258	1,199
Public	University of Wyoming	12,648	10,045	79.4%	2,603	20.6%	1,674	709
Public	Utah State University	28,622	25,259	88.3%	3,363	11.7%	4,292	1,265
Private	Vanderbilt University	12,567	6,883	54.8%	5,684	45.2%	1,607	208

Fall 2015 Part-Time Enrollment			2015-2016 Degrees Awarded				
Percentage of Total Students Enrolled Part Time	Percentage of Under-graduates Enrolled Part Time	Percentage of Graduates Enrolled Part Time	Associate's Degrees	Bachelor's Degrees	Master's Degrees	Doctorate Degrees	Professional Degrees
16.4%	8.0%	29.3%	0	4,044	2,359	346	705
8.9%	4.1%	21.7%	0	8,578	3,393	726	289
20.2%	14.8%	37.1%	0	5,367	1,264	468	434
10.5%	11.0%	47.2%	0	4,149	1,302	314	286
44.9%	0.0%	0.0%	0	233	191	22	267
9.4%	6.6%	18.2%	0	4,845	1,235	313	550
23.8%	21.8%	29.6%	26	2,800	1,352	147	392
21.8%	28.4%	20.8%	0	399	887	67	730
22.3%	14.7%	55.3%	0	2,630	666	82	0
12.2%	7.4%	24.4%	0	7,748	2,835	592	36
20.3%	7.3%	65.6%	44	6,232	1,338	298	39
5.4%	0.0%	5.4%	0	0	52	64	120
8.5%	5.8%	13.9%	0	3,065	1,265	216	583
5.8%	3.7%	9.7%	0	7,960	4,324	848	682
23.3%	14.4%	41.6%	0	8,584	3,178	804	1,018
12.5%	6.3%	35.0%	0	6,283	1,619	416	308
15.0%	6.8%	48.0%	0	3,945	852	307	135
14.9%	20.7%	13.1%	0	420	248	86	282
22.2%	15.9%	58.4%	0	3,372	661	130	65
9.3%	2.6%	46.5%	118	3,234	655	66	1
28.0%	24.5%	40.8%	0	4,231	1,179	200	320
17.2%	4.2%	39.8%	0	5,817	2,188	542	703
1.4%	0.1%	4.1%	0	2,764	1,058	216	172
14.9%	5.5%	18.0%	0	465	303	29	398
23.0%	14.9%	51.2%	0	4,400	1,642	210	146
9.9%	9.3%	13.7%	0	5,053	908	159	132
13.3%	10.2%	16.0%	0	3,503	4,228	540	665
11.1%	5.4%	22.2%	0	5,139	2,309	461	626
15.0%	9.9%	38.3%	0	3,342	544	97	155
14.7%	4.1%	28.7%	0	1,885	1,280	301	108
12.7%	6.4%	31.3%	3	6,279	1,628	317	431
28.0%	22.6%	43.3%	226	8,025	2,940	314	389
14.1%	3.2%	22.4%	0	5,325	7,909	714	864
12.1%	5.9%	34.9%	0	4,698	1,474	356	237
7.7%	7.7%	7.8%	0	10,165	3,229	896	490
38.1%	34.7%	59.7%	0	3,449	1,033	78	27
32.0%	21.1%	33.8%	0	423	539	113	393
10.5%	6.8%	11.8%	0	437	225	59	342
20.0%	17.1%	75.0%	0	141	3	0	0
25.0%	16.6%	27.6%	0	482	424	52	300
25.7%	0.0%	25.7%	0	0	98	98	221
27.4%	28.9%	23.0%	0	5,167	1,901	331	384
11.9%	8.9%	29.5%	0	2,462	387	78	143
8.9%	5.6%	16.9%	0	4,883	1,802	315	482
11.7%	8.6%	18.5%	0	8,654	3,588	632	518
10.3%	7.9%	16.6%	0	8,690	2,187	870	591
21.3%	16.4%	40.3%	0	2,333	448	99	117
36.4%	32.3%	66.7%	1,252	3,810	830	94	8
6.0%	0.9%	12.3%	0	2,178	1,554	322	364

Student Characteristics	Fall 2015 Headcount Enrollment						
Institutions with Over $40 Million in Federal Research, Alphabetically	Total Student Enrollment	Total Undergraduate Students	%	Total Graduate Students	%	First-time, Full-time Students	Full-time Transfer Students
Public Virginia Commonwealth University	30,918	23,741	76.8%	7,177	23.2%	3,984	1,767
Public Virginia Polytechnic Inst. and St. U.	32,663	25,384	77.7%	7,279	22.3%	6,315	965
Private Wake Forest University	7,837	4,871	62.2%	2,966	37.8%	1,284	35
Public Washington State Univ. - Pullman	29,686	24,470	82.4%	5,216	17.6%	4,625	2,094
Private Washington University in St. Louis	14,688	7,504	51.1%	7,184	48.9%	1,721	75
Public Wayne State University	27,140	17,587	64.8%	9,553	35.2%	2,320	1,210
Private Weill Cornell Medical College	1,037	0	0.0%	1,037	100.0%	0	0
Public West Virginia University	28,776	22,498	78.2%	6,278	21.8%	4,769	857
Private Woods Hole Oceanographic Inst.							
Private Yale University	12,385	5,532	44.7%	6,853	55.3%	1,363	24
Private Yeshiva University	6,194	2,740	44.2%	3,454	55.8%	771	18

Fall 2015 Part-Time Enrollment			2015-2016 Degrees Awarded				
Percentage of Total Students Enrolled Part Time	Percentage of Under-graduates Enrolled Part Time	Percentage of Graduates Enrolled Part Time	Associate's Degrees	Bachelor's Degrees	Master's Degrees	Doctorate Degrees	Professional Degrees
18.3%	15.2%	28.4%	0	5,321	1,549	306	412
8.7%	2.1%	31.8%	59	6,181	1,365	492	116
4.8%	1.3%	10.5%	0	1,339	875	58	295
15.9%	12.6%	31.2%	0	5,475	892	322	238
13.8%	9.1%	18.6%	5	2,308	1,819	266	428
34.0%	32.6%	36.5%	0	3,137	2,078	222	547
0.1%	0.0%	0.1%	0	0	58	58	105
12.5%	8.7%	26.2%	0	4,550	1,477	210	419
1.1%	0.4%	1.6%	0	1,589	1,818	411	299
16.2%	3.5%	26.3%	322	664	384	152	534

The Center Measures - National Rankings

	Institutions with Over $40 Million in Federal Research, Alphabetically	2017 No. of Measures in Top 25 Nationally	2017 No. of Measures in Top 26-50 Nationally	2016 No. of Measures in Top 25 Nationally	2016 No. of Measures in Top 26-50 Nationally
Public	Arizona State University	1	1	2	0
Public	Auburn University	0	0	0	0
Public	Augusta University	0	0	0	0
Private	Baylor College of Medicine	0	4	0	4
Private	Boston University	1	3	0	4
Private	Brandeis University	0	0	0	0
Private	Brown University	1	3	1	3
Private	California Institute of Technology	2	4	2	5
Private	Carnegie Mellon University	1	3	1	2
Private	Case Western Reserve University	0	3	0	3
Public	Clemson University	0	0	0	0
Public	Cleveland State University	0	0	0	0
Private	Cold Spring Harbor Laboratory	0	0	0	0
Public	Colorado State University - Fort Collins	0	0	0	0
Private	Columbia University	9	0	9	0
Private	Cornell University	4	5	4	5
Private	Dartmouth College	2	1	2	1
Private	Drexel University	0	0	0	0
Private	Duke University	7	2	8	1
Private	Emory University	3	5	2	6
Public	Florida International University	0	0	0	1
Public	Florida State University	0	1	0	1
Public	George Mason University	0	0	0	0
Private	George Washington University	0	0	0	2
Private	Georgetown University	0	1	0	2
Public	Georgia Institute of Technology	2	5	2	5
Private	Harvard University	9	0	9	0
Private	Icahn School of Medicine at Mount Sinai	1	2	1	2
Public	Indiana University - Bloomington	0	4	0	3
Public	Iowa State University	0	0	0	0
Private	Johns Hopkins University	7	2	6	3
Public	Kansas State University	0	0	0	0
Public	Louisiana State University - Baton Rouge	0	0	0	0
Private	Massachusetts Institute of Technology	9	0	9	0
Private	Medical College of Wisconsin	0	0	0	0
Public	Medical University of South Carolina	0	0	0	0
Public	Michigan State University	0	6	1	4
Public	Mississippi State University	0	0	0	0
Public	Montana State University - Bozeman	0	0	0	0
Public	Naval Postgraduate School	0	0	0	0
Public	New Jersey Institute of Technology	0	0	0	0
Public	New Mexico State University - Las Cruces	0	0	0	0
Private	New York University	3	5	3	5
Public	North Carolina State University	1	3	0	3
Private	Northeastern University	1	0	0	2
Private	Northwestern University	6	3	6	3
Public	Ohio State University - Columbus	6	2	5	3
Public	Oregon Health & Science University	0	1	0	1
Public	Oregon State University	0	0	0	0

2015 No. of Measures in Top 25 Nationally	2015 No. of Measures in Top 26-50 Nationally	2014 No. of Measures in Top 25 Nationally	2014 No. of Measures in Top 26-50 Nationally	2013 No. of Measures in Top 25 Nationally	2013 No. of Measures in Top 26-50 Nationally	2012 No. of Measures in Top 25 Nationally	2012 No. of Measures in Top 26-50 Nationally
1	0	1	0	1	1	0	1
0	0	0	0	0	0	0	0
0	0	0	0	0	0	0	0
0	3	0	3	0	3	0	3
0	4	1	3	2	2	1	3
0	0	0	0	0	0	0	1
1	3	1	3	0	3	1	3
2	4	3	2	2	4	2	4
1	2	0	2	0	3	0	3
0	4	0	4	0	3	0	4
0	0	0	0	0	0	0	0
0	0	0	0	0	0	0	0
0	0	0	0	0	0	0	0
0	1	0	0	0	0	0	0
9	0	9	0	9	0	9	0
4	5	3	6	4	5	5	4
2	1	2	1	2	1	2	1
0	0	0	0	0	0	0	0
9	0	8	1	8	1	8	0
3	5	3	5	3	5	3	5
0	0	0	0	0	0	0	0
0	1	0	0	0	1	0	1
0	0	0	0	0	0	0	0
0	0	0	0	0	1	0	0
0	1	0	2	0	1	0	2
3	5	2	4	2	5	3	4
9	0	9	0	8	1	8	1
0	4	0	2	0	2	0	2
0	3	0	3	0	3	0	3
0	0	0	0	0	1	0	1
6	3	8	1	7	2	6	3
0	1	0	0	0	0	0	0
0	0	0	0	0	0	0	0
9	0	9	0	9	0	9	0
0	0	0	0	0	0	0	0
0	0	0	0	0	0	0	0
1	4	0	6	0	6	0	5
0	0	0	0	0	0	0	0
0	0	0	0	0	0	0	0
0	0	0	0	0	0	0	0
0	0	0	0	0	0	0	0
0	0	0	0	0	0	0	0
3	5	4	4	4	5	3	4
0	4	0	4	0	2	0	2
0	1	0	1	0	0	0	0
6	3	6	3	6	3	6	3
6	2	6	2	4	3	5	3
0	1	0	0	0	1	0	1
0	0	0	0	0	1	0	0

The Center Measures - National Rankings

	Institutions with Over $40 Million in Federal Research, Alphabetically	2017 No. of Measures in Top 25 Nationally	2017 No. of Measures in Top 26-50 Nationally	2016 No. of Measures in Top 25 Nationally	2016 No. of Measures in Top 26-50 Nationally
Public	Pennsylvania State Univ. - Hershey Med. Ctr.	0	0	0	0
Public	Pennsylvania State University - Univ. Park	4	3	3	5
Private	Princeton University	4	3	4	2
Public	Purdue University - West Lafayette	2	4	1	5
Private	Rensselaer Polytechnic Institute	0	1	0	1
Private	Rice University	2	0	2	1
Private	Rockefeller University	1	1	1	1
Private	Rush University	0	0	0	0
Public	Rutgers University - New Brunswick	1	3	2	3
Public	San Diego State University	0	0	0	0
Private	Scripps Research Institute	0	3	1	2
Private	Stanford University	9	0	9	0
Public	Stony Brook University	0	0	0	0
Public	Temple University	0	0	0	0
Public	Texas A&M University - College Station	4	3	3	5
Private	Thomas Jefferson University	0	0	0	0
Private	Tufts University	1	0	1	0
Private	Tulane University	0	0	0	0
Public	Uniformed Services University of the HS	0	1	0	0
Public	University at Albany	0	0	0	0
Public	University at Buffalo	0	0	0	0
Public	University of Alabama - Birmingham	0	2	0	2
Public	University of Alabama - Huntsville	0	0	0	0
Public	University of Alaska - Fairbanks	0	0	0	0
Public	University of Arizona	0	7	0	6
Public	University of Arkansas for Medical Sciences	0	0	0	0
Public	University of California - Berkeley	7	2	7	2
Public	University of California - Davis	2	4	3	3
Public	University of California - Irvine	0	3	0	3
Public	University of California - Los Angeles	8	0	7	1
Public	University of California - Riverside	0	0	0	0
Public	University of California - San Diego	5	2	5	2
Public	University of California - San Francisco	6	1	6	1
Public	University of California - Santa Barbara	1	0	1	0
Public	University of California - Santa Cruz	0	0	0	0
Public	University of Central Florida	0	0	0	0
Private	University of Chicago	5	3	5	3
Public	University of Cincinnati - Cincinnati	0	3	0	1
Public	University of Colorado - Boulder	1	5	1	4
Public	Univ. of Colorado - Denver/Anschutz Med.	0	1	0	2
Public	University of Connecticut - Health Center	0	0	0	0
Public	University of Connecticut - Storrs	0	1	0	0
Private	University of Dayton	0	0	0	0
Public	University of Delaware	0	0	0	0
Public	University of Florida	3	4	3	4
Public	University of Georgia	0	1	0	1
Public	University of Hawaii - Manoa	0	0	0	0
Public	University of Houston - University Park	0	0	0	0
Public	University of Idaho	0	0	0	0

2015 No. of Measures in Top 25 Nationally	2015 No. of Measures in Top 26-50 Nationally	2014 No. of Measures in Top 25 Nationally	2014 No. of Measures in Top 26-50 Nationally	2013 No. of Measures in Top 25 Nationally	2013 No. of Measures in Top 26-50 Nationally	2012 No. of Measures in Top 25 Nationally	2012 No. of Measures in Top 26-50 Nationally
0	0	0	0	0	0	0	0
3	4	4	3	3	4	5	2
4	3	4	2	4	2	4	2
1	5	1	4	1	5	2	4
0	1	0	1	0	1	0	1
2	1	2	1	2	1	2	0
1	1	0	2	1	1	1	1
0	0	0	0	0	0	0	0
0	4	1	4	0	4	0	4
0	0	0	0	0	0	0	0
0	3	0	2	0	2	0	3
9	0	9	0	9	0	9	0
0	0	0	0	0	0	0	0
0	0	0	0	0	0	0	0
4	3	4	4	4	4	3	5
0	0	0	0	0	0	0	0
1	0	1	0	1	0	1	0
0	1	0	1	0	0	0	0
0	0	0	0	0	0	0	0
0	0	0	0	0	0	0	0
0	0	0	1	0	0	0	0
0	2	0	2	0	2	0	2
0	0	0	0	0	0	0	0
0	0	0	0	0	0	0	0
0	5	0	5	0	6	0	6
0	0	0	0	0	0	0	0
7	1	7	2	7	2	7	1
2	3	3	3	3	3	3	3
0	3	0	4	0	4	0	4
7	1	7	1	7	1	8	0
0	0	0	0	0	0	0	1
4	3	5	2	6	1	5	2
6	1	6	1	6	1	6	1
1	0	1	1	1	0	1	1
0	0	0	0	0	0	0	0
0	0	0	0	0	0	0	0
5	3	5	4	5	4	5	4
0	4	0	3	0	3	0	2
1	3	1	3	1	3	1	2
0	1	0	2	0	3	0	2
0	0	0	0	0	0	0	0
0	0	0	0	0	0	0	0
0	0	0	0	0	0	0	0
0	1	0	0	0	0	0	0
2	5	2	5	2	5	3	4
0	2	0	1	0	2	0	1
0	0	0	0	0	0	0	0
0	0	0	0	0	1	0	0
0	0	0	0	0	0	0	0

The Center Measures - National Rankings

	Institutions with Over $40 Million in Federal Research, Alphabetically	2017 No. of Measures in Top 25 Nationally	2017 No. of Measures in Top 26-50 Nationally	2016 No. of Measures in Top 25 Nationally	2016 No. of Measures in Top 26-50 Nationally
Public	University of Illinois - Chicago	0	0	0	0
Public	University of Illinois - Urbana-Champaign	3	4	3	4
Public	University of Iowa	0	3	0	3
Public	University of Kansas - Lawrence	0	0	0	1
Public	University of Kansas Medical Center	0	0	0	0
Public	University of Kentucky	0	1	0	0
Public	University of Louisville	0	0	0	0
Public	University of Maryland - Baltimore	0	0	0	0
Public	University of Maryland - Baltimore County	0	0	0	0
Public	University of Maryland - College Park	1	5	1	5
Public	University of Massachusetts - Amherst	0	0	0	1
Public	Univ. of Mass. Med. Sch. - Worcester	0	0	0	0
Private	University of Miami	0	1	0	1
Public	University of Michigan - Ann Arbor	8	1	8	1
Public	University of Minnesota - Twin Cities	6	2	6	2
Public	University of Missouri - Columbia	0	1	0	1
Public	University of Nebraska - Lincoln	0	0	0	1
Public	University of Nebraska Medical Center	0	0	0	0
Public	University of Nevada - Reno	0	0	0	0
Public	University of New Hampshire - Durham	0	0	0	0
Public	University of New Mexico - Albuquerque	0	0	0	0
Public	University of North Carolina - Chapel Hill	6	2	4	4
Private	University of Notre Dame	3	1	3	1
Public	University of Oklahoma - HSC	0	0	0	0
Public	University of Oklahoma - Norman	0	1	0	1
Public	University of Oregon	0	0	0	0
Private	University of Pennsylvania	9	0	9	0
Public	University of Pittsburgh - Pittsburgh	3	4	4	3
Public	University of Rhode Island	0	0	0	0
Private	University of Rochester	0	2	0	3
Public	University of South Carolina - Columbia	0	0	0	0
Public	University of South Florida - Tampa	0	2	0	2
Private	University of Southern California	6	3	6	3
Public	University of Tennessee - Knoxville	0	1	0	0
Public	University of Texas - Austin	4	4	4	4
Public	University of Texas - El Paso	0	0	0	0
Public	University of Texas HSC - Houston	0	0	0	0
Public	University of Texas HSC - San Antonio	0	0	0	0
Public	Univ. of Texas MD Anderson Cancer Center	2	1	1	2
Public	Univ. of Texas Medical Branch - Galveston	0	0	0	0
Public	Univ. of Texas SW Medical Center - Dallas	0	5	0	4
Public	University of Utah	0	5	0	4
Public	University of Vermont	0	0	0	0
Public	University of Virginia	1	2	1	4
Public	University of Washington - Seattle	7	1	7	1
Public	University of Wisconsin - Madison	7	1	7	1
Public	University of Wyoming	0	0	0	0
Public	Utah State University	0	0	0	0
Private	Vanderbilt University	3	4	4	3

2015 No. of Measures in Top 25 Nationally	2015 No. of Measures in Top 26-50 Nationally	2014 No. of Measures in Top 25 Nationally	2014 No. of Measures in Top 26-50 Nationally	2013 No. of Measures in Top 25 Nationally	2013 No. of Measures in Top 26-50 Nationally	2012 No. of Measures in Top 25 Nationally	2012 No. of Measures in Top 26-50 Nationally
0	1	0	0	0	0	0	0
5	2	3	4	3	4	3	4
0	4	1	3	0	4	0	7
0	1	0	1	0	1	0	0
0	0	0	0	0	0	0	0
0	0	0	0	0	0	0	0
0	0	0	0	0	0	0	0
0	2	0	1	0	0	0	1
0	0	0	0	0	0	0	0
1	5	1	4	1	5	1	5
0	0	0	0	0	0	0	0
0	1	0	1	0	2	0	2
0	1	0	1	0	1	0	1
8	0	8	0	8	1	8	0
6	2	4	4	6	2	6	2
0	1	0	1	0	1	0	1
0	0	0	0	0	0	0	0
0	0	0	0	0	0	0	0
0	0	0	0	0	0	0	0
0	0	0	0	0	0	0	0
0	0	0	0	0	0	0	0
6	2	6	2	5	3	6	2
3	1	3	1	2	1	2	1
0	0	0	0	0	0	0	0
0	0	0	1	0	0	0	1
0	0	0	1	0	0	0	0
8	1	8	1	9	0	9	0
5	2	4	4	3	5	4	4
0	0	0	0	0	0	0	0
0	3	0	3	0	5	0	4
0	0	0	0	0	0	0	0
0	0	0	0	0	0	0	0
6	3	5	4	6	3	6	3
0	1	0	1	0	2	0	1
4	4	4	4	5	3	5	2
0	0	0	0	0	0	0	0
0	0	0	0	0	0	0	0
0	0	0	0	0	0	0	0
1	2	1	2	1	2	1	2
0	0	0	0	0	0	0	0
0	4	0	4	0	6	0	7
0	5	0	5	1	4	0	3
0	0	0	0	0	0	0	0
1	3	2	4	3	2	1	5
7	1	7	1	7	1	7	1
6	2	7	1	7	1	7	1
0	0	0	0	0	0	0	0
0	0	0	0	0	0	0	0
4	4	4	4	4	4	4	4

The Center Measures - National Rankings

	Institutions with Over $40 Million in Federal Research, Alphabetically	2017 No. of Measures in Top 25 Nationally	2017 No. of Measures in Top 26-50 Nationally	2016 No. of Measures in Top 25 Nationally	2016 No. of Measures in Top 26-50 Nationally
Public	Virginia Commonwealth University	0	0	0	0
Public	Virginia Polytechnic Inst. and State Univ.	0	2	0	2
Private	Wake Forest University	0	0	0	0
Public	Washington State University - Pullman	0	0	0	0
Private	Washington University in St. Louis	4	4	4	4
Public	Wayne State University	0	0	0	0
Private	Weill Cornell Medical College	0	1	0	2
Public	West Virginia University	0	0	0	0
Private	Woods Hole Oceanographic Institution	0	0	0	0
Private	Yale University	8	1	8	1
Private	Yeshiva University	0	0	0	0

2015 No. of Measures in Top 25 Nationally	2015 No. of Measures in Top 26-50 Nationally	2014 No. of Measures in Top 25 Nationally	2014 No. of Measures in Top 26-50 Nationally	2013 No. of Measures in Top 25 Nationally	2013 No. of Measures in Top 26-50 Nationally	2012 No. of Measures in Top 25 Nationally	2012 No. of Measures in Top 26-50 Nationally
0	0	0	1	0	0	0	0
0	2	0	2	0	2	0	2
0	0	0	0	0	0	0	0
0	0	0	0	0	0	0	0
5	2	6	2	4	4	5	3
0	0	0	0	0	0	0	0
0	2	0	2	0	0	0	0
0	0	0	0	0	0	0	0
0	0	0	0	0	0	0	0
8	1	8	1	8	1	8	0
0	1	0	0	0	0	0	1

The Center Measures - Control Rankings

	Institutions with Over $40 Million in Federal Research, Alphabetically	2017 No. of Measures in Top 25 Among Privates/Publics	2017 No. of Measures in Top 26-50 Among Privates/Publics	2016 No. of Measures in Top 25 Among Privates/Publics	2016 No. of Measures in Top 26-50 Among Privates/Publics
Public	Arizona State University	2	5	2	5
Public	Auburn University	0	2	0	2
Public	Augusta University	0	0	0	0
Private	Baylor College of Medicine	4	2	4	3
Private	Boston University	6	2	5	3
Private	Brandeis University	0	7	0	7
Private	Brown University	5	4	4	5
Private	California Institute of Technology	7	2	8	1
Private	Carnegie Mellon University	6	3	5	4
Private	Case Western Reserve University	5	4	2	7
Public	Clemson University	0	1	0	2
Public	Cleveland State University	0	0	0	0
Private	Cold Spring Harbor Laboratory	0	4	0	4
Public	Colorado State University - Fort Collins	0	4	0	5
Private	Columbia University	9	0	9	0
Private	Cornell University	8	1	8	1
Private	Dartmouth College	4	4	3	5
Private	Drexel University	0	7	0	7
Private	Duke University	9	0	9	0
Private	Emory University	8	1	8	1
Public	Florida International University	0	0	0	1
Public	Florida State University	0	5	0	4
Public	George Mason University	0	1	0	0
Private	George Washington University	1	7	3	5
Private	Georgetown University	1	7	1	8
Public	Georgia Institute of Technology	7	2	7	1
Private	Harvard University	9	0	9	0
Private	Icahn School of Medicine at Mount Sinai	3	3	3	3
Public	Indiana University - Bloomington	2	6	3	2
Public	Iowa State University	0	5	0	6
Private	Johns Hopkins University	9	0	8	1
Public	Kansas State University	0	0	0	0
Public	Louisiana State University - Baton Rouge	0	2	0	3
Private	Massachusetts Institute of Technology	9	0	9	0
Private	Medical College of Wisconsin	0	4	0	4
Public	Medical University of South Carolina	0	0	0	0
Public	Michigan State University	5	3	4	4
Public	Mississippi State University	0	0	0	0
Public	Montana State University - Bozeman	0	0	0	0
Public	Naval Postgraduate School	0	0	0	0
Public	New Jersey Institute of Technology	0	1	0	0
Public	New Mexico State University - Las Cruces	0	0	0	0
Private	New York University	8	1	8	0
Public	North Carolina State University	3	6	2	7
Private	Northeastern University	2	5	1	7
Private	Northwestern University	9	0	9	0
Public	Ohio State University - Columbus	9	0	9	0
Public	Oregon Health & Science University	0	5	0	5
Public	Oregon State University	0	2	0	1

2015 No. of Measures in Top 25 Among Privates/Publics	2015 No. of Measures in Top 26-50 Among Privates/Publics	2014 No. of Measures in Top 25 Among Privates/Publics	2014 No. of Measures in Top 26-50 Among Privates/Publics	2013 No. of Measures in Top 25 Among Privates/Publics	2013 No. of Measures in Top 26-50 Among Privates/Publics	2012 No. of Measures in Top 25 Among Privates/Publics	2012 No. of Measures in Top 26-50 Among Privates/Publics
1	6	1	5	1	6	1	6
0	2	0	1	0	1	0	1
0	0	0	0	0	0	0	0
4	1	4	2	4	2	4	2
5	3	5	3	5	3	6	2
0	6	1	5	0	6	1	6
4	5	4	5	4	5	5	4
6	3	8	1	8	1	8	1
6	3	4	5	4	5	4	5
2	7	3	6	2	6	4	5
0	1	0	1	0	1	0	1
0	0	0	0	0	0	0	0
0	3	0	3	0	3	0	1
1	5	0	5	0	3	0	3
9	0	9	0	9	0	9	0
8	1	8	1	8	1	8	1
3	5	4	4	3	5	3	5
0	7	0	7	0	7	0	6
9	0	9	0	9	0	9	0
8	1	8	1	8	1	8	1
0	0	0	0	0	0	0	0
0	4	0	3	0	4	0	6
0	0	0	0	0	0	0	0
2	6	2	6	2	6	1	7
1	8	1	8	1	8	1	8
8	1	7	2	7	2	8	1
9	0	9	0	9	0	9	0
4	2	4	2	4	2	3	2
2	3	3	3	2	3	2	3
0	4	0	3	0	5	0	5
8	1	8	1	8	1	8	1
1	0	0	1	0	0	0	0
0	3	0	3	0	3	0	2
9	0	9	0	9	0	9	0
0	4	0	4	0	4	0	4
0	0	0	1	0	1	0	1
5	3	6	2	4	4	4	4
0	0	0	0	0	0	0	0
0	0	0	0	0	0	0	0
0	0	0	0	0	0	0	0
0	0	0	0	0	0	0	0
0	0	0	0	0	0	0	0
8	0	8	0	8	1	8	0
2	7	3	5	0	8	0	8
1	6	0	7	0	6	0	6
9	0	9	0	9	0	9	0
9	0	9	0	8	1	9	0
1	4	0	5	0	6	0	6
0	3	0	2	1	2	0	1

The Center Measures - Control Rankings

	Institutions with Over $40 Million in Federal Research, Alphabetically	2017 No. of Measures in Top 25 Among Privates/Publics	2017 No. of Measures in Top 26-50 Among Privates/Publics	2016 No. of Measures in Top 25 Among Privates/Publics	2016 No. of Measures in Top 26-50 Among Privates/Publics
Public	Pennsylvania State Univ. - Hershey Med. Ctr.	0	0	0	0
Public	Pennsylvania State University - Univ. Park	6	2	6	2
Private	Princeton University	7	2	7	2
Public	Purdue University - West Lafayette	5	4	6	3
Private	Rensselaer Polytechnic Institute	0	7	0	7
Private	Rice University	3	6	3	6
Private	Rockefeller University	3	4	2	4
Private	Rush University	0	3	0	2
Public	Rutgers University - New Brunswick	4	5	5	4
Public	San Diego State University	0	0	0	0
Private	Scripps Research Institute	5	0	4	1
Private	Stanford University	9	0	9	0
Public	Stony Brook University	1	4	0	5
Public	Temple University	0	0	0	1
Public	Texas A&M University - College Station	7	1	8	0
Private	Thomas Jefferson University	0	5	0	4
Private	Tufts University	1	8	1	8
Private	Tulane University	0	8	0	8
Public	Uniformed Services Univ. of the HS	1	1	0	1
Public	University at Albany	0	0	0	0
Public	University at Buffalo	0	5	0	5
Public	University of Alabama - Birmingham	2	1	1	3
Public	University of Alabama - Huntsville	0	1	0	1
Public	University of Alaska - Fairbanks	0	0	0	0
Public	University of Arizona	5	3	6	2
Public	University of Arkansas for Medical Sciences	0	0	0	0
Public	University of California - Berkeley	9	0	9	0
Public	University of California - Davis	5	4	6	3
Public	University of California - Irvine	2	4	2	4
Public	University of California - Los Angeles	9	0	9	0
Public	University of California - Riverside	0	2	0	1
Public	University of California - San Diego	9	0	8	1
Public	University of California - San Francisco	7	0	7	0
Public	University of California - Santa Barbara	1	5	1	4
Public	University of California - Santa Cruz	0	2	0	1
Public	University of Central Florida	0	1	0	0
Private	University of Chicago	9	0	9	0
Public	University of Cincinnati - Cincinnati	1	6	2	5
Public	University of Colorado - Boulder	5	3	4	4
Public	Univ. of Colorado - Denver/Anschutz Med.	1	4	2	3
Public	University of Connecticut - Health Center	0	0	0	0
Public	University of Connecticut - Storrs	1	2	0	3
Private	University of Dayton	0	2	0	2
Public	University of Delaware	1	1	1	1
Public	University of Florida	8	1	8	1
Public	University of Georgia	1	6	0	6
Public	University of Hawaii - Manoa	0	4	0	4
Public	University of Houston - University Park	0	5	0	4
Public	University of Idaho	0	0	0	0

2015 No. of Measures in Top 25 Among Privates/Publics	2015 No. of Measures in Top 26-50 Among Privates/Publics	2014 No. of Measures in Top 25 Among Privates/Publics	2014 No. of Measures in Top 26-50 Among Privates/Publics	2013 No. of Measures in Top 25 Among Privates/Publics	2013 No. of Measures in Top 26-50 Among Privates/Publics	2012 No. of Measures in Top 25 Among Privates/Publics	2012 No. of Measures in Top 26-50 Among Privates/Publics
0	0	0	0	0	0	0	0
8	0	8	1	7	1	6	3
7	2	7	2	7	2	7	2
5	4	5	3	6	2	6	2
0	7	0	7	0	7	0	8
3	6	4	5	3	6	4	5
2	4	3	3	3	3	2	4
0	2	0	2	0	3	0	3
3	6	3	6	2	5	1	7
0	0	0	0	0	0	0	0
4	0	4	0	4	0	4	0
9	0	9	0	9	0	9	0
0	5	0	6	0	3	0	4
0	1	0	1	0	0	0	0
7	1	8	1	8	1	8	1
0	4	0	4	0	4	0	4
1	8	1	8	1	8	1	8
0	7	0	7	0	7	0	7
0	0	0	0	0	0	0	0
0	0	0	0	0	0	0	1
0	4	0	6	0	6	0	6
1	3	2	1	2	2	2	2
0	0	0	0	0	0	0	0
0	0	0	0	0	0	0	0
4	4	4	4	5	3	6	2
0	0	0	0	0	0	0	0
9	0	9	0	9	0	9	0
5	3	6	3	5	4	6	3
2	5	3	3	1	5	2	5
9	0	9	0	9	0	9	0
0	2	0	2	0	3	0	2
8	1	7	2	8	1	7	2
7	0	7	0	7	0	7	0
1	4	1	4	1	5	1	4
0	1	0	1	0	1	0	1
0	1	0	0	0	0	0	0
9	0	9	0	9	0	9	0
2	5	2	5	3	4	2	5
3	4	4	2	3	4	3	4
1	4	1	3	2	4	1	4
0	0	0	0	0	0	0	0
0	1	0	2	0	2	0	1
0	2	0	2	0	2	0	2
1	1	1	0	1	3	1	1
8	1	8	1	8	1	8	1
1	6	0	6	1	4	1	3
0	5	0	5	0	4	0	3
0	3	0	3	1	4	0	3
0	0	0	0	0	0	0	0

The Center Measures - Control Rankings

	Institutions with Over $40 Million in Federal Research, Alphabetically	2017 No. of Measures in Top 25 Among Privates/Publics	2017 No. of Measures in Top 26-50 Among Privates/Publics	2016 No. of Measures in Top 25 Among Privates/Publics	2016 No. of Measures in Top 26-50 Among Privates/Publics
Public	University of Illinois - Chicago	0	4	0	5
Public	University of Illinois - Urbana-Champaign	8	1	9	0
Public	University of Iowa	2	6	2	6
Public	University of Kansas - Lawrence	0	3	1	3
Public	University of Kansas Medical Center	0	0	0	0
Public	University of Kentucky	1	3	0	6
Public	University of Louisville	0	1	0	1
Public	University of Maryland - Baltimore	0	4	0	4
Public	University of Maryland - Baltimore County	0	1	0	1
Public	University of Maryland - College Park	6	2	6	2
Public	University of Massachusetts - Amherst	0	3	1	1
Public	Univ. of Mass. Med. Sch. - Worcester	0	3	0	3
Private	University of Miami	3	4	3	4
Public	University of Michigan - Ann Arbor	9	0	9	0
Public	University of Minnesota - Twin Cities	9	0	9	0
Public	University of Missouri - Columbia	0	5	0	5
Public	University of Nebraska - Lincoln	0	3	1	2
Public	University of Nebraska Medical Center	0	0	0	0
Public	University of Nevada - Reno	0	0	0	0
Public	University of New Hampshire - Durham	0	0	0	0
Public	University of New Mexico - Albuquerque	0	2	0	2
Public	University of North Carolina - Chapel Hill	9	0	9	0
Private	University of Notre Dame	4	5	5	4
Public	University of Oklahoma - HSC	0	0	0	0
Public	University of Oklahoma - Norman	1	2	1	2
Public	University of Oregon	0	4	0	4
Private	University of Pennsylvania	9	0	9	0
Public	University of Pittsburgh - Pittsburgh	7	2	6	3
Public	University of Rhode Island	0	0	0	0
Private	University of Rochester	3	5	5	3
Public	University of South Carolina - Columbia	0	2	0	4
Public	University of South Florida - Tampa	0	6	0	6
Private	University of Southern California	8	1	8	1
Public	University of Tennessee - Knoxville	1	2	0	3
Public	University of Texas - Austin	8	1	8	1
Public	University of Texas - El Paso	0	0	0	0
Public	University of Texas HSC - Houston	0	1	0	0
Public	University of Texas HSC - San Antonio	0	0	0	0
Public	Univ. of Texas MD Anderson Cancer Ctr.	4	2	4	2
Public	Univ. of Texas Medical Branch - Galveston	0	0	0	0
Public	Univ. of Texas SW Medical Center - Dallas	4	3	3	4
Public	University of Utah	5	3	3	5
Public	University of Vermont	0	0	0	0
Public	University of Virginia	4	4	5	4
Public	University of Washington - Seattle	8	1	8	1
Public	University of Wisconsin - Madison	9	0	9	0
Public	University of Wyoming	0	0	0	0
Public	Utah State University	0	0	0	0
Private	Vanderbilt University	8	1	8	1

2015 No. of Measures in Top 25 Among Privates/Publics	2015 No. of Measures in Top 26-50 Among Privates/Publics	2014 No. of Measures in Top 25 Among Privates/Publics	2014 No. of Measures in Top 26-50 Among Privates/Publics	2013 No. of Measures in Top 25 Among Privates/Publics	2013 No. of Measures in Top 26-50 Among Privates/Publics	2012 No. of Measures in Top 25 Among Privates/Publics	2012 No. of Measures in Top 26-50 Among Privates/Publics
0	5	0	6	0	6	0	5
9	0	9	0	9	0	9	0
3	6	2	6	4	4	6	2
1	3	1	3	1	3	1	3
0	0	0	0	0	0	0	0
0	6	0	6	0	5	0	6
0	1	0	2	0	2	0	2
0	4	0	5	0	4	0	5
0	1	0	1	0	1	0	1
7	0	6	1	7	1	7	1
0	3	0	3	0	2	0	2
0	3	0	4	2	2	2	1
3	4	3	4	3	4	3	4
9	0	9	0	9	0	9	0
9	0	9	0	9	0	8	1
0	5	0	4	0	6	0	5
0	3	0	4	0	2	0	3
0	0	0	0	0	0	0	0
0	0	0	0	0	0	0	0
0	0	0	0	0	0	0	0
0	2	0	1	0	1	0	2
9	0	9	0	9	0	9	0
4	5	4	5	3	6	3	6
0	0	0	0	0	0	0	0
0	2	1	1	0	2	1	2
0	2	1	2	0	3	0	3
9	0	9	0	9	0	9	0
7	2	7	2	8	1	8	1
0	0	0	0	0	0	0	0
5	2	4	4	5	3	6	2
0	2	0	4	0	4	0	3
0	5	0	4	0	4	0	5
8	1	8	1	8	1	8	1
0	5	1	4	2	3	0	5
8	1	8	1	8	1	7	2
0	0	0	0	0	0	0	0
0	2	0	2	0	2	0	1
0	0	0	0	0	0	0	0
4	2	4	2	4	1	4	1
0	0	0	0	0	0	0	0
4	3	4	3	4	3	6	1
5	3	3	5	2	6	2	6
0	0	0	0	0	1	0	0
4	5	5	4	5	3	6	3
8	1	8	1	8	1	8	1
9	0	9	0	9	0	9	0
0	0	0	0	0	0	0	0
0	0	0	0	0	0	0	1
9	0	9	0	9	0	9	0

The Center Measures - Control Rankings

	Institutions with Over $40 Million in Federal Research, Alphabetically	2017 No. of Measures in Top 25 Among Privates/Publics	2017 No. of Measures in Top 26-50 Among Privates/Publics	2016 No. of Measures in Top 25 Among Privates/Publics	2016 No. of Measures in Top 26-50 Among Privates/Publics
Public	Virginia Commonwealth University	1	0	1	1
Public	Virginia Polytechnic Inst. and State Univ.	1	7	2	6
Private	Wake Forest University	0	7	0	6
Public	Washington State University - Pullman	0	6	0	4
Private	Washington University in St. Louis	9	0	9	0
Public	Wayne State University	0	0	0	0
Private	Weill Cornell Medical College	3	4	3	4
Public	West Virginia University	0	0	0	1
Private	Woods Hole Oceanographic Institution	0	4	0	4
Private	Yale University	9	0	9	0
Private	Yeshiva University	0	6	1	5

2015	2015	2014	2014	2013	2013	2012	2012
No. of Measures in Top 25 Among Privates/Publics	No. of Measures in Top 26-50 Among Privates/Publics	No. of Measures in Top 25 Among Privates/Publics	No. of Measures in Top 26-50 Among Privates/Publics	No. of Measures in Top 25 Among Privates/Publics	No. of Measures in Top 26-50 Among Privates/Publics	No. of Measures in Top 25 Among Privates/Publics	No. of Measures in Top 26-50 Among Privates/Publics
1	1	1	2	0	4	0	3
2	6	2	5	2	4	0	8
0	7	0	7	0	7	1	6
0	3	0	4	0	5	0	4
9	0	9	0	9	0	9	0
0	1	0	0	0	0	0	1
4	3	3	4	1	6	2	5
0	0	0	2	0	0	0	1
0	4	0	4	0	4	0	4
9	0	9	0	9	0	9	0
1	6	1	7	2	6	2	6

Federal Research with and without Medical School Research

	Institutions with Over $40 Million in Federal Research excluding Stand-Alone Medical Schools, Alphabetically	AAMC Med School	2015 Federal (x1000)	2015 AAMC Fed (x1000)	2015 Rank Incl AAMC	2015 Rank Excl AAMC	2014 Federal (x1000)	2014 AAMC Fed (x1000)	2014 Rank Incl AAMC	2014 Rank Excl AAMC
Public	Arizona State University		186,890	0	65	39	186,126	0	65	38
Public	Auburn University		47,939	0	149	125	49,739	0	149	126
Public	Augusta University	Yes	50,585	23,589	144	160	47,771	27,219	151	185
Private	Boston University	Yes	256,562	113,968	49	52	254,285	115,773	48	51
Private	Brandeis University		46,764	0	152	129	45,800	0	153	130
Private	Brown University	Yes	127,886	41,467	83	83	125,005	37,446	84	87
Private	California Institute of Technology		269,156	0	44	23	276,447	0	43	22
Private	Carnegie Mellon University		187,259	0	64	38	198,247	0	61	34
Private	Case Western Reserve University	Yes	307,960	251,043	36	117	328,548	265,930	29	112
Public	Clemson University		45,292	0	153	130	44,673	0	155	132
Public	Cleveland State University		41,721	0	157	133	44,139	0	156	133
Private	Cold Spring Harbor Laboratory		49,063	0	148	124	41,845	0	158	134
Public	Colorado State University - Fort Collins		213,685	0	54	32	206,958	0	56	33
Private	Columbia University	Yes	577,833	275,830	7	18	591,523	277,143	8	15
Private	Cornell University		277,163	0	41	20	299,320	0	36	20
Private	Dartmouth College	Yes	145,807	92,511	79	121	145,080	94,250	76	124
Private	Drexel University	Yes	67,226	24,660	126	132	75,557	9,434	122	108
Private	Duke University	Yes	558,566	318,274	9	27	556,847	318,028	10	28
Private	Emory University	Yes	346,534	199,294	25	50	329,254	199,084	27	54
Public	Florida International University	Yes	67,293	2,595	125	108	68,946	1,769	126	106
Public	Florida State University	Yes	133,569	4,855	82	56	140,995	3,413	79	52
Public	George Mason University		54,113	0	141	120	53,775	0	143	120
Private	George Washington University	Yes	135,667	19,172	81	66	139,148	17,636	82	58
Private	Georgetown University	Yes	87,268	74,601	105	219	99,567	82,261	103	204
Public	Georgia Institute of Technology		548,063	0	11	2	510,422	0	14	2
Private	Harvard University	Yes	530,382	153,831	13	8	554,944	170,892	11	8
Public	Indiana University - Bloomington	Yes	206,263	108,460	57	73	80,109	0	117	93
Public	Iowa State University		113,443	0	95	69	115,285	0	91	62
Private	Johns Hopkins University	Yes	1,988,993	445,116	1	1	1,936,953	443,740	1	1
Public	Kansas State University		66,632	0	127	106	64,565	0	129	109
Public	Louisiana State University - Baton Rouge		82,276	0	113	89	93,584	0	105	79
Private	Massachusetts Institute of Technology		486,650	0	15	4	480,991	0	16	4
Public	Michigan State University	Yes	256,228	9,194	50	26	247,970	14,634	49	29
Public	Mississippi State University		79,181	0	116	92	70,615	0	125	102
Public	Montana State University - Bozeman		62,827	0	132	109	66,770	0	128	107
Public	Naval Postgraduate School		71,987	0	123	101	89,284	0	109	84
Public	New Jersey Institute of Technology		50,554	0	145	122	51,853	0	146	123
Public	New Mexico State University - Las Cruces		78,253	0	120	96	80,247	0	116	92
Private	New York University	Yes	326,691	212,823	32	68	314,712	204,375	31	67
Public	North Carolina State University		196,058	0	60	36	177,722	0	70	41
Private	Northeastern University		78,379	0	119	95	77,401	0	120	97
Private	Northwestern University	Yes	385,868	232,322	24	48	385,888	224,480	24	46
Public	Ohio State University - Columbus	Yes	406,941	49,761	22	9	416,177	54,055	21	9
Public	Oregon State University		150,625	0	77	49	143,815	0	77	50
Public	Pennsylvania State University - Univ. Park		447,956	0	19	5	461,896	0	18	5
Private	Princeton University		157,867	0	75	47	163,805	0	72	44
Public	Purdue University - West Lafayette		209,005	0	56	34	227,857	0	53	30
Private	Rensselaer Polytechnic Institute		59,417	0	136	114	58,940	0	136	115
Private	Rice University		73,817	0	122	100	73,782	0	124	101

2013 Federal (x1000)	2013 AAMC Fed (x1000)	2013 Rank Incl AAMC	2013 Rank Excl AAMC	2012 Federal (x1000)	2012 AAMC Fed (x1000)	2012 Rank Incl AAMC	2012 Rank Excl AAMC	2011 Federal (x1000)	2011 AAMC Fed (x1000)	2011 Rank Incl AAMC	2011 Rank Excl AAMC
190,066	0	67	39	182,188	0	68	38	178,153	0	68	40
56,809	0	144	121	55,118	0	149	124	59,061	0	146	119
47,913	26,605	154	188	55,106	33,213	150	188	54,254	32,147	155	188
265,476	128,285	48	54	273,204	131,422	45	53	300,923	140,561	41	48
43,963	0	160	135	44,061	0	162	137	47,793	0	162	133
120,977	65,748	87	124	127,665	76,219	85	129	123,649	72,951	92	129
272,223	0	47	23	322,295	0	34	18	340,131	0	30	12
215,560	0	57	33	209,307	0	60	35	200,878	0	65	35
347,628	283,729	28	111	358,722	298,298	26	116	352,938	303,849	28	132
47,825	0	155	130	48,182	0	157	130	49,365	0	161	131
50,002	0	152	129	46,205	0	159	133	42,292	0	168	141
41,002	0	163	137	43,874	0	163	138	55,450	0	152	124
213,355	0	58	34	245,573	0	53	29	230,661	0	56	32
619,557	295,191	7	16	631,961	287,097	6	14	634,973	289,566	7	10
299,951	0	36	20	298,596	0	41	21	314,371	0	38	17
154,917	107,186	75	131	147,218	102,648	79	136	131,518	105,446	87	177
74,047	10,168	125	112	85,584	14,341	119	106	81,424	15,854	123	108
580,416	342,190	10	30	585,636	360,461	10	34	584,161	390,912	9	37
364,136	212,276	26	50	360,934	282,397	25	95	369,945	323,209	25	135
57,858	2,415	139	123	54,204	2,640	153	128	61,687	3,427	139	122
132,583	5,177	81	61	131,998	6,630	84	60	136,332	7,008	81	61
57,154	0	141	119	57,504	0	145	119	61,016	0	141	111
119,441	17,357	92	74	111,068	16,483	97	78	115,463	18,712	99	79
113,703	96,334	99	203	113,229	95,331	95	206	122,802	105,877	93	212
520,754	0	14	2	482,349	0	16	3	426,088	0	22	6
575,868	186,123	11	9	574,346	198,722	11	8	530,908	231,453	14	21
82,005	0	120	91	72,501	0	133	104	69,298	0	136	105
120,934	0	88	62	117,144	0	94	63	116,109	0	97	63
1,881,959	474,194	1	1	1,845,845	477,549	1	1	1,875,410	500,765	1	1
67,524	0	132	106	73,247	0	131	103	74,414	0	131	101
93,281	0	109	80	91,238	0	114	85	96,050	0	113	81
487,647	0	19	5	478,955	0	18	4	482,544	0	17	3
246,131	17,935	52	31	250,416	20,123	52	32	222,937	15,390	60	34
73,834	0	126	101	96,132	0	111	77	97,987	0	110	76
66,451	0	133	108	78,409	0	125	96	78,431	0	127	97
86,538	0	115	87	120,209	0	91	61	88,950	0	116	86
55,017	0	147	125	57,513	0	143	118	52,873	0	157	125
86,546	0	114	86	90,338	0	115	86	90,283	0	115	85
283,382	194,592	45	84	300,271	208,694	40	83	289,172	196,162	46	83
174,440	0	70	42	171,464	0	72	41	152,790	0	78	50
82,587	0	119	90	75,733	0	129	100	65,757	0	138	107
389,757	234,388	25	48	385,377	228,518	24	50	393,449	230,504	24	46
425,547	50,560	22	10	416,304	53,404	23	10	471,331	63,239	18	7
148,174	0	78	52	155,667	0	78	51	146,069	0	79	54
500,567	0	16	4	469,597	0	19	5	400,294	0	23	8
156,070	0	73	47	160,985	0	75	46	162,491	0	73	47
258,596	0	49	27	255,691	0	51	27	246,116	0	51	26
60,765	0	137	117	62,063	0	139	114	58,951	0	148	120
79,742	0	123	94	76,431	0	128	99	78,249	0	128	98

Federal Research with and without Medical School Research

	Institutions with Over $40 Million in Federal Research excluding Stand Alone Medical Schools, Alphabetically	AAMC Med School	2015 Federal (x1000)	2015 AAMC Fed (x1000)	2015 Rank Incl AAMC	2015 Rank Excl AAMC	2014 Federal (x1000)	2014 AAMC Fed (x1000)	2014 Rank Incl AAMC	2014 Rank Excl AAMC
Private	Rockefeller University		81,949	0	114	91	81,820	0	114	89
Public	Rutgers University - New Brunswick	Yes	320,311	47,981	35	22	355,116	42,392	25	17
Public	San Diego State University		43,526	0	154	131	44,807	0	154	131
Private	Scripps Research Institute		274,097	0	42	21	292,268	0	38	21
Private	Stanford University	Yes	645,633	411,680	4	28	608,342	366,231	4	27
Public	Stony Brook University	Yes	115,031	47,049	93	104	111,386	51,367	97	114
Public	Temple University	Yes	119,945	52,951	89	105	118,892	43,055	89	99
Public	Texas A&M University - College Station	Yes	291,714	14,231	38	19	298,489	0	37	23
Private	Tufts University	Yes	120,181	33,781	88	84	115,046	35,588	92	94
Private	Tulane University	Yes	84,143	23,605	109	112	94,287	25,285	104	104
Public	University at Albany		78,824	0	118	94	104,861	0	99	72
Public	University at Buffalo	Yes	174,146	27,092	70	51	185,144	28,169	66	48
Public	University of Alabama - Birmingham	Yes	325,008	184,555	33	53	276,112	170,690	45	71
Public	University of Alabama - Huntsville		66,564	0	129	107	73,913	0	123	100
Public	University of Alaska - Fairbanks		78,985	0	117	93	83,483	0	113	88
Public	University of Arizona	Yes	265,878	42,269	46	31	286,595	41,933	39	25
Public	University of California - Berkeley		342,042	0	26	11	309,305	0	33	18
Public	University of California - Davis	Yes	322,919	89,513	34	29	327,697	85,100	30	26
Public	University of California - Irvine	Yes	170,622	48,250	72	59	180,431	53,617	69	55
Public	University of California - Los Angeles	Yes	482,771	276,847	16	35	458,157	268,928	19	36
Public	University of California - Riverside	Yes	62,642	2,737	133	113	56,327	2,600	137	121
Public	University of California - San Diego	Yes	601,184	245,930	5	10	597,270	246,807	7	12
Public	University of California - Santa Barbara		114,596	0	94	67	119,816	0	87	60
Public	University of California - Santa Cruz		91,249	0	104	81	89,206	0	110	85
Public	University of Central Florida	Yes	81,788	5,022	115	97	64,323	7,590	130	117
Private	University of Chicago	Yes	290,776	180,683	39	70	276,237	168,641	44	68
Public	University of Cincinnati - Cincinnati	Yes	250,457	73,101	51	43	243,705	82,031	51	45
Public	University of Colorado - Boulder		341,828	0	27	12	302,877	0	34	19
Public	U. of Colorado - Denver/Anschutz Medical	Yes	266,147	144,216	45	60	277,209	156,914	42	59
Public	University of Connecticut - Storrs		91,837	0	103	80	80,317	0	115	91
Private	University of Dayton		74,548	0	121	99	63,881	0	131	110
Public	University of Delaware		109,258	0	97	71	111,933	0	96	65
Public	University of Florida	Yes	281,317	97,378	40	40	279,920	96,651	41	40
Public	University of Georgia		127,825	0	84	57	122,145	0	85	57
Public	University of Hawaii - Manoa	Yes	199,818	16,432	58	41	202,574	18,479	59	39
Public	University of Houston - University Park		54,516	0	140	119	55,574	0	138	118
Public	University of Idaho	Yes	49,591	0	147	123	49,423	0	150	127
Public	University of Illinois - Chicago	Yes	192,930	74,506	61	64	201,646	83,250	60	61
Public	University of Illinois - Urbana-Champaign		330,479	0	30	16	336,172	0	26	13
Public	University of Iowa	Yes	223,730	86,255	53	54	234,122	99,673	52	53
Public	University of Kansas - Lawrence		85,862	0	107	85	88,725	0	111	86
Public	University of Kentucky	Yes	145,097	49,066	80	76	140,450	47,963	80	81
Public	University of Louisville	Yes	66,100	43,342	130	177	63,258	39,871	132	171
Public	University of Maryland - Baltimore County		47,591	0	150	126	46,993	0	152	129
Public	University of Maryland - College Park		332,079	0	28	14	328,828	0	28	14
Public	University of Massachusetts - Amherst		97,206	0	101	74	102,682	0	101	74
Private	University of Miami	Yes	192,691	109,899	62	87	202,818	121,723	58	90
Public	University of Michigan - Ann Arbor	Yes	728,712	293,618	3	6	733,779	297,638	3	6
Public	University of Minnesota - Twin Cities	Yes	468,482	135,686	18	13	483,542	121,874	15	10

2013 Federal (x1000)	2013 AAMC Fed (x1000)	2013 Rank Incl AAMC	2013 Rank Excl AAMC	2012 Federal (x1000)	2012 AAMC Fed (x1000)	2012 Rank Incl AAMC	2012 Rank Excl AAMC	2011 Federal (x1000)	2011 AAMC Fed (x1000)	2011 Rank Incl AAMC	2011 Rank Excl AAMC
80,384	0	122	93	84,616	0	121	90	97,710	0	111	77
288,374	0	41	21	273,498	0	44	23	235,178	0	54	31
45,175	0	157	132	51,690	0	155	127	59,769	0	143	114
308,628	0	33	18	309,471	0	36	20	317,201	0	36	16
625,144	361,418	5	26	607,578	366,588	8	30	633,287	392,135	8	28
118,432	54,994	94	113	123,198	54,142	89	109	124,938	49,688	89	100
124,764	43,446	85	92	85,062	38,434	120	132	84,581	37,870	119	136
302,356	0	35	24	290,245	0	43	26	314,468	0	37	22
112,495	36,309	100	99	120,042	38,601	93	94	120,864	41,388	95	94
97,873	25,465	107	102	101,130	25,972	108	102	110,222	26,242	104	91
113,736	0	98	66	112,161	0	96	65	124,848	0	90	62
200,212	28,930	62	43	186,747	28,225	67	49	176,923	30,378	69	52
286,873	180,400	42	69	303,677	194,866	39	69	340,342	224,432	29	64
83,396	0	118	89	75,715	0	130	101	70,197	0	134	103
92,602	0	111	83	97,472	0	110	76	100,638	0	108	72
334,680	46,323	31	22	328,369	54,346	33	22	324,751	53,239	35	23
305,932	0	34	19	333,179	0	30	16	326,120	0	34	15
344,632	91,832	29	28	356,540	89,309	27	24	359,704	93,294	27	24
196,256	58,249	65	53	204,062	65,708	62	55	204,134	65,322	63	56
489,820	283,756	17	35	527,899	292,433	14	31	545,882	304,724	13	27
57,032	0	143	120	61,304	0	141	115	59,351	0	145	117
630,009	271,904	4	13	653,549	281,874	5	9	635,223	278,345	6	9
131,392	0	82	56	134,984	0	82	57	132,490	0	86	59
88,600	0	112	85	91,409	0	113	84	95,015	0	114	82
68,691	7,446	131	116	72,620	7,555	132	110	66,736	8,220	137	121
294,862	179,901	39	64	329,119	195,640	31	59	365,824	217,273	26	51
256,816	97,383	50	45	266,507	105,764	49	47	286,003	119,635	47	43
309,072	0	32	17	319,019	0	35	19	313,531	0	39	18
290,443	160,966	40	59	308,023	172,565	37	56	299,230	166,799	42	60
86,471	0	116	88	88,834	0	116	87	84,901	0	118	90
66,396	0	134	109	64,369	0	138	112	69,847	0	135	104
114,048	0	97	65	110,760	0	98	66	112,523	0	103	68
285,778	96,537	43	40	295,745	104,207	42	37	296,950	103,316	43	36
127,487	0	83	60	133,525	0	83	58	134,273	0	83	58
225,263	21,795	55	36	193,722	31,645	66	44	201,700	29,341	64	41
57,569	0	140	118	54,657	0	151	125	57,090	0	150	123
52,430	0	149	126	53,765	0	154	126	52,812	0	158	127
219,473	89,679	56	58	243,622	103,123	54	54	245,323	99,175	52	53
459,791	0	20	6	348,536	0	28	12	312,796	0	40	19
252,161	97,465	51	49	265,780	98,803	50	43	280,989	111,828	48	42
99,374	0	105	76	99,034	0	109	75	78,884	0	126	96
148,758	54,736	77	79	157,813	64,628	77	82	175,801	72,873	70	71
72,047	44,043	128	163	79,252	44,775	124	151	84,557	47,398	120	150
44,257	0	158	133	44,669	0	161	135	61,110	0	140	110
341,942	0	30	15	340,180	0	29	15	333,879	0	33	14
103,233	0	104	73	106,470	0	105	71	106,315	0	105	69
204,315	128,068	61	98	222,535	137,831	58	89	223,870	136,436	59	89
802,114	351,344	3	7	773,766	346,182	3	6	801,194	370,081	3	5
489,318	122,906	18	11	480,531	133,996	17	13	482,639	139,542	16	11

Federal Research with and without Medical School Research

	Institutions with Over $40 Million in Federal Research excluding Stand Alone Medical Schools, Alphabetically	AAMC Med School	2015 Federal (x1000)	2015 AAMC Fed (x1000)	2015 Rank Incl AAMC	2015 Rank Excl AAMC	2014 Federal (x1000)	2014 AAMC Fed (x1000)	2014 Rank Incl AAMC	2014 Rank Excl AAMC
Public	University of Missouri - Columbia	Yes	102,852	10,884	99	79	102,784	12,916	100	82
Public	University of Nebraska - Lincoln		94,763	0	102	78	93,190	0	106	80
Public	University of Nevada - Reno	Yes	49,977	13,482	146	138	50,904	18,516	147	144
Public	University of New Hampshire - Durham		83,106	0	111	86	89,640	0	107	83
Public	University of New Mexico - Albuquerque	Yes	151,619	54,920	76	75	151,082	50,456	75	75
Public	University of North Carolina - Chapel Hill	Yes	577,574	249,915	8	17	601,933	248,809	6	11
Private	University of Notre Dame		82,615	0	112	88	79,192	0	119	95
Public	University of Oklahoma - Norman		57,455	0	138	116	53,223	0	145	122
Public	University of Oregon		56,448	0	139	118	62,824	0	133	111
Private	University of Pennsylvania	Yes	597,791	370,570	6	30	606,115	380,930	5	31
Public	University of Pittsburgh - Pittsburgh	Yes	554,658	344,314	10	33	565,409	350,989	9	32
Public	University of Rhode Island		61,085	0	134	111	61,836	0	134	113
Private	University of Rochester	Yes	261,023	141,609	47	63	265,686	153,839	46	66
Public	University of South Carolina - Columbia	Yes	84,723	9,758	108	98	87,844	10,920	112	98
Public	University of South Florida - Tampa	Yes	196,215	59,162	59	55	205,155	59,544	57	49
Private	University of Southern California	Yes	408,105	149,851	21	24	421,887	155,039	20	24
Public	University of Tennessee - Knoxville		116,928	0	92	65	122,120	0	86	69
Public	University of Texas - Austin		331,388	81	29	15	313,955	0	32	16
Public	University of Texas - El Paso		40,334	0	158	134	34,528	0	166	141
Public	University of Utah	Yes	270,311	91,280	43	42	284,125	95,267	40	37
Public	University of Vermont	Yes	83,733	54,792	110	152	79,727	51,878	118	156
Public	University of Virginia	Yes	186,676	96,694	66	82	192,907	89,693	63	73
Public	University of Washington - Seattle	Yes	851,573	347,903	2	3	849,713	341,694	2	3
Public	University of Wisconsin - Madison	Yes	506,910	122,693	14	7	522,251	129,396	13	7
Public	University of Wyoming		47,232	0	151	128	39,778	0	162	136
Public	Utah State University		119,811	0	90	62	114,075	0	93	63
Private	Vanderbilt University	Yes	390,701	308,597	23	90	408,743	310,219	23	76
Public	Virginia Commonwealth University	Yes	123,665	52,213	86	102	119,507	51,909	88	105
Public	Virginia Polytechnic Inst. and State Univ.		191,080	0	63	37	198,092	0	62	35
Private	Wake Forest University	Yes	148,084	142,284	78	277	153,069	145,964	74	266
Public	Washington State University - Pullman		121,627	0	87	61	112,568	0	95	64
Private	Washington University in St. Louis	Yes	424,723	326,558	20	72	410,115	313,053	22	77
Public	Wayne State University	Yes	108,221	60,982	98	127	112,608	65,542	94	128
Public	West Virginia University	Yes	66,608	7,541	128	115	67,450	10,396	127	116
Private	Woods Hole Oceanographic Institution		172,995	0	71	44	177,616	0	71	42
Private	Yale University	Yes	471,381	343,791	17	58	475,585	349,194	17	56
Private	Yeshiva University	Yes	180,791	169,894	69	232	186,885	174,705	64	227

2013 Federal (x1000)	2013 AAMC Fed (x1000)	2013 Rank Incl AAMC	2013 Rank Excl AAMC	2012 Federal (x1000)	2012 AAMC Fed (x1000)	2012 Rank Incl AAMC	2012 Rank Excl AAMC	2011 Federal (x1000)	2011 AAMC Fed (x1000)	2011 Rank Incl AAMC	2011 Rank Excl AAMC
108,305	15,262	101	81	110,446	17,060	100	81	113,072	15,628	101	78
96,177	0	108	78	103,294	0	107	72	104,240	0	106	70
53,898	16,304	148	144	55,150	12,733	148	139	55,374	11,776	153	139
92,778	0	110	82	109,728	0	103	68	96,552	0	112	80
155,684	51,883	74	72	159,302	58,742	76	74	161,950	62,738	74	75
614,627	251,314	8	12	597,629	245,751	9	11	559,620	251,344	12	20
79,268	0	124	95	82,244	0	123	93	79,003	0	125	95
68,902	0	130	105	64,427	0	137	111	46,027	0	164	137
61,856	0	136	114	71,157	0	134	107	71,344	0	133	102
623,939	378,442	6	29	656,425	409,124	4	28	689,571	452,788	4	29
601,358	378,103	9	32	620,070	394,640	7	33	647,060	418,674	5	33
70,900	0	129	103	78,194	0	126	97	77,668	0	129	99
298,781	161,624	37	55	307,390	163,923	38	52	337,312	199,475	31	57
87,562	11,690	113	100	93,237	9,631	112	91	100,045	8,926	109	84
207,441	58,369	60	51	218,772	58,598	59	48	220,931	57,717	61	45
423,708	158,878	23	25	433,136	172,842	20	25	443,458	184,567	20	25
122,051	0	86	71	120,933	0	90	73	115,224	0	100	74
352,788	0	27	14	328,560	0	32	17	334,240	0	32	13
37,741	0	165	143	39,274	0	167	142	34,765	0	180	154
297,099	97,559	38	37	271,629	94,348	47	40	263,623	107,253	50	49
85,028	54,038	117	154	87,843	58,658	117	164	101,465	71,374	107	165
212,051	101,570	59	67	225,558	114,932	57	67	227,937	139,376	58	87
869,623	349,868	2	3	876,941	374,242	2	2	921,399	382,358	2	2
533,220	129,162	13	8	557,688	136,066	13	7	568,389	135,216	11	4
52,296	0	150	127	55,663	0	147	123	47,782	0	163	134
106,074	0	103	70	107,054	0	104	70	112,611	0	102	67
432,752	325,195	21	68	430,445	336,334	22	80	434,213	346,139	21	88
119,293	52,514	93	107	124,836	53,683	88	108	134,431	71,425	82	109
197,462	0	64	38	181,371	0	69	39	187,269	0	67	38
156,506	149,306	72	275	172,779	165,233	70	278	173,004	165,910	71	283
119,921	0	90	63	120,146	0	92	62	115,775	0	98	65
402,702	338,572	24	110	432,434	361,056	21	105	460,282	410,839	19	130
118,217	66,565	95	128	125,965	69,446	86	122	133,925	74,667	85	118
72,677	11,002	127	115	77,981	13,679	127	113	84,061	17,455	121	106
158,672	0	71	46	161,115	0	74	45	165,819	0	72	44
502,439	371,094	15	57	517,072	400,686	15	64	518,195	404,222	15	66
193,831	170,068	66	177	201,397	192,659	64	266	192,241	181,071	66	248

The Center for Measuring University Performance

Part III – The Top 200 Institutions

The following tables list the top 200 universities and colleges on each of the nine performance measures, along with National Merit and Achievement Scholars. (The Source Notes section provides detailed information on each of the 10 data elements.) Unlike the previous tables in Parts I and II, this section includes data for all academic institutions regardless of their federal research activity level.

The Center for Measuring University Performance provides each institution's rank nationally among all universities as well as its rank by institutional control (i.e., rank among private or public peers). In cases where several institutions tie for last place, we use a different cutoff point. For National Academy members, we list all institutions with at least two National Academy members among their faculty. Tables in this section include:

- **2015 Total Research Expenditures**

- **2015 Federal Research Expenditures**

- **2016 Endowment Assets**

- **2016 Annual Giving**

- **2016 National Academy Membership**

- **2016 Faculty Awards**

- **2016 Doctorates Awarded**

- **2015 Postdoctoral Appointees**

- **2015 SAT Scores**

- **2016 National Merit and Achievement Scholars**

Data found in these tables may not always match the figures published by the original source. *The Center for Measuring University Performance* makes adjustments, when necessary, to ensure that the data reflect the activity at a single campus rather than that of a multiple-campus institution or state university system. When data are missing from the original source, *The Center for Measuring University Performance* may substitute another figure if available. A full discussion of this subject, and the various adjustments or substitutions made to the original data, is in the Data Notes section of this report.

The Center for Measuring University Performance presents these tables, along with the prior years' top 200, as Microsoft Excel spreadsheets online at [http://mup.umass.edu].

The Top 200 Institutions – Total Research Expenditures (2015)

Top 1-50 Institutions in Total Research Expenditures	Total Research x $1000	National Rank	Control Rank	Institutional Control
Johns Hopkins University	2,299,057	1	1	Private
University of Michigan - Ann Arbor	1,300,340	2	1	Public
University of California - San Francisco	1,126,620	3	2	Public
University of Washington - Seattle	1,101,078	4	3	Public
University of California - San Diego	1,093,784	5	4	Public
Duke University	1,029,193	6	2	Private
University of California - Los Angeles	992,009	7	5	Public
Stanford University	969,643	8	3	Private
Harvard University	955,246	9	4	Private
University of North Carolina - Chapel Hill	939,252	10	6	Public
University of Wisconsin - Madison	938,366	11	7	Public
Massachusetts Institute of Technology	858,917	12	5	Private
University of Pittsburgh - Pittsburgh	852,333	13	8	Public
University of Minnesota - Twin Cities	844,016	14	9	Public
Texas A&M University - College Station	836,250	15	10	Public
University of Texas MD Anderson Cancer Center	833,406	16	11	Public
University of Pennsylvania	828,649	17	6	Private
Columbia University	826,010	18	7	Private
Yale University	792,953	19	8	Private
Georgia Institute of Technology	757,116	20	12	Public
University of California - Berkeley	748,139	21	13	Public
Ohio State University - Columbus	745,238	22	14	Public
University of California - Davis	706,087	23	15	Public
University of Florida	699,750	24	16	Public
Pennsylvania State University - University Park	683,003	25	17	Public
Washington University in St. Louis	680,150	26	9	Private
University of Southern California	650,457	27	10	Private
Cornell University	637,404	28	11	Private
Northwestern University	627,320	29	12	Private
Vanderbilt University	619,866	30	13	Private
University of Illinois - Urbana-Champaign	614,011	31	18	Public
Rutgers University - New Brunswick	607,257	32	19	Public
University of Arizona	592,874	33	20	Public
Emory University	574,472	34	14	Private
University of Texas - Austin	551,654	35	21	Public
Baylor College of Medicine	520,220	36	15	Private
Michigan State University	519,994	37	22	Public
University of Alabama - Birmingham	509,586	38	23	Public
University of Utah	509,409	39	24	Public
Icahn School of Medicine at Mount Sinai	508,353	40	16	Private
New York University	505,071	41	17	Private
University of Maryland - College Park	503,368	42	25	Public
Purdue University - West Lafayette	498,887	43	26	Public
Virginia Polytechnic Institute and State University	495,502	44	27	Public
North Carolina State University	462,347	45	28	Public
Indiana University - Bloomington	451,508	46	29	Public
University of Texas SW Medical Center - Dallas	438,824	47	30	Public
University of Iowa	423,528	48	31	Public
University of South Florida - Tampa	420,002	49	32	Public
University of Cincinnati - Cincinnati	408,412	50	33	Public

The Top 200 Institutions – Total Research Expenditures (2015)

Top 51-100 Institutions in Total Research Expenditures	Total Research x $1000	National Rank	Control Rank	Institutional Control
Arizona State University	403,708	51	34	Public
University of Colorado - Boulder	403,654	52	35	Public
University of Chicago	402,777	53	18	Private
University of Colorado - Denver/Anschutz Medical	400,515	54	36	Public
Case Western Reserve University	400,167	55	19	Private
Scripps Research Institute	384,161	56	20	Private
University of Maryland - Baltimore	379,465	57	37	Public
Boston University	372,267	58	21	Private
University at Buffalo	367,133	59	38	Public
Uniformed Services University of the Health Sciences	361,173	60	39	Public
California Institute of Technology	350,833	61	22	Private
University of Rochester	344,921	62	23	Private
University of Illinois - Chicago	344,619	63	40	Public
University of Virginia	339,813	64	41	Public
University of Georgia	330,273	65	42	Public
University of Miami	328,082	66	24	Private
University of Kentucky	325,558	67	43	Public
Oregon Health & Science University	325,268	68	44	Public
Rockefeller University	323,932	69	25	Private
University of California - Irvine	313,798	70	45	Public
University of Hawaii - Manoa	313,046	71	46	Public
Weill Cornell Medical College	309,015	72	26	Private
Colorado State University - Fort Collins	308,785	73	47	Public
Washington State University - Pullman	306,989	74	48	Public
Yeshiva University	306,174	75	27	Private
Iowa State University	295,635	76	49	Public
State Univ. of New York - Polytechnic Institute	295,313	77	50	Public
Brown University	286,332	78	28	Private
Louisiana State University - Baton Rouge	274,001	79	51	Public
Princeton University	272,379	80	29	Private
University of Nebraska - Lincoln	260,152	81	52	Public
University of Massachusetts Medical Sch - Worcester	250,338	82	53	Public
Medical University of South Carolina	243,534	83	54	Public
University of Missouri - Columbia	243,430	84	55	Public
Oregon State University	242,874	85	56	Public
Carnegie Mellon University	241,829	86	30	Private
Florida State University	237,427	87	57	Public
University of Texas Health Science Center - Houston	234,299	88	58	Public
University of Tennessee - Knoxville	233,650	89	59	Public
George Washington University	226,132	90	31	Private
University of New Mexico - Albuquerque	224,321	91	60	Public
Stony Brook University	219,485	92	61	Public
Mississippi State University	216,817	93	62	Public
Woods Hole Oceanographic Institution	216,592	94	32	Private
University of California - Santa Barbara	213,537	95	63	Public
Temple University	210,371	96	64	Public
Wayne State University	207,830	97	65	Public
Dartmouth College	203,660	98	33	Private
Medical College of Wisconsin	199,283	99	34	Private
University of Massachusetts - Amherst	197,183	100	66	Public

The Top 200 Institutions – Total Research Expenditures (2015)

Top 101-150 Institutions in Total Research Expenditures	Total Research x $1000	National Rank	Control Rank	Institutional Control
Virginia Commonwealth University	196,412	101	67	Public
University of South Carolina - Columbia	181,742	102	68	Public
Kansas State University	180,082	103	69	Public
Utah State University	173,848	104	70	Public
University of Texas Medical Branch - Galveston	173,506	105	71	Public
University of Kansas - Lawrence	172,406	106	72	Public
Wake Forest University	171,538	107	35	Private
University of Notre Dame	171,148	108	36	Private
University of Connecticut - Storrs	170,730	109	73	Public
University of Texas Health Science Ctr - San Antonio	170,277	110	74	Public
University of Central Florida	169,770	111	75	Public
University of Delaware	167,904	112	76	Public
Tufts University	162,510	113	37	Private
West Virginia University	160,560	114	77	Public
University of Louisville	160,199	115	78	Public
Georgetown University	157,308	116	38	Private
North Dakota State University	148,934	117	79	Public
University of California - Santa Cruz	147,518	118	80	Public
University of Nebraska Medical Center	145,009	119	81	Public
Rice University	141,935	120	39	Private
Tulane University	140,118	121	40	Private
University of Alaska - Fairbanks	139,605	122	82	Public
University of California - Riverside	136,493	123	83	Public
University of Oklahoma - Health Sciences Center	135,493	124	84	Public
Auburn University	132,970	125	85	Public
University of Arkansas for Medical Sciences	132,451	126	86	Public
University of New Hampshire - Durham	130,700	127	87	Public
Texas Tech University	128,554	128	88	Public
New Mexico State University - Las Cruces	127,000	129	89	Public
Oklahoma State University - Stillwater	126,607	130	90	Public
University of Houston - University Park	125,973	131	91	Public
Florida International University	124,631	132	92	Public
Drexel University	122,366	133	41	Private
Clemson University	120,858	134	93	Public
University of Arkansas - Fayetteville	120,679	135	94	Public
Thomas Jefferson University	119,631	136	42	Private
Northeastern University	115,664	137	43	Private
University of Vermont	114,090	138	95	Public
University at Albany	110,284	139	96	Public
Rensselaer Polytechnic Institute	102,122	140	44	Private
Montana State University - Bozeman	98,467	141	97	Public
New Jersey Institute of Technology	96,386	142	98	Public
University of Idaho	95,459	143	99	Public
University of Dayton	93,319	144	45	Private
University of Texas - Dallas	92,374	145	100	Public
University of Oklahoma - Norman	92,075	146	101	Public
Pennsylvania State University - Hershey Medical Ctr.	91,381	147	102	Public
George Mason University	89,845	148	103	Public
University of Rhode Island	86,139	149	104	Public
University of Kansas Medical Center	85,360	150	105	Public

The Top 200 Institutions – Total Research Expenditures (2015)

Top 151-200 Institutions in Total Research Expenditures	Total Research x $1000	National Rank	Control Rank	Institutional Control
University of Alabama - Huntsville	84,745	151	106	Public
Cold Spring Harbor Laboratory	84,653	152	46	Private
University of Nevada - Reno	83,385	153	107	Public
University of Connecticut - Health Center	80,891	154	108	Public
Georgia State University	79,813	155	109	Public
Rush University	79,048	156	47	Private
University of Maine - Orono	78,608	157	110	Public
University of Texas - El Paso	77,515	158	111	Public
San Diego State University	76,131	159	112	Public
University of Texas - Arlington	74,702	160	113	Public
Naval Postgraduate School	74,293	161	114	Public
Binghamton University	70,367	162	115	Public
Brandeis University	68,690	163	48	Private
University of Maryland - Baltimore County	67,944	164	116	Public
Augusta University	67,736	165	117	Public
Michigan Technological University	66,135	166	118	Public
University of Tennessee Health Science Center	65,771	167	119	Public
University of Oregon	65,226	168	120	Public
University of North Dakota	63,590	169	121	Public
University of Montana - Missoula	60,282	170	122	Public
Ohio University - Athens	57,786	171	123	Public
Southern Illinois University - Carbondale	57,509	172	124	Public
University of Massachusetts - Lowell	57,435	173	125	Public
South Dakota State University	57,433	174	126	Public
Colorado School of Mines	57,425	175	127	Public
Cleveland State University	56,683	176	128	Public
University of Wisconsin - Milwaukee	55,883	177	129	Public
University of Louisiana - Lafayette	55,250	178	130	Public
University of Wyoming	54,928	179	131	Public
University of Akron - Akron	54,089	180	132	Public
Wright State University - Dayton	53,881	181	133	Public
College of William and Mary	52,642	182	134	Public
City University of NY - City College	51,905	183	135	Public
University of Alabama - Tuscaloosa	51,555	184	136	Public
Indiana University - Purdue University - Indianapolis	51,479	185	137	Public
University of Texas - San Antonio	50,012	186	138	Public
Wichita State University	49,902	187	139	Public
Syracuse University	49,384	188	49	Private
Univ. of Maryland Center for Environmental Science	49,341	189	140	Public
University of Mississippi - Oxford	49,063	190	141	Public
Old Dominion University	48,418	191	142	Public
University of Toledo	48,391	192	143	Public
University of California System Admin Central Office	48,233	193	144	Public
Loyola University Chicago	47,000	194	50	Private
Louisiana State University HSC - New Orleans	46,840	195	145	Public
University of North Texas Health Science Center	46,335	196	146	Public
Howard University	45,764	197	51	Private
University of Puerto Rico - Medical Sciences	43,316	198	147	Public
Eastern Virginia Medical School	42,296	199	148	Public
University of Southern Mississippi	41,432	200	149	Public

The Top 200 Institutions – Federal Research Expenditures (2015)

Top 1-50 Institutions in Federal Research Expenditures	Federal Research x $1000	National Rank	Control Rank	Institutional Control
Johns Hopkins University	1,988,993	1	1	Private
University of Washington - Seattle	851,573	2	1	Public
University of Michigan - Ann Arbor	728,712	3	2	Public
Stanford University	645,633	4	2	Private
University of California - San Diego	601,184	5	3	Public
University of Pennsylvania	597,791	6	3	Private
Columbia University	577,833	7	4	Private
University of North Carolina - Chapel Hill	577,574	8	4	Public
Duke University	558,566	9	5	Private
University of Pittsburgh - Pittsburgh	554,658	10	5	Public
Georgia Institute of Technology	548,063	11	6	Public
University of California - San Francisco	535,457	12	7	Public
Harvard University	530,382	13	6	Private
University of Wisconsin - Madison	506,910	14	8	Public
Massachusetts Institute of Technology	486,650	15	7	Private
University of California - Los Angeles	482,771	16	9	Public
Yale University	471,381	17	8	Private
University of Minnesota - Twin Cities	468,482	18	10	Public
Pennsylvania State University - University Park	447,956	19	11	Public
Washington University in St. Louis	424,723	20	9	Private
University of Southern California	408,105	21	10	Private
Ohio State University - Columbus	406,941	22	12	Public
Vanderbilt University	390,701	23	11	Private
Northwestern University	385,868	24	12	Private
Emory University	346,534	25	13	Private
University of California - Berkeley	342,042	26	13	Public
University of Colorado - Boulder	341,828	27	14	Public
University of Maryland - College Park	332,079	28	15	Public
University of Texas - Austin	331,388	29	16	Public
University of Illinois - Urbana-Champaign	330,479	30	17	Public
Icahn School of Medicine at Mount Sinai	329,641	31	14	Private
New York University	326,691	32	15	Private
University of Alabama - Birmingham	325,008	33	18	Public
University of California - Davis	322,919	34	19	Public
Rutgers University - New Brunswick	320,311	35	20	Public
Case Western Reserve University	307,960	36	16	Private
Uniformed Services University of the Health Sciences	299,007	37	21	Public
Texas A&M University - College Station	291,714	38	22	Public
University of Chicago	290,776	39	17	Private
University of Florida	281,317	40	23	Public
Cornell University	277,163	41	18	Private
Scripps Research Institute	274,097	42	19	Private
University of Utah	270,311	43	24	Public
California Institute of Technology	269,156	44	20	Private
University of Colorado - Denver/Anschutz Medical	266,147	45	25	Public
University of Arizona	265,878	46	26	Public
University of Rochester	261,023	47	21	Private
Baylor College of Medicine	256,895	48	22	Private
Boston University	256,562	49	23	Private
Michigan State University	256,228	50	27	Public

The Top 200 Institutions – Federal Research Expenditures (2015)

Top 51-100 Institutions in Federal Research Expenditures	Federal Research x $1000	National Rank	Control Rank	Institutional Control
University of Cincinnati - Cincinnati	250,457	51	28	Public
Oregon Health & Science University	243,876	52	29	Public
University of Iowa	223,730	53	30	Public
Colorado State University - Fort Collins	213,685	54	31	Public
University of Maryland - Baltimore	211,773	55	32	Public
Purdue University - West Lafayette	209,005	56	33	Public
Indiana University - Bloomington	206,263	57	34	Public
University of Hawaii - Manoa	199,818	58	35	Public
University of South Florida - Tampa	196,215	59	36	Public
North Carolina State University	196,058	60	37	Public
University of Illinois - Chicago	192,930	61	38	Public
University of Miami	192,691	62	24	Private
Virginia Polytechnic Institute and State University	191,080	63	39	Public
Carnegie Mellon University	187,259	64	25	Private
Arizona State University	186,890	65	40	Public
University of Virginia	186,676	66	41	Public
University of Texas SW Medical Center - Dallas	183,787	67	42	Public
University of Massachusetts Med. Sch. - Worcester	183,588	68	43	Public
Yeshiva University	180,791	69	26	Private
University at Buffalo	174,146	70	44	Public
Woods Hole Oceanographic Institution	172,995	71	27	Private
University of California - Irvine	170,622	72	45	Public
Weill Cornell Medical College	168,103	73	28	Private
University of Texas MD Anderson Cancer Center	161,171	74	46	Public
Princeton University	157,867	75	29	Private
University of New Mexico - Albuquerque	151,619	76	47	Public
Oregon State University	150,625	77	48	Public
Wake Forest University	148,084	78	30	Private
Dartmouth College	145,807	79	31	Private
University of Kentucky	145,097	80	49	Public
George Washington University	135,667	81	32	Private
Florida State University	133,569	82	50	Public
Brown University	127,886	83	33	Private
University of Georgia	127,825	84	51	Public
University of Texas Health Science Center - Houston	125,890	85	52	Public
Virginia Commonwealth University	123,665	86	53	Public
Washington State University - Pullman	121,627	87	54	Public
Tufts University	120,181	88	34	Private
Temple University	119,945	89	55	Public
Utah State University	119,811	90	56	Public
Medical University of South Carolina	117,255	91	57	Public
University of Tennessee - Knoxville	116,928	92	58	Public
Stony Brook University	115,031	93	59	Public
University of California - Santa Barbara	114,596	94	60	Public
Iowa State University	113,443	95	61	Public
Medical College of Wisconsin	109,542	96	35	Private
University of Delaware	109,258	97	62	Public
Wayne State University	108,221	98	63	Public
University of Missouri - Columbia	102,852	99	64	Public
University of Texas Medical Branch - Galveston	98,050	100	65	Public

The Top 200 Institutions – Federal Research Expenditures (2015)

Top 101-150 Institutions in Federal Research Expenditures	Federal Research x $1000	National Rank	Control Rank	Institutional Control
University of Massachusetts - Amherst	97,206	101	66	Public
University of Nebraska - Lincoln	94,763	102	67	Public
University of Connecticut - Storrs	91,837	103	68	Public
University of California - Santa Cruz	91,249	104	69	Public
Georgetown University	87,268	105	36	Private
University of Texas Health Science Ctr. - San Antonio	85,940	106	70	Public
University of Kansas - Lawrence	85,862	107	71	Public
University of South Carolina - Columbia	84,723	108	72	Public
Tulane University	84,143	109	37	Private
University of Vermont	83,733	110	73	Public
University of New Hampshire - Durham	83,106	111	74	Public
University of Notre Dame	82,615	112	38	Private
Louisiana State University - Baton Rouge	82,276	113	75	Public
Rockefeller University	81,949	114	39	Private
University of Central Florida	81,788	115	76	Public
Mississippi State University	79,181	116	77	Public
University of Alaska - Fairbanks	78,985	117	78	Public
University at Albany	78,824	118	79	Public
Northeastern University	78,379	119	40	Private
New Mexico State University - Las Cruces	78,253	120	80	Public
University of Dayton	74,548	121	41	Private
Rice University	73,817	122	42	Private
Naval Postgraduate School	71,987	123	81	Public
University of Nebraska Medical Center	71,918	124	82	Public
Florida International University	67,293	125	83	Public
Drexel University	67,226	126	43	Private
Kansas State University	66,632	127	84	Public
West Virginia University	66,608	128	85	Public
University of Alabama - Huntsville	66,564	129	86	Public
University of Louisville	66,100	130	87	Public
University of Oklahoma - Health Sciences Center	65,463	131	88	Public
Montana State University - Bozeman	62,827	132	89	Public
University of California - Riverside	62,642	133	90	Public
University of Rhode Island	61,085	134	91	Public
Pennsylvania State University - Hershey Medical Ctr.	59,933	135	92	Public
Rensselaer Polytechnic Institute	59,417	136	44	Private
Thomas Jefferson University	58,536	137	45	Private
University of Oklahoma - Norman	57,455	138	93	Public
University of Oregon	56,448	139	94	Public
University of Houston - University Park	54,516	140	95	Public
George Mason University	54,113	141	96	Public
Rush University	52,193	142	46	Private
University of Arkansas for Medical Sciences	50,603	143	97	Public
Augusta University	50,585	144	98	Public
New Jersey Institute of Technology	50,554	145	99	Public
University of Nevada - Reno	49,977	146	100	Public
University of Idaho	49,591	147	101	Public
Cold Spring Harbor Laboratory	49,063	148	47	Private
Auburn University	47,939	149	102	Public
University of Maryland - Baltimore County	47,591	150	103	Public

The Top 200 Institutions – Federal Research Expenditures (2015)

Top 151-200 Institutions in Federal Research Expenditures	Federal Research x $1000	National Rank	Control Rank	Institutional Control
University of Wyoming	47,232	151	104	Public
Brandeis University	46,764	152	48	Private
Clemson University	45,292	153	105	Public
San Diego State University	43,526	154	106	Public
University of Connecticut - Health Center	43,512	155	107	Public
University of Kansas Medical Center	42,512	156	108	Public
Cleveland State University	41,721	157	109	Public
University of Texas - El Paso	40,334	158	110	Public
University of Tennessee Health Science Center	39,356	159	111	Public
Oklahoma State University - Stillwater	38,498	160	112	Public
Howard University	38,051	161	49	Private
City University of NY - City College	37,900	162	113	Public
University of North Dakota	37,457	163	114	Public
Georgia State University	36,843	164	115	Public
Louisiana State University HSC - New Orleans	36,027	165	116	Public
North Dakota State University	35,037	166	117	Public
University of Maine - Orono	35,033	167	118	Public
University of Montana - Missoula	33,617	168	119	Public
Colorado School of Mines	33,578	169	120	Public
University of Arkansas - Fayetteville	33,486	170	121	Public
University of Puerto Rico - Medical Sciences	31,889	171	122	Public
San Jose State University	31,250	172	123	Public
University of Mississippi Medical Center	31,018	173	124	Public
University of Texas - Dallas	30,776	174	125	Public
Morehouse School of Medicine	30,012	175	50	Private
U.S. Air Force Academy	29,417	176	126	Public
University of Massachusetts - Lowell	28,998	177	127	Public
Eastern Virginia Medical School	28,637	178	128	Public
Michigan Technological University	28,581	179	129	Public
South Dakota State University	28,488	180	130	Public
University of Alabama - Tuscaloosa	28,029	181	131	Public
Old Dominion University	27,857	182	132	Public
University of Mississippi - Oxford	27,779	183	133	Public
College of William and Mary	27,722	184	134	Public
Loyola University Chicago	27,380	185	51	Private
Saint Louis University - St. Louis	27,343	186	52	Private
University of Nevada - Las Vegas	26,970	187	135	Public
University of Texas - Arlington	26,858	188	136	Public
Wright State University - Dayton	26,814	189	137	Public
Syracuse University	26,769	190	53	Private
Florida A&M University	26,700	191	138	Public
University of Toledo	26,428	192	139	Public
Worcester Polytechnic Institute	25,743	193	54	Private
Illinois Institute of Technology	25,479	194	55	Private
Texas Tech University	25,458	195	140	Public
Stevens Institute of Technology	25,054	196	56	Private
University of Southern Mississippi	24,710	197	141	Public
University of Wisconsin - Milwaukee	24,222	198	142	Public
Portland State University	23,389	199	143	Public
University of Texas - San Antonio	23,108	200	144	Public

The Top 200 Institutions – Endowment Assets (2016)

Top 1-50 Institutions in Endowment Assets	Endowment Assets x $1000	National Rank	Control Rank	Institutional Control
Harvard University	34,541,893	1	1	Private
Yale University	25,408,600	2	2	Private
Stanford University	22,398,130	3	3	Private
Princeton University	22,152,580	4	4	Private
Massachusetts Institute of Technology	13,181,515	5	5	Private
University of Texas - Austin	10,935,781	6	1	Public
University of Pennsylvania	10,715,364	7	6	Private
Texas A&M University - College Station	9,944,936	8	2	Public
University of Michigan - Ann Arbor	9,743,461	9	3	Public
Northwestern University	9,648,497	10	7	Private
Columbia University	9,041,027	11	8	Private
University of Notre Dame	8,374,083	12	9	Private
University of Chicago	7,001,204	13	10	Private
Duke University	6,839,780	14	11	Private
Washington University in St. Louis	6,461,717	15	12	Private
Emory University	6,401,650	16	13	Private
University of Virginia	5,852,309	17	4	Public
Rice University	5,324,289	18	14	Private
University of Southern California	4,608,714	19	15	Private
Cornell University	4,524,419	20	16	Private
Dartmouth College	4,474,404	21	17	Private
University of California - Los Angeles	3,849,133	22	5	Public
University of California - Berkeley	3,845,281	23	6	Public
Vanderbilt University	3,822,187	24	18	Private
Ohio State University - Columbus	3,578,562	25	7	Public
University of Pittsburgh - Pittsburgh	3,524,904	26	8	Public
New York University	3,487,702	27	19	Private
Johns Hopkins University	3,381,281	28	20	Private
University of Minnesota - Twin Cities	3,280,681	29	9	Public
University of Washington - Seattle	2,968,013	30	10	Public
Brown University	2,963,366	31	21	Private
University of North Carolina - Chapel Hill	2,889,679	32	11	Public
University of Wisconsin - Madison	2,739,728	33	12	Public
Michigan State University	2,585,841	34	13	Public
Williams College	2,256,160	35	22	Private
Purdue University - West Lafayette	2,254,541	36	14	Public
University of Richmond	2,189,546	37	23	Private
University of California - San Francisco	2,112,014	38	15	Public
California Institute of Technology	2,106,724	39	24	Private
Boston College	2,064,300	40	25	Private
Amherst College	2,031,843	41	26	Private
Pomona College	1,984,931	42	27	Private
University of Rochester	1,927,573	43	28	Private
Rockefeller University	1,927,404	44	29	Private
Pennsylvania State University - University Park	1,912,254	45	16	Public
Georgia Institute of Technology	1,843,764	46	17	Public
Wellesley College	1,784,479	47	30	Private
Swarthmore College	1,746,962	48	31	Private
Carnegie Mellon University	1,708,618	49	32	Private
University of Texas SW Medical Center - Dallas	1,684,130	50	18	Public

The Top 200 Institutions – Endowment Assets (2016)

Top 51-100 Institutions in Endowment Assets	Endowment Assets x $1000	National Rank	Control Rank	Institutional Control
Case Western Reserve University	1,662,739	51	33	Private
Boston University	1,654,531	52	34	Private
Grinnell College	1,648,783	53	35	Private
Smith College	1,627,469	54	36	Private
Brigham Young University - Provo	1,571,803	55	37	Private
George Washington University	1,570,278	56	38	Private
Tufts University	1,562,968	57	39	Private
Virginia Commonwealth University	1,559,874	58	19	Public
University of Illinois - Urbana-Champaign	1,489,991	59	20	Public
Georgetown University	1,483,502	60	40	Private
Washington and Lee University	1,472,485	61	41	Private
University of Florida	1,461,347	62	21	Public
Texas Christian University	1,435,899	63	42	Private
Southern Methodist University	1,383,981	64	43	Private
Bowdoin College	1,339,981	65	44	Private
University of Delaware	1,261,790	66	22	Public
University of Iowa	1,259,309	67	23	Public
Weill Cornell Medical College	1,233,303	68	45	Private
University of Texas MD Anderson Cancer Center	1,212,099	69	24	Public
University of California - San Diego	1,176,581	70	25	Public
Tulane University	1,171,314	71	46	Private
University of Cincinnati - Cincinnati	1,165,522	72	26	Public
Lehigh University	1,162,711	73	47	Private
Syracuse University	1,156,828	74	48	Private
University of Kansas - Lawrence	1,150,623	75	27	Public
Baylor University	1,144,280	76	49	Private
Wake Forest University	1,141,211	77	50	Private
University of Kentucky	1,117,852	78	28	Public
Trinity University	1,084,908	79	51	Private
University of Utah	1,076,649	80	29	Public
Baylor College of Medicine	1,063,678	81	52	Private
Saint Louis University - St. Louis	1,053,035	82	53	Private
Berea College	1,050,680	83	54	Private
University of Georgia	1,016,732	84	30	Public
University of Oklahoma - Norman	1,003,434	85	31	Public
Middlebury College	1,000,598	86	55	Private
North Carolina State University	998,600	87	32	Public
Princeton Theological Seminary	995,553	88	56	Private
Indiana University - Bloomington	991,134	89	33	Public
University of California - Davis	965,805	90	34	Public
University of Tulsa	957,523	91	57	Private
Indiana University - Purdue University - Indianapolis	942,121	92	35	Public
Berry College	935,907	93	58	Private
Juilliard School	932,735	94	59	Private
Vassar College	928,812	95	60	Private
Washington State University - Pullman	907,828	96	36	Public
University of Arkansas - Fayetteville	898,908	97	37	Public
University of Nebraska - Lincoln	869,874	98	38	Public
University of Missouri - Columbia	869,566	99	39	Public
Brandeis University	866,778	100	61	Private

The Top 200 Institutions – Endowment Assets (2016)

Top 101-150 Institutions in Endowment Assets	Endowment Assets x $1000	National Rank	Control Rank	Institutional Control
Rutgers University - New Brunswick	865,867	101	40	Public
University of Miami	844,643	102	62	Private
Virginia Polytechnic Institute and State University	842,991	103	41	Public
Santa Clara University	840,706	104	63	Private
Colgate University	821,675	105	64	Private
Hamilton College (NY)	817,210	106	65	Private
College of William and Mary	803,698	107	42	Public
University of Alabama - Tuscaloosa	798,438	108	43	Public
Bryn Mawr College	797,121	109	66	Private
Loma Linda University	784,235	110	67	Private
Cooper Union for the Advancement of Science & Art	781,491	111	68	Private
Pepperdine University	781,341	112	69	Private
Oberlin College	770,271	113	70	Private
Wesleyan University	770,121	114	71	Private
Iowa State University	760,461	115	44	Public
University of Oregon	758,692	116	45	Public
University of Arizona	754,651	117	46	Public
Medical College of Wisconsin	748,862	118	72	Private
Rochester Institute of Technology	745,007	119	73	Private
Carleton College	738,136	120	74	Private
Lafayette College	733,244	121	75	Private
Bucknell University	722,425	122	76	Private
Denison University	716,180	123	77	Private
University of Louisville	715,689	124	47	Public
Colby College	710,659	125	78	Private
Claremont McKenna College	709,106	126	79	Private
Macalester College	700,189	127	80	Private
Northeastern University	693,025	128	81	Private
Howard University	685,775	129	82	Private
Colorado College	683,225	130	83	Private
College of the Holy Cross	680,993	131	84	Private
Texas Tech University	674,557	132	48	Public
Mount Holyoke College	667,595	133	85	Private
University of Houston - University Park	665,001	134	49	Public
Principia College	664,951	135	86	Private
MCPHS University	663,342	136	87	Private
Davidson College	661,926	137	88	Private
Icahn School of Medicine at Mount Sinai	659,261	138	89	Private
University of South Carolina - Columbia	655,469	139	50	Public
Drexel University	650,252	140	90	Private
Auburn University	646,624	141	51	Public
St. John's University (NY)	643,376	142	91	Private
Rensselaer Polytechnic Institute	634,916	143	92	Private
Yeshiva University	632,856	144	93	Private
Clemson University	621,294	145	52	Public
Fordham University	614,871	146	94	Private
DePauw University	614,568	147	95	Private
Arizona State University	612,590	148	53	Public
Furman University	609,731	149	96	Private
University of Denver	607,368	150	97	Private

The Top 200 Institutions – Endowment Assets (2016)

Top 151-200 Institutions in Endowment Assets	Endowment Assets x $1000	National Rank	Control Rank	Institutional Control
University at Buffalo	600,961	151	54	Public
University of Tennessee - Knoxville	597,475	152	55	Public
Florida State University	584,529	153	56	Public
University of Colorado - Boulder	583,190	154	57	Public
American University	576,919	155	98	Private
Oregon Health & Science University	570,485	156	58	Public
Villanova University	551,036	157	99	Private
Marquette University	550,106	158	100	Private
National University	545,681	159	101	Private
Rush University	538,823	160	102	Private
University of Mississippi - Oxford	536,563	161	59	Public
Loyola University Chicago	535,117	162	103	Private
University of Texas Medical Branch - Galveston	533,972	163	60	Public
University of South Alabama - Mobile	526,009	164	61	Public
Trinity College (CT)	524,259	165	104	Private
University of Oklahoma - Health Sciences Center	516,920	166	62	Public
West Virginia University	511,384	167	63	Public
Thomas Jefferson University	500,943	168	105	Private
University of California - Irvine	498,171	169	64	Public
Reed College	496,553	170	106	Private
Temple University	494,187	171	65	Public
Oregon State University	492,546	172	66	Public
University of Texas Health Science Ctr. - San Antonio	486,652	173	67	Public
Hillsdale College	482,289	174	107	Private
Ohio University - Athens	481,777	175	68	Public
University of Colorado - Denver/Anschutz Medical	479,474	176	69	Public
Whitman College	477,772	177	108	Private
Kansas State University	475,617	178	70	Public
University of Dayton	473,122	179	109	Private
Haverford College	471,744	180	110	Private
University of Vermont	467,702	181	71	Public
Worcester Polytechnic Institute	466,320	182	111	Private
University of Maryland - College Park	466,075	183	72	Public
University of Wyoming	458,486	184	73	Public
Pennsylvania State University - Hershey Medical Ctr.	449,943	185	74	Public
University of San Diego	449,795	186	112	Private
Creighton University	448,457	187	113	Private
Miami University - Oxford	446,795	188	75	Public
St. Olaf College	446,152	189	114	Private
Mississippi State University	444,485	190	76	Public
Virginia Military Institute	436,139	191	77	Public
University of Texas - Dallas	436,120	192	78	Public
University of Alabama - Birmingham	431,459	193	79	Public
University of St. Thomas (MN)	429,199	194	115	Private
DePaul University	420,056	195	116	Private
Louisiana State University - Baton Rouge	416,717	196	80	Public
College of the Ozarks	416,232	197	117	Private
Hofstra University	415,732	198	118	Private
Loyola Marymount University	413,724	199	119	Private
Miami Dade College	409,362	200	81	Public

The Top 200 Institutions – Annual Giving (2016)

Top 1-50 Institutions in Annual Giving	Annual Giving x $1000	National Rank	Control Rank	Institutional Control
Harvard University	1,187,530	1	1	Private
Stanford University	951,149	2	2	Private
University of Southern California	666,641	3	3	Private
Johns Hopkins University	657,293	4	4	Private
University of California - San Francisco	595,940	5	1	Public
Columbia University	584,809	6	5	Private
University of Pennsylvania	542,851	7	6	Private
University of Washington - Seattle	541,444	8	2	Public
Yale University	519,146	9	7	Private
Duke University	506,441	10	8	Private
University of California - Los Angeles	498,800	11	3	Public
New York University	461,150	12	9	Private
University of Chicago	443,305	13	10	Private
University of Michigan - Ann Arbor	433,776	14	4	Public
Cornell University	427,089	15	11	Private
Massachusetts Institute of Technology	419,752	16	12	Private
Northwestern University	401,679	17	13	Private
Ohio State University - Columbus	386,112	18	5	Public
University of Notre Dame	371,762	19	14	Private
University of California - Berkeley	348,865	20	6	Public
University of Texas - Austin	345,992	21	7	Public
University of Minnesota - Twin Cities	332,851	22	8	Public
University of Wisconsin - Madison	318,828	23	9	Public
University of North Carolina - Chapel Hill	308,694	24	10	Public
Texas A&M University - College Station	276,475	25	11	Public
Washington University in St. Louis	269,877	26	15	Private
Princeton University	267,876	27	16	Private
University of Oklahoma - Norman	252,996	28	12	Public
University of Virginia	245,392	29	13	Public
University of Florida	243,666	30	14	Public
University of Miami	236,334	31	17	Private
Dartmouth College	227,038	32	18	Private
University of Texas MD Anderson Cancer Center	208,482	33	15	Public
Brown University	207,725	34	19	Private
University of California - San Diego	206,873	35	16	Public
University of Utah	201,854	36	17	Public
Indiana University - Bloomington	195,908	37	18	Public
Emory University	192,700	38	20	Private
University of Iowa	192,262	39	19	Public
University of Arizona	186,870	40	20	Public
California Institute of Technology	182,869	41	21	Private
University of Texas SW Medical Center - Dallas	181,153	42	21	Public
Michigan State University	176,131	43	22	Public
University of Kentucky	163,919	44	23	Public
University of Cincinnati - Cincinnati	162,076	45	24	Public
University of Colorado - Boulder	160,445	46	25	Public
University of Illinois - Urbana-Champaign	159,693	47	26	Public
Case Western Reserve University	158,323	48	22	Private
Oregon Health & Science University	156,961	49	27	Public
Boston University	156,941	50	23	Private

The Top 200 Institutions – Annual Giving (2016)

Top 51-100 Institutions in Annual Giving	Annual Giving x $1000	National Rank	Control Rank	Institutional Control
Carnegie Mellon University	155,302	51	24	Private
Georgetown University	153,384	52	25	Private
Purdue University - West Lafayette	151,217	53	28	Public
University of Kansas - Lawrence	149,771	54	29	Public
Louisiana State University - Baton Rouge	147,998	55	30	Public
Pennsylvania State University - University Park	147,570	56	31	Public
University of Maryland - College Park	146,044	57	32	Public
Vanderbilt University	143,605	58	26	Private
Indiana University - Purdue University - Indianapolis	143,199	59	33	Public
Arizona State University	140,417	60	34	Public
University of Oregon	136,295	61	35	Public
University of Georgia	133,881	62	36	Public
North Carolina State University	129,948	63	37	Public
Georgia Institute of Technology	129,304	64	38	Public
University of California - Davis	129,224	65	39	Public
University of Pittsburgh - Pittsburgh	127,155	66	40	Public
Boston College	126,209	67	27	Private
Icahn School of Medicine at Mount Sinai	120,327	68	28	Private
Rutgers University - New Brunswick	118,493	69	41	Public
Auburn University	118,477	70	42	Public
University of Missouri - Columbia	113,079	71	43	Public
University of Rochester	107,297	72	29	Private
University of Colorado - Denver/Anschutz Medical	106,963	73	44	Public
Baylor University	104,676	74	30	Private
Washington State University - Pullman	103,845	75	45	Public
Rice University	102,977	76	31	Private
George Washington University	101,391	77	32	Private
University of California - Santa Barbara	101,177	78	46	Public
University of Nebraska - Lincoln	100,542	79	47	Public
Virginia Polytechnic Institute and State University	100,057	80	48	Public
Tulane University	98,919	81	33	Private
Oklahoma State University - Stillwater	98,781	82	49	Public
University of Houston - University Park	98,449	83	50	Public
Southern Methodist University	98,113	84	34	Private
Oregon State University	97,101	85	51	Public
Kansas State University	96,626	86	52	Public
University of South Carolina - Columbia	94,103	87	53	Public
University of Alabama - Tuscaloosa	91,942	88	54	Public
University of Nebraska Medical Center	91,702	89	55	Public
University of Tennessee - Knoxville	91,456	90	56	Public
Clemson University	90,623	91	57	Public
Syracuse University	90,319	92	35	Private
Iowa State University	90,148	93	58	Public
Wake Forest University	88,787	94	36	Private
University of Alabama - Birmingham	88,043	95	59	Public
Weill Cornell Medical College	85,207	96	37	Private
University of Louisville	85,186	97	60	Public
San Diego State University	79,781	98	61	Public
University of Mississippi - Oxford	78,853	99	62	Public
Baylor College of Medicine	77,605	100	38	Private

The Top 200 Institutions – Annual Giving (2016)

Top 101-150 Institutions in Annual Giving	Annual Giving x $1000	National Rank	Control Rank	Institutional Control
Stony Brook University	76,704	101	63	Public
University of Arkansas - Fayetteville	76,693	102	64	Public
Florida State University	75,413	103	65	Public
Texas Christian University	75,303	104	39	Private
West Virginia University	74,882	105	66	Public
University of California - Irvine	73,657	106	67	Public
Williams College	72,707	107	40	Private
Mississippi State University	69,763	108	68	Public
University of Nevada - Reno	69,521	109	69	Public
University of Oklahoma - Health Sciences Center	69,440	110	70	Public
Virginia Commonwealth University	69,180	111	71	Public
University of California - Santa Cruz	69,052	112	72	Public
George Mason University	67,940	113	73	Public
Texas Tech University	67,727	114	74	Public
Rockefeller University	67,659	115	41	Private
University of New Mexico - Albuquerque	66,077	116	75	Public
University of Connecticut - Storrs	65,620	117	76	Public
Lehigh University	63,678	118	42	Private
Temple University	62,254	119	77	Public
Villanova University	61,468	120	43	Private
University of Vermont	61,407	121	78	Public
Drexel University	60,905	122	44	Private
Wayne State University	60,708	123	79	Public
Tufts University	60,405	124	45	Private
College of William and Mary	59,542	125	80	Public
Berea College	59,150	126	46	Private
Western Michigan University	58,492	127	81	Public
Wellesley College	58,275	128	47	Private
University of Maryland - Baltimore	57,911	129	82	Public
Brandeis University	57,593	130	48	Private
Smith College	57,431	131	49	Private
University of Delaware	56,843	132	83	Public
Thomas Jefferson University	56,821	133	50	Private
Northeastern University	56,292	134	51	Private
University of Texas Health Science Center - Houston	55,453	135	84	Public
Marquette University	54,437	136	52	Private
University of Illinois - Chicago	53,815	137	85	Public
Claremont McKenna College	53,418	138	53	Private
Worcester Polytechnic Institute	51,811	139	54	Private
Davidson College	51,212	140	55	Private
University of Wyoming	49,374	141	86	Public
Santa Clara University	48,921	142	56	Private
Washington and Lee University	48,355	143	57	Private
Chapman University	47,237	144	58	Private
University of Texas - Dallas	46,825	145	87	Public
College of the Holy Cross	46,724	146	59	Private
Mount Holyoke College	46,364	147	60	Private
Fordham University	46,182	148	61	Private
U.S. Military Academy	46,041	149	88	Public
Creighton University	45,948	150	62	Private

The Top 200 Institutions – Annual Giving (2016)

Top 151-200 Institutions in Annual Giving	Annual Giving x $1000	National Rank	Control Rank	Institutional Control
University of Denver	45,806	151	63	Private
University of South Florida - Tampa	45,583	152	89	Public
University of Texas Medical Branch - Galveston	44,659	153	90	Public
Medical University of South Carolina	44,310	154	91	Public
Colorado State University - Fort Collins	42,798	155	92	Public
Barnard College	42,513	156	64	Private
University of Hawaii - Manoa	42,209	157	93	Public
University of Tulsa	41,267	158	65	Private
Wesleyan University	40,968	159	66	Private
University of Texas Health Science Ctr. - San Antonio	40,458	160	94	Public
Middlebury College	40,370	161	67	Private
Westmont College	40,343	162	68	Private
Oberlin College	39,886	163	69	Private
Pomona College	39,498	164	70	Private
Yeshiva University	39,298	165	71	Private
Miami University - Oxford	37,940	166	95	Public
Rensselaer Polytechnic Institute	37,798	167	72	Private
University of Kansas Medical Center	37,443	168	96	Public
University of San Diego	36,830	169	73	Private
University at Buffalo	36,219	170	97	Public
University of Akron - Akron	35,932	171	98	Public
Bowdoin College	35,696	172	74	Private
Pennsylvania State University - Hershey Medical Ctr.	35,472	173	99	Public
University of San Francisco	35,382	174	75	Private
University of Mississippi Medical Center	35,308	175	100	Public
University of Missouri - Kansas City	35,104	176	101	Public
Hamilton College (NY)	35,094	177	76	Private
University of Nevada - Las Vegas	34,865	178	102	Public
Virginia Military Institute	34,556	179	103	Public
Utah State University	34,359	180	104	Public
California Polytechnic State Univ - San Luis Obispo	33,735	181	105	Public
Skidmore College	32,818	182	77	Private
University of Massachusetts - Amherst	32,805	183	106	Public
York College Pennsylvania	32,245	184	78	Private
Amherst College	32,099	185	79	Private
Portland State University	31,866	186	107	Public
Sewanee-The University of the South	31,734	187	80	Private
City University of NY - Hunter College	31,162	188	108	Public
Colby College	31,106	189	81	Private
Gonzaga University	30,971	190	82	Private
Loyola University Chicago	29,596	191	83	Private
Illinois Institute of Technology	29,486	192	84	Private
Columbus State University	28,995	193	109	Public
Furman University	28,933	194	85	Private
Colgate University	28,922	195	86	Private
Biola University	28,611	196	87	Private
U.S. Air Force Academy	28,545	197	110	Public
University of North Dakota	27,965	198	111	Public
Gustavus Adolphus College	27,954	199	88	Private
Butler University	27,870	200	89	Private

The Top 200 Institutions – National Academy Membership (2016)

Top 1-46 Institutions in National Academy Membership	Number of Members	National Rank	Control Rank	Institutional Control
Harvard University	382	1	1	Private
Stanford University	340	2	2	Private
Massachusetts Institute of Technology	267	3	3	Private
University of California - Berkeley	230	4	1	Public
Columbia University	136	5	4	Private
University of California - San Francisco	133	6	2	Public
Princeton University	126	7	5	Private
University of California - San Diego	119	8	3	Public
University of Pennsylvania	118	9	6	Private
Yale University	117	10	7	Private
California Institute of Technology	114	11	8	Private
University of Michigan - Ann Arbor	113	12	4	Public
University of Washington - Seattle	110	13	5	Public
Johns Hopkins University	101	14	9	Private
University of California - Los Angeles	100	15	6	Public
University of Wisconsin - Madison	77	16	7	Public
University of Chicago	70	17	10	Private
University of Texas - Austin	70	17	8	Public
Duke University	67	19	11	Private
Cornell University	63	20	12	Private
University of California - Santa Barbara	58	21	9	Public
New York University	56	22	13	Private
University of Illinois - Urbana-Champaign	56	22	10	Public
Rockefeller University	51	24	14	Private
University of Southern California	48	25	15	Private
Washington University in St. Louis	48	25	15	Private
University of California - Davis	46	27	11	Public
Carnegie Mellon University	43	28	17	Private
Northwestern University	42	29	18	Private
University of Minnesota - Twin Cities	41	30	12	Public
University of North Carolina - Chapel Hill	38	31	13	Public
Rutgers University - New Brunswick	36	32	14	Public
University of Texas SW Medical Center - Dallas	36	32	14	Public
Vanderbilt University	34	34	19	Private
Ohio State University - Columbus	33	35	16	Public
Texas A&M University - College Station	32	36	17	Public
University of Pittsburgh - Pittsburgh	32	36	17	Public
Emory University	31	38	20	Private
Georgia Institute of Technology	31	38	19	Public
University of California - Irvine	30	40	20	Public
University of Arizona	29	41	21	Public
University of Colorado - Boulder	29	41	21	Public
Pennsylvania State University - University Park	28	43	23	Public
Purdue University - West Lafayette	28	43	23	Public
Weill Cornell Medical College	28	43	21	Private
Gerstner Sloan-Kettering Grad. Sch. of Biomed. Sci.	27	46	22	Private
Scripps Research Institute	27	46	22	Private
University of Maryland - College Park	27	46	25	Public

The Top 200 Institutions – National Academy Membership (2016)

Top 49-87 Institutions in National Academy Membership	Number of Members	National Rank	Control Rank	Institutional Control
University of Florida	26	49	26	Public
Baylor College of Medicine	25	50	24	Private
Rice University	24	51	25	Private
University of Virginia	23	52	27	Public
Arizona State University	22	53	28	Public
Case Western Reserve University	22	53	26	Private
University of Rochester	22	53	26	Private
Brown University	21	56	28	Private
North Carolina State University	21	56	29	Public
University of Utah	21	56	29	Public
Icahn School of Medicine at Mount Sinai	20	59	29	Private
University of Iowa	20	59	31	Public
Boston University	19	61	30	Private
Dartmouth College	16	62	31	Private
Michigan State University	14	63	32	Public
Stony Brook University	14	63	32	Public
University of Colorado - Denver/Anschutz Medical	14	63	32	Public
Virginia Polytechnic Institute and State University	14	63	32	Public
Indiana University - Bloomington	13	67	36	Public
University of Miami	13	67	32	Private
Yeshiva University	13	67	32	Private
Tufts University	12	70	34	Private
Brandeis University	11	71	35	Private
George Washington University	11	71	35	Private
University of Texas MD Anderson Cancer Center	11	71	37	Public
City University of NY - City College	10	74	38	Public
Oregon Health & Science University	10	74	38	Public
University of Hawaii - Manoa	10	74	38	Public
University of Houston - University Park	10	74	38	Public
Georgetown University	9	78	37	Private
Iowa State University	9	78	42	Public
University of California - Riverside	9	78	42	Public
University of California - Santa Cruz	9	78	42	Public
University of Maryland - Baltimore	9	78	42	Public
University of Massachusetts - Amherst	9	78	42	Public
University of Missouri - Columbia	9	78	42	Public
University of Oregon	9	78	42	Public
Washington State University - Pullman	9	78	42	Public
Colorado State University - Fort Collins	8	87	50	Public
Drexel University	8	87	38	Private
Florida State University	8	87	50	Public
University at Buffalo	8	87	50	Public
University of Cincinnati - Cincinnati	8	87	50	Public
University of Delaware	8	87	50	Public
University of South Florida - Tampa	8	87	50	Public

The Top 200 Institutions – National Academy Membership (2016)

Top 94-120 Institutions in National Academy Membership	Number of Members	National Rank	Control Rank	Institutional Control
Howard University	7	94	39	Private
Rensselaer Polytechnic Institute	7	94	39	Private
University of Alabama - Birmingham	7	94	56	Public
University of Georgia	7	94	56	Public
University of Massachusetts Med. Sch. - Worcester	7	94	56	Public
University of Illinois - Chicago	6	99	59	Public
University of Tennessee - Knoxville	6	99	59	Public
Virginia Commonwealth University	6	99	59	Public
Wake Forest University	6	99	41	Private
Cold Spring Harbor Laboratory	5	103	42	Private
Morehouse School of Medicine	5	103	42	Private
Oregon State University	5	103	62	Public
Temple University	5	103	62	Public
Texas Tech University	5	103	62	Public
University of Kansas - Lawrence	5	103	62	Public
University of New Mexico - Albuquerque	5	103	62	Public
University of Texas Health Science Ctr. - San Antonio	5	103	62	Public
Colorado School of Mines	4	111	68	Public
Illinois Institute of Technology	4	111	44	Private
Lehigh University	4	111	44	Private
Thomas Jefferson University	4	111	44	Private
Uniformed Services University of the Health Sciences	4	111	68	Public
University of Connecticut - Health Center	4	111	68	Public
University of Notre Dame	4	111	44	Private
University of Texas - Dallas	4	111	68	Public
University of Texas Health Science Center - Houston	4	111	68	Public
Boston College	3	120	48	Private
Clark University (MA)	3	120	48	Private
Mayo Clinic School of Medicine	3	120	48	Private
Medical College of Wisconsin	3	120	48	Private
Naval Postgraduate School	3	120	73	Public
Northeastern University	3	120	48	Private
Oklahoma State University - Stillwater	3	120	73	Public
Rush University	3	120	48	Private
Rutgers University - Newark	3	120	73	Public
Southern Methodist University	3	120	48	Private
University of Arkansas - Fayetteville	3	120	73	Public
University of Nebraska - Lincoln	3	120	73	Public
University of Texas - Arlington	3	120	73	Public
University of Texas Medical Branch - Galveston	3	120	73	Public
Wayne State University	3	120	73	Public
Woods Hole Oceanographic Institution	3	120	48	Private

The Top 200 Institutions – National Academy Membership (2016)

Institutions with 2 National Academy Members	Number of Members	National Rank	Control Rank	Institutional Control
Brigham Young University - Provo	2	136	56	Private
Chapman University	2	136	56	Private
Charles R. Drew University of Medicine and Science	2	136	56	Private
Clemson University	2	136	81	Public
Drew University	2	136	56	Private
Florida Atlantic University	2	136	81	Public
Florida International University	2	136	81	Public
George Mason University	2	136	81	Public
Louisiana State University - Baton Rouge	2	136	81	Public
Medical University of South Carolina	2	136	81	Public
Meharry Medical College	2	136	56	Private
Pardee RAND Graduate School	2	136	56	Private
Pennsylvania State University - Hershey Medical Ctr.	2	136	81	Public
Rowan University	2	136	81	Public
Stevens Institute of Technology	2	136	56	Private
Syracuse University	2	136	56	Private
Tulane University	2	136	56	Private
University of Alaska - Fairbanks	2	136	81	Public
University of Kansas Medical Center	2	136	81	Public
University of Kentucky	2	136	81	Public
University of Louisville	2	136	81	Public
University of Nevada - Reno	2	136	81	Public
University of Rhode Island	2	136	81	Public
University of Vermont	2	136	81	Public
University of Wyoming	2	136	81	Public
West Virginia University	2	136	81	Public

The Top 200 Institutions – Faculty Awards (2016)

Top 1-46 Institutions in Faculty Awards	Number of Awards	National Rank	Control Rank	Institutional Control
Harvard University	66	1	1	Private
Stanford University	48	2	2	Private
University of Michigan - Ann Arbor	48	2	1	Public
University of Illinois - Urbana-Champaign	38	4	2	Public
University of California - Berkeley	36	5	3	Public
University of Washington - Seattle	35	6	4	Public
University of Pennsylvania	34	7	3	Private
Massachusetts Institute of Technology	33	8	4	Private
University of California - San Francisco	28	9	5	Public
University of North Carolina - Chapel Hill	28	9	5	Public
Yale University	28	9	5	Private
Purdue University - West Lafayette	27	12	7	Public
University of Minnesota - Twin Cities	27	12	7	Public
University of Wisconsin - Madison	27	12	7	Public
Columbia University	25	15	6	Private
Duke University	25	15	6	Private
Northwestern University	25	15	6	Private
University of California - San Diego	25	15	10	Public
Pennsylvania State University - University Park	22	19	11	Public
University of California - Los Angeles	22	19	11	Public
Johns Hopkins University	21	21	9	Private
Ohio State University - Columbus	21	21	13	Public
University of Chicago	21	21	9	Private
University of Southern California	21	21	9	Private
Cornell University	20	25	12	Private
North Carolina State University	20	25	14	Public
Princeton University	20	25	12	Private
Arizona State University	19	28	15	Public
Georgia Institute of Technology	19	28	15	Public
Emory University	18	30	14	Private
New York University	18	30	14	Private
University of Texas - Austin	18	30	17	Public
University of Pittsburgh - Pittsburgh	17	33	18	Public
University of Tennessee - Knoxville	17	33	18	Public
Brown University	16	35	16	Private
Carnegie Mellon University	16	35	16	Private
Indiana University - Bloomington	16	35	20	Public
University of Colorado - Boulder	16	35	20	Public
University of Notre Dame	16	35	16	Private
Washington University in St. Louis	16	35	16	Private
University of California - Irvine	15	41	22	Public
University of Connecticut - Storrs	15	41	22	Public
University of Florida	15	41	22	Public
University of Utah	15	41	22	Public
University of California - Davis	14	45	26	Public
University of Arizona	13	46	27	Public
University of Cincinnati - Cincinnati	13	46	27	Public
University of Maryland - College Park	13	46	27	Public
University of South Florida - Tampa	13	46	27	Public
Vanderbilt University	13	46	20	Private

The Top 200 Institutions – Faculty Awards (2016)

Top 51-92 Institutions in Faculty Awards	Number of Awards	National Rank	Control Rank	Institutional Control
Case Western Reserve University	12	51	21	Private
Michigan State University	12	51	31	Public
Rutgers University - New Brunswick	12	51	31	Public
University of California - Riverside	12	51	31	Public
University of Texas SW Medical Center - Dallas	12	51	31	Public
University of Illinois - Chicago	11	56	35	Public
University of Massachusetts Med. Sch. - Worcester	11	56	35	Public
Boston University	10	58	22	Private
Oregon State University	10	58	37	Public
Scripps Research Institute	10	58	22	Private
Washington State University - Pullman	10	58	37	Public
Weill Cornell Medical College	10	58	22	Private
Dartmouth College	9	63	25	Private
Florida State University	9	63	39	Public
Northeastern University	9	63	25	Private
University of Georgia	9	63	39	Public
University of Iowa	9	63	39	Public
University of New Mexico - Albuquerque	9	63	39	Public
California Institute of Technology	8	69	27	Private
George Washington University	8	69	27	Private
Rice University	8	69	27	Private
Stony Brook University	8	69	43	Public
Texas A&M University - College Station	8	69	43	Public
Tufts University	8	69	27	Private
University of California - Santa Barbara	8	69	43	Public
University of California - Santa Cruz	8	69	43	Public
University of Central Florida	8	69	43	Public
University of Massachusetts - Amherst	8	69	43	Public
University of Nebraska - Lincoln	8	69	43	Public
University of Oregon	8	69	43	Public
Brandeis University	7	81	31	Private
Gerstner Sloan-Kettering Grad. Sch. of Biomed Sci.	7	81	31	Private
Iowa State University	7	81	51	Public
Kansas State University	7	81	51	Public
Rockefeller University	7	81	31	Private
University of Colorado - Denver/Anschutz Medical	7	81	51	Public
University of Houston - University Park	7	81	51	Public
University of Kentucky	7	81	51	Public
University of Missouri - Columbia	7	81	51	Public
University of Virginia	7	81	51	Public
Utah State University	7	81	51	Public
College of William and Mary	6	92	59	Public
New York University School of Medicine	6	92	34	Private
Rutgers University - Newark	6	92	59	Public
Texas State University - San Marcos	6	92	59	Public
Tulane University	6	92	34	Private
University at Buffalo	6	92	59	Public
University of New Hampshire - Durham	6	92	59	Public
University of Texas - Arlington	6	92	59	Public
Virginia Polytechnic Institute and State University	6	92	59	Public

The Top 200 Institutions – Faculty Awards (2016)

Top 101-121 Institutions in Faculty Awards	Number of Awards	National Rank	Control Rank	Institutional Control
Auburn University	5	101	66	Public
Boise State University	5	101	66	Public
Clemson University	5	101	66	Public
Drexel University	5	101	36	Private
Fordham University	5	101	36	Private
Georgia State University	5	101	66	Public
Icahn School of Medicine at Mount Sinai	5	101	36	Private
Illinois Institute of Technology	5	101	36	Private
Mayo Clinic School of Medicine	5	101	36	Private
Syracuse University	5	101	36	Private
Temple University	5	101	66	Public
University of Arkansas - Fayetteville	5	101	66	Public
University of Hawaii - Manoa	5	101	66	Public
University of Miami	5	101	36	Private
University of Rochester	5	101	36	Private
University of South Carolina - Columbia	5	101	66	Public
University of Texas - Dallas	5	101	66	Public
University of Vermont	5	101	66	Public
West Virginia University	5	101	66	Public
Western Michigan University	5	101	66	Public
American University	4	121	44	Private
Baylor College of Medicine	4	121	44	Private
California Polytechnic State Univ. - San Luis Obispo	4	121	78	Public
Colorado School of Mines	4	121	78	Public
Colorado State University - Fort Collins	4	121	78	Public
Middlebury College	4	121	44	Private
Oregon Health & Science University	4	121	78	Public
Rensselaer Polytechnic Institute	4	121	44	Private
Rutgers University - Camden	4	121	78	Public
San Francisco State University	4	121	78	Public
San Jose State University	4	121	78	Public
Texas Tech University	4	121	78	Public
U.S. Naval Academy	4	121	78	Public
University of Alabama - Tuscaloosa	4	121	78	Public
University of Delaware	4	121	78	Public
University of Kansas - Lawrence	4	121	78	Public
University of Montana - Missoula	4	121	78	Public
University of Oklahoma - Norman	4	121	78	Public
University of Texas - San Antonio	4	121	78	Public
Worcester Polytechnic Institute	4	121	44	Private
Yeshiva University	4	121	44	Private

The Top 200 Institutions – Faculty Awards (2016)

Institutions with 3 Faculty Awards	Number of Awards	National Rank	Control Rank	Institutional Control
Barnard College	3	142	50	Private
California State University - Fullerton	3	142	93	Public
City University of NY - Bernard M. Baruch College	3	142	93	Public
Columbia College - Chicago	3	142	50	Private
Florida International University	3	142	93	Public
Fort Lewis College	3	142	93	Public
George Mason University	3	142	93	Public
Harvey Mudd College	3	142	50	Private
Howard University	3	142	50	Private
Ithaca College	3	142	50	Private
Jacksonville State University	3	142	93	Public
James Madison University	3	142	93	Public
Lehigh University	3	142	50	Private
Louisiana State University - Baton Rouge	3	142	93	Public
Loyola University Chicago	3	142	50	Private
Mills College	3	142	50	Private
Missouri University of Science and Technology	3	142	93	Public
Montana State University - Bozeman	3	142	93	Public
New Jersey Institute of Technology	3	142	93	Public
New School	3	142	50	Private
Northern Arizona University	3	142	93	Public
Oberlin College	3	142	50	Private
Oklahoma State University - Stillwater	3	142	93	Public
Portland State University	3	142	93	Public
San Diego State University	3	142	93	Public
Stevens Institute of Technology	3	142	50	Private
University of Alabama - Birmingham	3	142	93	Public
University of Denver	3	142	50	Private
University of Idaho	3	142	93	Public
University of Maryland - Baltimore County	3	142	93	Public
University of North Carolina - Charlotte	3	142	93	Public
University of North Texas	3	142	93	Public
University of Rhode Island	3	142	93	Public
Villanova University	3	142	50	Private
Wake Forest University	3	142	50	Private
Wayne State University	3	142	93	Public

The Top 200 Institutions – Doctorates Awarded (2016)

Top 1-50 Institutions in Doctorates Awarded	Number of Degrees	National Rank	Control Rank	Institutional Control
University of Texas - Austin	896	1	1	Public
University of Wisconsin - Madison	870	2	2	Public
University of Michigan - Ann Arbor	848	3	3	Public
Ohio State University - Columbus	807	4	4	Public
University of Minnesota - Twin Cities	804	5	5	Public
University of California - Los Angeles	775	6	6	Public
Stanford University	763	7	1	Private
Purdue University - West Lafayette	727	8	7	Public
University of Illinois - Urbana-Champaign	726	9	8	Public
University of Florida	723	10	9	Public
University of Southern California	714	11	2	Private
Harvard University	713	12	3	Private
Texas A&M University - College Station	705	13	10	Public
Arizona State University	674	14	11	Public
Nova Southeastern University	670	15	4	Private
Pennsylvania State University - University Park	659	16	12	Public
Massachusetts Institute of Technology	646	17	5	Private
University of Washington - Seattle	632	18	13	Public
Rutgers University - New Brunswick	620	19	14	Public
University of Maryland - College Park	592	20	15	Public
Columbia University	587	21	6	Private
Boston University	579	22	7	Private
University of California - Berkeley	576	23	16	Public
University of North Carolina - Chapel Hill	542	24	17	Public
University of Pennsylvania	540	25	8	Private
Duke University	537	26	9	Private
Michigan State University	533	27	18	Public
Georgia Institute of Technology	531	28	19	Public
University of California - San Diego	529	29	20	Public
Johns Hopkins University	528	30	10	Private
University of Georgia	526	31	21	Public
University of Arizona	524	32	22	Public
North Carolina State University	518	33	23	Public
University of California - Davis	513	34	24	Public
Cornell University	497	35	11	Private
Virginia Polytechnic Institute and State University	492	36	25	Public
New York University	489	37	12	Private
Indiana University - Bloomington	485	38	26	Public
University of Iowa	468	39	27	Public
Northwestern University	467	40	13	Private
University of Pittsburgh - Pittsburgh	461	41	28	Public
City University of NY - The Graduate Center	442	42	29	Public
University of Missouri - Columbia	416	43	30	Public
Yale University	411	44	14	Private
University of Colorado - Boulder	410	45	31	Public
University of Chicago	396	46	15	Private
University of California - Irvine	393	47	32	Public
Florida State University	386	48	33	Public
Alliant International University	382	49	16	Private
Princeton University	373	50	17	Private

The Top 200 Institutions – Doctorates Awarded (2016)

Top 51-98 Institutions in Doctorates Awarded	Number of Degrees	National Rank	Control Rank	Institutional Control
University of Houston - University Park	358	51	34	Public
University of Tennessee - Knoxville	356	52	35	Public
Stony Brook University	350	53	36	Public
University of California - Santa Barbara	346	54	37	Public
University of Illinois - Chicago	346	54	37	Public
Louisiana State University - Baton Rouge	344	56	39	Public
University at Buffalo	340	57	40	Public
University of Utah	331	58	41	Public
Iowa State University	327	59	42	Public
Carnegie Mellon University	323	60	18	Private
Texas Tech University	323	60	43	Public
George Mason University	322	62	44	Public
Vanderbilt University	322	62	19	Private
Washington State University - Pullman	322	62	44	Public
University of Connecticut - Storrs	320	65	46	Public
University of South Carolina - Columbia	317	66	47	Public
University of Virginia	315	67	48	Public
University of Kansas - Lawrence	314	68	49	Public
University of South Florida - Tampa	314	68	49	Public
University of Kentucky	313	70	51	Public
University of Nebraska - Lincoln	307	71	52	Public
Virginia Commonwealth University	306	72	53	Public
University of North Texas	304	73	54	Public
University of Rochester	301	74	20	Private
University of Central Florida	299	75	55	Public
University of Massachusetts - Amherst	298	76	56	Public
University of Cincinnati - Cincinnati	284	77	57	Public
University of Delaware	283	78	58	Public
Auburn University	272	79	59	Public
Washington University in St. Louis	266	80	21	Private
George Washington University	264	81	22	Private
Oklahoma State University - Stillwater	256	82	60	Public
Temple University	256	82	60	Public
Emory University	251	84	23	Private
Colorado State University - Fort Collins	249	85	62	Public
University of Alabama - Tuscaloosa	240	86	63	Public
University of California - Riverside	239	87	64	Public
Brown University	235	88	24	Private
Clemson University	233	89	65	Public
Case Western Reserve University	230	90	25	Private
Georgia State University	223	91	66	Public
Wayne State University	222	92	67	Public
University of Miami	216	93	26	Private
University of Notre Dame	216	93	26	Private
Drexel University	214	95	28	Private
Oregon State University	214	95	68	Public
Rice University	211	97	29	Private
Saint Louis University - St. Louis	210	98	30	Private
University of Oklahoma - Norman	210	98	69	Public
West Virginia University	210	98	69	Public

The Top 200 Institutions – Doctorates Awarded (2016)

Top 101-149 Institutions in Doctorates Awarded	Number of Degrees	National Rank	Control Rank	Institutional Control
University of Hawaii - Manoa	204	101	71	Public
Liberty University	202	102	31	Private
University of New Mexico - Albuquerque	200	103	72	Public
University at Albany	193	104	73	Public
California Institute of Technology	190	105	32	Private
University of Texas - Arlington	188	106	74	Public
Northeastern University	186	107	33	Private
Teachers College at Columbia University	184	108	34	Private
Medical University of South Carolina	181	109	75	Public
Kansas State University	179	110	76	Public
Southern Illinois University - Carbondale	179	110	76	Public
University of Arkansas - Fayetteville	178	112	78	Public
Claremont Graduate University	176	113	35	Private
University of California - Santa Cruz	174	114	79	Public
University of Texas - Dallas	174	114	79	Public
University of Nevada - Las Vegas	166	116	81	Public
University of Memphis	160	117	82	Public
Kent State University - Kent	159	118	83	Public
University of Oregon	159	118	83	Public
Boston College	155	120	36	Private
Mississippi State University	153	121	85	Public
Yeshiva University	152	122	37	Private
Florida International University	151	123	86	Public
Old Dominion University	151	123	86	Public
University of North Carolina - Greensboro	151	123	86	Public
Maryville University of Saint Louis	150	126	38	Private
University of Alabama - Birmingham	149	127	89	Public
University of Louisville	147	128	90	Public
Regent University	144	129	39	Private
Syracuse University	144	129	39	Private
University of Wisconsin - Milwaukee	144	129	91	Public
Rensselaer Polytechnic Institute	142	132	41	Private
University of Southern Mississippi	142	132	92	Public
Ohio University - Athens	137	134	93	Public
Loyola University Chicago	136	135	42	Private
Tufts University	135	136	43	Private
Tulane University	135	136	43	Private
University of Toledo	135	136	94	Public
Binghamton University	132	139	95	Public
University of Nevada - Reno	130	140	96	Public
St. John's University (NY)	129	141	45	Private
East Tennessee State University	127	142	97	Public
Carlos Albizu University - San Juan	126	143	46	Private
Lehigh University	126	143	46	Private
Fordham University	125	145	48	Private
Georgetown University	124	146	49	Private
University of Akron - Akron	124	146	98	Public
University of Texas - San Antonio	124	146	98	Public
University of California - San Francisco	123	149	100	Public
University of Colorado - Denver/Anschutz Medical	123	149	100	Public

The Top 200 Institutions – Doctorates Awarded (2016)

Top 151-200 Institutions in Doctorates Awarded	Number of Degrees	National Rank	Control Rank	Institutional Control
Northern Illinois University	121	151	102	Public
University of North Carolina - Charlotte	121	151	102	Public
Western Michigan University	121	151	102	Public
Fielding Graduate University	120	154	50	Private
University of Missouri - Kansas City	120	154	105	Public
University of Denver	118	156	51	Private
University of Mississippi - Oxford	116	157	106	Public
Colorado School of Mines	115	158	107	Public
North Dakota State University	115	158	107	Public
University of South Dakota	114	160	109	Public
University of Texas Health Science Center - Houston	113	161	110	Public
Missouri University of Science and Technology	109	162	111	Public
Baylor University	108	163	52	Private
Texas Woman's University	108	163	112	Public
Brigham Young University - Provo	107	165	53	Private
Catholic University of America	106	166	54	Private
New Mexico State University - Las Cruces	105	167	113	Public
Florida Atlantic University	103	168	114	Public
Loma Linda University	101	169	55	Private
University of Puerto Rico - Rio Piedras	100	170	115	Public
Shenandoah University	99	171	56	Private
University of Wyoming	99	171	116	Public
Howard University	98	173	57	Private
University of Texas SW Medical Center - Dallas	98	173	117	Public
University of Rhode Island	97	175	118	Public
Indiana University of Pennsylvania	96	176	119	Public
University of Massachusetts - Lowell	96	176	119	Public
Duquesne University	95	178	58	Private
A.T. Still University of Health Sciences	94	179	59	Private
Baylor College of Medicine	94	179	59	Private
Utah State University	94	179	121	Public
Palo Alto University	92	182	61	Private
Lamar University	91	183	122	Public
University of Northern Colorado	89	184	123	Public
Dartmouth College	87	185	62	Private
Indiana University - Purdue University - Indianapolis	87	185	124	Public
Illinois Institute of Technology	86	187	63	Private
Jackson State University	86	187	125	Public
Michigan Technological University	86	187	125	Public
University of Nebraska Medical Center	86	187	125	Public
San Diego State University	85	191	128	Public
Brandeis University	83	192	64	Private
Indiana State University	82	193	129	Public
Portland State University	82	193	129	Public
University of Maryland - Baltimore County	82	193	129	Public
Wilmington University (DE)	80	196	65	Private
Southern Methodist University	79	197	66	Private
University of Texas - El Paso	78	198	132	Public
University of Vermont	78	198	132	Public
Azusa Pacific University	77	200	67	Private
Tennessee State University	77	200	134	Public

The Top 200 Institutions – Postdoctoral Appointees (2015)

Top 1-50 Institutions in Postdoctoral Appointees	Number of Postdocs	National Rank	Control Rank	Institutional Control
Harvard University	5,674	1	1	Private
Stanford University	2,264	2	2	Private
Johns Hopkins University	1,679	3	3	Private
Massachusetts Institute of Technology	1,493	4	4	Private
University of Michigan - Ann Arbor	1,299	5	1	Public
University of California - San Diego	1,250	6	2	Public
Columbia University	1,249	7	5	Private
University of Washington - Seattle	1,205	8	3	Public
University of California - Berkeley	1,184	9	4	Public
Yale University	1,157	10	6	Private
University of California - San Francisco	1,041	11	5	Public
University of California - Los Angeles	1,016	12	6	Public
University of Colorado - Boulder	911	13	7	Public
University of Pennsylvania	901	14	7	Private
University of California - Davis	833	15	8	Public
University of North Carolina - Chapel Hill	803	16	9	Public
University of Wisconsin - Madison	765	17	10	Public
University of Minnesota - Twin Cities	752	18	11	Public
Northwestern University	746	19	8	Private
New York University	680	20	9	Private
University of Florida	679	21	12	Public
University of Pittsburgh - Pittsburgh	664	22	13	Public
Icahn School of Medicine at Mount Sinai	643	23	10	Private
Emory University	642	24	11	Private
University of Texas MD Anderson Cancer Center	637	25	14	Public
Vanderbilt University	629	26	12	Private
Ohio State University - Columbus	619	27	15	Public
Texas A&M University - College Station	615	28	16	Public
Washington University in St. Louis	615	28	13	Private
University of Chicago	586	30	14	Private
Duke University	584	31	15	Private
Mayo Clinic Graduate School of Biomedical Sciences	576	32	16	Private
Scripps Research Institute	573	33	17	Private
University of Texas SW Medical Center - Dallas	562	34	17	Public
California Institute of Technology	552	35	18	Private
University of Illinois - Urbana-Champaign	542	36	18	Public
Baylor College of Medicine	537	37	19	Private
Princeton University	526	38	20	Private
Cornell University	502	39	21	Private
North Carolina State University	497	40	19	Public
University of Maryland - College Park	496	41	20	Public
University of Utah	487	42	21	Public
University of Southern California	475	43	22	Private
Michigan State University	471	44	22	Public
University of Arizona	471	44	22	Public
Boston University	421	46	23	Private
University of Virginia	420	47	24	Public
Purdue University - West Lafayette	389	48	25	Public
University of Texas - Austin	370	49	26	Public
Pennsylvania State University - University Park	366	50	27	Public

The Top 200 Institutions – Postdoctoral Appointees (2015)

Top 51-100 Institutions in Postdoctoral Appointees	Number of Postdocs	National Rank	Control Rank	Institutional Control
Indiana University - Bloomington	365	51	28	Public
Weill Cornell Medical College	354	52	24	Private
University of Massachusetts Medical School - Worcester	348	53	29	Public
University of Iowa	346	54	30	Public
University of Maryland - Baltimore	325	55	31	Public
Rutgers University - New Brunswick	306	56	32	Public
University of California - Santa Barbara	306	56	32	Public
University of Cincinnati - Cincinnati	303	58	34	Public
Iowa State University	299	59	35	Public
University of California - Irvine	297	60	36	Public
Oregon Health & Science University	292	61	37	Public
Rockefeller University	292	61	25	Private
University of Colorado - Denver/Anschutz Medical	288	63	38	Public
Yeshiva University	283	64	26	Private
University of South Florida - Tampa	282	65	39	Public
Case Western Reserve University	271	66	27	Private
University of Houston - University Park	264	67	40	Public
Rice University	263	68	28	Private
Stony Brook University	263	68	41	Public
University of Miami	258	70	29	Private
Arizona State University	257	71	42	Public
University at Buffalo	256	72	43	Public
Colorado State University - Fort Collins	254	73	44	Public
Brown University	252	74	30	Private
University of Alabama - Birmingham	252	74	45	Public
University of Georgia	250	76	46	Public
Georgia Institute of Technology	237	77	47	Public
University of Texas Health Science Center - Houston	237	77	47	Public
University of Hawaii - Manoa	234	79	49	Public
University of Rochester	233	80	31	Private
Virginia Polytechnic Institute and State University	225	81	50	Public
University of Kentucky	221	82	51	Public
University of Illinois - Chicago	214	83	52	Public
Oregon State University	212	84	53	Public
Texas Tech University	207	85	54	Public
University of Nebraska - Lincoln	205	86	55	Public
Dartmouth College	204	87	32	Private
Florida State University	202	88	56	Public
Virginia Commonwealth University	194	89	57	Public
Carnegie Mellon University	193	90	33	Private
University of California - Riverside	190	91	58	Public
Tufts University	182	92	34	Private
Medical University of South Carolina	178	93	59	Public
Washington State University - Pullman	175	94	60	Public
Temple University	167	95	61	Public
University of Texas Health Science Center - San Antonio	167	95	61	Public
University of Missouri - Columbia	165	97	63	Public
Augusta University	159	98	64	Public
Sanford-Burnham Medical Research Institute	157	99	35	Private
University of Kansas - Lawrence	149	100	65	Public

The Top 200 Institutions – Postdoctoral Appointees (2015)

Top 101-151 Institutions in Postdoctoral Appointees	Number of Postdocs	National Rank	Control Rank	Institutional Control
Louisiana State University - Baton Rouge	148	101	66	Public
Kansas State University	146	102	67	Public
Wayne State University	146	102	67	Public
University of Massachusetts - Amherst	144	104	69	Public
Cold Spring Harbor Laboratory	143	105	36	Private
University of Tennessee - Knoxville	136	106	70	Public
Tulane University	133	107	37	Private
University of Oklahoma - Norman	133	107	71	Public
University of Delaware	132	109	72	Public
University of South Carolina - Columbia	129	110	73	Public
University of California - Santa Cruz	125	111	74	Public
University of New Mexico - Albuquerque	124	112	75	Public
University of Notre Dame	124	112	38	Private
Irell & Manella Graduate School of Biological Sciences	119	114	39	Private
Thomas Jefferson University	117	115	40	Private
Northeastern University	114	116	41	Private
George Washington University	111	117	42	Private
Georgetown University	109	118	43	Private
University of Connecticut - Storrs	109	118	76	Public
University of Nebraska Medical Center	108	120	77	Public
University of Louisville	107	121	78	Public
University of Oregon	105	122	79	Public
University of Connecticut - Health Center	104	123	80	Public
University of Tennessee Health Science Center	103	124	81	Public
University of Texas Medical Branch - Galveston	102	125	82	Public
University of Kansas Medical Center	100	126	83	Public
Woods Hole Oceanographic Institution	99	127	44	Private
Brandeis University	95	128	45	Private
Drexel University	93	129	46	Private
Southern Illinois University - Carbondale	87	130	84	Public
Wake Forest University	87	130	47	Private
University at Albany	86	132	85	Public
University of Vermont	86	132	85	Public
Rensselaer Polytechnic Institute	83	134	48	Private
University of Oklahoma - Health Sciences Center	83	134	87	Public
Louisiana State University HSC - New Orleans	82	136	88	Public
University of Texas - Dallas	80	137	89	Public
University of Nevada - Reno	78	138	90	Public
Clemson University	77	139	91	Public
Georgia State University	76	140	92	Public
Florida International University	75	141	93	Public
Pennsylvania State University - Hershey Medical Center	70	142	94	Public
University of Arkansas - Fayetteville	69	143	95	Public
University of Maryland - Baltimore County	67	144	96	Public
Medical College of Wisconsin	66	145	49	Private
Colorado School of Mines	65	146	97	Public
Northern Illinois University	64	147	98	Public
University of Akron - Akron	60	148	99	Public
University of Texas - Arlington	60	148	99	Public
Saint Louis University - St. Louis	59	150	50	Private
University of Texas - El Paso	58	151	101	Public

The Top 200 Institutions – Postdoctoral Appointees (2015)

Top 152-200 Institutions in Postdoctoral Appointees	Number of Postdocs	National Rank	Control Rank	Institutional Control
University of North Texas	56	152	102	Public
North Dakota State University	55	153	103	Public
University of Wyoming	54	154	104	Public
Oklahoma State University - Stillwater	53	155	105	Public
Syracuse University	52	156	51	Private
Mississippi State University	51	157	106	Public
Montana State University - Bozeman	51	157	106	Public
University of Central Florida	51	157	106	Public
University of Idaho	51	157	106	Public
West Virginia University	51	157	106	Public
Loma Linda University	50	162	52	Private
City University of NY - City College	47	163	111	Public
Rutgers University - Newark	47	163	111	Public
University of Mississippi - Oxford	46	165	113	Public
University of New Hampshire - Durham	46	165	113	Public
Loyola University Chicago	45	167	53	Private
George Mason University	44	168	115	Public
Boston College	43	169	54	Private
Kent State University - Kent	43	169	116	Public
New Jersey Institute of Technology	42	171	117	Public
University of Mississippi Medical Center	42	171	117	Public
Utah State University	42	171	117	Public
University of Alabama - Tuscaloosa	41	174	120	Public
Auburn University	40	175	121	Public
University of California - Merced	40	175	121	Public
University of Texas - San Antonio	39	177	123	Public
University of Alaska - Fairbanks	37	178	124	Public
Albany Medical College	36	179	55	Private
University of Montana - Missoula	36	179	125	Public
Baylor University	34	181	56	Private
San Diego State University	33	182	126	Public
Uniformed Services University of the Health Sciences	33	182	126	Public
University of Nevada - Las Vegas	33	182	126	Public
University of Rhode Island	32	185	129	Public
Creighton University	31	186	57	Private
Illinois Institute of Technology	31	186	57	Private
Old Dominion University	31	186	130	Public
University of Toledo	31	186	130	Public
Worcester Polytechnic Institute	31	186	57	Private
Binghamton University	30	191	132	Public
South Dakota State University	30	191	132	Public
University of South Alabama - Mobile	30	191	132	Public
Indiana University - Purdue University - Indianapolis	29	194	135	Public
Missouri University of Science and Technology	29	194	135	Public
University of North Carolina - Charlotte	29	194	135	Public
Brigham Young University - Provo	28	197	60	Private
East Carolina University	28	197	138	Public
Rush University	28	197	60	Private
Louisiana State University - Shreveport	27	200	139	Public
Rosalind Franklin University of Medicine and Science	27	200	62	Private
University of Massachusetts - Lowell	27	200	139	Public
University of North Carolina - Greensboro	27	200	139	Public

The Top 200 Institutions – SAT Scores (2015)

Top 1-50 Institutions in Median SAT Scores	Median SAT Score	National Rank	Control Rank	Institutional Control
California Institute of Technology	1550	1	1	Private
Franklin W. Olin College of Engineering	1520	2	2	Private
University of Chicago	1520	2	2	Private
Yale University	1515	4	4	Private
Massachusetts Institute of Technology	1505	5	5	Private
Harvard University	1500	6	6	Private
Princeton University	1490	7	7	Private
Stanford University	1485	8	8	Private
Vanderbilt University	1485	8	8	Private
Harvey Mudd College	1480	10	10	Private
Columbia University	1475	11	11	Private
Rice University	1475	11	11	Private
Brown University	1465	13	13	Private
University of Pennsylvania	1465	13	13	Private
University of Notre Dame	1460	15	15	Private
Washington University in St. Louis	1460	15	15	Private
Webb Institute	1460	15	15	Private
Amherst College	1457	18	18	Private
Duke University	1455	19	19	Private
Carnegie Mellon University	1450	20	20	Private
Dartmouth College	1445	21	21	Private
Johns Hopkins University	1445	21	21	Private
Pomona College	1445	21	21	Private
Tufts University	1445	21	21	Private
Northeastern University	1440	25	25	Private
Northwestern University	1440	25	25	Private
Williams College	1440	25	25	Private
Claremont McKenna College	1435	28	28	Private
Swarthmore College	1435	28	28	Private
Cornell University	1430	30	30	Private
Haverford College	1425	31	31	Private
Georgetown University	1410	32	32	Private
Vassar College	1410	32	32	Private
Georgia Institute of Technology	1405	34	1	Public
Case Western Reserve University	1400	35	34	Private
Grinnell College	1400	35	34	Private
Washington and Lee University	1400	35	34	Private
Carleton College	1390	38	37	Private
University of Michigan - Ann Arbor	1390	38	2	Public
Wellesley College	1390	38	37	Private
Middlebury College	1385	41	39	Private
Reed College	1385	41	39	Private
Rensselaer Polytechnic Institute	1385	41	39	Private
University of Southern California	1385	41	39	Private
Emory University	1380	45	43	Private
University of California - Berkeley	1380	45	3	Public
Jewish Theological Seminary of America	1373	47	44	Private
Boston College	1365	48	45	Private
Colby College	1365	48	45	Private
Scripps College	1364	50	47	Private

The Top 200 Institutions – SAT Scores (2015)

Top 51-101 Institutions in Median SAT Scores	Median SAT Score	National Rank	Control Rank	Institutional Control
Brandeis University	1360	51	48	Private
College of William and Mary	1360	51	4	Public
Macalester College	1360	51	48	Private
New York University	1360	51	48	Private
Tulane University	1360	51	48	Private
U.S. Air Force Academy	1360	51	4	Public
University of North Carolina - Chapel Hill	1360	51	4	Public
Barnard College	1355	58	52	Private
Oberlin College	1355	58	52	Private
University of Virginia	1355	58	7	Public
Bryn Mawr College	1350	61	54	Private
Colgate University	1350	61	54	Private
Davidson College	1350	61	54	Private
Colorado School of Mines	1340	64	8	Public
Rose-Hulman Institute of Technology	1340	64	57	Private
Southern Methodist University	1340	64	57	Private
University of Miami	1340	64	57	Private
University of California - San Diego	1335	68	9	Public
Stevens Institute of Technology	1333	69	60	Private
Kenyon College	1330	70	61	Private
Lehigh University	1325	71	62	Private
University of California - Los Angeles	1325	71	10	Public
Babson College	1320	73	63	Private
Rhodes College (TN)	1320	73	63	Private
Trinity University	1320	73	63	Private
University of Richmond	1320	73	63	Private
Wheaton College (IL)	1320	73	63	Private
University of Maryland - College Park	1315	78	11	Public
Whitman College	1310	79	68	Private
Binghamton University	1307	80	12	Public
Boston University	1305	81	69	Private
Santa Clara University	1305	81	69	Private
Brigham Young University - Provo	1300	83	71	Private
Bucknell University	1300	83	71	Private
Hillsdale College	1300	83	71	Private
Ohio State University - Columbus	1300	83	13	Public
University of Tulsa	1300	83	71	Private
University of Wisconsin - Madison	1300	83	13	Public
Villanova University	1300	83	71	Private
George Washington University	1290	90	76	Private
Lafayette College	1290	90	76	Private
Occidental College	1290	90	76	Private
University of Texas - Austin	1290	90	15	Public
Centre College	1280	94	79	Private
Hendrix College	1280	94	79	Private
St. Olaf College	1280	94	79	Private
U.S. Military Academy	1280	94	16	Public
U.S. Naval Academy	1280	94	16	Public
University of Illinois - Urbana-Champaign	1280	94	16	Public
University of Minnesota - Twin Cities	1280	94	16	Public
New College of Florida	1275	101	20	Public

The Top 200 Institutions – SAT Scores (2015)

Top 102-150 Institutions in Median SAT Scores	Median SAT Score	National Rank	Control Rank	Institutional Control
Rhode Island School of Design	1270	102	82	Private
Thomas Aquinas College	1270	102	82	Private
Stony Brook University	1265	104	21	Public
U.S. Coast Guard Academy	1265	104	21	Public
University of Pittsburgh - Pittsburgh	1265	104	21	Public
University of Texas - Dallas	1265	104	21	Public
Zaytuna College	1263	108	84	Private
Fordham University	1260	109	85	Private
Miami University - Oxford	1260	109	25	Public
Missouri University of Science and Technology	1260	109	25	Public
Saint Louis University - St. Louis	1260	109	85	Private
University of Denver	1260	109	85	Private
University of Florida	1260	109	25	Public
Clemson University	1250	115	28	Public
Yeshiva University	1250	115	88	Private
American University	1245	117	89	Private
North Carolina State University	1245	117	29	Public
University of Washington - Seattle	1245	117	29	Public
Baylor University	1240	120	90	Private
Butler University	1240	120	90	Private
College of Wooster	1240	120	90	Private
Illinois Institute of Technology	1240	120	90	Private
Illinois Wesleyan University	1240	120	90	Private
Milwaukee School of Engineering	1240	120	90	Private
Texas Christian University	1240	120	90	Private
Truman State University	1240	120	31	Public
University of Georgia	1240	120	31	Public
Bentley University	1235	129	97	Private
California Polytechnic State Univ. - San Luis Obispo	1235	129	33	Public
University of Connecticut - Storrs	1235	129	33	Public
City University of NY - Bernard M. Baruch College	1230	132	35	Public
Rochester Institute of Technology	1230	132	98	Private
Soka University of America	1230	132	98	Private
Skidmore College	1227	135	100	Private
Rutgers University - New Brunswick	1225	136	36	Public
University of California - Santa Barbara	1225	136	36	Public
Auburn University	1220	138	38	Public
DePauw University	1220	138	101	Private
Drake University	1220	138	101	Private
Florida State University	1220	138	38	Public
John Brown University	1220	138	101	Private
Marquette University	1220	138	101	Private
Taylor University	1220	138	101	Private
U.S. Merchant Marine Academy	1220	138	38	Public
University of Alabama - Huntsville	1220	138	38	Public
University of Colorado - Boulder	1220	138	38	Public
University of Massachusetts - Amherst	1220	138	38	Public
University of Tennessee - Knoxville	1220	138	38	Public
College of New Jersey	1215	150	45	Public
Willamette University	1215	150	106	Private

The Top 200 Institutions – SAT Scores (2015)

Top 152-190 Institutions in Median SAT Scores	Median SAT Score	National Rank	Control Rank	Institutional Control
Mercer University	1210	152	107	Private
New Jersey Institute of Technology	1210	152	46	Public
Pepperdine University	1210	152	107	Private
St. Univ. of New York - Coll. of Env. Sci and Forestry	1210	152	46	Public
University of Dallas	1210	152	107	Private
University of Maryland - Baltimore County	1210	152	46	Public
University of San Diego	1210	152	107	Private
Virginia Polytechnic Institute and State University	1210	152	46	Public
Berry College	1205	160	111	Private
Calvin College	1205	160	111	Private
Covenant College	1205	160	111	Private
Creighton University	1205	160	111	Private
Emerson College	1205	160	111	Private
Hope College	1205	160	111	Private
Kettering University	1205	160	111	Private
Loyola Marymount University	1205	160	111	Private
Loyola University Chicago	1205	160	111	Private
Michigan Technological University	1205	160	50	Public
Purdue University - West Lafayette	1205	160	50	Public
South Dakota School of Mines and Technology	1205	160	50	Public
St. Louis College of Pharmacy	1205	160	111	Private
University of Alabama - Tuscaloosa	1205	160	50	Public
University of California - Davis	1205	160	50	Public
University of Dayton	1205	160	111	Private
University of Missouri - Columbia	1205	160	50	Public
University of Oklahoma - Norman	1205	160	50	Public
University of St. Thomas (MN)	1205	160	111	Private
Drexel University	1203	179	123	Private
Elon University	1200	180	124	Private
University of Massachusetts - Lowell	1200	180	57	Public
University of South Carolina - Columbia	1200	180	57	Public
Chapman University	1195	183	125	Private
Pennsylvania State University - University Park	1195	183	59	Public
State Univ. of New York - College at Geneseo	1195	183	59	Public
University of Delaware	1195	183	59	Public
University of Portland	1195	183	125	Private
University of Vermont	1195	183	59	Public
Grove City College	1193	189	127	Private
Birmingham-Southern College	1190	190	128	Private
Cornell College	1190	190	128	Private
Drury University	1190	190	128	Private
Gonzaga University	1190	190	128	Private
Lipscomb University	1190	190	128	Private
Luther College	1190	190	128	Private
New Mexico Institute of Mining and Technology	1190	190	63	Public
Samford University	1190	190	128	Private
Syracuse University	1190	190	128	Private
Texas A&M University - College Station	1190	190	63	Public
University of Evansville	1190	190	128	Private
Valparaiso University	1190	190	128	Private
Wofford College	1190	190	128	Private

The Top 200 Institutions – National Merit Scholars (2016)

Top 1-53 Institutions in National Merit Scholars	Number of Scholars	National Rank	Control Rank	Institutional Control
University of Oklahoma - Norman	279	1	1	Public
University of Chicago	277	2	1	Private
Harvard University	233	3	2	Private
University of Southern California	230	4	3	Private
Vanderbilt University	220	5	4	Private
Stanford University	179	6	5	Private
Northwestern University	168	7	6	Private
University of California - Berkeley	161	8	2	Public
University of Florida	158	9	3	Public
University of Alabama - Tuscaloosa	155	10	4	Public
Massachusetts Institute of Technology	154	11	7	Private
University of Minnesota - Twin Cities	150	12	5	Public
Yale University	147	13	8	Private
University of Pennsylvania	134	14	9	Private
Purdue University - West Lafayette	125	15	6	Public
Texas A&M University - College Station	122	16	7	Public
University of Texas - Dallas	119	17	8	Public
Princeton University	117	18	10	Private
Arizona State University	109	19	9	Public
Duke University	106	20	11	Private
Brown University	100	21	12	Private
University of Kentucky	99	22	10	Public
Cornell University	81	23	13	Private
Northeastern University	81	23	13	Private
Baylor University	80	25	15	Private
University of Central Florida	77	26	11	Public
University of Texas - Austin	74	27	12	Public
Case Western Reserve University	72	28	16	Private
Brigham Young University - Provo	71	29	17	Private
Columbia University	67	30	18	Private
Rice University	67	30	18	Private
Auburn University	60	32	13	Public
University of Michigan - Ann Arbor	60	32	13	Public
Boston University	56	34	20	Private
Carnegie Mellon University	55	35	21	Private
Georgia Institute of Technology	55	35	15	Public
University of Maryland - College Park	55	35	15	Public
Emory University	54	38	22	Private
Indiana University - Bloomington	52	39	17	Public
Carleton College	50	40	23	Private
Tufts University	50	40	23	Private
University of Cincinnati - Cincinnati	50	40	18	Public
Dartmouth College	49	43	25	Private
Johns Hopkins University	47	44	26	Private
University of Arkansas - Fayetteville	45	45	19	Public
California Institute of Technology	44	46	27	Private
Clemson University	43	47	20	Public
Fordham University	43	47	28	Private
University of Arizona	43	47	20	Public
University of California - Los Angeles	43	47	20	Public
University of Mississippi - Oxford	43	47	20	Public
University of Notre Dame	43	47	28	Private
Harvey Mudd College	41	53	30	Private

The Top 200 Institutions – National Merit Scholars (2016)

Top 54-104 Institutions in National Merit Scholars	Number of Scholars	National Rank	Control Rank	Institutional Control
Tulane University	39	54	31	Private
University of Georgia	39	54	24	Public
Mississippi State University	37	56	25	Public
University of Miami	36	57	32	Private
University of Nebraska - Lincoln	36	57	26	Public
University of South Carolina - Columbia	36	57	26	Public
Iowa State University	35	60	28	Public
Rutgers University - New Brunswick	35	60	28	Public
Michigan State University	34	62	30	Public
Georgetown University	33	63	33	Private
University of Utah	33	63	31	Public
Washington University in St. Louis	33	63	33	Private
University of Tulsa	30	66	35	Private
University of Illinois - Urbana-Champaign	29	67	32	Public
University of Virginia	29	67	32	Public
University of North Carolina - Chapel Hill	28	69	34	Public
Liberty University	26	70	36	Private
Macalester College	26	70	36	Private
University of Iowa	26	70	35	Public
Louisiana State University - Baton Rouge	25	73	36	Public
Rensselaer Polytechnic Institute	25	73	38	Private
University of Houston - University Park	25	73	36	Public
University of Pittsburgh - Pittsburgh	25	73	36	Public
Stony Brook University	24	77	39	Public
University of Rochester	24	77	39	Private
University of Washington - Seattle	23	79	40	Public
Florida State University	22	80	41	Public
Oberlin College	22	80	40	Private
University of Alabama - Birmingham	22	80	41	Public
University of Louisville	20	83	43	Public
University of New Mexico - Albuquerque	20	83	43	Public
Grinnell College	19	85	41	Private
Ohio State University - Columbus	19	85	45	Public
Southern Methodist University	19	85	41	Private
University of California - San Diego	19	85	45	Public
University of Tennessee - Knoxville	19	85	45	Public
West Virginia University	19	85	45	Public
University of Kansas - Lawrence	18	91	49	Public
George Washington University	17	92	43	Private
University of Idaho	17	92	50	Public
University of Wisconsin - Madison	17	92	50	Public
Wheaton College (IL)	17	92	43	Private
Williams College	17	92	43	Private
Bowdoin College	16	97	46	Private
Miami University - Oxford	16	97	52	Public
Pennsylvania State University - University Park	16	97	52	Public
Missouri University of Science and Technology	15	100	54	Public
New York University	15	100	47	Private
Texas Tech University	15	100	54	Public
Washington and Lee University	15	100	47	Private
Franklin W. Olin College of Engineering	14	104	49	Private
Pomona College	14	104	49	Private
Rose-Hulman Institute of Technology	14	104	49	Private
St. Olaf College	14	104	49	Private

The Top 200 Institutions – National Merit Scholars (2016)

Top 108-148 Institutions in National Merit Scholars	Number of Scholars	National Rank	Control Rank	Institutional Control
Calvin College	13	108	53	Private
Harding University	13	108	53	Private
Oklahoma State University - Stillwater	13	108	56	Public
University of Missouri - Columbia	13	108	56	Public
Montana State University - Bozeman	12	112	58	Public
University of Richmond	12	112	55	Private
University of South Florida - Tampa	12	112	58	Public
Boston College	11	115	56	Private
Brandeis University	11	115	56	Private
Rochester Institute of Technology	11	115	56	Private
University of Dallas	11	115	56	Private
University of North Texas	11	115	60	Public
Furman University	10	120	60	Private
Kenyon College	10	120	60	Private
University of Colorado - Boulder	10	120	61	Public
University of Nevada - Reno	10	120	61	Public
University of Vermont	10	120	61	Public
Virginia Commonwealth University	10	120	61	Public
Wayne State University	10	120	61	Public
Colorado State University - Fort Collins	9	127	66	Public
Hendrix College	9	127	62	Private
Hillsdale College	9	127	62	Private
Rhodes College (TN)	9	127	62	Private
Trinity University	9	127	62	Private
University of Oregon	9	127	66	Public
Worcester Polytechnic Institute	9	127	62	Private
Amherst College	8	134	67	Private
Davidson College	8	134	67	Private
Haverford College	8	134	67	Private
Lehigh University	8	134	67	Private
North Carolina State University	8	134	68	Public
Oregon State University	8	134	68	Public
Truman State University	8	134	68	Public
Villanova University	8	134	67	Private
College of Charleston	7	142	71	Public
Colorado College	7	142	72	Private
New College of Florida	7	142	71	Public
North Dakota State University	7	142	71	Public
Oklahoma Christian University	7	142	72	Private
Swarthmore College	7	142	72	Private
Colby College	6	148	75	Private
Kansas State University	6	148	74	Public
Lawrence University	6	148	75	Private
Louisiana Tech University	6	148	74	Public
Marquette University	6	148	75	Private
Michigan Technological University	6	148	74	Public
Middlebury College	6	148	75	Private
Santa Clara University	6	148	75	Private
Smith College	6	148	75	Private
Texas Christian University	6	148	75	Private
University of Maine - Orono	6	148	74	Public
Whitman College	6	148	75	Private

The Top 200 Institutions – National Merit Scholars (2016)

Institutions with at least 4 National Merit Scholars	Number of Scholars	National Rank	Control Rank	Institutional Control
Centre College	5	160	83	Private
Claremont McKenna College	5	160	83	Private
College of William and Mary	5	160	78	Public
Drake University	5	160	83	Private
Gustavus Adolphus College	5	160	83	Private
Loyola University Chicago	5	160	83	Private
Saint Louis University - St. Louis	5	160	83	Private
University of Evansville	5	160	83	Private
Valparaiso University	5	160	83	Private
American University	4	169	91	Private
Ball State University	4	169	79	Public
Belmont University	4	169	91	Private
Benedictine College	4	169	91	Private
California Polytechnic State Univ - San Luis Obispo	4	169	79	Public
College of Wooster	4	169	91	Private
Creighton University	4	169	91	Private
Drexel University	4	169	91	Private
Lewis & Clark College	4	169	91	Private
Mount Holyoke College	4	169	91	Private
Occidental College	4	169	91	Private
Ohio University - Athens	4	169	79	Public
Ouachita Baptist University	4	169	91	Private
Reed College	4	169	91	Private
Scripps College	4	169	91	Private
Southwestern University	4	169	91	Private
University of California - Davis	4	169	79	Public
University of Missouri - Kansas City	4	169	79	Public
University of Southern Mississippi	4	169	79	Public
University of St. Thomas (MN)	4	169	91	Private
Wichita State University	4	169	79	Public

Source Notes

Total Research Expenditures
Federal Research Expenditures
Source: Higher Education Research and Development
(HERD) Survey, FY 2015

Each year, the National Science Foundation (NSF) collects data from hundreds of academic institutions on expenditures for research and development in science and engineering fields and classifies them by source of funds (e.g., federal government, state and local government, industry, etc.). These data are the primary source of information on academic research and development (R&D) expenditures in the United States. Included in this survey are all activities specifically organized to produce research outcomes that are separately budgeted and accounted for. This "organized research" may be funded by an external agency or organization ("sponsored research") or by a separately budgeted organizational unit within the institution ("university research"). This report excludes activities sponsored by external agencies that involve instruction, training (except training in research techniques, which is considered organized research), and health service, community service or extension service projects.

All Federally Funded Research Labs (FFRLs) are excluded from these academic expenditures data, including the following: Jet Propulsion Laboratory (California Institute of Technology); Los Alamos National Lab, Lawrence Livermore Lab, Lawrence Berkeley Lab (University of California); Software Engineering Institute (Carnegie Mellon); Argonne National Laboratory (University of Chicago); National Astronomy and Ionospheric Center (Cornell); Ames Laboratory (Iowa State University); Lincoln Laboratory (MIT); Plasma Physics Lab (Princeton); and SLAC National Accelerator Laboratory (Stanford). The NSF data no longer classify the Applied Physics Lab (APL) at Johns Hopkins as an FFRL, but federal funds support the vast majority of research conducted there. The APL makes up more than one-half of Johns Hopkins' total federal R&D expenditures.

While inconsistencies in reporting (known and unknown) do exist here, as in any survey of this type, problems arise mostly when one breaks out the data by source of funds. NSF expects institutions to use year-end accounting records to complete this report, and there are nationally recognized accounting guidelines for higher education institutions. However, there are also countless variations in institutional policy that determine whether the university reports a particular expenditure as coming from one source or another, or possibly not counted at all. Take federal formula funds for agriculture (e.g., Hatch-McIntire, Smith-Lever) as an example. We conducted an informal survey of the appropriate institutions in the Association of American Universities (AAU) and found that two out of eleven land grants did not include any of these federal funds in their 1997 NSF data, while others included all or some of these monies. Because these funds make

up a very small percentage of the total research expenditures in any given year, the impact on our total research rankings is slight. The agriculture formula funds will have a somewhat greater, but still small, impact on the federal research rankings.

We believe that the reporting inconsistencies in the data are relatively minor when using the total research expenditures and the federal research expenditures component. Federal and state government audits of institutional accounting make deceptive practices highly unlikely, even though these entities do not audit the NSF data directly. NSF goes to great lengths to verify the accuracy of the data, especially federal expenditure data—checking them against several other federal agencies that collect the same or similar information. In fact, all major federal agencies and their subdivisions submit data to NSF identifying research obligations to universities each year. Historically, the NSF data have tracked very closely the data reported by universities. Further, for their National Patterns of R&D Resources series, NSF prefers to use the figures reported by the performers of the work (that is, academic institutions, industry, nonprofits) because they believe that the performers are in the best position to accurately report these expenditures.

In some sections of this report, these expenditure data are deflated to constant 1983 dollars to show real change over time. While NSF uses the Gross Domestic Price (GDP) implicit price deflator in its reports on federal trends in research, we use the Higher Education Price Index (HEPI) because of its narrower focus. Originally developed by Research Associates of Washington and currently managed by Commonfund Institute, the HEPI illustrates the effect of inflation on college and university operations. [1] In contrast, the GDP implicit price deflator is based on change in the entire U.S. economy and, as noted by NSF itself, "[its] use more accurately reflects an 'opportunity cost' criterion [i.e., the value of R&D in terms of the amount of other goods and services that could have been spent with the same amount of money], rather than a measure of cost changes of doing research." [2]

Endowment Assets

Source: NACUBO-Commonfund Study of Endowment, endowment market value as of June 30, 2016.

Institutions report the market value of their endowment assets as of June 30 to three different sources, and they quite often use three different values. For this project, we use the NACUBO-Commonfund Study of Endowment because of NACUBO's long history of reporting endowments of higher education institutions, their emphasis on using audited financial statements, and their focus on net assets (i.e., includes returns on investments and excludes investment fees and other withdrawals). NACUBO conducts its study annually and reports the results each February in the Chronicle of Higher Education.

Another source for endowment assets is the Council for Aid to Education's (CAE) annual Voluntary Support of Education (VSE) survey, cosponsored by the Council for Advancement and Support of Education (CASE) and the National Association of Independent Schools. The VSE survey is useful as a secondary resource because it provides more single-campus data than the other two sources. For those institutions that report a system-wide total to NACUBO, we often use the VSE data to calculate a campus' percentage contribution to the entire system, applying that factor to the NACUBO figure. In other cases, we may substitute the VSE figure when the institution indicates that this is a good data source.

The National Center for Education Statistics (NCES) Integrated Postsecondary Education Data System (IPEDS) Finance Survey also collects information on endowment assets. IPEDS data are released later than other two sources and are used when NACUBO nor VSE figures are unavailable.

In our inaugural report of *The Top American Research Universities* in 2000, we noted the wide variation in the reporting of endowment market value between all three sources. An examination of the 1997 endowment figures showed only one university (University of North Carolina at Chapel Hill) had submitted the same figure to each of the three organizations. In a more recent study of major research universities, we found about one-third of the all institutions report identical figures but just seven universities in our over $40 million federal research group. In the earlier study, we found that endowment assets reported to IPEDS tended to be lower than NACUBO or VSE data, but this is no longer true. In general, the greater the endowment the likelihood that the figures reported to the three sources will vary. Both studies found no consistent pattern to explain reporting variations among the institutions.

Annual Giving

Source: Council for Aid to Education's Voluntary Support of Education (VSE) Survey, FY 2016.

The Council for Aid to Education (CAE), formerly an independent subsidiary of RAND, has produced the Voluntary Support of Education (VSE) Survey since 1957. The annual giving data include all contributions actually received during the institution's fiscal year in the form of cash, securities, company products, and other property from alumni, non-alumni individuals, corporations, foundations, religious organizations, and other groups. Not included in the totals are public funds, earnings on investments held by the institution, and unfulfilled pledges.

CAE's VSE Data Miner service, available online, provides 11 years of data for all participating institutions. Although this is a

subscription-based service and requires a user ID and password, limited access is available online at [http://www.cae.org/vse].

National Academy Members

Source: National Academy of Sciences, National Academy of Engineering, and National Academy of Medicine membership directories for 2016.

One of the highest honors that academic faculty can receive is membership in the National Academy of Sciences (NAS), the National Academy of Engineering (NAE), or the National Academy of Medicine (NAM), formerly known as the Institute of Medicine. All three are private, nonprofit organizations and serve as advisors to the federal government on science, technology, and medicine. Nominated and voted on by active members, newly elected members of these organizations receive life terms. Individuals elected to membership come from all sectors—academia, industry, government, and not-for-profit agencies or organizations. Member election dates are in February (NAE), April (NAS), and October (NAM).

The data collected for these rankings use active or emeritus members at their affiliated work institution, as reported in the online membership directories. In all cases, we were able to determine the specific campus for individual members. We re-check institutional affiliation annually to account for established members who have changed employers or whose membership is no longer active.

Faculty Awards in the Arts, Humanities, Science, Engineering, and Health

Source: Directories or web-based listings for multiple agencies or organizations.

For this category, we collect data from several prominent grant and fellowship programs in the arts, humanities, science, engineering, and health fields. Included in this measure are:

- American Council of Learned Societies (ACLS) Fellows, 2015-16
- Beckman Young Investigators, 2016
- Burroughs Wellcome Fund Career Awards, 2016
- Cottrell Scholars, 2016
- Fulbright American Scholars, 2016-17
- Getty Scholars in Residence, 2016-17
- Guggenheim Fellows, 2016
- Lasker Medical Research Awards, 2016
- MacArthur Foundation Fellows, 2016

- National Endowment for the Humanities (NEH) Fellows, 2017

- National Humanities Center Fellows, 2016-17

- National Institutes of Health (NIH) MERIT (R37), FY 2016

- NSF CAREER awards, 2016

- Newberry Library Long-term Fellows, 2016-17

- Pew Scholars in Biomedicine, 2016

- Robert Wood Johnson Policy Fellows, 2016-17

- Searle Scholars, 2016

- Sloan Research Fellows, 2016

- Woodrow Wilson Fellows, 2016-17

While the vast majority of these programs clearly identify a particular campus, in a few instances we used the institution's web-based phone directory to determine the correct campus.

Doctorates Awarded

Source: NCES IPEDS Completions Survey, doctoral degrees awarded between July 1, 2015, and June 30, 2016.

Each year, universities report their degrees awarded to the NCES in the IPEDS Completions Survey. IPEDS provides straightforward instructions for reporting doctoral degrees awarded, and we do not find any inconsistencies in reporting among the universities included in our rankings. IPEDS asks each institution to identify the number of Doctor of Education, Doctor of Juridical Science, Doctor of Public Health, and Doctor of Philosophy degrees awarded between July 1 and June 30.

Most institutions in our study submit degree data by campus or offer doctoral degrees solely or primarily at the main campus.

In addition to doctorate degrees, we present degrees awarded at other levels—associate's, bachelor's, master's, and professional degrees—in the Student Characteristics table.

Postdoctoral Appointees

Source: NSF/Division of Science Resource Statistics (SRS) Survey of Graduate Students and Postdoctorates in Science and Engineering, Fall 2015.

Each year, NSF and NIH collect data from all institutions offering graduate programs in any science, engineering, or health field. The Survey of Graduate Students and Postdoctorates in Science and Engineering (also called the Graduate Student Survey or GSS) reflects graduate enrollment and postdoctoral employment at the beginning of the academic year. Postdoctorates are defined

in the GSS as "individuals with science and engineering PhD's, MD's, DDS's or DVM's and foreign degrees equivalent to U.S. doctorates who devote their primary effort to their own research training through research activities or study in the department under temporary appointments carrying no academic rank." The definition excludes clinical fellows and those in medical residency training programs unless the primary purpose of their appointment is for research training under a senior mentor.

In the methodological notes for this survey,[3] NSF indicates that it verifies the data with the institutional coordinator when dramatic year-to-year fluctuations are noted. In addition, in this data set, it is unclear whether an institution has actually reported zero postdocs or NSF has simply assigned a zero for non-response (rather than imputing by using prior-year or peer data, as described in NSF methodological notes). This year, in cases where we suspect it is not a true zero, we left the field blank.

Although each doctorate-granting campus submits data separately, NSF often aggregates them in its published reports. In all cases, we obtain the single-campus data for these schools directly from NSF.

SAT Scores

Source: NCES IPEDS Survey, SAT and ACT scores for Fall 2015.

IPEDS reports the 25th and 75th percentiles for verbal and quantitative SAT I scores for most institutions in our study. For our measure, we calculated the median of that range. Some institutions report the ACT instead of the SAT to IPEDS and some report both. We selected the test which has the greatest percentage of students reporting. To convert ACT scores, we use a conversion table provided by The College Board[4] to generate a comparable SAT equivalent score. When an institution submits neither an SAT nor ACT score, we substitute data from other national data sources.

Other Measures of Undergraduate Quality

National Merit and Achievement Scholars

Source: The 2015-16 National Merit Scholarship Corporation Annual Report, which reflects the 2016 freshman class.

The National Merit Scholarship Corporation (NMSC) is an independent, nonprofit organization that awards scholarships to the nation's outstanding high school seniors based on their academic achievement, qualifying test scores, high school principal and counselor recommendations, and their activities, interests, and goals. The NMSC names approximately 15,000 National Merit Finalists each February. Of these, about 8,000 will receive a National Merit $2,500 Scholarship, a corporate-sponsored scholarship, or a college-sponsored scholarship.

Until it was discontinued in 2015, National Achievement Scholars were selected and funded in a similar fashion and represented the nation's outstanding African-American students. Ideally, the National Hispanic Scholars Program should also be included in this category, but it does not track the enrollment of its scholarship winners. Should it do so in the future, we will include these students in our data. In this study, Merit and Achievement scholarships are credited to the main campus if the NMSC Annual Report does not indicate a branch campus.

While the number of National Merit and National Achievement award winners in the entering class provides an indication of the attractiveness of a university's undergraduate program to outstanding students, it is also an indicator that is sensitive to institutional policies on financial aid. Because the number of Merit Scholars is small, relatively small changes in institutional aid policies can have a significant impact on the number of National Merit Scholars enrolling in institutions. The average SAT score provides a broader-based and more reliable measure of overall undergraduate quality; for those reasons, we prefer the SAT scores to the number of National Merit and Achievement Scholars as an indicator of undergraduate quality.

Institutional Characteristics

Medical Schools

Source: NCES IPEDS Completions Survey, MD degrees awarded between July 1, 2015, and June 30, 2016.

Although the IPEDS Institutional Characteristics Survey does have a "medical" field that indicates whether an institution grants a medical degree, we choose not to use its data because it includes medical degrees in Veterinary Medicine, Dentistry, and other professional health-related fields. For our measure, we determined whether a particular campus awarded any MD degrees during the academic year. If the institution did not submit any data to IPEDS for that year, we then looked at whether it was accredited by the American Medical Association to determine whether the institution has a medical school.

Land Grant Institutions

Source: National Association of State Universities and Land Grant Colleges.

The first Morrill Act in 1862 appropriated federal funds for universities to provide agricultural and technical education to their citizens. A second Morrill Act in 1890 expanded eligibility to include several historically black colleges and universities, and in 1994 several Native American tribal colleges were recognized as land grant institutions. Today, there is at least one land grant institution in each state and U.S. territory and in the District of Columbia. Of the 106 institutions, most are public universities.

Federal land grant institutions receive both federal and state dollars in support of their agricultural and extension activities.

While land grant status technically applies to some university systems, such as the University of California and the University of Nebraska, for our study we designate as land grant institutions only those schools that actually perform that function (e.g., UC-Berkeley, UC-Davis, UC-Riverside, Nebraska-Lincoln). In these cases, the land grant field will identify whether an institution is part of a system-wide land grant and whether the vast majority of the activity occurs on that campus. For example, UC-Davis is coded as "Yes-System" while UCLA is coded as "No-System."

Research Focus

NSF/SRS Survey of R&D Expenditures at Universities and Colleges, FY 2015.

In addition to reporting expenditure data by source of funds, NSF identifies in what major disciplines the money is expended. In the Research by Discipline table we provide the proportion of total and federal expenditures in each discipline for those institutions with more than $40 million in federal research. These data are useful for developing groups of similar institutions for peer analysis.

The Institutional Characteristics table provides a summary measure of an institution's research strength and concentration based on these discipline-level expenditures. Universities with 95-100% of their federal research dollars spent in one particular discipline are coded as "all." We identify institutions with 75-94% in one area as "heavy" and label those with 50-74% of their expenditures concentrated as "strong." Other universities with 25-49% in one or more disciplines we describe as "moderate." A few institutions (but none in the more than $40 million group) have expenditures distributed fairly evenly across the disciplines; those we code as "mixed."

In some cases, where an institution reports as a multi-campus entity, we made adjustments to break out the discipline-level expenditure data by single campus. Typically, this involved moving all or a portion of the life sciences expenditures to the health or medical center campus. IPEDS fall enrollment and graduate degrees by discipline data also were used to help in this effort.

While these data offer some insight as to the research structure of a university, their usefulness is limited. For example, we may be tempted to use the life sciences as a surrogate for medical research, but we must remember that they also include agricultural and biological sciences. Further, the growing trend toward multidisciplinary and interdisciplinary projects may make it more difficult for universities to accurately reflect expenditures by discipline or sub-discipline. We choose not to break out these sub-disciplines because the data are increasingly prone to error as further adjustments are made.

Student Characteristics

Fall Enrollment

Source: NCES IPEDS Fall Enrollment Survey, 2015.

Each November, institutions report their current fall headcount enrollment to the IPEDS Fall Enrollment Survey. Enrollment figures include both degree seeking and non-degree seeking students. We provide the headcount enrollment by level as presented by IPEDS, along with the percentage of those attending part-time. Graduate students include those seeking specialist degrees in engineering and education. First professional students include those seeking degrees in medical fields, such as Chiropractic, Dentistry, Medicine, Optometry, Osteopathic Medicine, Pharmacy, Podiatry, and Veterinary Medicine, as well as those seeking degrees in Law and Theology.

Each campus in our study submits enrollment data by campus, except for the few institutions identified in our Data Notes section. Because this is an informational item and not one of our nine quality measures, we did not attempt to adjust these figures.

Federal Research with and without Medical School Research

AAMC Federal Research

Source: Association of American Medical Colleges

The Association of American Medical Colleges collects data on federally sponsored research at medical colleges through on the Liaison Committee on Medical Education (LCME) Part I-A, Annual Financial Questionnaire. We calculate each medical school's federal R&D by summing the recorded dollars and a portion of the relative administrative costs. We exclude the not-recorded dollars.

Footnotes

1 About HEPI, Commonfund Institute
(Online: http://www.commonfund.org/CommonfundInstitute/HEPI)

2 National Patterns of R&D Resources, 2003: Technical Notes
(Online: http://www.nsf.gov/statistics/nsf05308/appa.htm)

3 Survey Methodology: Survey of Graduate Students and Postdoctorates in Science and Engineering
(Online: http://www.nsf.gov/statistics/srvygradpostdoc/)

4 ACT and SAT Concordance Tables, November 6, 2009
(Online: http://www.research.collegeboard.org/publications)

Data Notes

The raw data used for *The Top American Research Universities* project—obtained from federal agencies and national organizations—often contain information on single-campus institutions, multiple-campus institutions, and state university systems, without clearly identifying the distinctions. This makes national comparisons difficult and unreliable.

To increase the validity and usefulness of these data, we adjusted the original reported figures, when necessary, to ensure that all data represent the strength of a single-campus institution. MUP Center bases its adjustments on information gathered from the reporting agency or from the university itself. In cases where the published data represent a single campus, we do not adjust the data. When the data represent more than one campus, we first attempt to obtain a figure directly from the National Science Foundation (NSF) (for research expenditures and post-doctorates), from the institution itself, or from the university system office that submitted the data. If unavailable from those primary sources, we use an estimated or substitute figure derived from information found on the institution's website.

If the institution provides an estimate representing at least 97% of the originally published figure, we credit the full amount to the main campus. Otherwise, we use the estimate provided by the institution.

MUP Center does not adjust the private university data because of multi-campus or system-wide reporting. We treat all private universities in this study as single-campus institutions because, while some may have multiple campuses, they are generally in or around a single city and considered an integral part of the main campus. Furthermore, private institutions generally do not break out their data by regional, branch, or affiliated campus as often happens with public institutions.

The following tables outline the various adjustments or substitutions that we made to the original data. The tables list institutions alphabetically and include both private and public universities. For the purpose of this report, we provide notes for institutions with more than $40 million in fiscal year 2015 federal research.

Data Notes for Universities with Over $40 Million in Federal Research

University / Statistics	Original Data (dollars in thousands)	MUP Data (dollars in thousands)	Comments
Arizona State University			
2016 Doctorates		674	Combined IPEDS reported data.
Auburn University			
2016 Endowment		646,624	Estimate at least 97% is main campus.
2016 Giving		118,477	Estimate at least 97% is main campus.
Cleveland State University			
2016 Endowment		72,700	Substituted 2016 VSE. Did not report to NACUBO.
Colorado State University - Fort Collins			
2016 Giving		42,798	Used 2016 IPEDS. Did not report to VSE.
Cornell University			
2015 Federal R&D	445,266	277,163	Estimate 62.2% based on university documents.
2015 Total R&D	946,419	637,404	Estimate 67.3% based on university documents.
2016 Endowment	5,757,722	4,524,419	Substituted 2016 IPEDS.
2016 Giving	588,262	427,089	Estimate 72.6% based on 2016 IPEDS.
Icahn School of Medicine at Mount Sinai			
2016 Endowment		659,261	Used 2016 IPEDS. Did not report to NACUBO, VSE.
2016 Giving		120,327	Used 2016 IPEDS. Did not report to VSE.
Indiana University - Bloomington			
2016 Endowment	1,986,464	991,134	Substituted 2016 IPEDS.
2016 Giving	360,936	195,908	Estimate based on IPEDS and university documents.
Kansas State University			
2015 SAT			Does not require SAT/ACT.
Louisiana State University - Baton Rouge			
2016 Endowment	781,833	416,717	Substituted 2016 VSE.
Medical College of Wisconsin			
2016 Giving		19,028	Used 2016 IPEDS. Did not report to VSE.
Michigan State University			
2015 Endowment	2,673,652	2,672,822	Revised 2015 NACUBO data.
New Mexico State University - Las Cruces			
2016 Endowment		214,778	Estimate at least 97% is main campus.
Ohio State University - Columbus			
2016 Endowment		3,578,562	Estimate at least 97% is main campus.
2016 Giving		386,112	Estimate at least 97% is main campus.

Data Notes for Universities with Over $40 Million in Federal Research

University / Statistics	Original Data (dollars in thousands)	MUP Data (dollars in thousands)	Comments
Pennsylvania State University - Hershey Medical Center			
2015 Federal R&D	507,889	59,933	Estimate 11.8% based on university documents.
2015 Postdocs	436	70	Estimate 16% based on university documents.
2015 Total R&D	774,384	91,381	Estimate 11.8% based on university documents.
2016 Endowment	3,602,312	449,943	Substituted data from published documents.
2016 Giving	197,064	35,472	Estimate 18.0% based on university documents.
Pennsylvania State University - University Park			
2015 Federal R&D	507,889	447,956	Estimate 88.2% based on university documents.
2015 Postdocs	436	366	Estimate 84% based on university documents.
2015 Total R&D	774,384	683,003	Estimate 88.2% based on university documents.
2016 Endowment	3,602,312	1,912,254	Substituted data from published documents.
2016 Giving	197,064	147,570	Estimate 74.9% based on university documents.
Purdue University - West Lafayette			
2016 Endowment		2,254,541	Estimate at least 97% is main campus.
2016 Giving		151,217	Estimate at least 97% is main campus.
Rockefeller University			
2016 Giving		67,659	Used 2016 IPEDS. Did not report to VSE.
Rush University			
2016 Giving		3,070	Used 2016 IPEDS. Did not report to VSE.
Rutgers University - New Brunswick			
2016 Endowment	1,083,665	865,867	Substituted 2016 IPEDS.
2016 Giving	139,404	118,493	Estimate 85.0% based on university documents.
Temple University			
2015 SAT			Does not require SAT/ACT.
Texas A&M University - College Station			
2015 Federal R&D		291,714	Now include Texas A&M HSC with main campus.
2015 Total R&D		836,250	Now include Texas A&M HSC with main campus.
2016 Endowment	10,539,526	9,944,936	Substituted 2016 VSE.
Thomas Jefferson University			
2016 Endowment		500,943	Substituted 2016 VSE. Did not report to NACUBO.
University of Alabama - Birmingham			
2016 Endowment	1,220,781	431,459	Substituted 2016 VSE.
University of Alabama - Huntsville			
2016 Endowment	1,220,781	71,053	Substituted 2016 VSE.

Data Notes for Universities with Over $40 Million in Federal Research

University / Statistics	Original Data (dollars in thousands)	MUP Data (dollars in thousands)	Comments
University of Alaska - Fairbanks			
2016 Endowment	285,257	173,372	Estimate 61% based on IPEDS.
University of Arizona			
2015 SAT			Does not require SAT/ACT.
University of Arkansas for Medical Sciences			
2016 Endowment		31,733	Used 2016 IPEDS. Did not report to NACUBO, VSE.
2016 Giving		24,655	Used 2016 IPEDS. Did not report to VSE.
University of California - Berkeley			
2016 Endowment	1,585,935	3,845,281	Substituted 2016 VSE.
University of California - Davis			
2016 Endowment	325,497	965,805	Substituted 2016 VSE.
University of California - Los Angeles			
2016 Endowment	1,803,671	3,849,133	Substituted 2016 VSE.
University of California - Riverside			
2016 Endowment	129,185	191,420	Substituted 2016 VSE.
University of California - San Diego			
2016 Endowment	536,134	1,176,581	Substituted 2016 VSE.
University of California - San Francisco			
2016 Endowment	1,138,815	2,112,014	Substituted 2016 VSE.
University of California - Santa Cruz			
2016 Endowment	8,341,073	162,211	Substituted 2016 VSE.
University of Cincinnati - Cincinnati			
2016 Endowment		1,165,522	Estimate at least 97% is main campus.
University of Colorado - Boulder			
2016 Endowment	1,062,664	583,190	Substituted data from published documents.
2016 Giving	281,482	160,445	Estimate 57.0% based on university documents.
University of Colorado - Denver/Anschutz Medical			
2016 Endowment	1,062,664	479,474	Substituted data from published documents.
2016 Giving	281,482	106,963	Estimate 38.0% based on university documents.
University of Connecticut - Health Center			
2015 Federal R&D	135,349	43,512	Estimate 32.1% based on university documents.
2015 Total R&D	251,621	80,891	Estimate 32.1% based on university documents.
2016 Doctorates	336	16	Estimate based on university factbook.
2016 Endowment	377,171	83,260	Estimate 27% based on IPEDS substitution and published documents.
2016 Giving	72,367	6,747	Estimate 9.3% based on university documents.

Data Notes for Universities with Over $40 Million in Federal Research

University / Statistics	Original Data (dollars in thousands)	MUP Data (dollars in thousands)	Comments
University of Connecticut - Storrs			
2015 Federal R&D	135,349	91,837	Estimate 67.9% based on university documents.
2015 Total R&D	251,621	170,730	Estimate 67.9% based on university documents.
2016 Doctorates	336	320	Estimate based on university factbook.
2016 Endowment	377,171	275,335	Estimate 73% based on IPEDS substitution and published documents.
2016 Giving	72,367	65,620	Estimate 91.7% based on university documents.
University of Hawaii - Manoa			
2016 Endowment		271,180	Estimate at least 97% is main campus.
University of Houston - University Park			
2016 Endowment	741,825	665,001	Substituted 2016 VSE.
University of Illinois - Chicago			
2016 Endowment	2,290,995	287,188	Substituted 2016 VSE.
University of Illinois - Urbana-Champaign			
2016 Endowment	2,290,995	1,489,991	Substituted 2016 VSE.
University of Kansas - Lawrence			
2015 Federal R&D	128,374	85,862	Estimate 66.9% based on university documents.
2015 Postdocs	249	149	Estimate 60% based on university documents.
2015 Total R&D	257,766	172,406	Estimate 66.9% based on university documents.
2016 Doctorates	336	314	Estimate based on KS Board of Regents data book and IPEDS Completions.
2016 Endowment	1,475,158	1,150,623	Estimate 78% of 1,496,474 reported in IPEDS based on public documents.
2016 Giving	187,214	149,771	Estimate 80.0% based on university documents.
University of Kansas Medical Center			
2015 Federal R&D	128,374	42,512	Estimate 33.1% based on university documents.
2015 Postdocs	249	100	Estimate 40% based on university documents.
2015 Total R&D	257,766	85,360	Estimate 33.1% based on university documents.
2016 Doctorates	336	22	Estimate based on KS Board of Regents data book and IPEDS Completions.
2016 Endowment	1,475,158	345,852	Estimate 22% of 1,496,474 reported in IPEDS based on public documents.
2016 Giving	187,214	37,443	Estimate 20.0% based on university documents.
University of Maryland - Baltimore			
2016 Endowment	968,861	254,733	Substituted 2016 VSE.
University of Maryland - Baltimore County			
2016 Endowment	968,861	78,101	Substituted 2016 VSE.

Data Notes for Universities with Over $40 Million in Federal Research

University / Statistics	Original Data (dollars in thousands)	MUP Data (dollars in thousands)	Comments
University of Maryland - College Park			
2016 Endowment	280,322	466,075	Substituted 2016 VSE.
University of Massachusetts - Amherst			
2016 Endowment	734,166	287,213	Substituted 2016 VSE.
University of Massachusetts Medical School - Worcester			
2016 Endowment	734,166	183,435	Substituted 2016 IPEDS.
2016 Giving		7,550	Used 2016 IPEDS. Did not report to VSE.
University of Michigan - Ann Arbor			
2016 Endowment		9,743,461	Estimate at least 97% is main campus.
2016 Giving		433,776	Estimate at least 97% is main campus.
University of Minnesota - Twin Cities			
2016 Endowment		3,280,681	Estimate at least 97% is main campus.
2016 Giving	345,640	332,851	Estimate 96.3% based on IPEDS and university documents.
University of Missouri - Columbia			
2016 Endowment	1,459,991	869,566	Substituted 2016 VSE.
University of Nebraska - Lincoln			
2016 Endowment	1,475,091	869,874	Substituted 2016 IPEDS.
2016 Giving	214,459	100,542	Estimate 46.9% based on 2016 IPEDS.
University of Nebraska Medical Center			
2016 Endowment	1,475,093	223,753	Substituted 2016 IPEDS.
2016 Giving	214,459	91,702	Estimate 42.8% based on 2016 IPEDS.
University of New Hampshire - Durham			
2016 Endowment		330,131	Used 2016 IPEDS. Did not report to NACUBO, VSE.
2016 Giving		14,372	Used 2016 IPEDS. Did not report to VSE.
University of Oklahoma - Health Sciences Center			
2015 Federal R&D	122,918	65,463	Estimate 53.3% based on university documents.
2015 Total R&D	227,568	135,493	Estimate 59.5% based on university documents.
2016 Endowment	1,520,354	516,920	Estimate 34% based on published documents.
2016 Giving	322,436	69,440	Estimate 21.5% based on 2016 IPEDS.
University of Oklahoma - Norman			
2015 Federal R&D	122,918	57,455	Estimate 46.7% based on university documents.
2015 Total R&D	227,568	92,075	Estimate 40.5% based on university documents.
2016 Endowment	1,520,354	1,003,434	Estimate 66% based on published documents.
2016 Giving	322,436	252,996	Estimate 78.5% based on 2016 IPEDS.

Data Notes for Universities with Over $40 Million in Federal Research

University / Statistics	Original Data (dollars in thousands)	MUP Data (dollars in thousands)	Comments
University of Rochester			
2015 SAT			Did not report SAT/ACT.
University of Tennessee - Knoxville			
2015 Federal R&D		116,928	Now include UT Institute of Ag with Knoxville campus.
2015 Total R&D		233,650	Now include UT Institute of Ag with Knoxville campus.
2016 Endowment	1,099,634	597,475	Substituted 2016 VSE.
University of Texas - Austin			
2016 Endowment	24,203,213	10,935,781	Substituted 2016 VSE.
University of Texas - El Paso			
2016 Endowment	24,203,213	218,880	Substituted 2016 VSE.
University of Texas Health Science Center - Houston			
2016 Endowment	24,203,213	336,086	Substituted 2016 VSE.
University of Texas Health Science Center - San Antonio			
2016 Endowment	24,203,213	486,652	Substituted 2016 VSE.
University of Texas MD Anderson Cancer Center			
2016 Endowment	24,203,213	1,212,099	Substituted 2016 VSE.
University of Texas Medical Branch - Galveston			
2016 Endowment	24,203,213	533,972	Substituted 2016 VSE.
University of Texas SW Medical Center - Dallas			
2016 Endowment	24,203,213	1,684,130	Substituted 2016 VSE.
University of Vermont			
2016 Endowment		467,702	Substituted 2016 VSE. Did not report to NACUBO.
University of Washington - Seattle			
2016 Endowment		2,968,013	Estimate at least 97% is main campus.
2016 Giving		541,444	Estimate at least 97% is main campus.
University of Wisconsin - Madison			
2016 Endowment	2,419,161	2,739,728	Substituted 2016 VSE.
Utah State University			
2015 Endowment	314,688	314,668	Revised 2015 NACUBO data.
Wake Forest University			
2015 SAT			Does not require SAT/ACT.
Washington State University - Pullman			
2016 Endowment		907,828	Estimate at least 97% is main campus.
2016 Giving		103,845	Estimate at least 97% is main campus.

Data Notes for Universities with Over $40 Million in Federal Research			
University / Statistics	Original Data (dollars in thousands)	MUP Data (dollars in thousands)	Comments
Wayne State University			
2015 Endowment	306,319	307,569	Revised 2015 NACUBO data.
Weill Cornell Medical College			
2015 Federal R&D	445,266	168,103	Estimate 37.8% based on university documents.
2015 Total R&D	946,419	309,015	Estimate 32.7% based on university documents.
2016 Endowment	5,757,722	1,233,303	Substituted 2016 IPEDS.
2016 Giving	588,262	85,207	Estimate 14.5% based on 2016 IPEDS.
Yeshiva University			
2015 Endowment	1,061,440	680,327	Revised 2015 NACUBO data.

The Center for Measuring University Performance Publications

The Top American Research Universities. (MUP Center Reports, 2000-2016). [http://mup.umass.edu/publications]

American Research Universities in an Era of Change: 2006-2015, 2016.

What's in a Name? The Classification of Research Universities, 2015.

Tracking Academic Research Funding: The Competitive Context for the Last Ten Years, 2014.

The Best American Research Universities Ranking: Four Perspectives, 2013.

Measuring Research Performance: National and International Perspectives, 2012.

Moving Up: The Marketplace for Federal Research in America, 2011.

In Pursuit of Number One, 2010.

Research University Competition and Financial Challenges, 2009.

Competition and Restructuring the American Research University, 2008.

Rankings, Competition, and the Evolving American University, 2007.

Deconstructing University Rankings: Medicine and Engineering, and Single Campus Research Competitiveness, 2005.

Measuring and Improving Research Universities: TheCenter at Five Years, 2004.

The Sports Imperative in America's Research Universities, 2003.

University Organization, Governance, and Competitiveness, 2002.

Quality Engines: The Competitive Context for Research Universities, 2001.

The Myth of Number One: Indicators of Research University Performance, 2000.

Improving student success using technology-based analytics. *Diversity & Democracy*, Volume 17, Number 1 (2014) by Elizabeth D. Capaldi. [http://aacu.org/diversitydemocracy/2014/winter/phillips]

Rainer and Julie Martens Invited Lecture: Research Universities—the Next Five Years, *Kinesiology Review*, Volume 3, Issue 1 (2014), 4-12 by John V. Lombardi. [http://journals.humankinetics.com/kr-back-issues/kr-volume-3-issue-1-february]

Leading the University: The Roles of Trustees, Presidents, and Faculty, *Change*, 45:1 (2013), 24-32 by Richard Legon, John V. Lombardi, and Gary Rhoades. [http://www.changemag.org/Archives/Back%20Issues/ 2013/January-February%202013/leading-the-university-abstract.html]

Improving Advising Using Technology and Data Analytics, *Change*, 45:1 (2013), 48-55 by Elizabeth D. Phillips. [http://www.changemag.org/Archives/Back Issues/2013/January-February 2013/improving-advising-full.html]

How Universities Work, Baltimore: Johns Hopkins (2013) by John V. Lombardi.

Performance and Costs in Higher Education: A Proposal for Better Data. *Change*, April, 23, 8-15 (2011) by Elizabeth D. Capaldi and Craig. W. Abbey. [http://www.changemag.org/Archives/Back%20Issues/2011/March-April%202011/better-data-full.html]

Intellectual Transformation and Budgetary Savings through Academic Reorganization. *Change*, July/August, 19-27. (2009) by Elizabeth D. Capaldi. [http://www.changemag.org/Archives/Back%20Issues/July-August%202009/full-intellectual-budgetary.html]

Improving Graduation Rates: A Simple Method That Works, *Change*, 38:4 (2006), 44-58 by Elizabeth D. Capaldi, John Lombardi, and Victor Yellen. [http://jvlone.com/A%20Simple%20Method_Change2006.pdf]

Using National Data in University Rankings and Comparisons (*TheCenter Reports*, June 2003) by Denise S.Gater. [http://mup.umass.edu/gaternatldata.pdf]

A Review of Measures Used in U.S. News & World Report's "America's Best Colleges" (*TheCenter* Occasional Paper) by Denise S. Gater. [http://mup.umass.edu/Gater0702.pdf]

TheCenter Top American Research Universities: An Overview (*TheCenter Reports*, 2002) by Diane D. Craig. [http://mup.umass.edu/TARUChina.pdf]

The Competition for Top Undergraduates by America's Colleges and Universities (*TheCenter Reports*, 2001) by Denise S. Gater. [http://mup.umass.edu/gaterUG1.pdf]

The Use of IPEDS/AAUP Faculty Data in Institutional Peer Comparisons (*TheCenter Reports*, 2001) by Denise S. Gater and John V. Lombardi [http://mup.umass.edu/gaterFaculty1.pdf]

Toward Determining Societal Value Added Criteria for Research and Comprehensive Universities (*TheCenter Reports*, 2001) by Roger Kaufman. [http://mup.umass.edu/kaufman1.pdf]

U.S. News & World Report's Methodology (*TheCenter Reports*, 2001, Revised) by Denise S. Gater. [http://mup.umass.edu/usnews.html]

A Decade of Performance at the University of Florida (1990-1999) (University of Florida, 1999) by John V. Lombardi and Elizabeth D. Capaldi [http://mup.umass.edu/10yrPerformance.html]

The Center for Measuring University Performance Advisory Board

Chaouki T. Abdallah
Executive Vice President for Research
Professor of Electrical & Computer Engineering
Georgia Institute of Technology

Arthur M. Cohen
Professor Emeritus
Division of Higher Education
Graduate School of Education and Information Studies
University of California, Los Angeles

Larry Goldstein
President, Campus Strategies, LLC

Gerardo M. Gonzalez
Dean Emeritus
Professor, Educational Leadership and Policy Studies
School of Education
Indiana University

Roger Kaufman
Professor Emeritus, Educational Psychology and Learning
Florida State University
Director, Roger Kaufman & Associates
Distinguished Research Professor
Sonora Institute of Technology

Winfred M. Phillips
Executive Chief of Staff
Professor of Mechanical Engineering
Don and Ruth Eckis Professor of Biomedical Engineering
University of Florida

The Center for Measuring University Performance Staff

John V. Lombardi
MUP Center Director
Professor of History, University of Massachusetts Amherst
President Emeritus, University of Florida

Craig W. Abbey
Research Director, MUP Center
Associate Vice President and
Director of Institutional Analysis
University at Buffalo

Diane D. Craig
Research Associate, MUP Center
University of Florida

Lynne N. Collis
Administrative Services, MUP Center

Notes

Notes

Notes